It's a Wonderful World

Appreciations

A great friend since 1989, Khalid Ansari is a very humble, soft-spoken and sensible person. He is somebody whom you would like to seek guidance from.

He is a master of journalism. His columns are interesting, insightful and knowledgeable. Above all, he is a man of class.

—**Zaheer Abbas**, Former cricket captain of Pakistan

A specimen of an aristocratic, social being, Khalid Ansari is very upright and down to earth. He is someone who has always cared for sports in India.

Remarkably fit and a workaholic, he is a very restless individual, forever on the lookout for new ventures and avenues. All in all, he is a very good friend.

—**Bishan Singh Bedi**, Legendary spin bowler and former test captain of India

What strikes me the most about Khalid A-H Ansari is the felicity with which he writes on varied subjects: be it politics, culture, business, social issues or even wars. And of course, cricket. He is a true pro. To say he calls a spade a spade may sound too trite. For him, issues are more important than personalities and that's why he is different from many of his ilk.

—**Inderjit Singh Bindra**, Former BCCI President and current Principal Advisor of the ICC

My first impressions of Khalid when we first met were that of a man who was honest, sincere and a professional journalist with a great love and passion for the game and plenty of knowledge. I soon came to realize that he is well respected not only in India but in all cricket-playing nations.

I can truly say there is no third umpire needed on that decision!

—**Billy Bowden**, Former ICC umpire

I have known for some time that Mr Khalid Ansari is one of India's leading cricket writers. I have noticed that he has a special feel for the game. Mr Ansari is highly critical of Team India when matters go out of hand but he is quick with his praise when his country's cricketers make India proud.

—**Greg Chappell**, Former Australian batsman and coach of India

I first met Khalid Ansari in the early '90s when I started writing for his newspaper *Mid-Day*.

I have come to appreciate his love for the game and his desire to contribute thought-provoking pieces to a newspaper that prides itself on maintaining high standards.

We have dined out together a few times and I really look forward to these occasions for the conversation, overstuffed kulcha and spicy kebabs.

—**Ian Chappell**, Former captain of Australia

I never felt that I was talking to a journalist when I spoke to Khalid. He was never trying to extract things out of you and he never left you with that 'Oh, what have I said' feeling after an interview.

Khalid's rise has been gradual and good. And he has been decent all the way.

—**Nari Contractor**, Former Test captain of India

There is no greater challenge for a journalist and writer than to maintain a freshness of mind and thought over a long period.

To this end, Khalid Ansari has been the most successful and, as a consequence, I suspect this splendid body of his work will be well received and resonate with readers for many years to come.

—**Mike Coward**, Australian cricket journalist, commentator, author and historian

When I first met Khalid in the early 1970s, I was struck by his great dressing sense, which made him stand out in any crowd.

He and his wife made a lovely couple, and it was a pleasure to spend evenings with them. Khalid was not one of those who came to the press box and ranted away. We discussed things, and those evenings were enjoyed and will be cherished.

—**Kapil Dev**, Legendary all-rounder and captain of the Indian cricket team that won the 1983 World Cup

I read Khalid Ansari's works even before I played for India. I first met him in 1996 and got to know him over the years. You can make out that he is a person who cares and has a balanced view of the game.

Khalid is a great supporter of Indian cricket, yet not sensationalistic in his writings. He's also supported Indian cricketers whenever they've been wronged.

—**Rahul Dravid,** Former captain and current Head Coach of India

Khalid has been a friend and a good one. He did a lot for cricketers and did not expect anything in return. He has been straightforward and never afraid to speak his mind. If there is someone out of line, Khalid will sure put him in place.

Khalid is a truly special person whom I've had the pleasure and privilege of calling one of my dearest friends over the zillion years that we've known each other.

—**Farokh Engineer,** Former wicketkeeper-batsman of India and the Lancashire County Cricket Club in England

I first got to know Khalid Ansari in the 1970s when journalists were a very special breed and Khalid certainly belonged to that era. He always enjoyed this trust and had the knack for quoting accurately in interviews, without hurting anyone's feelings. He appealed to me straightaway.

I have considered him to be a special, true friend. His honesty and high integrity have helped him reach many milestones in the media world, and the magazines and newspapers he pioneered were a reflection of his own character—reliable and truthful.

—**Ranjit Fernando,** Former Sri Lankan wicketkeeper-batsman and current member of the Coaching Committee of Sri Lanka

Khalid bhai always had the betterment of cricketers at heart. He cared for sports and is a great human being.

—**Karsan Ghavri,** Former Test and ODI cricketer of India

Khalid Ansari is a gentleman I have seen and observed in the cricketing world for many years.

Since I have grown to know Khalid I can safely say the word 'gentleman' is used in the true definition of the word.

Khalid has been a great friend, with whom I have spent memorable and pleasant hours away from the game.

—**Michael Holding**, Former Jamaican cricketer who played for the West Indies

Khalid Ansari's contribution to sports development has probably gone unnoticed. The Mid-Day/Petra Foundation programme of sponsoring the Malaysian Under-15 cricket team to Mumbai and the Maharashtra junior squash team to Kuala Lumpur is just one of the examples of his love and devotion to sport. Thank you, Khalid, for your contribution to sport at all levels.

—**H.R.H. Tunku Imran**, Malaysian sports administrator, former President of the Olympic Council of Malaysia and the Commonwealth Games Federation and honorary Member of the International Olympic Committee

I have known Khalid Ansari since 1977, when I came to Bombay for the first time. I have always had great respect for him as a person and as a sportswriter. What emerges from his writings is his passion for sports in general, and cricket in particular. When people read his works, they might not necessarily agree with him, but they certainly feel his passion for sport and enjoy the richness and variety of his experience.

—**Imran Khan**, Former cricketer who led the Pakistan team to victory in the 1992 Cricket World Cup and current Prime Minister of Pakistan

It is an honour to be asked to write an appreciation for the outstanding contribution that Khalid Ansari has made to sports and cricket in particular.

I have been fortunate to have received a lot of information on cricket through his writings and have read many of his articles and books on the subject. I rate Khalid Ansari amongst the best leaders in communication and quality within the demands of our sport.

—**Bob Merriman**, Former president of Cricket Australia and Cricket Victoria

The first aspect which struck me about Khalid when I first met him in 1974 was that he came across as very trustworthy—a quality which is very hard to find in such an environment.

Our association developed and it was he who was solely responsible for giving me the opportunity to express my cricketing views through articles in his publication, *Sportsweek*.

Our bond became even stronger because, when dealing with the press in India, I've always looked at him as 'The Godfather.' Not just because of his respected views, but I was always very impressed with his sense of dressing!

—**Sir Vivian Richards,** Former cricketer of the West Indies and widely regarded as one of the best batsmen of all time

Khalid A-H Ansari has been an alert eye to Indian sports ever since he started the popular magazine *Sportsweek*, which ran for two decades.

As a field journalist, his tremendous vision and commitment to sports have stood out. Having vision alone does not take you far. It's your ability to turn that vision into reality which counts in the end. Khalid Ansari has done that and that is why his contribution to sports is significant.

—**Sachin Tendulkar,** Former cricketer of India who served as captain of the national team, arguably India's greatest batsmen ever and Padma Shri recipient

Khalid wrote, and still does, from his heart. If there's an issue on which the public needs an expert view, you can be assured that it will not miss him. He has contributed immensely to sports through his writings which have been critical yet unbiased.

He also guided the Squash Racquets Association of Maharashtra for the sport he dearly loves, as the beads of sweat would suggest in case you bump into him at one of the sports clubs in Mumbai.

—**Dilip Vengsarkar,** Former Indian Test captain and selector

I have always enjoyed Khalid Ansari's company and encouragement. We've had some very convivial evenings on tours. It was nice to get away, talk a little bit of cricket, have a nice meal and have a good laugh. I wish him all the best.

—**John Wright,** Former captain of New Zealand and coach of Team India

I have known Khalid Ansari for many years. A committed sports lover, he has contributed immensely to sport. I got to know him well when he worked with me in the All-India Council of Sports (AICS), in which he was a great asset. We spent many a long and convivial hour discussing sport in different parts of the country where the AICS met.

—**Late Field Marshal S.H.F.J. Manekshaw,**
First Indian army officer to be promoted to rank of Field Marshal, acknowledged hero of the Bangladesh war against Pakistan

It's a Wonderful World

A Memoir

KHALID A-H ANSARI

RUPA

Published by
Rupa Publications India Pvt. Ltd 2022
7/16, Ansari Road, Daryaganj
New Delhi 110002

Sales Centres:
Allahabad Bengaluru Chennai
Hyderabad Jaipur Kathmandu
Kolkata Mumbai

Copyright © Khalid A-H Ansari 2022
Photos courtesy: Author's collection
Illustrations courtesy: Richie Ryall (South Africa)

While every effort has been made to trace copyright holders and obtain permission, this has not been possible in all cases; any omissions brought to our attention will be remedied in future editions.

All rights reserved.
No part of this publication may be reproduced, transmitted, or stored in a retrieval system, in any form or by any means, electronic, mechanical, photocopying, recording or otherwise, without the prior permission of the publisher.

The views and opinions expressed in this book are the author's own and the facts are as reported by him which have been verified to the extent possible, and the publishers are not in any way liable for the same.

ISBN: 978-93-5520-101-0

First impression 2022

10 9 8 7 6 5 4 3 2 1

Printed at Parksons Graphics Pvt. Ltd, Mumbai

The moral right of the author has been asserted.

This book is sold subject to the condition that it shall not, by way of trade or otherwise, be lent, resold, hired out, or otherwise circulated, without the publisher's prior consent, in any form of binding or cover other than that in which it is published

In gratitude to my parents who taught me that greatness comes not from accident of birth but through nobility of purpose, selfless endeavour and service to one's fellow human beings.

Jab Upar Wala Meherbaan To Gadha Pehelwan

Contents

Foreword	*xxi*
Introduction	*xxiii*
Preface	*xxvii*
Eureka!	*xxxi*
Positive Forces	*xxxv*
Prologue	*xxxix*

ONE
THE STORY BEGINS...

The Beginning	3
Partition	12
Early Childhood	16
St Mary's (SSC) High School	19
Childhood Influences	25
Early Upbringing	27
My Father	30
St Xavier's College	32
Wanderlust	35
To Seek, to Strive, to Find…and Not to Yield	40
Jab Miya Beewi Raazi (When Husband and Wife Are in Agreement)	43

TWO
THE FAMILY

Tarique, Alya and Imaan	47
Sharique, Emraan and Safiya	49
Tehzeeb, David, Noah and Leah	51
Memories are Made of This	54
Nanavati Case	56
Stirring a Hornet's Nest	59
Test of Character	62
Making Life Hell	65

THREE
IN EDUCATION WE TRUST

Contemporary Education	69
A Fulfilling Experience	71
The Byculla Connection	73
Urdu, Beloved Urdu	75

FOUR
ACROSS THE BORDER

Pakistani Journos	81
'Hey Guys, Woman!'	84
Zaheer Abbas aka *Zaheer, Ab Bas Karo*	88
Omar Qureshi, Commentator Par Excellence	91
Zulfikar Ali Bhutto: the Mediocre Right-Handed Batsman	93
Farooq Mazhar: the Punjabi Munda	95
'*Saheeb*, the White Man's Burden, *Saheeb*'	97
Air Marshal Nur Khan: the 'Man of Steel'	100

FIVE
LEARNING LESSONS THE HARD WAY

Stanford University	105
New Horizons	107
School of Hard Knocks	109
Prohibition	112
'You Bloody Communist'	115

'That Ansari—Let Him Live There, Die There' — 117
Flower Power — 120
No Bed of Roses — 126

SIX
LAUT KE BUDDHU GHAR KO AAYE
(The Innocents Return Home)

A Son Disowned! — 131
J. Walter Thompson — 132
Queen Bee — 135
A Visit by Chacha Nehru — 137
The Kiss — 140
The Yokel Returns Home — 142
Press Institute of India — 145

SEVEN
AND HERE COMES *SPORTSWEEK*

Sportsweek — 151
Sheer Lunacy — 154
A Mission — 159
Notable Writers — 163
Doing Our Bit for Sports — 166
Sportsweek Awards — 168
The 'Value for Money' Magazine — 170
Burning My Candle at Both Ends — 171

EIGHT
SPORTS IN MY INK

Olympic Games — 177
1982 Asian Games, New Delhi — 180
The 'Hitting Out' Column — 182
The Unsporting Indian — 189
It's 'Do or Die' for Us — 191
From Olympian Heights to Stygian Depths — 193
Causes of India's Hockey Decline — 194
Not All Fun and Games — 196

Sachin: Born to Bat	198
'Crisp 'n' Crackling'	202

NINE
SIGHTS, SMELLS AND SOUNDS

The Communicators	207
The Infamous Vaseline Incident	208
Forty-Seven Large Scotches	210
In a Lighter Vein	214
Parsi-Monious	217
A Vast Wasteland	221
Of Two-Fingered Salutes Down Under	224
Four Seasons in a Day	227
The Chappells	232
Lord's—among the Best	233
Sydney Cricket Ground	236
Wanderers	239
Bada Rona Aata Hai (Feel Like Shedding Tears)	242
We Came Down from the Trees for the Booze	245
'…Make it Fish and Chips'	247
All-Time Cricketing Greats	250
Hockey Despair	253
Asiad Chronicle	256

TEN
A MAD DREAM TO START A DAILY NEWSPAPER

Advertising, Advertising	263
Mid-Day	267
Strike	273
Ye Hai Bambai Meri Jaan (This is Bombay, My Dear)	276
'Call It Bloody "Midnight"'	282
Mid-Day's Plan For Citizens (ACT), 1983	285
'Will You Accept Bombay's Challenge, Madam PM?'	289
JRD and Palkhivala	292
Jugaad	295

ELEVEN
THE BOLD(S) AND THE BEAUTIFUL(S)

Field Marshal 'Sam Bahadur' Manekshaw	301
Arjuna Awards	305
Rajmata Gayatri Devi of Jaipur	307
La Lollo: the Most Beautiful Woman in The World	309
'Lasting Beauty' Goldie Hawn	311

TWELVE
'PHOREN' JAUNTS

UK, Bahamas, Cuba	315
Commonwealth Heads of Government Meeting (CHOGM)	317
New York	318
Havana, Cuba	319
NAM Summit, Harare, 1986	320
'The Most Hated Man in Africa'	322
Greece, Yugoslavia, Poland, 1986	324
John Major	328
With President Abdul Kalam, 2005	329
'Sedition' Charge	331

THIRTEEN
KHALEEJ TIMES

The 'Indian Butcher' in Dubai	337
Uneven Playing Field	341
Working to Plan	346
Kanz Communications, Dubai	348

FOURTEEN
BONDS OF FRIENDSHIP

The Little Master	353
'Rooky' Engineer	358
Bishan Bedi	362
Kapil Dev Nikhanj	367
Dilip Vengsarkar	370
Squash Exchange with Malaysia	372

Mid-Day A-H Ansari Squash Academy	373
Raju Chainani	374
Tunku 'Pete' Imran	375
The Grand Prix	377
My Dear Friend, Behram—RIP	379

FIFTEEN
THE WAR AND THE MOUNTAINS

Kargil Indo-Pak War, 1999	383
If There Be Heaven on Earth...	386
Call to Paes, Bhupathi to Dedicate Win to Kargil Jawans	388
The Mountains Beckon Again	390

SIXTEEN
AND THEN WE MET...

Bringing in the New Millennium Down Under	397
Zeyna, Zeynasan	399

SEVENTEEN
YOU WIN SOME, YOU LOSE SOME

The Asian Age	405
Special Executive Magistrate	408
Ambassadorship	409
Padma Shri	410
Sheriff of Mumbai	413

EIGHTEEN
LIFE IS BEAUTIFUL AND FULL OF SURPRISES

Think Big, Think Presidential	417
Mid-Day Anniversary Celebrations	421
A New Year in the Air	423
Inquilab Golden Jubilee	425
There Once Was...Squash	427

NINETEEN
PURSUITS...

'Run For Fun'—a Mass Movement for Fitness	433
CHAMPS Foundation	435
Terry Fox Run	436
Cricket Club of India	438
Bombay Gymkhana	439
Eyeball to Eyeball with Datta Samant	443
Supremacy Surrendered	445
Mumbai Club Life	448
In Memory of a Dear Friend and Champion	452

TWENTY
UNITED COLOURS OF NATIONS

United Nations	457
The UN General Assembly	459
Nikita Khrushchev	462
Dismantling of Glasnost, Perestroika	464
United Nations Preparatory Committee (PrepCom), New York	468
Earth Summit, Rio de Janeiro, 1997	471

TWENTY-ONE
THE GAME CALLED LIFE

Return to Mumbai	475
'Doin' What Comes, Natur'lly'	477
A Crisis of Grave Magnitude	480
Achilles Heel	484
Writing on the Wall	487
Life Down Under, Mate	489
Giving Back to Society	492
Afterthoughts	495
Epilogue	516
Index	521

Foreword

It has been 50 years since I first met Khalid Ansari. He was then the editor of the sports weekly magazine called *Sportsweek* and had come over to interview me after my return from the West Indies tour. He had come with his sons and daughter, and the thing that I remember was how he had put me at ease and the respect with which he greeted my parents. That immediately warmed me towards him and we did a terrific interview, even if I say so myself. There were no awkward questions. He didn't act as if he was smarter than me, which he was and is, but was genuinely interested in my growth as a cricketer up to that point in my career.

There was none of that reticence that sometimes comes while speaking to journalists because he would respect the confidence someone had reposed in him and knew that they talked to him as an individual and not as a media person. For some, everything was about a story and byline; on the advice of our seniors, we quickly learnt to distinguish between who you could talk to as a person and who was a media person 24/7.

Over the years, our relationship changed from a professional one to that of being friends, and after my retirement from the game, I was pleasantly surprised when he asked me to come onboard *Sportsweek* as the editor. I enjoyed writing, and still do, but being the editor meant having a completely different perspective about other sports. Fortunately, not only did I have Khalid and his two sons, Tarique and Sharique, but also a team of top-class sports writers, and we all shared the same vision of India as a sporting nation to reckon with.

That vision is slowly but surely coming to fruition.

My badminton partner Gautam Thakkar, who sadly passed away too soon, had invited me to be a member of the Saturday club at the Bombay Gymkhana and it was there that I got to know Khalid even better. During those lunches, no topic was off-limits and the eclectic bunch that had gathered there often had an opinion on just about everything. There was plenty of leg-pulling, and in a setting like that one can truly get to know the true character of a person—if they can laugh at themselves and take a joke, they are alright. Khalid gave as good as he got, especially from Nana Chudasama, who has also unfortunately left us, and the banter at those lunches was always invigorating as well as informative as there were brains from all walks of life in that small Saturday club.

Knowing his passion for sports and his concern for sportspersons, it was a no brainer for me to ask him, along with Nana Chudasama, to become a trustee of the CHAMPS Foundation. The foundation looks to assist and help those Indian sportspersons who are in the twilight of their lives and are struggling after retirement. His advice was always spot on and most insightful.

What stands out about Khalid is his zest for life. To this day, he travels around the world, taking in the sights and sounds and experiencing what different countries and cultures are about. He lives his life to the fullest and squeezes the maximum out of every single day, things we should all learn from him and strive to do.

His autobiography will be like him—no holds barred—and will be a thrilling read to the end that will leave us feeling, *'wish I had a life like this...'*

—Sunil Gavaskar

Introduction

A picture of Khalid Ansari jogging on the Dadar overbridge with the police commissioner of the city is imprinted in my mind's eye. Since the commissioner in question was me, the year must be either 1982, 1983, 1984 or 1985, I cannot recollect which. I am certain, though, that it was some sporting event because neither Khalid nor I would otherwise be out jogging in Dadar. I do not know where my friend did his jogging but I did it daily on the public roads outside my official residence on the Narayan Dabholkar Road.

Khalid Ansari began his career in *Inquilab*, the Urdu daily started by his freedom fighter father, Abdul Hamid Ansari, in 1937. After his undergraduate studies in Mumbai, Khalid obtained a master's in Journalism and Mass Communication from Stanford University, California, US.

On returning to India, he established the Mid-Day Multimedia Ltd which published Asia's leading afternoon newspaper *Mid-Day* in two languages from Mumbai, New Delhi, Bengaluru and Pune, and the *Sunday Mid-Day*, besides the *Inquilab*, the Urdu language daily. He also started *Sportsweek*, which became India's leading sports magazine for two decades between 1969 and 1989. Simultaneously, Khalid was Chairman of M.C. Media Ltd, a group whose undertakings included F.M. radio broadcasting (a joint venture with BBC London) in eight Indian cities.

The Ansari family sold off majority holding in Mid-Day Multimedia Ltd a few years ago, but not before my friend Khalid had left an impression on the country's sports scene. The more importance sports were given in the press, the more motivation it would create to participate and excel in that world—Khalid understood this principle. Sports unite citizens like only wars against enemies of our country can. When India competes in cricket against a foreign team, cricket lovers, and even those not particularly fixated on the game, watch the match anxiously. Irrespective of creed, caste, gender, language, region or political leaning, they are on tenterhooks till our team wins, and conversely, really feel the loss when we lose! Sporting events are substitutes for war, but are, of course, an infinitely more civilized form of combat.

Barring the 1992 Olympics in Barcelona, Khalid Ansari has covered every Olympics since the 1972 games in Munich. He was at Montreal in 1976, Moscow in 1980, Los Angeles in 1984, Seoul in 1988, Atlanta in 1996, Sydney in 2000, Athens in 2004 and Beijing in 2008, literally travelling across the globe in pursuit of the greater glory of sports.

Khalid Ansari was a member of the Organizing Committee of the Commonwealth Games held in New Delhi in 2010 till he resigned for personal reasons arising out of allegations of malfeasance on the part of some senior members of the Committee. He is chairman emeritus of the Squash Racquet Association of Maharashtra (SRAM) and an honorary life member of the Cricket Club of India (CCI), an honour that I too, incidentally, share with him courtesy the legendary Raj Singh Dungarpur.

When the Asian Games were held in Delhi in 1982, Khalid was appointed editor of *Asiad Chronicle*, the official publication of that year's Games. Khalid is the author of three books, *Cricket and Cricketing Greats*, *Sachin: Born to Bat* and *Cricket at Fever Pitch*, and editor of *Wills Tribute to Excellence: Champions of One-Day Cricket*. For his devotion and dedication to sports, Khalid was made a member of the All India Council of Sports that was at the time presided over by General P.P. Kumaramangalam and Field Marshal Sam Manekshaw.

The world of sports was not the only thing that concerned Khalid Ansari, though it was his first love. Khalid covered the foreign visits of presidents Fakhruddin Ali Ahmed, Giani Zail Singh and A.P.J. Abdul Kalam, as well as those of prime ministers Rajiv Gandhi and Atal Bihari Vajpayee. He was also a member of the Indian delegation of the 1989 United Nations General Assembly held in New York.

Khalid Ansari was interested in environmental issues as well. In 1994 he started the *Earth Times* at the headquarters of the United Nations in New York and published the *Earth Summit Times*, the official UN newspaper of the 'Earth Summit' in Rio de Janeiro, Brazil. My own brother, who attended that summit in Rio, told me that the newspaper was read with interest by most delegates. Incidentally, Khalid was also appointed the managing editor and executive editor of the *Khaleej Times* in Dubai, a position that reflected his extensive experience and varied interests in the field of journalism. He covered the Commonwealth Heads of Government Meeting in the Bahamas in 1985, the NAM conference in Harare in 1986, the Kargil War in 1999 and the Fijian coup d'état in 2000.

No wonder he was recognized by his alma maters, Mumbai's St Xavier's College and the Government Law College as a distinguished alumnus of each of these prestigious institutions of learning. He was also elected president of both the Bombay Gymkhana and the Rotary Club of Bombay Mid-Town.

However, the Padma Shri conferred by the government in 2001 for his contributions to journalism and sports undoubtedly represents the pinnacle of Khalid's achievements.

Khalid started the Abdul Hamid Ansari Charitable Trust in memory of his revered freedom-fighter father. The trust has since been converted into a foundation that is involved in animal welfare, conducts eye camps in slum areas and municipal schools, and sponsors vocational education to more than 500 girls belonging to the underprivileged classes in the cities of Mumbai and Pune every year.

As a trustee of the CHAMPS Foundation, founded by former Indian cricketer, Sunil Gavaskar, he has helped many retired Indian sportspeople in need. All in all, a memorable life lived by a true gentleman who was voted 'Gentleman of the Year' in 1988 by *Gentleman* magazine. But Khalid Ansari has been a gentleman not only in 1988 but in all seasons for all times.

—Julio Ribeiro

Preface

JAB UPAR WALA MEHERBAAN TO GADHA PEHELWAN
When the One Above showers His blessings,
the donkey thinks he's the king.

—Proverb in Indian folklore

When the suggestion to write these memoirs was first mooted in the last millennium by Rajan Mehra of Rupa Publications, my immediate reaction was: 'Thanks, but no thanks.'

'Isn't the act of writing about oneself crass, egoistic, narcissistic, likely to degenerate into a vulgar "I did this and that," pat-my-own-back hagiography?' I asked. On the spur of the moment, Rajan even suggested that the book be titled along the lines of 'Memoirs of an Indian Muslim.'

'I'm hardly a Muslim,' I retorted, 'although I follow the tenets of the religion I was born into. And I'm *uber* proud to be an Indian, as Islam exhorts its followers to be faithful to the country they live in.'

'In any case, who will want to read about me?' I asked Rajan, replicating the reply of good friend, the puckish Field Marshal S.H.F.J. 'Sam' Manekshaw, when I had previously made a similar suggestion to him saying he write his autobiography to serve as an inspiration for future generations. Summoning all my powers of persuasion, I had tried to buttress my proposal to him by quoting the memorable lines by Henry Wadsworth Longfellow:

> Lives of great men all remind us
> We can make our lives sublime,
> And, departing, leave behind us
> Footprints on the sands of time

'No chance, Khalid… Over my dead body,' he had replied in a tone of finality, 'I know too bloody much.'

My entreaties fell on deaf years for many years thereafter. I tried to convince him that he wouldn't have to endure embarrassment over writing about himself and that all he would have to do was talk, at his convenience, into a speaking device which I would be happy to transcribe for him to edit for publication in the form of an 'As told to…' biography.

But, forgive the pun, the field marshal stuck to his guns.

He passed away without leaving behind for posterity, an authorized record of his brave and inspirational deeds and glimpses into his colourful personality.

As a wannabe historian, one who strongly believes that records of men of substance and their deeds should be passed down in history, I had previously made a similar suggestion to Mumbai businessman 'Mota'—the eldest of four brothers of the high-profile Chudasama family. There were three other brothers, apart from Mota: 'Nana' (a former sheriff of Mumbai), 'Jinka' (a Pune businessman) and 'Chota' (a PR honcho at the Air India office in New York), each one a bloomin' character in his own right.

'Great idea,' replied the amiable, but eccentric, Mota wryly, after prolonged reflection upon my proposal, 'we'll sell four copies between us'—a frightening prospect as far as this effort was concerned!

However, I did succeed in persuading, after considerable effort, and helping New York-based Anil Nayar, the legendary Indian squash champion, and his wife, Jean, to publish his eminently readable autobiography.

To return to this memoir, Javed (Siddiqui) Akhtar, well-known basketball player and journalist, who had worked with me at *Sportsweek* and *Mid-Day* for over a decade, startled me one day with an out-of-the-blue proposal. He had just returned to Mumbai (then, Bombay) from Saudi Arabia, where he had worked with the

Saudi Gazette for many years.

'*Bhaijan*' (Brother—he always addressed me thus), 'I know how you feel about not writing about yourself, but I would very much like to write your biography,' he pleaded, 'especially since your family and mine go back decades.' (His father had worked with mine since the latter started the *Inquilab* in 1937.)

Struck by his sincerity of purpose, I told him I didn't have the heart to refuse as long as I didn't have to write about myself in first person singular, and that an 'As told to…' format was acceptable.

Javed and I commenced work on the project in real earnest, spending many hours together: he shooting questions at me at random, in no particular sequence, and me replying to the best of my ability within the constraints of memory. Progress was slow but steady until tragedy struck and Javed, God's own man, honest to the core and as sincere as they come, passed away suddenly, leaving behind a devoted wife and two sons.

Fast-forward to the years following my retirement and return to Mumbai from Sydney, where my wife Zeyna and I had resided intermittently for 10 years, my family and friends were now nudging me to pick up the threads from where Javed had left. But Javed's painstaking handwritten notes were nowhere to be found.

My friend and collaborator on three books, Clayton Murzello, cricket historian and award-winning sports editor of *Mid-Day*, who is presently a member of the Mumbai Cricket Association (MCA) museum committee, offered to help, as is his wont. He recommended for the project, Devendra Prabhudesai, author of six biographies, including those of Sunil Gavaskar and Rahul Dravid, and script writer of documentaries on Sachin Tendulkar's hundredth and two-hundredth Tests.

Prabhudesai very kindly agreed. He drew up a list of contents, following which I commenced work on this project. As I laboured to unearth details of the largely unknown background of my late father, who started life as an orphan but went on to play an important role in our country's freedom movement for which he was named '*fakhr-e-sahafat*' (pride of journalism), it soon became evident that the proposed 'As told to…' format of the memoir was not feasible.

For one thing, despite all his impressive credentials as a biographer, it would have been extremely difficult, if not impossible, for Prabhudesai to collect adequate details of my father's life, something that only I could do, given the decades-old chronological distance, not to mention dissonance in political, cultural and lingual mindsets. Moreover, for better or worse, nobody knows me better than myself—warts and all. (Reminds one of the naughty confessions made by a male celebrity: 'Next to myself, I like Marilyn Monroe best.')

It would have also been extremely difficult to communicate my innumerable intimate negative traits to a third person and expect him to adequately capture the subtle nuances without embarrassment to himself! After all, this project was certainly *not* going to be a soapy, unctuous, wah-wah, shabash, roses-all-the-way autobiography. The more I agonized over it, the more I became convinced that an autobiographical format (much as I detested the thought of having to grind the first person singular 'I' to dust), was the best way to go. So it became a Hobson's choice—even though there aren't very many synonyms for 'I', 'me', 'myself', 'yours truly' and 'this writer' in the English language.

That said, as I perused voluminous files of my published articles in *Sportsweek* and *Mid-Day* for these memoirs, I came across an abundance of articles about me in *other* publications written by *other* people. Moreover, I stumbled upon correspondence. This was a godsend route that has saved me ginormous amounts of awkwardness.

The solution to this dilemma reminds me of Archimedes, the Greek mathematician, physicist, engineer, inventor and astronomer, who was so thrilled by his discovery in the bathtub that he immediately hopped out of the bath and ran onto the streets to inform the king, shouting out loudly, 'Eureka, eureka, I've found it, I've found it!' By reproducing, verbatim, other peoples' published or written correspondence, I have been able quote relevant material without qualms, thereby avoiding considerable personal embarrassment.

Moreover, instead of piggybacking narratives of two lifetimes (my father's, in brief, and my own) in strict chronological order, I have endeavoured to present an admixture of sequential events of importance and matters of acquired knowledge and personal experience.

Eureka!

I stumbled upon the homespun expression about the donkey from Urdu/Hindi folklore when I was grappling with the dilemma of how to overcome the mortifying problem of avoiding writing repeatedly in the first person singular.

Why not create an alter ego or the Other Self to serve as a bulwark, a shield, medium of benevolence, an intermediary from embarrassment? Why not make the poor donkey, hapless personification of stupidity in society, a rampart against my continuing self-consciousness? Why not, in all good faith, let *him* be my Other Self and let *him* absorb, as if by osmosis, all the finger-pointing—as well as glory—that may come my way for any seeming transgressions of modesty?

It was indeed an enormous eureka moment!

The more I thought about it, the more thrilled I was—especially since upon doing some research, I discovered that the expression does huge injustice to the poor donkey who is nowhere near as stupid as the expression makes it out to be. The pitiful *gadha* (donkey) with the ludicrous bray, unfairly considered the stupidest creation in the animal kingdom in Indian folklore, is the object of widespread ridicule.

There have been centuries-old misconceptions worldwide regarding the donkey's intelligence, influenced by colloquial language; comparisons with mules or asses (scientific name: *Equus asinus*) are sometimes made to insult a person's intelligence, hence the term asinine.

A 2013 study by The Donkey Sanctuary, a British charity devoted to welfare of the donkey, found that the much-maligned animal has an excellent memory, and a great ability to learn and solve problems at the same rate as dolphins and dogs. In fact, among equines—horses, zebras and donkeys—they are considered the smartest on parameters of problem-solving and deduction (connecting cause and effect), memory and trainability. Donkeys generally have small family groupings much like deer. Although they have been selectively bred over time, they will never submit completely to an alpha (dominant person).[1]

And yet, 74 per cent of people in a YouGov survey do not think of a donkey as 'intelligent' and believe that comparisons with donkeys 'sometimes act as a means of insulting human intelligence.' Animal behaviourist Ben Hart also postulated that, 'when compared to horses, they show more subtle body language when in pain or distress. Donkeys also have a strong sense of self-preservation and are unwilling to do things that they perceive as dangerous. The donkeys' stoic nature, minimal body language, and their natural propensity to freeze when threatened or frightened, combined with a reluctance to put themselves at risk, results in donkeys commonly being mislabelled as stupid or stubborn. I believe anyone that calls a donkey stupid, has simply been outsmarted by one!'[2]

The more I thought about it, the more my heart bled for the poor donkey.

So why not make the hapless donkey my alter ego? Why not make *him*, instead of me the metaphorical raison d'être—the purpose—of this tale? After all is it not a timeworn belief that we are all the makers of our own destiny?

And, as compensation for his miseries, have the Maker bless the donkey with the gift, as in many a phenomenon in nature's incomprehensible scheme of things, to pass them on to mortals for reasons known only to itself.

By doing so, along with the device of having other people speak on my behalf through quotations (as explained earlier), I have certainly

---

[1]'How Intelligent are Donkeys?', The Donkey Sanctuary, https://www.thedonkey sanctuary.org.uk/what-we-do/knowledge-and-advice/for-owners/understanding-donkey-characteristics/how-intelligent-are-donkeys. Accessed on 28 October 2021.
[2]'Donkeys Revealed As a British Favourite Despite "Stubborn" Myth', The Donkey Sanctuary, https://www.thedonkeysanctuary.org.uk/news/donkeys-revealed-as-a-british-favourite-despite-stubborn-myth. Accessed on 28 October 2021.

spared myself huge discomfiture and, hopefully but more importantly, the reader insufferable annoyance over my potential abuse of the first person singular.

And so it has come to pass.

◆

In these memoirs I have tried to present a cocktail of some gyan (wisdom), dollops of unserious but hopefully enlightening personal anecdotes, frothy bon mots, *gup-shup* (natter) and news.

Most of all, I have endeavoured to make this a fun book with a serious underpinning of personal tough-as-nails experiences, from which readers will benefit, hopefully.

What started out as a biography has perforce taken the avatar of a memoir. I sincerely hope that after my best efforts, the reader will not be bored to tears, and on the contrary enjoy this tale of the Gadha who thinks he is *pehalwan*.

Enjoy!

Positive Forces

International publishing phenomenon Paulo Coelho, author of the seminal *The Alchemist*, who has sold more than 165 million copies worldwide and is the most translated living author and proponent of what he terms the 'Life Force', posits that within ourselves we all have the necessary strength to find our own destiny.

It is Coelho's belief that there are, in nature, positive forces waiting to be tapped for our own good and that it is up to us to do so and realize our full potential. In *The Alchemist*, Coelho teaches us about the essential wisdom of listening to our hearts, of learning to read the omens strewn along life's path and, above all, of following our dreams.

'Follow your dreams even if it means going through some nightmares,' he extrapolates.

In *Aleph*, Coelho invites us to consider the meaning of our own personal journeys—are we where we want to be, doing what we want to do?

The late Indian president A.P.J. Abdul Kalam once famously said, 'You have to dream before your dreams come true.'

I may have acquired fragments of knowledge along the way but as Alfred Tennyson would have us believe: 'Knowledge comes, but wisdom lingers.' Like many of us, in my twilight years, I find myself still grappling with the mysteries and complexities of life, which saints, savants and seers have attempted to unravel since life began millions of years ago.

What is it all about? What is the purpose of life, of existence, of reward and punishment for the way we conduct ourselves? Is there such a thing as predestiny? If so, why? Is there an afterlife: heaven, hell and purgatory? A veritable gallimaufry of questions to which there seem to be no definitive rational and convincing answers at times—at least as far as this ignoramus is concerned!

Self-proclaimed agnostic Khushwant Singh propounds his own belief in typical confrontational manner in *There Is No God*, the titles of one of his best sellers. Given the gift of free thought and free will, atheists, as also agnostics, have their own absolute convictions, and so do theologians, scientists, rationalists and believers of abracadabra sorcery, mumbo-jumbo occultism and the like.

There are omnists and pantheists. And there are cults, some of which are certainly not peaceful, but positively evil aggregations that take delight in engaging in wanton extortion, fraud, rape and even murdering their own members. They too are, after all, children of the same God who created our Universe!

Not having had the privilege of studying theology, I too, like many of us, am entrapped in the vortex of this unending mystery. The older I get chronologically, the smaller I feel intellectually, and the more increasingly bewildered I get about the concept of karma—of destiny, of reward and punishment in this seemingly harsh and ugly world. Like many of my friends and acquaintances, I ask myself: if we are indeed created in the image of the Maker, why are we so inhumane to our fellow human beings and God's other creations in the animal kingdom and other multifarious species?

Atal Bihari Vajpayee, who in my opinion, is the greatest statesman and prime minister India has ever had, and with whom I had the privilege to attend the 1988 session of the 159-member United Nations General Assembly as a delegate, told the world body: 'We hope the world will act in the spirit of enlightened self-interest.' Sadly, the operative word 'enlightened' is conspicuous by its absence in the performance of that august body, as also in its predecessor's, the League of Nations, which failed precisely for this reason, with crass self-interest being the only raison d'être of member nations.

The history of Homo sapiens is replete with instances of man's cruelty to man, animals and birds, of wars and disputes over land, power, religion, genocides, holocausts. Why, why, why? Why are evil and corrupt people rewarded and the good, compassionate, loving ones made to suffer? Why, as in Oscar Wilde's *The Picture of Dorian Gray*, does Dorian, despite his hedonistic lifestyle, remain forever young, while his painting ages and fades frighteningly, as is the case in real life?

Why, in real life, do serial killers, terrorists, confidence tricksters, murderers, rapists and criminals of all hues thrive and prosper while looking deceptively radiant and youthful, even as the virtuous age and wither, even die, prematurely?

How about the so-called 'children of a lesser God?' Also, babies and innocent children who suffer for no fault of their own, those born prematurely who are physically or cognitively disabled?

How does one explain horrific acts of demented people, like the 30-year-old British nurse Lucy Letby of Chester, once the face of a £3 million fund-raising campaign for the Nursing and Midwifery Council, who is accused of murdering eight newborn babies and of trying to murder 10 more? Again: why, why, why?

Mirza Ghalib, arguably the greatest Urdu poet of all time, once lamented, *albeit* in an altogether different romantic context: *'Ya Ilahi ye maajra kya hai?'* (What is this riddle, O Lord Above?)

All conventional religions, and I speak basically about the one I was born into and have grown up with, provide invaluable guidelines about right and wrong, about how one should live one's life for the greater good of the greatest numbers, but the enigma, the ongoing mystery about the real purpose of life, continues to be elusive.

On a personal note, I often also wonder: why does the Maker look so kindly—consistently—upon this Gadha, meaning yours truly. You too will, by the time you've finished reading these memoirs!

You will understand why I'm still unable to fathom the mystery of the seemingly wanton lavishment of so much munificence upon a single individual in his lifetime. Is it 'alignment of stars,' 'accident of birth,' 'being at the right place at the right time,' even 'karma' (if you are so inclined)? None of them pass the litmus test of science, logic, rationality.

The only plausible explanation seems to lie in the subtitle of the chapter: *'Upar wala meherbaan to gadha pehelwan'* (When the One Above showers His blessings, the donkey thinks he's the king).

Positive Forces

Prologue

Dhundta phirta hun main 'Iqbal'
Apne aap ko,
Aap hi goya musaafir
Aap hi manzil hun main

(I keep wandering to discover my true self,
I am the traveller, and also the destination.)

—Allama Iqbal, legendary Urdu poet

I was born in a lower middle-class family to Abdul Hamid Nizamuddin (not much is known about his background except that he started life as an orphan in Mumbai) and Amina Begum (background also unknown except that her family hailed from Hubli, educational and industrial hub in Karnataka) in the rundown Nagpada/Madanpura neighbourhood near Byculla, which continues to be home to the local Ansari community.

Traditionally, the Ansaris were hand weavers whose ancestry is generally believed to go back to the Arab Ansar tribe which helped Prophet Muhammad flee during the Hejira from Mecca to Medina in AD 622, to escape religious persecution by Meccan Arabs. However, according to columnist and former *Mid-Day* editor-in-chief Aakar Patel, who later became executive director of Amnesty International, India, Ansaris are a 'converts from the Vankar caste of weavers. Many are from Uttar Pradesh, which they are thought to have fled after the

1857 mutiny. The British chopped off the thumbs of these rebellious weavers, and so making them useless in their profession. The Ansaris moved to Bhiwandi, outside Bombay, making it one of the largest weaving centres of the world.' He goes on: 'The Ansaris of Mid-Day did not make their money from weaving but from newspapers. The founder was Abdul Hamid Ansari, who wrote and published the Urdu [then] weekly Inquilab.'[1]

Hardly anything is known about my ancestry (even to myself), except that my grandfather, Nizamuddin, was a school teacher who migrated from Barabanki in UP to Marol, near Andheri, in Mumbai. It is also known that Nizamuddin had three sons of whom Abdul Hamid was the youngest.

On the topic of ancestry: a chance meeting with an American professor of history during a trip abroad a few years ago, led me (eager to trace my ancestry) and my wife Zeyna to embark upon an endeavour to ascertain our ancestral journey going back an awesome 120,000 years via the National Geographic society's Genographic Project.[2]

The study is rather esoteric—briefly put, although findings of the pioneering study going back to the very early beginnings of Homo sapiens on Earth are obscure, analyses of DNA going back 150,000 years reveal that the world population, now confirmed as having originated in Africa, shares one common maternal ancestor: a Mitochondrial Eve. Her male counterpart was a Y-chromosome Adam.

The fascinating study breaks down the migration of our ancestors (possibly from Ethiopia in Africa) to all corners of the globe, region-wise into various branches, from a set of 18 world regions, with information gleaned from a simple sputum test, determining one's entire genome and enabling determination of both parents' information. Percentages of the subjects reflect both recent influences and ancient

---

[1] Aakar Patel, 'The Muslim businessmen of India', DNA, 16 May 2010, https://www.dnaindia.com/india/comment-the-muslim-businessmen-of-india-1383602. Accessed on 29 October 2021.
[2] 'The Genographic Project® Geno 2.0 Next Generation Helix Product Privacy Policy', National Geographic, https://www.nationalgeographic.com/pages/article/genographic. Accessed on 28 October 2021.

genetic patterns in DNA due to how groups migrated to and from different regions, mixing for hundreds or even thousands of years. The South Asia component of the study, which most Indians belong to, represents the first migration from Africa through the Indian subcontinent.

My genetic makeup is 60 per cent Southern Asian, 29 per cent Central Asian and 9 per cent Southeast Asian and Oceania. As for closer ancestry, my knowledge is zilch.

My first wife, Rukya is daughter of former Mumbai police commissioner Sheikh Hussain (he was given the title of *Khan Bahadur*, meaning 'brave tiger') and Khatija, who was from Sawantwadi, Maharashtra. My second wife Zeyna is 77 per cent east European, 16 per cent Anatolian and 6 per cent Southern European. She was born to Yugoslav parents in London, who migrated to New Zealand in the last century.

All I know about my immediate ancestry is that my father studied at a school founded by Sir Mohamed Yusuf, proprietor of Bombay Steam Navigation Company, for the sons and orphans of seafarers in Nhava island, off Mumbai 'as a debt of gratitude to the seafaring community who had served bravely and loyally on the Company's ships.'[3] The school was also established for the purpose of encouraging the progeny of the seafaring community, irrespective of their caste or religion, to follow in the footsteps of their predecessors.

Later in life, when freedom fighter Abdul Hamid had made a mark in life, he was made a trustee of this school where he studied.

The orphan from Nhava Sheva went on to be called *mujahid-e-azaadi* (soldier of freedom) and *fakhr-e-sahafat* (pride of journalism).

---

[3]'Training Ship Rahaman: Background', https://web.archive.org/web/201309272 12837/http://tsrahaman.org/background.html. Accessed on 28 October 2021.

ONE

THE STORY BEGINS...

The Beginning

From sketchy records and word-of-mouth transmission, it seems that towards the end of the nineteenth century, Abdul Hamid's father Hafiz Nizamuddin migrated to Mumbai and married Banni Begum.

According to Javed Jamaluddin, to whom I am grateful for the scholarly research that went into writing my father's biography from which I have reproduced extracts liberally, Abdul Hamid, the youngest of Hafiz Nizamuddin and Banni Begum's five children (three sons and two daughters), was born on New Year's Eve, 1906. Abdul Hamid had a cousin, Abdul Rahim, who had lost his parents quite early. Nizamuddin adopted Abdul Rahim.

Abdul Hamid's life was full of ups and downs ever since he lost both his parents when he was only 10 years old, until his death in 1972. Immediately after her husband's death, his shattered mother, also lost a son and daughter, while her eldest child, Abdul Rehman joined the British army and left for Baghdad. She was heartbroken and died pining for her children.

Abdul Hamid and Abdul Rahim were brought up by their sister and brother-in-law. Nearly five years later, Abdul Rehman came back from the war and took on the responsibility of looking after his two brothers. Since his army allowance was not enough to send the brothers to school, Abdul Rehman sent the boys to an orphanage set up by Sir M.D. Yusuf. There, Abdul Hamid learnt carpentry and Abdul Rahim, weaving. Abdul Hamid passed the Urdu final and three classes of English and left the orphanage for further studies.

Abdul Rehman was again entrusted with the task of looking after his two brothers. Abdul Rahim was not interested in further studies and took up employment at a printing press, while Abdul Hamid secured admission at the Anjuman Islam School. He also studied for some time at the Khairul Islam Orphanage, which he supported financially, along with other underprivileged schools, after the *Inquilab* daily became a success.

After his intermediate exams, Abdul Hamid discontinued his studies. He gave tuitions and worked as a teacher for a short period at a municipal school in Madanpura, near Byculla in central Mumbai, where he shared a room with his brother and cousin. The chowk at Byculla Bridge under the flyover, where six important roads intersect, is now called the Abdul Hamid Ansari Chowk.

Becoming self-sufficient with the passage of time and wishing to have more children after his firstborn (me), in 1937, Abdul Hamid requested wife Amina, who could not bear any more children, permission to remarry according to Muslim tenet, without which he would not have been able to take on a second wife. Bismillah Begum bore him five children: Salma, Shahid, Najma, Mujahid and Raashid.

Salma, now widowed, Mujahid and Raashid live in the US. Najma, a divorcee with three children, resides in Mumbai. Shahid died in a car crash near Kalyan at the age of 23.

Although the second marriage succeeded in its professed intention of expanding the family, unsurprisingly it proved to be dysfunctional, a fact that Abdul Hamid regretted and termed 'the biggest mistake of my life.' It wrought havoc with my psyche. But more on that later.

◆

After India's Independence in 1947, Abdul Hamid wrote in his column: 'I bow my head before the Almighty in gratitude for all that I have today. By God's grace, *Inquilab* has reached new heights. I have overcome many hurdles to reach here. I keep mentioning these hurdles in my column "Qissa-e-dard sunate hain hum, kyon ke majboor hain hum" (I narrate my tale of woe since I am helpless).'

'Qissa-e-dard' was a great favourite not just with readers of the

Inquilab, but also with intellectuals, the literati and journalists from all over the country. Through the column, Abdul Hamid not only guided Muslims on social and political matters, but also exposed those who were misleading the Muslim community in the name of religion. He took it upon himself to bring about changes in social and religious attitudes.

At a function at Mumbai's YMCA, Abdul Hamid said: 'The problem staring in our faces today is that of communalism. We should all work for unity and national integration.'

It is estimated that Abdul Hamid wrote over 300 columns (many of which, sadly, lie in a moth-eaten state and are thereby irretrievable) championing various causes ranging from national integration, communal harmony, the importance of teaching and learning Hindi and Marathi, the education of orphans and girls, to solidarity with the weaker sections of society; he wrote on corruption, religious obscurantism, civic issues and much more.

Javed Jamaluddin, author of my father's biography *Abdul Hameed Ansari, Revolutionary Journalist and Freedom Fighter,* which won the Maharashtra State Urdu Sahitya Academy award, writes in the book:[1]

> Abdul Hamid Ansari's greatest quality was that he was a fighter in the true sense of the word. A balanced individual, who always carefully weighed the pros and cons of any situation, he threw himself whole-heartedly into the freedom struggle against the British knowing fully well that the path was strewn with obstacles.
>
> For years he was involved in nationalistic activities, including the Salt Satyagraha (non-violent resistance) without caring about the consequences. He was sentenced to imprisonment many times for his—and the *Inquilab's*—political pursuits between 1920 until Independence in 1947.

The foreword of the book is written by Dr Rafiq Zakaria, eminent scholar, former minister and Member of Parliament and my friend and mentor. The following are some excerpts from that section of the book:

---

[1]Javed Jamaluddin, *Abdul Hameed Ansari: Revolutionary Journalist and Freedom Fighter,* Popular Prakashan, 2004.

Abdul Hamid Ansari was a crusader who emerged victorious due to sheer hard work and determination.

An epitome of perseverance and self-sacrifice, he left an indelible mark on journalism and on the hearts and minds of his readers.

During these sad times when voices of communalism have become strident and the Muslim community's very identity as Indians is being questioned, Abdul Hamid Ansari's life and message to modern India become very relevant.

He was a true patriotic Indian. A freedom fighter and a newspaper man to the core, his liberalism easily towered over smaller minds and parochial elements. He forded the waters of prejudice of the majority community and the narrow-mindedness of his own community to pioneer a new path.

He successfully laid the foundation of *Inquilab*, which has been a beacon as well as the voice of the progressive Muslim community, and later was the inspiration for his son Khalid Ansari's *Mid-Day*. Both are benchmarks in Indian journalism today.

This book brings to our attention how a brave and fearless soldier of the Indian freedom struggle and revolutionary journalist was ignored and remained unappreciated despite his great service to the nation.

Unfortunately, the participation of Indian Muslims in the Indian struggle is often ignored. It is sad that after the Congress came to power, it completely ignored Mr Ansari who devoted the best years of his life to the country and its people. The Congress party should have assessed Mr Ansari's contributions, but it never happened. He could have made a mark in politics had the Congress given him a chance. His contribution was hardly acknowledged.

Money, position and power were never important to Abdul Hamid. His magnificent obsession was service to the country, followed by promotion of the Urdu language. He must be turning in his grave at the systemic manner in which the beautiful language is being obliterated in the country, because it is said to be the exclusive language of Muslims, which it, decidedly, is not.

Mr Ansari's life is an inspiration to one and all. Jamaluddin's book brings to our attention how a brave and fearless soldier of the Indian freedom movement was ignored and remained unappreciated despite his great services to the nation.

According to Jamaluddin, 'Mr Ansari never got his due. For him, journalism was a passion. He not only worked hard to make the Urdu language popular among the masses, but also introduced offset printing technology for the first time in the country.'

◆

As the Indian National Congress, under the guidance of Mahatma Gandhi, mounted up on the efforts to free the country from foreign rule, Abdul Hamid Ansari jumped into the fray with characteristic missionary zeal. A fiery, passionate speaker, at mohalla and street corner meetings, he exhorted his passive compatriots in the Congress and Muslim League—then often at loggerheads with each other—to sink their differences and join hands for the common cause of freedom. His fervent involvement with India's fight for freedom saw Abdul Hamid work with various groups such as Mehfil Afzal Payambari resulting in his incarceration by the British on a number of occasions.

During the freedom struggle, Abdul Hamid worked alongside Hafiz Ali, Bahadur Khan, Barristers Zahur Ahmed Allahabadi, Moinuddin Harris, Abdul Hamid Nomani and the Ali brothers. He was then initiated into journalism by Hafiz Ali who cherry-picked him to join the popular Urdu daily *Akhbar-e-Hilal* and was soon elevated to the position of editor, which resulted in him being sent to jail several times because of his fiery editorials during this period. Imprisoned at Pune's notorious Yerawada Central Jail after the Salt Satyagraha, Abdul Hamid raised his voice against the treatment of prisoners. His jail term was consequently extended but resulted in political prisoners being given a few facilities after that incident.

All his friends from Mumbai, including Harilal Mahimtura, who went on to become a presidency magistrate in Mumbai and activist Vithalbhai Jhaveri, were released but Abdul Hamid had to spend two more years at Yerawada Jail. He was, however, far from chastised and continued his revolutionary work in prison. This resulted in some changes being brought about in the functioning of the jail.

Abdul Hamid's provocative, in-your-face demeanour was expectedly anathema to the colonial masters and he was made to serve three prison sentences during the Khilafat movement at Mumbai's Arthur Road and Pune's Yerawada where his run-ins with the guards, jailors and officials became the stuff of legend, especially among the freedom-fighter inmates.

Political prisoners were randomly and regularly tortured at Yerawada. When Abdul Hamid raised his voice against this, the jailor subjected him to harsh treatment. He was made to perform back-breaking manual labour and thrown into solitary confinement. He then went on an indefinite hunger strike. As a result, when other prisoners were released after the Gandhi-Irwin pact, Abdul Hamid was held back.

A jamadar—Vilayat Khan—was appointed to look after the prisoners in solitary confinement. Khan, a cruel man who tried to dissuade Abdul Hamid from the hunger strike which went on for 17 days, asked him to request for a pardon in exchange for his freedom. But Abdul Hamid refused and instead ended up influencing Khan by saying that Islam did not preach unkindness: 'I opted to die fighting for the nation, which was the right thing to do according to Islamic norms. A true Muslim will always be true to the nation of his birth and will lay down his life for the nation. I would never stoop so low as to ask for pardon. I would rather die with dignity.'[2]

In the biography, Jamaluddin writes, 'After this, Khan started treating Abdul Hamid with compassion. He would permit him to come out of his cell for a walk and some fresh air. On one occasion, Khan slipped half a dozen sweet limes into his cell. While thanking Khan for his kindness, Abdul Hamid urged him not to do so because this went against the principles of satyagraha (non-cooperation). By now Khan had become Abdul Hamid's supporter and confidante. Jail superintendent Major Martin once approached him and asked him to beg for pardon and leave the Congress. Abdul Hamid refused the

---

[2]Javed Jamaluddin, *Abdul Hameed Ansari: Revolutionary Journalist and Freedom Fighter*, Popular Prakashan, 2004. p. 39.

offer and a few days later he was informed that his demands have been accepted, following which he ended his fast.'

While in prison, Abdul Hamid learnt Marathi, Gujarati and English. He also read up on religion and the world political situation. After completing his term, Abdul Hamid again plunged into the freedom movement. In Jamaluddin's words, 'Abdul Hamid, like gold, emerged brighter from the fire of adversity. He went on to become an eminent person in social and political circles in Mumbai. During this period, he made up his mind about what he wanted to be and how he would go about achieving it. He learnt to cope with adversity and always turned difficult situations around. And he treated everyone with respect and dignity.'

The rest, as they say, is history with the *Inquilab*, in time, (according to the Audit Bureau of Circulation) becoming India's premier, most widely circulated, respected and influential newspaper in the country.

It was during the Quit India movement that Abdul Hamid met noted freedom fighters Abid Ali Jaferbhai and Salehbhai Abdul Kader. The former was then living abroad but returned to India to join the freedom movement. Abid Ali became a personal favourite of Jawaharlal Nehru and went on to become a minister in the Central government and represented India at the International Labour Organization (ILO) in Geneva.

Impressed with the young journalist's ardent nationalism and zeal, which bordered on the missionary, as well his passionate writing ability, Jaferbhai and Salehbhai decided to sponsor an Urdu daily newspaper with Abdul Hamid solely in charge, to spearhead the nationalist movement among the Muslims of Mumbai. They remained Abdul Hamid's soulmates and mentors until their deaths.

The paper was called the *Inquilab* meaning 'revolution' to reflect the objective and spirit of the freedom movement reflected in the stirring slogan *Inquilab Zindabad* (long live the revolution).

The early editions were printed in ramshackle Ghas Galli on Lamington Road before moving to Nagpada, where it was printed for many years, on a dilapidated hand-fed sheet printing machine (this was before the advent of rotary) that churned out one set of four out of the total of six/eight pages.

All pages of the *Inquilab* were written by hand on a specially coated yellow paper which were then transferred onto stone by a massive hand press before being moved to the antediluvian printing press—literally, the Stone Age days which shall remain forever etched in my memory. He was ever the printer's devil, who stalked the newspaper's newsroom and press room with unabated curiosity and of whom it may be said that he had printer's ink in his veins!

The newspaper's reputation was built on hard-headed, no-nonsense honesty and sincerity of purpose. Abdul Hamid made *Inquilab* the vehicle for addressing issues concerning the common man. It was the voice of the poor, needy and helpless sections of society.

He was an admirer of Abul Kalam Azad, and despite thinking very highly of him, he didn't see eye to eye with him on many issues. On this subject, he once said, 'I think journalists and political leaders should be pulled up for their misdeeds. These very people claim to be the guides and leaders of the public. If they indulge in objectionable behaviour, their followers should be made aware of it.'

Luminaries of the Urdu language such as Ali Sardar Jafri, Sahir Ludhianvi, Majrooh Sultanpuri, Shakeel Badayuni, Kaifi Azmi, Firaq Gorakhpuri, Zoe Ansari (who was also editor of the *Inquilab* for some years), Yusuf Khan (Dilip Kumar) and music director Naushad were his close friends but he was unsparing in his criticism of them, whenever he believed it was warranted.

Though Abdul Hamid and Majrooh Sultanpuri were at loggerheads from time to time, after his death in 1972, Sultanpuri said of him: 'I did not share a very cordial relationship with Abdul Hamid Ansari. We were in fact engaged in a battle (over the issue of converting Urdu into the Devanagari script). And my personal experience with him has shown that whenever he opposed anyone or anything, he did it with passion and fearlessness.'[3]

And, at a condolence meeting, Sahir Ludhianvi said of Abdul Hamid, 'Affluent people start newspapers these days and the masses have no choice or say in the matter. But Abdul Hamid's efforts have

---

[3]Javed Jamaluddin, *Abdul Hameed Ansari: Revolutionary Journalist and Freedom Fighter*, Popular Prakashan, 2004.

evolved into an enormous revolution. His paper is the voice of the nation. He has kept the flame of Urdu journalism burning. His initiative has been instrumental in keeping the language alive in the hearts of the common man. Secularism, democracy and minority rights were very close to Abdul Hamid Ansari's heart. And we are confident that *Inquilab* will take this forward.'

Senior journalist Khalil Zahid once remarked, 'Abdul Hamid's hold over the Urdu-speaking public was so great that he could easily change mindsets through his writings and influence political and social decisions. His only dream was to mould his newspaper according to the sentiments of the common man. The hardships that he faced in the orphanage, jail and the narrow bylanes of Madanpura, brought him closer to the poor and needy.'

Partition

'I'll not migrate to Pakistan as long as even one Muslim is left on Indian soil. A true Muslim can never think of leaving his country. I shall continue to live in India even if I have to sacrifice my life for this cherished goal of mine.'

—Revolutionary journalist and freedom fighter Abdul Hamid Ansari

When India gained Independence in 1947, Abdul Hamid steadfastly refused to migrate to Pakistan. He provided guidance to his loyal readers throughout the World War II years. Despite turbulence and vicissitudes, he remained steadfast to the various causes he espoused, such as patriotism, national integration, women's education, promotion of the Urdu language, even as he promoted the causes of brotherhood and peaceful coexistence against the evil forces of communalism after the trauma of the Partition.

Through the Inquilab Relief Fund, which he started, Abdul Hamid collected funds for the victims of riots in West Bengal, Pune, Bhiwandi, Nizamabad, Gulbarga, Hazratbal and the earthquake in Bihar. Due to his ardent belief that he was the custodian of the money collected through the relief efforts, Abdul Hamid was meticulous in his account keeping and published in the *Inquilab* details of every rupee collected, and later handed it over to the beneficiaries in public.

At the same time, he shamed organizations such as the Jamiat Ulema-e-Hind (which he exposed for misappropriating funds raised for victims of the riots in Bengal) and the Bombay Weavers' Co-Operative Society, which embezzled public money. Some of the office bearers were his friends, but his professional responsibility overcame personal considerations. 'It is my duty to expose corruption,' he once said at a public meeting.

Recalls Haroon Khushtar, a reporter with *Inquilab*: 'On January 18, 1956, Abdul Hamid and I went to CP Tank and Girgaum to cover the riots and arson. Tension was at its peak and I was fully aware that Abdul Hamid would not be scared of the merciless killings, police firings and tear gas shell. We scooped the story from areas which were considered extremely dangerous for non-Maharashtrians.'

Although the primary focus of the *Inquilab* was on national and local news, late in life, Abdul Hamid remembered with pride that it was his paper that broke the news of Stalin's death on 5 March 1953 and how he came perilously close to dumping the entire print-run of that day's issue over confusion regarding the veracity of the death (over which he had taken a huge gamble so that the paper could be the first to report the news), over the wires.

Being a municipal corporator (he was elected to the BMC with the highest number of votes to date in the history of the civic body), Abdul Hamid had his hand on the pulse of the metropolis. In an editorial titled 'Life in Bombay' he wrote, 'Renowned English author and critic G.K. Chesterton once said that London seems beautiful from a distance. The same applies to Bombay as well. The entire country is in awe of the city. Bombay's beauty, its wealth, skyscrapers, cinema halls, buses and electric trains and, not to forget the film industry, hold a lot of attraction for everyone. But those who live here know that, in reality, the city is ugly, filthy, and heartless. Because Bombay provides employment opportunities and it attracts everyone—from labourers of South India to farmers from UP and Bihar. As a result, Bombay is bursting at its seams with people.'

A true Mumbaikar who spoke fluent Marathi, Abdul Hamid addressed Mumbai's gargantuan problems through the *Inquilab*, but it must be conceded that his ultimate contribution was negligible, given the power politics in the BMC.

Abdul Hamid Ansari, the orphan boy from Madanpura and one-man band of printer, publisher, editor and street vendor must also get credit for pioneering a revolution in the newspaper printing industry.

In 1965, the *Inquilab* became the first Indian newspaper to graduate from lithography to rotary offset. This achievement is monumental, especially when one considers the fact that Abdul Hamid did not initially have the ₹2.25 lakhs to buy the sub-standard Planeta sheet-fed offset press from erstwhile East Germany. A loyal employee of 25 years even offered him ₹50,000, his life savings, which left him tearful, but he politely refused.

Many mishaps ensued, including the interminable and inexplicable delay in the shipment of the equipment from East Germany, which arrived in damaged condition and had to be replaced, following a two-year battle with the suppliers.

Payment for the final instalment was enabled by the then presidency magistrate and friend Harilal Mahimtura's wife Veena and the sale of his wife Amina Begum's jewellery for ₹35,000, which she had saved over 27 years from her monthly household allowance.

Explaining his reasons for not taking a loan, despite offers of help from high-placed political friends and the Maharashtra State Finance Corporation (MSFC), Abdul Hamid said, 'I do not wish to lose my freedom of expression…nor do I want people to make allegations that I take sides or refrain from criticizing the government for personal gain.'

Wear and tear caused during the storage and shipment of the machine led to further delay and a consequent deterioration in his heart condition. It was aggravated by the death of Shahid, his eldest son by his second marriage, in a car accident near Kalyan, which brought on two heart attacks.

◆

But Abdul Hamid was undaunted and continued his steadfast battles for various cherished causes with a missionary zeal until his death. In 1972 he left behind me, then 35 years old, two grandsons—Tarique, aged 11, and Sharique, 9—and a granddaughter, Tehzeeb, aged 2.

Sadanand Shetty, founder and chairman of Fouress Corporation, the Bengaluru-based conglomerate; businessman Firoz Baldiwala;

my friends and fellow Rotarians were of invaluable help in getting bank loans for the printing press. Without their selfless help, it could not have been possible for us to break away from the shackles of antiquated printing.

Congratulating the *Inquilab* group at the historic installation of the press at which Maharashtra Vasantrao Naik presided and actor Dilip Kumar, an old associate of Abdul Hamid, was chief guest, R.K. Karanjia of Blitz Publications remarked: 'Urdu journalism and its journalists have not let the fire in their pens die out even for a moment. It is indeed laudable that Urdu journalists (like Abdul Hamid Ansari) have not only kept alive the tradition of social awareness, but have taken a step forward. Now *Inquilab* will be printed by the offset process and will bring greater glory to the journalistic world.'

Early Childhood

Khudi ko kar buland itna ki har taqdeer se pehle
Khuda bande se khud pooche bata teri raza kya hain

(Elevate yourself so high before each Destiny that
God may ask you, 'Tell me, what is your desire?')

—Allama Iqbal

I don't know much about my childhood except that I was born when my parents were living on Ripon Road (now Maulana Azad Rd) between Nagpada Junction and Madanpura, close to Jacob Circle in Central Mumbai.

I was sent to St Agnes Primary (Convent of Jesus and Mary) on Clare Road, Byculla, close to home; it was a girls' school but admitted a few boys in the infant and primary classes.

I've often wondered if this could have been the reason I've always been an unabashed admirer of all things beautiful (females of the species included!), since childhood influences are said to last a lifetime.

At that time, boys had to leave St Agnes after the second standard. My career at the primary school was cut short by two years because of what were at the time termed 'double promotions'—in my case not because I was extraordinarily bright but, according to my mother, a *seedha-sadha* (naïve), obedient boy who always stood up when speaking to elders and, by implication, appealed to the maternal instincts of the teachers.

I mention this seemingly inconsequential detail, not out of braggadocio or levity, but for a reason. I was convinced it was unfair for me in terms of scholastic achievement to be two years younger than my classmates. I was 15 when I passed out of St Mary's school, comparatively weaker physically and wet behind my ears. Many of my classmates were old enough to shave, smoke cigarettes clandestinely and terrorize those younger, with impunity.

'Double promotions' can be counterproductive in a harsh, competitive, rough-and-tumble environment like the one at St Mary's, in which bullying was par for the course. It may have toughened some of the boys but made me introverted and insecure when dealing with the older, brawnier street-smart bullies.

Growing up, our play area next to the ramshackle building (grandiosely named Imperial Mansions) where we lived and where the neighbourhood children played barefoot cricket, football, hockey, seven tiles and 'robbers and thieves' was congested. An uneven narrow two-way street, it was called Macbeth Lane (Batak Gully or Ducks Lane) because ducks belonging to the East Indian community, waddled there without check and were often felled by a truant cricket sixer, much to the owners' chagrin.

In this sports nursery, the raison d'être for street games was one—to win. The proceedings, however, were largely friendly and played in fair spirit. In Australia, the most essential quality in a budding champion is the 'mongrel' quality, one which talent scouts look for most among young cricketers, apart from ability. I was fortunate to possess this competitive spirit, but was certainly no champ, the acme of my sporting achievement being representing my school St Mary's, and St Xavier's College, Mumbai, under Nari Contractor, and succeeding him as cricket captain of Government Law College.

Reasonably fleet-footed, an 11-second 100-metre sprinter, I was crowned all-round champion athlete at Government Law College in 1959 but, try as I might, Tara Malkani, the state sprint champion, always finished a few nanoseconds ahead of me at the Maharashtra state level. My coach was the legendary Jal Pardiwala, at the then impressive NSCI Stadium, Worli, under the Rajkumari Amrit Kaur scheme, but Tara was just too fleet-footed for me. Later in 1972, I was privileged to spend quality time with 'Jalbhai' at the ill-starred Olympic Games—the first of nine that I was privileged to see in the call of duty.

St Mary's (SSC) High School

Although each one of us at St Mary's hated to lose, what separated us from others was the fact that we were taught to always play fair and by the rules—this was before the advent of John Lever's 'Vaseline', Michael Atherton's 'sawdust-in-pocket' and Steven Smith's, David Warner's and Cameron Bancroft's ball-tampering *badmaashi*.[4]

For us St Mary's boys, the memorable words of elegant early-twentieth-century golf writer Grantland 'Granny' Rice were inviolable:

> For when the One Great Scorer comes to write against your name,
> He marks—not that you won or lost—But how you played the game.

When crafting those felicitous words, Rice certainly could not have been thinking of the likes of the golf-addict former president of a powerhouse country, who is notorious for cheating shamelessly on the golf course!

During my childhood, my father was totally immersed in the freedom movement and had neither the time, nor much education or

---

[4]The above incidents of skulduggery are reminiscent of the time an Indian cricket captain would, at the toss, invariably swiftly pick up the coin from the turf, remarking to his counterpart: 'Sorry skip, you've lost the toss again!'

understanding of the higher scholastic standards prevalent in Mumbai. I was moved to St Mary's School, Mazagaon. An average student, I was woefully weak in algebra and geometry, proficient in English and generally at par with the rest of the class at science, maths, geography and history, but just couldn't come to terms with the interminably boring dates in European history.

Given his irregular work hours and rather parlous financial situation, my father thought it unnecessary for me, all of 7, to attend school by taking the bus. Situated on Nesbit Road, Mazagaon, St Mary's was a good 50-minute walk each way from home via Badak Gully, Clare Road, Shepherd Road and Nesbit Bridge. My father also believed firmly that strenuous physical activity should be a sine qua non for young bodies. He dearly loved me but, despite living in the same house, I was lucky if I even saw him once a week! At the time, we had a live-in attendant, Aminbhai, belonging to the Sidi tribe from Janjira, near Alibaug, but originally descended from enslaved people who were brought from Africa by the Nawab. Aminbhai doted on me and, in cahoots with my affectionate uncle Abdul Rahman, spoiled me rotten with an unending supply of chocolates that made a sorry mess of my teeth, necessitating many painful visits to a dentist.

Aminbhai was tasked with walking me to school and back every day. Later, when he passed away, I followed the same route on my own until my final year.

In hindsight, the exercise of walking to school and back did me a power of good and I enjoyed the passing parade so much that when my sons—Tarique and Sharique—started attending Cathedral School near Fort, they were required to walk uphill, rather than be driven, with their bulging school backpack, to the bus stop at Malabar Hill Post Office from home, Cosmopolis, on Nepean Road. It was the same drill on their return from school. It must be said to their credit that not once did they ask why they were required to climb the hill lugging their books when their friends and classmates living in the area, if not driven all the way to school and back, had their help carry their bags to the bus-stop.

Most of the students at St Mary's were also from a lower middle-class background. Our fees were consequently much lower, stemming from the fact that we pursued the Indian Senior School Certificate curriculum whereas examination papers of the *burra sahibs* (big boys) of the senior Cambridge section across the Mazagaon Bridge were marked in England.

My father paid ₹12 a month as fees in my 12th standard as opposed to the ₹75 paid by parents of Senior Cambridge section boys like Iqbal Chagla, who went on to step into his illustrious lawyer father M.C. Chagla's shoes, and later, Azim Premji, the IT whizz-kid. The passage of time has dimmed memories of school but 'the days of our youth were indeed days of our glory,' as legendary poet George Byron wrote. The sands of time have taken a heavy toll on our school colleagues: only two St Mary's alumni remain in touch—Narendra Shetty (Executive Chairman, Haldyn Glass Works) and Bipin Hardi (Chief Engineer, Carnival Cruises, US).

At school there was also the genial Captain Reza Beg (Commander, Air India), champion marathon runner, who entered the *Guinness Book of Records* by becoming the first pilot in world commercial airline history to be reinstated after being dismissed from service following a serious heart condition. He swore to return to his job and, after prolonged medical treatment and physiotherapy, regained his commercial pilot's licence and won a celebrated legal battle against the airline, thereby setting a precedent in the industry. A bon vivant and good friend, Captain Beg migrated with Kolkata-born wife Leonie to Auckland, New Zealand, where he passed away in 2020.

Then there was Dom Moraes, son of redoubtable *Times of India* editor Frank Moraes.

'Hello ol' chap, we do have a hot sun in India!' we would taunt him after his observation about the oppressive weather at an inter-section cricket match soon after he had arrived from a trip to Ol' Blighty, where he won the Hawthornden Prize for literature.

Getting my Secondary School Certificate at the age of 15 presented me a dilemma of Himalayan proportions. With father busy as ever, and no relative, elder family member or friend in the whole wide world except those in the dysfunctional step-family, none of whom, in any case, were educated enough to be able to guide, I had to make my own decisions regarding choice of educational career.

The selection turned out to be a no-brainer, a one-horse race, since the only criterion applied by friends (none of whom were any the wiser), was not the fact of the distinguished alumni but the girls in south Mumbai colleges—exclusively in terms of looks and sociability. Academic excellence was a pitiable last among the yardsticks applied! George Bernard Shaw was spot on when he famously declared 'youth is wasted on the young.'

My friends and I were convinced, for some strange reason, that the billiards salon adjacent to our school was a 'shady' place frequented by drunks, roughnecks and gamblers, which was entirely incorrect. We derived a strange thrill from walking up and down past the main door to sneak a peek at the proceedings inside the dimly lit hall in the hope of unravelling the profound mystery, such was our innocence up to almost the sixth standard.

◆

To assert that the rivalry between the two St Mary's sections on the field of play was bitter would be a gross understatement. Looked down upon by the privileged boys from across the road, it gave us, the 'poor, underprivileged boys', who competed with messianic zeal, unalloyed joy to thrash the 'snobs' (an unfair description to be honest, since they were not!).

That said, the 'play fairly—but there's no glory in coming second' mindset became good preparation for some of us to cope with the battles ahead in life. Looking back over the years, this fierce drive to excel also manifested itself in the scholastic achievements of many students from our section, many of whom have excelled in their endeavours.

◆

I was deeply saddened recently to find, as I drove past my beloved alma mater, that the playground, the fountainhead of well-rounded mental, physical and emotional character development of thousands of proud St Mary's students over the years, had succumbed to Mammon, to the lure of filthy lucre and converted into an eyesore of a housing colony.

That apart, I shall forever remain grateful to St Mary's and sincerely hope that the 156-year-old Jesuit institution lives up to its motto '*Immaculata*' meaning 'pure', 'whole' and 'untouched'. Apart from receiving holistic secondary school education of a lofty standard, which has been the foundation of whatever I have learnt at respected centres of learning in India and abroad, it inculcated in me, at an impressionable age, certain values, virtues and verities without which I could never have realized my true potential.

For this I gratefully thanked the Jesuit priests of St Mary's school and St Xavier's college during my acceptance speech at a function at the college to honour past students. I have no pretensions of being an orator, but hope my words seemed sincere enough, if nothing else!

I also made it a point to draw attention to the poor salaries that teachers/professors of both institutions are paid. Stressing the invaluable roles they play in imparting education, shaping young minds and building character, I implored the authorities to address the problem.

For the strict, disciplinarian Catholic priests who ran the school with an admixture of admirable no-nonsense strict adherence to 'Catholic' values (in the sense of being universal) and compassion, the virtues of probity and rectitude were paramount. (On a recent visit to my alma mater, I was delighted to find, upon probing, that most of the cherished values inculcated in us as students continue to this day).

Their mission was character-building. The old chestnut, 'Do unto others as you would have others do to you' still retained its original sanctity before being unfortunately distorted, in society at large, to 'Do to others before they do to you.' Very early in life we were taught the meaning of Sir Walter Scott's memorable poem *Marmion*: 'Oh what a tangled web we weave, when first we practise to deceive.'

Our day at school started with the Lord's prayer in assembly. There was strong emphasis—not on narrow, sectarian religious teaching, but on moral science, the universality of religion and its true meaning in everyday life.

In what would be an anomaly in India today, we had courses in moral science and, later, civics at St Xavier's College, where I had the privilege to learn at the feet of devoted purveyors of knowledge, wisdom, gyan to keep us within the straight and narrow tramlines of responsible behaviour in public.

The concept of an honours system, as prevails in certain Western countries, was as yet unknown but, at a time when corporal punishment was the norm in Jesuit schools, there was no question of sparing the rod and spoiling the child! A few whacks from the wooden 'palm striker' succeeded in keeping the roguish, smart alecs in line.

It would be churlish of me to not commend the Jesuit Catholic institutions, which have been rendering selfless service to the cause of Indian education and but for whose sincerity, hard work and devotion, the list of luminaries who passed out from their institutions would not have been possible.

Also, I must take up cudgels in their defence against the calumny being spread, especially on social media, accusing them of proselytization. In all my 12 years at St Mary's School and St Xavier's College, I have never come across a single proven case of conversion nor have I met anybody who has been. While conceding that there may have been the odd case somewhere, it is grossly unfair to allege that the problem is endemic.

The mischief mongers among us who follow an agenda of divisiveness and disaffection, spread poison and hatred through misinformation among our otherwise peaceful and secular people should be dealt with in the severest possible manner.

Childhood Influences

I shall never forget the invaluable role that my dear childhood friend, mentor and exemplar Jaffer Mansuri (he later changed his surname to Durazi after his Bahraini pearl fisherman grandfather) played in my upbringing. He showed me the right and virtuous path away from the deleterious influences of youth, and constantly inspired me to have a purpose in life, to shun mediocrity and strive for excellence. He constantly showered me with gifts of books, especially the classics and amusing bon mots.

Thanks to him, a quotation remain etched in my memory:

> *In the lexicon of youth, which fate reserves for a bright manhood, there is no such word as fail.*
>
> —Edward Bulwer-Lytton

I had this nugget of wisdom framed and hung outside my two sons' bedroom door, when they were studying at Cathedral School, Mumbai, for them to see—and be inspired by—first thing after they woke up in the morning.

They haven't admitted in so many words if they were inspired or not, but if one were to go by their achievements, the answer is fairly obvious!

◆

To revert to the narrative: with my father getting even more deeply immersed in the cataclysmic public life following the euphoria of

Independence in 1947, and nobody in our family to guide me in my desire to go for further education upon passing my secondary school certificate at the jejune age of 15, I felt adrift in a sea of increasing self-doubt, low self-esteem and confusion.

Sans any sex education at school worth the name—except for hushed whispers, 'nod-nod, wink-wink,' 'fake news' sources of information—I was thrown into a maelstrom of confusion upon reaching puberty, with its attendant mental, physical and emotional complexities.

To make matters worse, my father, desirous of fathering more children after me, requested my mother for permission to remarry, since she could not bear any more children. Being an ever-accommodating wife, my mother capitulated graciously, blissfully unaware of the cataclysm that this released genie would wreak.

Early Upbringing

To expect any husband to treat two wives equally, a precondition for taking a second wife as laid down by Islam, is oxymoronic: in essence, a contradiction of terms.

Two wives vying for the constant love and attention of one and the same husband in the same household is a recipe for disaster. Expecting happiness in such a situation is akin to discovering the Yeti or finding the Loch Ness monster.

And so was it for me, a mentally confused and devastated teenager, living in trauma with two mothers in a smallish two-bedroom flat. I'm sure my second mother had some laudable qualities—only she didn't show them, or perhaps I didn't recognize any.

Although my grandfather was a teacher of religion, my father was extremely liberal in his religious beliefs, nationalistic politics being his sole and most important concern in life.

In my parents' lexicon, the five-letter words 'm-o-n-e-y' and 'g-r-e-e-d' were the most evil and corrosive words, the root of all evil. They taught me at a young age to forgive, but never forget since it is important in life to learn from one's experiences. In the words of George Santayana, 'Those who cannot remember the past are condemned to repeat it.'

My half-siblings and I were raised in a, what may be termed, non-denominational manner and were encouraged to respect all religions and celebrate all religious festivals, but rites and rituals were unacceptable. That is why, all through life my friends have belonged to diverse faiths, colours, cultures and spoken different languages. My children have been taught to follow the same tenets in life.

Despite possessing what appeared to be an obsessive-compulsive personality where nationalism and egalitarianism were concerned, my father, despite his rather limited education, taught me the importance of balance, especially when forming value judgements. He was a rationalist with an overt disdain for cant and shibboleth.

◆

This reminds me of the time when my father, two of his friends and I were driving back to Mumbai via Pune. On the route was this tomb of a Muslim saint to which devotees flock to witness what is termed a 'miracle'—seven (or perhaps nine) people standing around a large, heavy, spherical stone are said to be able to lift it with only a forefinger each.

We dutifully stood around the hefty stone in a group, as sanctimoniously directed by the organizers of the drama, forefingers below the stone, took a deep breath which they said was essential and, as per our conspiracy hatched earlier, chanted: '*Ya shaitan Ali Bawa*' (the Devil) and, hey presto, the stone was hoisted shoulder-high on our fingers!

Unsurprisingly, the ringmasters of the deception were not amused and almost stoned us out of the sanctum sanctorum.

Ever the hardcore sceptic, my father later attributed the 'miracle' to a simple principle in physics, according to which force, if applied from equal and opposite directions, enables the lifting of heavy objects. The taking of that deep breath, according to him, was necessary for the application of equal force from opposite directions. I never got around to ascertaining the veracity of what may have been his half-baked theory but, if anything, it confirmed my suspicion of miracles, religious hocus-pocus, god-men and miracle workers of all hues.

Around this time in life, I chanced upon a proverb, presumably the translation of one in Arabic. I found the words to be as amusing as profound and something I have treasured all these years:

He who knows and knows not he knows,
Is asleep, awaken him;
He who knows not and knows he knows not,
Is a child, enlighten him:
He who knows and knows he knows,
Is a wise man, follow him:
He who knows not, and knows not he knows not,
Is a fool, shun him.

My Father

My father abjured extremism and always chose the middle, betwixt and between path. When asked to mediate in any dispute, his predilection was always for a 'much can be said on both sides,' sentiment, a diplomatic maxim I shamelessly adopted with amazing results. Also, when choosing to avoid expressing an opinion on a controversial subject, I learnt to phlegmatically use the expression 'the jury is still out...' which the British, masters in the art of diplomacy, have mastered. It has helped extricate me from many an awkward situation.

As may be expected under the circumstances, I loved my father dearly and was convinced that the feeling was mutual, perhaps more so because I saw so little of him in my formative years. He was my hero, and I longed for his closeness, for his loving and caring touch, which unfortunately never materialized. The causes he espoused as a journalist were his magnificent obsession. Whatever little time he was left with had to be divided between his two families—sadly, to the detriment of both.

I hungered for my father's appreciation of my academic and sporting achievements at school. He once confided to one of his close friends that it was his belief that success can go to young peoples' heads and that it was imperative not to praise them to their faces. In my assessment, as a young student I did not realize that he loved me with his entire being and, deep down inside, was proud of me, as indeed was my mother, a paragon of virtue. I now realize that my continuing lack of self-confidence in life and my insatiable hunger for appreciation is directly attributable to this aspect.

Looking back, this strange unrequited childhood hunger for recognition—not for whatever little I may have achieved in material terms but—to be acknowledged as what I considered myself to be, a good, compassionate, God-fearing human being in a harsh, ugly world, became a compulsion and the source of a feeling of acute inadequacy. So obsessive was this need that, instead of taking umbrage over an incensed remark by a Dubai-based Pakistani journalist to the effect that I was 'disgustingly honest,' I was overjoyed and retorted, 'What would you give to be like me?'

With the passage of time, my parents' *takiya kalam* (leitmotif) 'forgive people but don't forget incidents' became my lodestar in life.

St Xavier's College

To return to St Xavier's and a major decision-making time again—this time for the selection of courses for the two-year programme after intermediate leading up to the bachelor's degree.

Again, on the advice of close friends (many of whom were from the business community), I opted for Economics only to discover I had no interest in—nor head for—matters concerning money and finance. Finding myself totally out of my depth I beat a hasty retreat. Deprived of any experienced and knowledgeable source of advice, my personal preference fell upon English literature, one of the few streams I felt I had an aptitude for.

The professors who taught us—coincidentally both named Menezes—were masters of their craft and, apart from making us au fait with the refinements and nuances of the beautiful language starting with the Olde English (Anglo-Saxon) period, then continuing with the Middle English, Renaissance, Neoclassical, Romantic, Victorian, Edwardian, Georgian, Modern and the Postmodern periods, they lovingly infected us with their own felicity.

In the words of Carl Malamud, president and founder of Public. Resource.Org, 'Students should be able to access materials they need to educate themselves with, with the full support of their institutions, instead of being forced to fend for themselves in the wilds of the Internet.'[5]

---

[5]Carl Malamud, 'Who May Swim in the Ocean of Knowledge?' *The Wire*, 2 March 2018, https://thewire.in/education/who-may-swim-in-the-ocean-of-knowledge. Accessed on 29 October 2018.

Unfortunately, one of the Menezeses would spray the front benches with a shower of sputum in the course of his passionate lectures but that didn't dissuade his forgiving *shagirds* (students) from keeping only the front row of benches unoccupied out of respect for his scholarship.

We, their students, will remain forever indebted to the professors Menezes for energizing us with a similar love for the language which has become the premier lingua franca of the world but, alas, is fast losing its pristine purity in its native land, as lamented by Prof. Higgins in the stage musical *My Fair Lady*. (Based on George Bernard Shaw's *Pygmalion*, *My Fair Lady* is widely acknowledged by the cognoscente as the 'perfect' musical.)

My two years at St Xavier's College studying English for the bachelor's degree surely ranks among the most enjoyable times in my academic life, what with being able to indulge my love of cricket and actually playing for the college team and simultaneously luxuriating in a kaleidoscope of marvellous works of literature.

The behemoth that is the St Xavier's College library provided access to the many-splendoured world of English literature. It reminded one of the immortal words of physicist and mathematician, Isaac Newton, just before he died: 'I do not know what I may appear to the world, but to myself I seem to have been only like a boy playing on the seashore…while the great ocean of truth lay all undiscovered before me.'

As it turned out, my decision to seek admission in St Xavier's College in Mumbai was fortuitous in terms of quality of education and not strictly because of my Lothario friends' paradigm of female sociability.

Because of the conspicuous absence of any female contacts in my social life (except for a loving, but sadly ineffectual and guileless, mother in a dysfunctional family dominated by a stepmother, whose sole mission in life, understandably, was the material welfare of her own offspring), with no close relatives; half-sisters with whom my relationship was, at best, lukewarm; no aunts, cousins or even female family friends; and utterly lacking in self-confidence as I was, I tended to be hopelessly introverted and not 'the life of the party' type that appealed to the upper-crust set.

Later in life, when decisions regarding choice of schools had to be made for sons Tarique and Sharique and daughter Tehzeeb, one of the important criteria my (first) wife Rukya and I adhered to was that the school/s:

- should be co-educational given that both she and I had been to gender-segregated schools: she to the St Agnes High School, followed by the girls-only Sophia College (for her bachelor's) and I to St Mary's all-boys' school, followed by a college (St Xavier's), where my own personal contact with girls was a big cypher. This had resulted in both of us becoming exceedingly timorous in the presence of people of the other sex.
- should have a mixed student body in terms of economic background, since we had both attended schools that catered very largely to the economically-challenged strata of society, resulting in both of us developing a sense of comparative financial inadequacy and
- should have a student body with a mix of students from different nationalities

Wanderlust

In a contrast with college, my family and home life went downhill, my sense of solitude seemingly unending. A welcome relief came in the form of college 'study tours,' as they were called, to places of tourist interest in different parts of the country. It was, perhaps, my father's way to help me escape the stifling home environment but it also helped open my eyes to the richly rewarding joy of travel and the wondrous world beyond my immediate surroundings.

The alluring, full-page colour advertisements of Canadian Club Whisky in *Life* magazine featuring explorers and world travellers enjoying sundowners at exotic destinations instilled a wanderlust which refused to go away like the accursed COVID-19 from planet Earth.

Similarly, I'm also indebted to the column 'Improve Your Word Power' in *Reader's Digest* magazine which opened my eyes to the fascinating and unbounded world of semantics and its branch, linguistics.

◆

The inexpensive cattle-class train journey to Darjeeling (home of Tenzing Norgay, the first man to climb Mount Everest, along with Sir Edmund Hillary of New Zealand) was a great education. The trips to Kashmir, Mount Abu, Ajmer, Jaipur and Udaipur, even distant Colombo, Kandy, Sigiriya and Nuwara Eliya in Sri Lanka, although arduous, were immensely educative.

The trip to Ajmer was an experience of a lifetime. *Bella notte* (Italian for 'beautiful night')—the breathtaking, star-spangled night we experienced at Ajmer Railway station, was reminiscent of Vincent Van Gogh's magnum opus oil on canvas painting called just that, *The Starry Night*. Incidentally, the song 'Loveliest Night of the Year' with reference to *Bella Notte*, sung in 1951 by Mario Lanza, continues to linger in my mind's eye because of nature's incomparable ethereal pyrotechnics at run-down Ajmer station that night.

It was infinitely more spectacular than even the aurora borealis near the North Pole (which, incidentally, many years later turned out to be a huge disappointment because of the gross ineptitude of the Norwegian liner, which was a stop-at-all ports fishing trawler. You win some, lose some!).

College tours meant eating barely edible food, drinking impure water and anodyne tea and sleeping in bargain-basement price beddings on floors of filthy, rickety, third-class train coaches. But so exhilarating was the camaraderie, so educationally rewarding the experience in terms of widening mental horizons, not to mention getting to know female college mates at close quarters, that the next trip was booked out by us men no sooner had we returned from the previous one!

> That was the time we joked to our friends that Winston Churchill's World War II aphorism from 1939 about Russia being 'a riddle wrapped in a mystery, inside an enigma' was not originally a put-down of the country but of the female of the species!

◆

On the subject of travel, among the more memorable trips taken by Zeyna and me was the one we took before COVID times to Jalandhar for a wedding and to unforgettable Amritsar with Le Corbusier's nondescript Chandigarh en route.

I must make special mention of the indescribable feeling of heightened inner tranquillity that the Harmandir Sahib 'abode of God'

Golden Temple inspires. At the temple, management of visitors and the langar (communal free kitchen) is flawless, the premise, spotless and the number of daily pilgrims (pre-COVID 19) who are fed, in excess of 100,000.

A trip to the Indo-Pakistan border at Wagah (Zeyna's first, my second) to witness the Beating Retreat ceremony was an eminently bizarre and senseless display of faux juvenile chest-thumping and muscle-flexing. It is hyped in tourist brochures as a 'symbol of cooperation and brotherhood between the two countries,' but, in reality, is the opposite—if the delirious, xenophobic and almost hysterical shrieks of 'Jai Hind' countered by 'Pakistan Zindabad' were anything to go by!

◆

To return to where we were:

Bitten by the travel bug, and driven by an urge to continue my honeymoon with travel and tourism, I foolishly decided to try my hand at becoming a part-time travel guide even as I pursued my bachelor's degree. More importantly, as one's pocket money at home was meagre as it was, one was hardly in a position to turn up one's nose at the pittance!

My knowledge of ancient Indian history was laughable, of comparative religions and mythology, worse, and of Marathi, abysmal. After undergoing a brief but meaningless training course at the Government of India tourism office at Churchgate in Mumbai, I managed to pass the examination and was immediately sent on my first assignment as guide to a 20-something group of perfervid Americans.

The tourists turned out to be much better read and knowledgeable about Mumbai than even my trainers and examiners. They kept up a raucous and, for me, terrifying barrage of incisive questions concerning matters like the origin of Banganga Tank on Malabar Hill, its legend dating back to the Ramayana, architectural complexities of the aqueduct at Hanging Gardens, the multitudinous flora and fauna of the city. I had zero answers given my insular background and the fact that I had not been taught about such things. Bluffing my way out was hardly the solution, so I ignominiously faked a bad case of food poisoning, ran the fastest 100 and 200 metres like Usain Bolt and, once out of sight, hailed a taxi home never to return to the tourist office again.

That must have been the only time an Indian tourist guide went missing in action and, hand on my heart, it must rank among the most humiliating and dishonourable experiences of my life!

◆

My parents offered me the opportunity to continue my studies after graduation and I jumped at it since the academic bug had bitten me and, more importantly, because of the bang-up social life at college that meant I got two more years at co-educational St Xavier's.

In those days, the rules of Mumbai University permitted students to simultaneously pursue two parallel courses, namely, a master's degree as well as a bachelor's law degree. By now my mind had been made up to emulate my father's example and become a journalist.

In the naïve, but not altogether illogical, belief that knowledge of political science and law would be assets in my chosen profession (law to prevent involvement in lawsuits!), I took the leap, following the dictum that at times you must leap before you look, or you never leap at all.

◆

For the master's degree, we were required to study political theory, Indian government and politics, public administration and international relations, the last-named taught by a Prof. Iyer, whose grasp of the subject was nothing short of brilliant.

I shall never forget the two lady professors of the department—both ardent and redoubtable Gandhians—Dr Aloo Dastur and Dr Usha Mehta, whose passion for teaching was infectious and who were keen that I write a thesis on the Mahatma for a PhD degree but I had, by then, made other plans.

◆

Many years later, a veteran professor of Mumbai University offered to get me a doctorate for a sum of money, saying that I would have to do no work at all and that the dissertation would be written by a proxy! My then deceased parents would have been delighted had I 'earned' the doctorate, but their predictable response to the actual situation, had they been alive, made it a contemptible no-brainer.

Among my fellow-students at the university was Syed Ali Bilgrami of the distinguished Bilgrami clan of Hyderabad, Bhagwan Hiranandani (who went on to become a Queen's Counsel in London but passed away prematurely), Nilambari and Hansa of Mansa (former princesses of Mansa state in Saurashtra) and Lakshmi Shastri, a real bright spark who married Dr Jayadratha Shastri and mothered the irrepressible cricket Test captain turned successful India coach Ravi Shastri.

To Seek, to Strive, to Find... and Not to Yield

My father's financial situation improved—but only slightly and slowly—and although he could do with some assistance in his newspaper business, he selflessly felt that I should study further, though he could definitely not afford to send me to any American—forget Ivy League—college.

In those days, the university fees were nowhere near the obscene levels at which they are today. In 1961, when I studied at Stanford for my master's degree, the annual fee was $1,200, which approximates to $10,552 today, after allowance for inflation. However, the fee today runs to around $75,000 per annum which lead to young graduates being indebted for years to repay study loans and, in some cases, even committing suicide.

◆

Another instance of being at the right place at the right time came at the next major milestone of my life: when I had to take the critical decision regarding selection of American university—I had been admitted to three out of the four that I had applied to.

One had heard of the formidable reputations of Ivy League universities in the US. I haven't the faintest idea why they're called 'schools' when they are, in fact, colleges.

Again, with nobody among family or friends to guide and advise,

I was truly at my wit's end and my innumerable visits to the United States Information Service (USIS) proved to be infructuous. In the words of the Beatles' hit song:

> He's a real nowhere man
> Sitting in his nowhere land
> Making all his nowhere plans for nobody
> Doesn't have a point of view
> Knows not where he's going to
> Isn't he a bit like you and me?

◆

In those days, the editorial staff at the *Inquilab* would graciously pass on to me invitations to social events of relative inconsequence. One such invitation saw me at a soiree at a flat in the Mark Haven building.[6]

I must have come across as a 'little boy lost'[7] in a largish gathering of adults. Seeing me by myself, a gentleman who gave the appearance of being the host came across, introduced himself and asked (also possibly ascertaining whether I had crashed the party) what a tyro was doing in a crowd of seasoned journalists.

He turned out to be a Mr Adrian Miller who was head of USIS in Mumbai. 'Stanford, of course,' Miller replied, without batting an eyelid, when asked which of the three universities he would choose if he were in my shoes. As luck would have it, he was a graduate of Stanford which, apart from the fact that it was located in sunny, beautiful California, was also on top of my wish list.

I remember my father had to borrow money from two friends to pay my first quarter fee since I was late in applying for a scholarship.

In another manifestation of luck, or whatever one may term it, the tuition fee at Stanford went up steeply at Stanford after—only *after*—my first quarter, for which my father paid and, as with all American universities, have been rising astronomically ever since.

---

[6] A building adjacent to the Taj Mahal Palace hotel in Apollo Bunder, Mumbai
[7] After William Blake's poem of the same name about a small child who gets lost in the woods while he is out searching for his father

Thanks to my educational background at St Mary's High School and St Xavier's College (especially as regards the English language), I didn't have any serious problems coping with the journalism, advertising and mass communication courses at Stanford. At the end of the first quarter, I applied for the Samuel Jackson Jr Fellowship and was infinitely relieved to be chosen, which meant that I did not have to pay any tuition fee thereafter until my graduation and that greatly reduced the enormous burden on my father.

On my return home, and in keeping with my newly acquired faux American values, I offered to repay my father the money that he had so painstakingly borrowed for me. Steeped in older traditional values which maintained that it is the father's duty to look after his family, he was so offended he didn't speak to me for a week!

◈

Jab Miya Beewi Raazi
(When Husband and Wife Are in Agreement)

There was, of course, one seemingly insurmountable obstacle: my parents, like innumerable others at that time, were adamant I shouldn't go abroad for studies without first getting married, lest I return with a memsahib (white lady) as my wife.

All my protestations were futile, my logic refuted cogently, especially by my mother who was keen that I should marry a desi (Indian) girl from a 'respectable' family—religion or class no bar—as the classified matrimonial ads in the money-spinning 'Hatched, Matched, Dispatched' columns of the popular *Times of India* promised.

I was pathologically opposed to the concept of an arranged marriage and since I was desperate to study at Stanford, I capitulated to the extent of stipulating that I be allowed to meet Rukya (short for Ruqaiyya) Shaikh. She was a shy and beautiful graduate of Sophia College, Mumbai, and daughter of retired pre-Independence police commissioner, Khan Bahadur Shaikh Hussain. The proposal came via a family doctor, Dr Edward D'Cruz, who was known to both families.

Dr D'Cruz was spot-on in his judgement: Rukya and I, then both in our early 20s and, although not quite 'Made for Each Other,' were compatible enough for both of us to agree to the proposed marriage.

In my star-struck eyes, she was just the right choice for me—she was good-natured; shy, but at the same time, outgoing to the right degree; English-speaking with the right amount of Anglo-Indian mix.

As a result of an education at St Agnes Convent, she was imbued with the same religious values as me and seemed the kind of person who would be a good mother to our children. Very importantly for a prospective Muslim wife, her eyes were demurely focused at her toes. I had no doubt that my parents, my mother especially, would like to have her as *bahu* (daughter-in-law).

Rukya and I met just a few times, going for drives to the sylvan United Services Club in the Colaba area where we spent our limited time, since a strict curfew had been imposed by her father, watching the cloud formations and sunsets, which are particularly romantic during the Mumbai monsoons.

There's a popular Hindi saying, especially popular among Bollywood screenplay writers, *'jab miyan beewi raazi, to kya karega qazi?'* (when prospective husband and wife are willing, what choice does the priest have?)

And, as was meant to be, Rukya and I were wed under traditional Muslim rites by Mumbai's legendary Qazi Murghay at my house, as was the custom in both our families, on 27 July 1960 (incidentally qazis are not my favourite people—but that's another story!).

Sadly, we were also meant to split up, amicably, after a happy and mutually respectful union of 43 years, which exemplary wife and mother Rukya glorified by giving birth to three wonderful children—two sons, Tarique and Sharique and a daughter, Tehzeeb.

Rukya and I remain the best of friends.

TWO

THE FAMILY

Tarique, Alya and Imaan

All my three children, Tarique, Sharique and Tehzeeb, studied at the co-educational Cathedral and John Connon School in Mumbai for reasons mentioned in the earlier chapter.

A sprinter of merit, Tarique excelled at his studies and went on to become head boy of the school for two consecutive years, the only student to have had that distinction in the 160-year-old history of the institution. Tarique's honour came about partly because of a change in the system of education but largely because of his leadership qualities and ability to guide and counsel fellow students who had emotional problems brought on, in many cases, by drugs. He gained admission to Notre Dame University in the US and graduated with a degree in business management. He then returned to Mumbai and got involved in the family business with tremendous zeal and conspicuous success. Not only was he involved in its day-to-day running, but he also started many satellite Mid-Day Multimedia Ltd ventures engaged in commercial printing and outdoor advertising. He was also responsible for starting FM radio services in seven Indian cities in collaboration with BBC Radio.

He married Anu Bose, daughter of the late Rupen and Kumud Bose (née Thorat). They have a daughter, Alya, and a son, Imaan. Alya was head girl and, like both her parents, a champion athlete. Following her schooling at JB Petit High School in Mumbai and United World College of South East Asia (UWCSEA) in Singapore, she went on to pursue a bachelor's degree at Macalester College in the US. She is now studying for her PhD in Comparative Literature, Moving Image and Media Studies. She is co-convenor for the Moving Image and Media Studies Graduate Group (2020–21), and co-chair of the Cultural Studies and Comparative Literature Graduate Student Association Media and Cultural Studies at the University of Minnesota, Minneapolis.

Following the sale of the family printing and publishing businesses, Tarique settled down and currently lives in Indonesia with his eight-year-old 'jungle boy' (because he loves nature) Imaan. Tarique sits on the advisory board of the Keough School of Global Affairs at the University of Notre Dame, US.

Sharique, Emraan and Safiya

Born in Mumbai's Breach Candy Hospital, two years to the day after Tarique, my second son Sharique is a seemingly shy but an inwardly warm human being. His smile says it all! Blessed with a heart of gold, a trait he has indubitably inherited from his mother Rukya, he has, unfortunately, had a rough ride in life.

Sharique got his bachelor of commerce degree from K.C. College in Mumbai. He then went on to get a bachelor's degree in printing technology from Rochester Institute of Technology (RIT), New York, and later a master's, also from RIT.

He met fellow student Kimberley Donaldson at RIT and later tied the knot with her in Rochester. After a stint in Alexandria, Virginia, they moved to Buffalo in New York, where he started Chakra Communications, an electronics publishing firm which continues to this day. The young couple were blessed with two children—Emran and Safiya. Tragically and very prematurely, Kim succumbed to cancer.

Disaster struck again in June 2018 when Sharique suffered a major heart attack at home in Buffalo. Fortunately, timely mouth-to-mouth resuscitation by his children saved him, but delay in admitting him to hospital because of distance, traffic and time, resulted in hypoxia (a deficiency in the supply of oxygen to the brain).

Zeyna and I were in Europe when we received the shattering news. Cutting our holiday short, we rushed to Buffalo only to be told by the heart specialist, in a seemingly uncaring and matter-of-fact manner, that there was no 'hope' for Sharique.

Hitherto a disbeliever of miracles (or whatever you choose to call them!), I am no longer a sceptic: not only did Sharique survive, by God's grace, he is now on his feet, able to swim and workout in the gym with 80 per cent of his mental and physical faculties in good shape. Now retired, he lives in Mumbai with his mother Rukya. He is blessed to have as dear friend and companion, Soma Rao, a graduate in medicine and his schoolmate from Cathedral School.

Another close friend of Sharique's is Shahab Durazi, who is rated among India's leading women's fashion designers. His father Jaffer was my childhood friend and later, mentor during my adolescence.

Sharique's son Emraan, now 23, graduated from Marquette University, Milwaukee, in 2019 and works at a political think tank in Washington DC; his daughter Safiya, now 22, will graduate from the University of Buffalo, New York, this year and plans to pursue a career in psychology.

Tehzeeb, David, Noah and Leah

Tehzeeb was born on 24 July 1969, the day Commander Neil Armstrong and his module pilot Edwin 'Buzz' Aldrin landed the Apollo Lunar Module Eagle on the Moon.

Friends suggested it would be appropriate to name the new-born daughter 'Mehjabeen,' (meaning 'beautiful as the moon' or 'a beloved person' in Arabic) but we opted for the Urdu 'Tehzeeb,' the Persian word meaning 'refinement, edification and reformation' in English.

> Although Armstrong's famous words upon landing, 'That's one small step for man, one giant leap for mankind' have become historic, he later clarified that that wasn't what he had planned to say.
>
> He explained that there was a word lost in his now-legendary one-liner: 'That's one small step for "a" man.' It's just that people didn't hear the 'a'.
>
> An unverifiable naughty version would have us believe that Wunkind, a close friend of Neil Armstrong, was arduously propositioning a lady whom he desperately wanted to marry. Uninterested, she consistently rejected his amorous advances with the words: 'No way—only when man lands on the Moon!'
>
> And thereby hangs a tale! Armstrong's historic words, after his epic feat by way of rejoicing for friend, Wunkind, were garbled in transmission—and the name 'Wunkind' was mistaken for 'mankind!'

◆

Tehzeeb, the youngest, is a blithe, seemingly light-hearted happy camper on the outside, but a no-nonsense mother on the inside, who believes in speaking her mind.

After schooling in Mumbai and a year in Pennsylvania, US, under a Rotary Exchange programme, Tehzeeb graduated from Elmira University, New York, with a degree in International Relations. After working at the *Earth Times*, a newspaper covering sustainable development and the environment (which I edited for its publisher Ted Kheel in its nascent stage at the headquarters of the United Nations in 1994), she now works as a trademark analyst in New Jersey.

Tehzeeb's husband, David Grossman, also got his bachelor's degree from Elmira College and a master's degree from Columbia University. David is the global director of trademark surveillance services for an American brand protection firm.

David and Tehzeeb have two children. Noah, 23, who graduated from Bucknell University, Pennsylvania, in 2019, has followed in his father's footsteps and also works for a brand protection firm in New York as consultant. Leah, now 20, is pursuing a bachelor's degree in Neuroscience at Colgate University, New York. The family lives in Morristown, New Jersey.

◆

Full credit must go to Tarique for steering the family ships, the *Inquilab* and *Mid-Day*, through stormy seas with exemplary skill and—after he and I had seen the writing on the wall consequent to the havoc being wrought by electronic media on its print counterpart—adroitly negotiating a transfer of ownership of the newspapers to Jagran Prakashan in 2012.

Sometimes I say I am like a barber who only knows how to cut hair, so for me—a person who only knows newspaper publishing—the collapse of any publication is a heartrending occurrence.

Seeing the financial woes and, worse, closure of some of the legendary newspaper titles in India and abroad, is, for me, poignant since I have often skated on thin ice and know a little about how the heart of a newspaper beats.

◆

I'm grateful to Rukya and, while they were growing up, all my children for the extreme patience and understanding with which they accepted having to endlessly wait in our car on the way home after dinner or an evening out together, even though they were exceedingly tired, while I stopped by at the office to attend to an urgent production or editorial matter. Not once, over years of having to endure this torture—especially as my children were so young—did they show even the slightest sign of disapproval. I'd like them to know that I'm greatly appreciative of everything.

Tehzeeb, David, Noah and Leah

Memories are Made of This

A lasting memory is that of a joint decision with Rukya to give up our apartment in a prestigious building called 'Cosmopolis' on Nepean Sea Road, Malabar Hill, Mumbai, where we resided after my stint at the J. Walter Thomson (JWT) advertising agency, following my return from Stanford University.

By way of background: I first worked in Mumbai as an understudy to my father in 1962 at the *Inquilab*. My attachment to the paper was, at best, lukewarm, and my father and I had diametrically opposite views regarding the running of newspapers. In any case, my knowledge of the Urdu language was passable, and I had my own ambition, fostered in the US, of starting my own publication, but in the English language.

My father was devastated seeing my disinterest in the *Inquilab*, his baby, which he had nursed with exemplary love and devotion through the most turbulent times during the freedom struggle. (Meanwhile, my father had also started *Shaam*, meaning 'evening,' an afternoon Urdu daily, which never really set the Arabian Sea on fire—it was started more out of nationalistic fervour than financial prudence, and *Kahkashan* meaning 'constellation of stars,' a weekly Urdu film magazine.)

He was extremely keen that I work with him on his magnificent obsessions, his publications. *Kahkashan* was edited by the renowned Shamim Zuberi and became an extremely popular Urdu film publication nation-wide and was a close second to *Shama* of New Delhi, where the Urdu language was much more widely spoken than in Mumbai.

Matters came to a head in the words of the old Frank Sinatra favourite:

> When an irresistible force such as you
> Meets an immovable object such as me
> You can bet as sure as you live
> Something's gotta give
> Something's gotta give
> Something's gotta give

A stubborn chip off the old block, I was not prepared to relent, and we decided to part ways, which led to me leaving my parental home sans roof over my head, along with wife Rukya and three-month-old son Tarique, who had been born at Stanford.

I'm indebted to St Xavier's college mate Amir Curmally (his family owned the Mumbai landmark music store, *Rhythm House*, at Kala Ghoda), for facilitating my first job—at the J. Walter Thomson advertising agency—when I was desperately in need of providing food and shelter to Rukya and Tarique, after my falling out with my father.

I shall remain ever grateful to Amir. He's a sincere friend—my lifebuoy, my saviour!

◆

Four years later, with time having healed wounds and my father keeping indifferent health as the result of two heart attacks, I decided to 'kiss and make up' and return to him and the *Inquilab* with the objective of taking over from him, which had always been his desire, anyway. At the time, I was working as an accounts director, servicing clients such as Tata Sons, Hindustan Lever, Ciba Geigy, Larsen and Toubro, Goodlass Nerolac, India Tobacco Company and others and was allotted a company flat at Kemp's Corner. We had to vacate the flat and find a new roof over our heads.

Nanavati Case

Those of an earlier generation will recall the salacious whodunit saga of Commander Kawas Manekshaw Nanavati allegedly shooting dead his English wife Sylvia's businessman paramour Prem Ahuja at the latter's Jeevan Jyot flat on Nepean Sea Road flat on 27 April 1959.

The trial (with shades of the more recent Sheena Bora, Sunanda Pushkar and Sushant Singh mysteries, and the alleged Arnab Goswami suicide abetment brouhaha) held the nation enthralled for five years after which the Commander was covertly placed on parole in a Lonavala bungalow (100 km away from Mumbai).

Mysteriously, as can happen in India, the perpetrator of the crime of passion was pardoned and allowed to emigrate to Canada with his wife and three children.

◆

The unwritten agreement between my father and me, as a condition to my return to *Inquilab,* was predicated by the understanding that we would live apart. Our decision to surrender the JWT India House company flat meant that wife Rukya, I and infant son Tarique would have to find a different place to live in.

After great effort, and many refusals because of our name, we found a beautiful flat in Cosmopolis, a coveted building on Nepean Sea Road on leafy, prestigious Malabar Hill in 1970. It belonged to P.N. Sarma, managing director of Ogilvy, Benson and Mather, the leading advertising agency, which created the award-winning Fevicol ad and numerous other award-winning campaigns.

Unable to afford to *buy* a flat, we decided to take his flat on the then prevalent leave and license (L and L) basis upon P.N.'s written assurance that we could stay there indefinitely since he was planning to retire and relocate to Bengaluru, where he owned property, as long as we paid our L and L dues regularly and maintained the place in good order. This was Rukya's pre-condition since she didn't fancy the prospect of having to move again, with bag, baggage and school-going kids.

It so transpired that P.N. succumbed to a heart attack, leaving behind a widow and two young school-going sons. It didn't take Rukya and me much time to decide that we could not possibly continue living in the apartment under the changed circumstances.

Our friends, almost without exception, advised us not to surrender the flat since the law was incontrovertibly on our side; it was then worth a substantial fortune by Malabar Hill standards; and no licensees, not even from the behemoth multi-nationals, were relinquishing their mannas from heaven. 'Name even one large corporation that is giving up leave and license premises…and you are hardly in their league,' they argued. Our more outspoken friends thought we were morons who had taken leave of our senses for even contemplating giving up the flat, especially after the character assassination campaign against us. But, my parents' mantra, their badge of honour—which they always wore with unrelenting pride that 'g-r-e-e-d,' that abominable five-letter word should always be shunned—prevailed in the ultimate analysis.

To our great shock, this brought us face to face with the lamentable reality that it is not at all easy in India for a family with a Muslim surname to get a roof over its head in this so-called international and secular metropolis.

After many rejections, as soon as we revealed our Muslim family names, we were surprisingly taken for inspection, by Mumbai's then leading real estate agent, Bhagwandas & Co., to the very same beautiful three-bedroom Jeewan Jyot apartment of the Commander Nanavati-Prem Ahuja notoriety, mentioned above.

Terms were negotiated, and Rukya and I were about to sign on the dotted line when the young estate agent, keen not to let this deal fall through, enthusiastically volunteered the information that the scenic bedroom overlooking the sea was the one ('yes, the VERY one') in which the dashing navy commander had achieved retribution. One need not mention that we changed our minds about signing the deal, post-haste.

Rukya and I never regretted this decision: our lives changed dramatically after that, exemplifying the adage that good deeds beget just reward—in this very world—and one does not have to wait until the 'next life,' (whatever that means) for recompense.

Stirring a Hornet's Nest

To continue with the subject of rectitude: for my father, the giving of bribes ('speed money' as it is euphemistically called in corporate parlance) was as distasteful as accepting it, a principle which often worked to his disadvantage.

My Western background, with its emphasis on hard-headed 'so be it...get on with it, irrespective of the means,' practicality, should normally have made corruption in business matters an unavoidable and, therefore, acceptable fact of life. But, in reality, traditional idealistic family principles made it an absolute no-no, often to the great detriment of our businesses. Friends labelled these principles foolish, but such was the reality.

To give one instance, at the risk of seemingly washing dirty linen in public but because it is pertinent to illustrate my indebtedness to my parents in my upbringing: unfortunately, my father didn't understand the need for estate planning and left behind his succession matters in a chaotic state, given the complexities and, if I may add absurdities of Muslim Personal Law. On the face of it, the elementary but, in my opinion unjust, principle of primogeniture, should have simplified the issue of succession after my father's passing in 1972. On the contrary, it stirred a hornet's nest of horrible proportions with my half-siblings making—under misguided advice from self-proclaimed relatives and well-wishers who popped up from nowhere—preposterous claims as to their share in the estate, which was, in reality dinky but, gargantuan in their newly opened star-struck eyes.

The age-old gambit of palm-greasing could have settled the issue to my total satisfaction in no time in our Indian legal scheme of things, but introspection as to what my father would have wanted me to do under the circumstances, made any doubts about the modus operandi a no-brainer. Instead, I took the advice of a dear friend, Arvind Shah, of Chimanlal Paper Company: 'Give more than is their due and sleep in peace,' he told me unhesitatingly.

I shall remain forever indebted to Arvind bhai for his sagacious advice. For good measure, I went a step further and, offering to forget the past and the hurtful litigation my siblings had initiated against me, undertook to look after my stepmother, stepsister, Najma and her three children for the rest of my life, which I have continued to do.

My stepmother passed away in 2018 but, I might say for the record, that Najma and her three children still receive a monthly cheque from me even though she has a regular rental income from three properties that she now owns in suburban Mumbai, a metropolis in which prices are absurdly steep. But I have no doubt my parents are proud of me, wherever they may be!

There may be, perhaps, just a tad bit too much backslapping happening here, but this should be recorded for posterity: unbeknownst to the rest of the family, ever since my father's death in 1972, I have, as sole trustee and of my own accord, looked after Inquilab Manzil (the building he left behind), paid its taxes, looked after its repairs and maintenance, collected rent from tenants and the like. A trusted associate from *Inquilab*'s parent group, Aziz Khatri, who cut his professional teeth with us some 50 years ago and saw the birth and maturity of all our publications—*Sportsweek, Mid-Day, Sunday Mid-Day*, the Delhi and Pune editions of *Mid-Day, Sunday Mid-Day* (Bengaluru), Gujarati *Mid-Day* and *Turfite* (the horse-racing weekly)—continues to help us look after the property despite his poor health.

Imagine my step-siblings' surprise and delirious joy when I informed them, recently (following intimations of mortality and knowing that my parents would have fully approved of my decision), that they have shares in the property, which for them was a real bonanza, given their rather precarious financial situations.

I also got them to agree that, contrary to the Islamic tenet that male descendants are entitled to twice the amount that their female family members are, the total proceeds from sale of any property will be shared in *equal* measure, regardless of any unjust Muslim law stipulations.

Test of Character

Another test of character came in 1985, when some of my staff members decided to leave *Mid-Day* (which I started in 1979—more of this later) and join my then chief reporter and extremely popular columnist Behram Contractor at the rival publication, *The Afternoon Despatch & Courier*, a tabloid founded by him and bankrolled by the late industrialist Kamal Morarka of Gannon Dunkerley and other major business enterprises.

This happened at a time when our perennially limited resources and hand-to-mouth, rob Peter to pay Paul, existence had me scrambling every month to raise enough money to pay the staff their salaries *on time* (another cardinal principle passed down by my father). I was also under pressure to purchase newsprint and a million other expenses—big and small—to ensure regular and timely publication; it made life hellish, to say the least.

The separation arose out of Contractor's demand that he be elevated to the post of chief editor of the paper. I did not agree to this—in my opinion, though he was undeniably a humour columnist par excellence with a huge fan readership, he did not possess the background, scholarship, editorial experience or sophistication to become chief editor of a newspaper of *Mid-Day*'s stature.

To cut a long story short: while it was perfectly in order in a free country for staff to decide whether to stay or leave to join the rebel newspaper, in my view, the tactics resorted to by the instigators of the move, at this critical juncture, were reprehensible.

I do not point a finger at anybody in particular, but among the dirty tricks resorted to, was the stealing of file photographs and invaluable reference material from the *Mid-Day* archives, an indispensable asset for any newspaper worth its salt, which we had built and expanded with great effort over the years.

Thanks to the hard work and devotion of my editorial staff—editor Binod Rao, news editor K.N. Radhakrishan, chief reporter Manu Desai, Javed Akhtar, Gopi Baskaran, Sharad Kotnis and, later, editors Anil Dharker, Bacchi Karkaria, Rahul Singh, Ayaz Menon and Aakar Patel—we were able to hold our own, even as the upstart resorted to scurvy tactics such as false circulation claims and the like.

This period saw a steady growth in the paper's circulation because of aggressive news breaks and special investigative stories (such as the kidney transplant scam) under editors like Bacchi Karkaria, Rahul Singh, Aakar Patel and the late Anil Dharker. During this time, Shobhaa De wrote an eminently thought-provoking daily column for a number of years.

Mid-Day was the only paper in the city to report, continuously and extensively, on Terrorist and Disruptive Activities (Prevention) Act courts and the Justice B.N. Srikrishna Commission inquiry into the Bombay Riots of 1992–93.

Each of the original *Sportsweek* staff members has left their distinctive imprint, while helping build circulation and consequent advertising revenue. However, Ayaz Memon has had the longest umbilical cord relationship with the group. He merits special mention for his long and devoted association with our organization.

Ayaz joined *Sportsweek* as a sub-editor on probation in November 1979 and was confirmed in April 1980. He rose to become a news editor in 1985 and associate editor in 1987. In 1989, Memon left to join the *Independent*, belonging to *The Times of India* stable. He rejoined *Mid-Day* as editor of Special Projects in 1991 (when I was away in Dubai), becoming an editor in September 1993, a post he retained till March 2000. Ayaz has gone on to carve a niche for himself as a respected freelance newspaper columnist and television cricket commentator with a wide following. We at *Inquilab*,

Sportsweek and *Mid-Day* have always considered him one of us and I, in particular, am delighted to see him do so well in all that he has undertaken.

Making Life Hell

Going back in the time machine: as expected, the arrival of my five half-siblings, in fairly quick succession through my father's second wife, made life hell for me.

With my father working extremely long hours, day-after-day, and with my mother in even worse emotional condition than me (physical, too, as she suffered from tuberculosis), I became mentally troubled. Bereft of self-worth, I kept losing weight, appetite and my youthful memory.

I was well and truly sucked into the swirling, seemingly unending vortex of melancholia. It sounds maudlin but, to be honest, many were the nights when I would go to bed with 'tears on my pillow', as the classic oldie goes.

My own mother was almost universally called an 'angel.' Loving, caring and compassionate to a fault, she was the archetypal 'suffering in silence' wife of the Indian movies of the time. Predictably, there were disputes and differences aplenty between the two wives, invariably ending in my mother, ever the sacrificing spouse, relenting to demands that were often unreasonable and even absurd.

Emotionally, I have taken after my mother—she too, was ubersensitive and given to depths of sorrow. I started despairing life and became terribly despondent. Due to a heightened sense of helplessness, nervousness and irritability, I developed dysphemia, a stammer stemming, in my case, from lack of self-confidence.

A short course in public speaking called 'Nervous Tension Aids

Eloquence' at a public speaking institute at Charni Road in south Mumbai, which I stumbled upon accidentally, helped somewhat, but the problem of nervousness persists to this day. Only I know that the confident demeanour I have been able to cultivate when compelled to address a public gathering is skin deep, but I derive comfort from the fact that I am in the distinguished company of great communicators like Mahatma Gandhi.

It is said that the man who was instrumental in spreading the gospel of ahimsa, the cardinal principle of non-violence in Hinduism, Buddhism and Jainism, and played a pioneering role in India's freedom movement, initially had panic attacks with symptoms like blurred vision and trembling when practising as a lawyer in South Africa.

Thomas Jefferson, the third American president; Richard Branson, among other things, reputedly one of the world's highest-paid public speakers; golfer Tiger Woods; British comedian Rowan Atkinson (Mr Bean), Prince Harry and singer Adele are also victims of the condition that some people consider a disability.

On a personal note, I was amazed to discover that the illustrious mass communications authority Professor Wilbur Schramm, my guru at Stanford University, also stammered but only when imparting his gyan to his awestruck class.

◆

THREE

IN EDUCATION WE TRUST

Contemporary Education

One of my criticisms of contemporary education in India is that it calls for specialization at too early an age in college careers.

During earlier times, the first two years at college, irrespective of the area of specialization chosen by the student, were devoted *compulsorily* to the Humanities, which basically consisted of languages, the arts, literature, philosophy, religion and history. They were subsequently expanded to include political science, psychology, sociology, law and religion, depending upon the college and state university.

It was only after the intermediate stage that students could specialize—for two years—in their chosen field, leading up to graduation. This diverse mix generally made for a balanced, universal cocktail of knowledge and information, which produced comparatively well-rounded personalities rather than ones with blinkered (I use the expression with respect!) expertise in just one discipline or area of specialization to the exclusion of all others.

It can be argued that the earlier system produced jacks of all trades and masters of none. That said, the spirit of enquiry engendered in a fresh mind by exposure to a multiplicity of subjects from diverse disciplines in a liberal arts programme, if only in two years in college, can only be of inestimable benefit. As Samuel Johnson said: 'Curiosity is one of the most permanent and certain characteristics of a vigorous intellect.'

On balance and after meticulous consideration of the pros and cons, I incline towards the former system since it enables informed clarity of thought based on access to multidimensional reference points, logical analysis stemming from a broad understanding of the awesome complexities of the nature of life (of 'cabbages and kings') and balanced judgement pertaining to many more and diverse spheres of knowledge.

Curricula must perforce change with the radical evolution in the 'atmospherics' of the lives of people. To be fair, sea changes have been made in the field of education in India over the years and the system is vastly different today.

This is not to deride the present system, given the outstanding progress in diverse disciplines of human endeavour. Homo sapiens have progressed spectacularly in matters material since the second Industrial Revolution, especially in the fields of electronics, science, medicine, commerce and technology.

But progress in matters spiritual has been, woefully, tardy. I'm tempted to attribute this to the cutting off of the link to humanistic disciplines.

A Fulfilling Experience

With its then mix of liberal study courses, education in the first and second years at St Xavier's was a fulfilling experience even as I revelled inwardly in the diverse mix of subjects such as logic, English literature, political science and sociology. The quality of English language teaching was of an exceedingly high order. Whatever I learnt about English literature was engendered at St Xavier's largely by two professors, as previously mentioned.

There was the dour, punctilious Professor Colaco, whose command over the English language was formidable. And of course, my favourite, the flamboyant Professor Aguiar, he with the appropriate first name Theophilus, ugly pock-marked skin but the suavity and deportment of a French movie star, the voice of Jose Ferrer in his award-winning role in *Cyrano de Bergerac* and the diction of an English university don. Apart from English, he also taught a course which went by the name of Logic. The passage of time dims memory but all that one remembers is that Logic was described in the college brochure, roughly as 'hard to understand, very challenging but enjoyable.' The description must surely have been written by an advertising copywriter who knew the power of words that could motivate desired action.

The course did persuade: some of my friends and I rose to the bait but, looking back, the course undeniably helped produce a mindset of logical thought process lasting a lifetime.

Although Nature had bypassed Professor Aguiar in the looks department, for his suavity, he was, by far, the pin-up boy for the girl students. When launching *Mid-Day* in 1979, I visited the then ageing Professor Aguiar at his Byculla home to request him to write a column on the English language for the paper. Gracious as ever, he played the perfect host but declined because of infirmity. Disappointed, I then approached Sabi Merchant, who accepted and wrote an extremely popular column called 'Mind Your Language' for *Mid-Day* for many years.

Later, when I took a three-year sabbatical in Dubai, UAE to run the *Khaleej Times* (the leading English language newspaper of the Middle East) as managing director and executive editor, I introduced Sabi's, as also columns of the legendary Khushwant Singh and amiable maverick Bejan Daruwala, to the large Indian expatriate population of the Middle East, all of which combined almost led to the newspaper's circulation spiralling out of the graph!

The Byculla Connection

Professors Colaco and Aguiar both lived in Byculla, as did internationally renowned singer Sir Cliff Tony Brent (born Bretagne) and Nagpada-born, but London-based, property and Internet entrepreneurs David and Simon Reuben.

With a net worth of £21.5 billion, the Reuben brothers are second in the 2020's *Sunday Times* list of the richest people in Britain, behind the Hinduja brothers—Srichand and Parmanand Gopichand—and household goods and technology magnate Sir James Dyson.

Dare I mention in the same breath that yours truly was born exactly two years to the day before start of World War II not far from the same plebeian Byculla, Mumbai neighbourhood as the Reuben brothers.

> **INDIA-BORN CELEBRITIES**
>
> As a matter of information, among those who were born in Mumbai but achieved fame abroad were renowned scholar Homi K. Bhabha; short story writer, novelist, poet and journalist Rudyard Kipling; prime minister of Ireland Leo Varadkar; print and television journalist Fareed Zakaria; pharmaceutical company entrepreneur Yusuf Hamied and actor Merle Oberon (born Estelle Merle O'Brien Thompson).
>
> Then there were those born elsewhere in India: novelist and poet William Makepeace Thackeray, (Kolkata), England Test cricket captain, later Baron, Colin Cowdrey (Ootacamund),

Hollywood stars Julie Christie (Assam) and Vivien Leigh (Kolkata), singer Cliff Richard (Lucknow), Freddie Mercury (born Farrokh Balsara in Zanzibar; studied in Panchgani, Maharashtra) and Engelbert Humperdinck (in the then Madras), actor Ben Kingsley (born as Krishna Pandit Bhanji in Yorkshire, England, but to Indian parents).

It is not generally known that the score of the 007 theme, featured in the 1971 James Bond film, Dr No, which still captivates audiences worldwide, was adapted from a composition by British musical theatre celebrity Monty Norman and was based on an adaptation of the novel *A House for Mr Biswas* by illustrious Trinidad and Tobago-born British writer of Indian origin V.S. Naipaul.

Urdu, Beloved Urdu

My major regret in life has been that my doting, but work-obsessed, father, who devotedly championed the cause of the mellifluous Urdu language, did not see the need for me to learn it, except in a rather half-hearted manner at home.

This sufficed for me to supervise the *Inquilab* after my father's demise, but was hardly enough to make a speech in, as I was pushed into when attending a college function. I still cringe when I remember the embarrassment.

Many years later, in 1978, Sharad Pawar broke away from the Congress party to form a coalition with the Janata Party and named it the National Congress Party. He kindly offered me (an apolitical animal if ever there was one!) a ticket to contest the Parliamentary election.

The prospect of having to campaign in Hindi/Urdu at public meetings was terrifying enough. But I discovered later that the offer was made (a) because I was a 'Muslim,' (b) owned an Urdu newspaper which catered largely to the sizeable Muslim community of Mumbai and (c) was for a constituency, the majority residents of which were Muslims. It elicited a polite refusal from me that, given the craze for election tickets in our country, must rank as perhaps the most spontaneous in the history of Indian democracy!

In any case my oratorical—or shall I say, my fire-breathing, rabble-rousing demagogic—skills, negative attributes in my own book but prime requisites in the shark-infested cesspool of politics, were abysmal and my political ethos lamentably awry.

When you consider the fact that my father owned and published India's leading Urdu newspaper with a large Urdu-speaking staff, I consider it a shame that my grasp of the language is as pitiful as it is at best, passable—but, thankfully, not *'khali pili kaiko bom marta hai Bambaiya'* (why are you shouting like this only).

This shall always remain a mystery, especially in view of my family *mahol* (milieu) being profoundly Urdu and Muslim-centric, with regular visitors at home being eminent poets and littérateurs such as Ali Sardar Jafri, Sahir Ludhianvi, Kaifi Azmi, Shakeel Badayuni, Majrooh Sultanpuri, Hasrat Jaipuri, actor Dilip Kumar, musician Naushad and their ilk.

I can only put it down to my father's misguided belief that the education I was receiving at English medium St Mary's was good enough for me. Be that as it may, it left me no time for the study of Urdu under a private tutor at home. School homework was very time-consuming. Extremely frequent were the days when my hapless tutor, Mr Alam, had to return home without imparting any Urdu lesson since his ward had been assigned a heavy load at school.

Only I am to blame for the fact that I'm an ignoramus in the Urdu language (my mother tongue), a linguistic and cultural Anglo Indian, a *neem hakeem khatra-e-jaan* (half doctor—a danger to your life). With a little effort I could have made the time but there was no pot of gold at the end of the rainbow at home, as there was at school, namely the exam results for promotion to the next higher class.

This brings to mind an anecdote narrated by my dear friend General Danny Misra, a resident director of Bengaluru's sylvan West End Hotel in the 1970s, who passed away at the turn of the century. He was a pucca old-school Lucknowi who spoke impeccable Urdu and was proud of it! He was also an excellent raconteur and had a vast collection of yarns, which he narrated with rare panache. One of them (in Urdu) went as follows:

> There was this nouveau riche bumpkin who arrives on a train at Lucknow station. Twirling his handlebar moustache he haughtily emerges out of the station and, seeing a rickshawala, yells out impudently: *'Abey rickshawale, chale ga?'* (Hey, rickshawala, are you free?)

Replies the rickshawala (reverentially): '*Huzoor, khadim aap ki khidmat mein haazir hai—kahaan jaayega?*' (Sir, I am your servant and at your service—where would you like to go?)

'*Gomti Nagar—kitne paise lega?*' (Gomti Nagar [a posh residential area in Lucknow], how much will you charge?' asks the yokel haughtily.)

'*Hum kahaan aap se paise maang rahe hain? Jo marzi ho, dijye ga...qubool hoga.*' (Where am I demanding any money? You may give whatever you choose and it will be acceptable).

'*Seedhay jawaab de, ulloo ke patthe. Tum sab ek jaise ho. Abhi meethi baat karta hai, baad mein hamara gala katega.*' (Give a proper answer, nincompoop...you are all alike...talking sweet now and will slit my throat later).

Unable to bear the rude talk any longer, the rickshawalla replies in a whisper: '*Zara aahesta bolye janaab...kahin ghoda na sun le.*' (Kind sir, please speak softly, the horse may hear you!)

Such is the purity, richness, refinement of a dulcet language which is being systematically destroyed by misinformed, misguided elements who consider what is essentially hybrid Hindustani and Persian (it was a court and official/legal language down the years in our history), but has tragically been stigmatized as the language of 'the enemy.'

The hotheads responsible for this linguistic genocide fail to realize that Urdu, conspicuously a secular language, was the mother tongue of millions of Hindus in undivided India notably in the reconstituted states of Punjab, Hyderabad, Haryana and Himachal Pradesh.

Some of its greatest, most prominent, prolific and popular proponents and practitioners have been non-Muslims, namely Firaq Gorakhpuri, Krishan Chander, Munshi Premchand, Rajinder Singh Bedi, B.S. Jain Jauhar, Ameer Chand Bahar, Bhagwan Das Ejaz, Sohan Rahi, Indra Mohan Kaif, Deepak Qamar, Asha Prabha, Inder Shabnam, Kamini Devi, Navroz Kotwal (he is Parsi), as is Peenaz Masani, the renowned ghazal singer), P.P. Srivastava, Pratpal Singh Betaab and Preeta Vajpayee among many others.

Khushwant Singh, the legend, was an unapologetic lover of the language, especially Urdu poetry. Kuldeep Nayar, doyen of Urdu journalism, who was a good friend, edited the *Tej* Urdu newspaper in New Delhi for many years with distinction and went on to become our high commissioner in the UK, once lamented with great prescience, 'Every time I see a Hindu funeral procession, I tell myself: "There goes another Urdu newspaper reader, another one of a dying breed, never to be replaced."'

FOUR

ACROSS THE BORDER

Pakistani Journos

Speaking of Pakistani journalists—and I've had the mixed fortune of getting to know many of them at various events in different parts of the world: they do not know the first thing about press freedom.

The suave cricket commentator Chisty Mujahid is balanced but, by and large, the others are disconcertingly chauvinistic. Their mental horizons are conspicuously myopic, their news sense pathetic, their command of the English language execrable and their understanding of the nuances of international law and politics annoyingly blinkered. It is impossible to have an intelligent, unbiased conversation with most of them.

By and large, I found the Urdu language media across the border to be refreshingly hail-fellow-well-met and have had the privilege of being invited to many homes for delicious, although monotonous, biryani meals.

This reminds me of hockey legend Randhir Singh Gentle telling me in Karachi: '*yaar Khalid, yahaan biryani kha ke thak gaye. Lekin mehmaan nawazi lajawaab hai. Roz kahin na kahin dawaat hoti hai. Ab to yeh naubat aa pauhanchi hai ke sirf chota hazri ke liye waqt bacha hai.*' (Khalid, one is tired of eating biryani here. But the hospitality is without parallel—I've reached a stage where I only have time left for early morning tea.)

That said, once they've befriended you, their warmth and affability is *sans pareil* (having no equal), as it is, indeed, on the Indian side of the border where Pakistani journalists are concerned.

A notable exception was a bumptious, but celebrated, English-language radio commentator and chief executive of a multinational company, who rather fancied his looks. Being uppity, he was rather unpopular with many of his colleagues, some of whom spread the canard that his wife, a glamorous, friendly and chatty—therefore misunderstood—lady in that country's male chauvinist society 'had slept with the entire cricket Pakistani team, including the 12th man.'

He was my least favourite media person, especially after my run-in with him at a welcome reception for the Indian team at which he hectored me by saying that it was 'illogical' for an educated Muslim like me to continue living in a backward Hindu country like India and that I would be much happier in Pakistan. Sport is said to build bridges between people. It certainly didn't where this smug moron was concerned!

From my experience, there were two notable exceptions to this jaundiced mindset: both were proud sons in uniform of their respective countries, which incidentally went to war against each other, namely S.H.F.J. Manekshaw and Air Marshal Nur Khan of Pakistan. True to their calling, they were disciplined to the hilt and went to war when their country called upon them to do so. But once, armed hostilities had ceased, they bore no animosity towards citizens of the enemy country. Interestingly, both were called upon to head influential sports bodies in their respective countries and, were distinguished examples of my personal belief that sports can demolish barriers and build bridges even between people at war with each other.

The field marshal was often at pains to recount incidents testifying to his mutual admiration by, and for, people across the border, as did the air marshal, especially in his dealings with me, I may add—the fact that both he and I were Muslims had nothing to do with it. We respected each other, as he did other Indians, as individuals and for no other reason.

CALLING YOUR PM 'A BLOODY FOOL'

This reminds me of a joke which Natwar Singh, former external affairs minister of India in Indira Gandhi's government, recounted at the function of our Inquilab Publications group to celebrate its golden jubilee.

The story goes that two senior journalists—one Indian, the other Pakistani—were discussing freedom of the press in their respective countries.

'We're proud of our press freedom,' says the Indian. 'I can call my prime minister a 'fool' and nothing will happen to me.'

Not to be outdone, the journalist from across the border retorts: 'That's no big deal. Even I can call *your* prime minister a bloody fool in my column and nothing will happen to me.'

'Hey Guys, Woman!'

Speaking of cultural differences, the Indian media, on the 1978–79 cricket tour of Pakistan had been invited to a reception by Indian ambassador K.S. Bajpai at a rundown hotel, flaunted as 'the most modern in Faisalabad (formerly Lyallpur),' a town known for its textiles.

Among members of the Indian media, were widely travelled men of the world (with a glad eye for attractive ladies!) such as the irrepressible joker Dicky Rutnagur (*Daily Telegraph*, London), romantic at heart K. Niran Prabhu (*The Times of India*, Mumbai) and the puckish London School of Economics-educated Kishore Bhimani (*The Statesman*, Kolkata).

Being perhaps the most orthodox city in a country of strict Islamic values, spectators at the Faisalabad India-Pakistan Test were strictly segregated, prompting the Casanovas in the Indian media party to complain of 'sore eyes' for not even being able to set eyes on a single lady in that hick town for a week!

The television set was on at the soiree as we made inane conversation, sipping our soft drinks. Suddenly somebody yelled, 'Hey guys, woman!'

All eyes turned to the TV screen, which showed a *female* news reader. Such is the lot of hard-working, itinerant—and occasionally 'starved'—cricket columnists.

◆

My first contact with a Pakistani journalist came about when Khalid Butt, a cherubic PR official of the Pakistan cricket board, tasked with looking after the Indian press party, received us upon arrival at Karachi airport.

He greeted each member of the Indian press party with a warm fraternal *khush amdeed* (welcome) hug at the tarmac and drove us to the arrivals lounge in a swanky limousine. This was the first time that I had ever been accorded such a reception—and that, too, in a country with which my own has a chequered, blow-hot-blow-cold relationship.

While as a *baraati* (member of a wedding procession) and member of a press party on an official VIP visit to a foreign country, I have been 'received' on state visits by presidents Fakhruddin Ali Ahmed, Zail Singh and A.P.J. Abdul Kalam, as well as prime ministers Rajiv Gandhi and Atal Bihari Vajpayee, this was the first, and only, time that I had been received in my own right.

◆

By way of prelude to what follows, I might mention that before boarding the flight from New Delhi, I had enclosed some money for the visa fee in my passport, which I sent with my travel agent to the Pakistan embassy. After stamping the visa, the passport was returned to the agent who, for some strange reason (perhaps intending to return the balance amount to me), put the money back in the passport and returned both items to me. Unaware of what I had done, I presented my passport—and money—to the immigration official at New Delhi airport who, again surprisingly, did not notice the enclosed money while stamping the passport and returned it to me. I duly put the passport away in my bag before boarding the flight to Karachi.

Having submitted our press party's passports to the officials at Karachi, Khalid Butt, he of proud Kashmiri background, was helping us retrieve our baggage, when an announcement on the loudhailer said I was wanted at the passport counter—not a pleasant prospect, and in Pakistan of all places!

Given the fact that we were *mehmaan* (guests—who are inordinately respected in the Islamic tradition), and that, too, of none other than Air Marshal Nur Khan, Khalid Butt explained the circumstances, and

I was allowed to proceed. I must confess that during Butt's ('ifs' and 'buts') encounter with the passport officials, I was on tenterhooks with frightening visions of being sentenced to 'sing the Jailhouse Rock' at Pakistan's notorious Central Mianwali prison, the equivalent of Tihar in Delhi.

For those with a penchant for the macabre: according to the *Dawn* (1 February 2015), former Pakistani prime minister Zulfikar Ali Bhutto, although declared not guilty of murder, was first incarcerated at Mianwali prison, under orders from president Zia-ul-Haq, then moved to Rawalpindi Jail where he was hanged by Tara Masih, who has since then gone down in Pakistani folklore. Incidentally, hangmen in Pakistan are traditionally of the Christian faith.

Customs officials are not my favourite people. I am discomfited by their generally officious and condescending demeanour and get the awful feeling I am being singled out on suspicion. However, on balance, I must confess this is a greatly unfair figment of my imagination, since I am invariably waved through, in no small measure thanks to my increasingly grey hair, I imagine.

◆

To continue on the topic of airport experiences, some years ago, my wife Zeyna and I, on holiday in Turkey at the time, received the terrible news that my son Sharique, who was living in Buffalo, New York, had had a serious heart attack.

We cut short our holiday and rushed to the US. Upon arrival at JFK airport en route to Buffalo, we were awaiting immigration clearance. Zeyna, who is considerably younger than me and a holder of both British and Australian passports, was subjected to detailed questioning about why she wished to enter the US, where she would be staying, with whom, etc.

Then came my turn, and, voila, my passport was stamped, and I waved through with nary a question. Taken aback, I asked the officer the reason for my preferential treatment, to which he pointed at my grey hair and replied, 'Because of your age, sir.' As though an 80-year-old with a giveaway Muslim name—since Muslims are often given 'preferential' treatment in that country—cannot be a terrorist in the 'land of the free and the home of the brave,' as its national anthem would have us believe!

Old age *does* have its advantages sometimes!

◈

That said, two encounters with customs officials linger in memory and may be the cause of my irrational disconcertment.

The first was at Moscow's Sheremetyevo airport, where I had arrived for the politics-riven 1980 Olympics (at the height of the Cold War) and was subjected to chilling inquisitorial treatment for carrying a copy of the American *Time* magazine.

The second was, during transit, at Tel Aviv's Ben Gurion airport when the cold, searing, suspicious scrutiny of the customs officials raised terrifying images of what Mossad operatives are reportedly capable of.

I now realize my illogical visions of being incarcerated, given the full monty, and locked up in the local equivalents of San Francisco's San Simeon prison (now disused) were perhaps grossly uncalled for and the result of being at the wrong place at the wrong time. But I must admit that my illogical trepidations have not abated with time.

Coming back to Khalid Butt and my unpleasant brush with the law in Karachi, the incident sparked the start of an informal relationship that was to last through many wonderful sporting exchanges on either side of the border, as also abroad at the Olympics and Asian Games, courtesy hockey and cricket, the great sporting levellers.

I have many warm memories of Butt's visit to Mumbai for the Hockey World Cup. Khalid was enchanted by the metropolis and struck by the similarity between the city, and his own Karachi.

Zaheer Abbas aka *Zaheer, Ab Bas Karo*

I remember Zaheer Abbas, the indescribably elegant Pakistani batsman, who hit his first purple patch against India in Pakistan in 1977–78, went on to captain Pakistan and play two series for World XI in Australia (along with my rambunctious friend Farokh 'Rookie' Engineer). He represented his country as the last president of the International Cricket Council (ICC) (as the position itself was abolished in 2016).

Upon arrival at Mumbai airport, he exclaimed: '*Yaar, tumahara shehr to bilkul hamare Karachi jaisa hai!*' (Buddy, your city is just like our Karachi!).

Zaheer had come to Mumbai from his native Karachi for his friend Sunil Gavaskar's birthday and that is when he and I struck up a friendship. Rukya and I invited him back to India and stay with us at our *ghareeb khana* ('humble abode,' as the expression in Urdu goes).

Although 'Zed' couldn't accept our invitation, his parents did a few years later and spent a memorable week with us. They live on the seafront in Karachi and so were particularly enamoured with the similar view from our home on Warden Road. They were also very impressed with the secularism implicit in the fact that it was situated between Haji Ali Mosque on the sea and the Mahalaxmi Temple. 'We get blessings from both sides,' I said to their great amusement. Zaheer, nicknamed the 'Asian Don Bradman' did return to Mumbai with his

Kanpur-born second wife Rita Luthra (named Samina Abbas after marriage), years later. For cricket aficionados interested in such trivia, three other Indian Test captains—Lala Amarnath, Sunil Gavaskar and Bishan Singh Bedi—have their *sasural* (in-laws' homes) in the once-thriving industrial town of Kanpur.

It is said that Zed's first wife was convinced that 70 per cent of his fan mail came from India, despite the defeats he inflicted on the Indian team during their tour of Pakistan in 1982–83, prompting Sunil Gavaskar to recall that his team would refer to him as '*Zaheer, ab bas karo*' (Zaheer, that's enough).

Zed and Samina (her father, K.C. Luthra, was a friend of Zaheer's father, Shabbir Abbas) returned to Mumbai a few years later when they, my wife Zeyna and I spent a delightful 'down memory lane' evening at our home over cocktails. We followed that up with a Parsi meal at the CCI and a screening of *Lagaan* at the hoary, but now-defunct, Eros Cinema. It only strengthened their love for our city and their resolve to revisit, which has, since then, unfortunately not materialized because of political reasons.

Moral and Professional Dilemmas

This brings to mind an incident concerning Zed during the controversial 1983 Bangalore Test between the arch-rivals, which ended in a farcical finish following Pakistan captain Zaheer Abbas's churlish attempt to deny Gavaskar a century. But despite my belief in professional responsibility, even obligation, to tell the *whole* story, I shall refrain from writing about this one—I believe it was extremely personal, shared with me due to implicit trust placed in me, and therefore constitutes 'privileged' information.

Another such professional dilemma arose during Bishan Bedi's team's tour of Australia in 1978–78, which Australia won 3–2 with the home team eking out a 47-run victory in the decisive final Test at Adelaide on the last day. India had registered their first Test win in Australia during the series earlier on the tour by a thumping 222 runs at Melbourne, followed by another by an innings and 2 runs at Sydney.

An incident at the Barossa Valley vineyards on the rest day of the final Test in Adelaide was instrumental in India losing the Test—and series 2–3—albeit against an enfeebled Australia side, because of its best players having switched to Kerry Packer's World Series Cricket. Only two journalists were privy to the crucial incident. One of them, Kishore Bhimani, has passed away and I am honour-bound professionally to not divulge it. But I must confess, it has been an agonizing journalistic, as well as moral, dilemma between respecting the public's right to know and an individual's right to privacy. As I am the sole custodian of the secret, honouring it has become a no-brainer for me.

A third incident in point was a crisis of conscience during the 2006 Melbourne Commonwealth Games. I was a member of a group of journalists staying at the 125-year-old, Victorian Windsor Oberoi hotel, favoured by us because of its Indian connection and proximity to the Melbourne Cricket Ground (MCG) where the Games were being held.

Midway through the Games' schedule I was made privy by a senior hotel manager to an incident involving an official of the Indian contingent, alleging rape of a member of the hotel staff. The accused was an official of the Indian contingent, and the allegation was made by the hotel authorities. Nobody else among the press corps, staying at any of the hotels or elsewhere, was aware of the incident which would most certainly have been a red-hot explosive story.

My dilemma was whether to 'scoop' the masala story, a mouth-watering 'exclusive' answer to the prayers of any reporter worth his salt, one which would have been gleefully picked up by the large press and electronic media contingent from the 71 countries participating in the Games. To scoop or not to scoop? On the one hand was national honour, since the despicable alleged culprit was Indian and, on the other, was my professional obligation to inform my readers of the incident, no matter how shameful! With the time difference between Melbourne and the headquarters (Mumbai) being five and a half hours, I had time on my side. Nevertheless, with the option of burying my head in the sand also available, a decision had to be taken and fairly urgently, given the press deadline.

Looking back, I still wonder if I took the correct call to kill my story. All things considered, I feel I was right in giving precedence to national honour.

Omar Qureshi, Commentator Par Excellence

There was also the urbane and erudite Mumbai-born cricket writer Omar Qureshi, who, along with Zulfikar Ali Bhutto (he later became prime minister of Pakistan) studied at the Cathedral and John Connon School. Along with Jamsheed Marker, Omar was lord and master of all he surveyed on Pakistani radio and subsequently on television. He was a member of the Indian Medical Service before Partition, and later, columnist for *Dawn*, *Pakistan Times* and *The Guardian* (UK). An ardent Indophile, he wrote nostalgic pieces of his times in Mumbai and Delhi and authored many books. Qureshi later became the public relations manager of Pakistan International Airlines (PIA or Perhaps I'll Arrive Airline, as I used to teasingly refer to it to my Pakistani friends).

In 1978, after my initial meeting with Air Marshal Nur Khan during the Champions Trophy in Karachi, he very kindly extended me an invitation to Pakistan for the Indian Test cricket team's forthcoming tour of that country. Omar Qureshi was specially flown down by the air marshal (who was then also president of their cricket and squash associations/federations) with a personal couriered invitation, which I was more than happy to accept.

As that was his first visit to Mumbai—the city of his birth—after

Partition, Omar was like a child, taking in the sights and sounds with wide-eyed, unalterable mien. 'Love is lovelier the second time around...' Omar would croak the song memorialized by Frank Sinatra. 'I've fallen in love again with your city, Khalid...' Omar Qureshi would gush, 'wish I'd never gone away.'

At the airport, when returning to his home in Karachi, Omar embraced me warmly and, with tears in his eyes, promised to 'return soon, inshallah.'

But, alas, it was not to be.

When I went back to Pakistan for the Friendship Series cricket tournament, I tried to meet Omar but was advised against it by his close journalist friends since he was 'in rather poor shape.' His 'there's no mañana (tomorrow), lifestyle,' aggravated by years of heavy smoking, had taken a heavy toll. The man who had taken a principled stand against the imposition of martial law in his country in the '60s, passed away, following a stroke, at his Clifton Beach home in Karachi in 2005.

Zulfikar Ali Bhutto: the Mediocre Right-Handed Batsman

Coming to Zulfikar Ali Bhutto, whom I referred to earlier: before migrating to Pakistan, he was a member of the landmark CCI, the cricket ground that is named after Michael Herbert Rudolf Knatchbull, fifth son of Baron Brabourne, who was governor of Bombay between 1933–37 and later, acting governor-general of India. Brabourne laid the foundation stone of the Brabourne Stadium in 1936 after conducting negotiations for the land with Anthony de Mello of the CCI.

As a student at St Xavier's College, Bhutto used to practise at the Sunder Cricket Club nets in Cross Maidan opposite the historic Azad Maidan on which the Bombay Gymkhana stands. He was said to be a mediocre right-handed batsman.

Incidentally, I too used to practise at the same ground during my college days in the '50s, under the watchful eye of much-loved groundsman Narayan Kabadi. I would practise there in the hope that I might catch the eyes of the legendary Vinoo Mankad and Dattu Phadkar and umpire Ahmed M. Mamsa, who would occasionally drop by at the nets. But try as I did, I just wasn't good enough to be noticed!

Bhutto joined the CCI, but was not selected to play for the club team. He was expelled from the club at a special general meeting of members, at which the momentous decision was also taken, at then President Vijay Merchant's behest, to not agree to the demand by the Bombay Cricket Association (BCA; and now known as the Mumbai Cricket Association) for an increase in the number of seats for the members of its parent body. This prompted the BCA president Sheshrao Wankhede to sever ties with the CCI. Being a minister in the Maharashtra state government, he used his enormous clout and built a stadium that was named after him, almost a cricket ball's throw away from the world-famous Brabourne.

Farooq Mazhar: the Punjabi Munda

Among the Pakistani journalists whom I got to know very well was Farooq Mazhar, the archetypal, burly Punjabi *munda* (smart blighter) with an imposing twirling moustache and grandiloquent voice, who was as soft at heart as he was fearsome on the exterior. Highly respected among his *biradari* (brotherhood), Farooq was a household name in the world of Pakistani hockey and cricket as an Urdu journalist and radio and television commentator.

I had the good fortune to befriend Farooq at the inaugural Champions Trophy tournament, several cricket and hockey matches and nine Olympic Games. At each of these events, Farooq and I (we had a unique, unspoken bond) would get together with journalists from all over the world and discuss cricket and hockey, magnificent obsessions for both of us, until the proverbial cows came home.

At the 1982 Hockey World Cup held in Mumbai, Farooq Mazhar was elected president, and I, vice-president (self-styled president for 'vice') of the International Sports Writers Association (IHSWA) of international hockey writers, which was part of the International Hockey Federation (FIH). Until then, the IHSWA had been monopolized by a Eurocentric clique, which, in Farooq's and my opinion, needed to be overhauled and replaced by a more geographically diverse body of hockey journalists with the interest of the game at heart.

Being able to break the stranglehold of an entrenched monopoly and replacing it with an eclectic body of hockey writers from almost every continent was, for the two of us, most gratifying to say the least. In our efforts, we were helped greatly by Geerhard de Grooth—the third angle of the triangle—who, being Dutch, a European, was considered a renegade by the colonial masters who had controlled international hockey at the highest level for years on end.

Along with changes in the playing surface (the switch to AstroTurf) and in its rules, the pristine nature of the beautiful game, with all its elegant dribbling, dexterity, athleticism, body swerves and feints and also ingenious short-pass positional tactics, swung world hegemony to the bigger, stronger and fitter European countries such as Germany, the Netherlands, Spain and England.

Having lost touch with Farooq (I last met him in Dubai many years ago) and unaware of his failing health, I was truly aggrieved to learn of his passing away. In spite of the fact that we were both fiercely nationalistic, especially as regards matters concerning sport, we were sincere friends.

'*Saheeb*, the White Man's Burden, *Saheeb*'

Geerhard de Grooth was a businessman from 'den Haag' (the Hague) and amateur hockey writer who, in time, must certainly have broken all records for covering hockey matches, both men's and women's, given the sport's popularity in the Netherlands and its standing in the world.

We first met at the Munich Olympics of 1972 and regularly thereafter at international hockey tournaments around the world. 'Gerry,' as he was known as, was a real character, a sui generis chipmunk with a quirky sense of humour. Puckish beyond description, his sense of the comical knew no bounds as regards language or gestures and with total disregard for the sensitivities of his audience or the victims of his jokes. He christened a colleague, who was 6 feet 7 inches tall, with the name 'Tiny,' and his favourite equivalent for 'goodbye' was 'see you at the funeral.'

Many of his stories were in embarrassingly bad taste, but his animated rendering in Dutch-laced English and *andaaz-e-bayaan* (manner of delivery) would invariably bring the house down.

◆

On one occasion, in Mumbai, when I was dropping Gerry at his hotel after an evening of side-splitting laughter, he made a remark, which I, being rather intolerant at that time and not knowing him too well, considered offensive, and ordered him and his Dutch colleague out of my car.

He called early the next morning to apologize for his 'disgraceful' manners. So transparently contrite was he, even as he cracked joke after joke in the course of his apology, that it would have taken a person with a heart of stone, to not forgive him as he pleaded.

Forgive, but never forget, as my mother taught me! I'm sure many people will not agree...but this has been my way. And I'm happy with the results and the peace of mind it has brought me. We became best friends thereafter, helped by the fact that he began to understand and respect Indian sensibilities concerning humour.

On one occasion when he was seeing me off at Amsterdam's Amstelveen airport, he was so overcome saying *vaarwel* ('farewell' in Dutch) as he embraced me, that he choked while calling me his best friend *('mijn beste vriend')* adding 'forever' and 'as long as I live' in Dutch. We then decided to make it a point to meet every time we were in each other's part of the world, even if it meant travelling a reasonable distance to do so.

I'll never forget the time Gerry rang the doorbell at our Bombay home at an unearthly hour, without prior intimation and looking like Death warmed up, after a particularly uncomfortable and exhausting flight. 'Here I am,' he announced, flashing a smile. '...keeping my promise!' He was on his way to an assignment in Sri Lanka, a place he dearly loved, largely because of its colonial past, as the Island of Serendipity used to be a Dutch colony.

'But you didn't have our address,' my wife interjected.

'No problem for this Dutchman,' he replied. 'I remembered the location from my last time in Bombay. When I got into a taxi at the airport, I said: "Take me to the mosque in the middle of the sea."'

'The mosque in the middle of the sea?' The driver was confused, so I told him 'just drive into the city towards the Taj Hotel and I will find it. When we came to the junction near your home (which I recognized), I got off, wandered around a bit—I am travelling with only this bag—and, voila, there was your front gate!'

◆

When I next visited Amsterdam, Gerry was waiting at the airport arrivals enclosure and, as I emerged, ran towards me, grabbed the trolley from me and, cockily striding a few metres ahead of me, shouted repeatedly for all the world to hear: 'Saheeb, it's the White Man's burden, Saheeb…'

That was Geerhard de Grooth: bon vivant, hilarious mime, prankster sans frontiers. I suspected he had a case of ADHD (Attention Deficit Hyperactivity Disorder), but his zest for life more than compensated for it.

He went out of my life as mysteriously as he had entered it. I have tried my best to contact him, to meet his charming wife Susan and cricketer-son Tim (he represented Netherlands in the World Cricket Cup) but have had no success.

I sincerely hope Gerry is happy and well, wherever he may be.

Air Marshal Nur Khan: the 'Man of Steel'

Cricket *dewaane* (aficionados) who had the good fortune of crossing the border to witness the 2004 Friendship Cricket Series, the brainchild of the late Atal Bihari Vajpayee, will forever cherish warm memories of the genuine hand of friendship extended to all of us at every step wherever we went in that country.

On a personal note: given my allergy to jingoistic politics, I've had some extremely close Pakistani friends from the world of sport. Prominent among them was Air Marshal Nur Khan.

Born into a military family of the Punjabi Awan tribe in Attock, he completed his education from Aitchison College and later graduated from the famed Rashtriya Indian Military College in Dehradun. A three-star air officer, he fought for the Allies in World War II and distinguished himself in the Six-Day War in the Middle East, later becoming Commander-in-Chief of the Pakistan Air Force.

After retirement from the armed forces, Nur Khan (known as the 'Man of Steel' and remembered for overpowering a hijacker on a domestic Pakistan Airlines plane) became the most respected sport administrator in his country as head of its cricket, hockey and squash national bodies, in all of which they were numero uno in the world.

We were introduced during the Champions Trophy hockey tournament held in Karachi in 1980—incidentally at the Lahore home of legendary Pakistani singing nightingale, Noor Jahan. Former cricket captain Abdul Hafeez Kardar, the (then retired) dashing all-rounder Fazal Mahmood, and a textile magnate/budding politician called Nawaz Sharif (who later went on to become prime minister of Pakistan) were also present.

Nur Khan's and my passion for sport struck a chord that lasted many years. He never visited India but always played gracious host—at his elegant home in Lahore and at Campo de Polo (Buenos Aires, Argentina) during the IHF Hockey World Cup in 1978.

◈

Similarly, my good friend Tunku Imran of Malaysia was president of the Malaysian Cricket Association and the national hockey and squash bodies. Now a retired office-bearer of the ICC and former president of the International Olympic Association and the Commonwealth Games Federation, he was simultaneously an executive board member of the ICC and emeritus president of the World Squash Federation (WSF).

Tunku Tan Sri Dato' Seri Imran ibn Almarhum Tuanku Ja'afar al-Haq—to use his full name but who is known to his good friends as 'Pete'—is the second son of Ja'afar, elected monarch of Negeri Sembilan, one of the 13 states of Malaysia, who was king of Malaysia from 1994 to 1999.

But more about Pete later.

FIVE

LEARNING LESSONS THE HARD WAY

Stanford University

To return to Stanford University: it has produced perhaps the largest number of Fulbright, Marshall and Rhodes scholars and members of the United States Congress, as also 74 living billionaires and 17 living astronauts.

The university also counts among its alumni, Padma Bhushan Azim Premji, who graduated in Business and is popularly known as the Czar of the Indian IT industry, and Sundar Pichai, CEO of Alphabet Inc and its subsidiary Google Inc.

Like former US president John F. Kennedy, Mukesh Ambani also attended Stanford, but did not graduate. Ambani, India's richest individual with an estimated net worth of US$89.7 billion (as of 2021) enrolled for an MBA but, according to the university's website, withdrew in 1980 to help his father build Reliance, which at the time was still a (fast-)growing enterprise and not the behemoth it is today. His daughter Isha, however, obtained her MBA from Stanford in 2018.

Azim Premji had to drop out of the university because of the sudden death of his father but he completed the requirements of his degree via correspondence later.

As a matter of information, among prominent college dropouts from Indian colleges, who are now billionaires in their country are media baron Dr Subhash Chandra, Gautam Adani (of Adani group), Mukesh Jagtiani (Dubai-based Landmark group), P.N.C. Menon (NRI and owner of Bangalore-based construction company Sobha

Developers), and Vinod Goenka (DB Realty, incidentally, linked to the 2G scam in India).

Other distinguished dropouts include Bill Gates (Microsoft), Steve Jobs and Steve Wozniak (Apple), March Zuckerberg (Facebook) and Henry Ford.

New Horizons

My wife Rukya's and my journey from Mumbai to Naples, Italy on board the Lloyd Triestino liner *Asia*, continuing on to New York on her sister ship *Saturnia* was a memorable experience. This was after I obtained my master's and LLB degrees in Mumbai and moved to Stanford University for further academic pursuits.

We were both travelling abroad for the first time in our lives, and that too, by sea. Being innocents in foreign lands, never before had we spent time—anywhere—with people other than our own fellow Indians. By-products of the Raj, we were initially in awe of fair-skinned foreigners who, when we got to know them better, were surprisingly convivial. The biggest thrill was to be served at the table by fair-skinned waiters which took some getting used to. Being natives of Mumbai, we took the ubiquitous Cairo beggars and flies in our strides, but were gobsmacked by the Suez Canal, an engineering marvel.

But we were truly humbled by the mind-boggling wonder of the world, the Pyramids: their size, strength, proportions and awesome human ingenuity regarding concept and execution; they were indeed a thrilling reminder of limitless human potential.

We spent a night in transit at Naples (our first sighting of a European city) at a dingy hotel, the best we could afford, in a seedy portside district inhabited by pimps and prostitutes, and which was more rundown than Mumbai's Bapu Khote Street. And that is saying something! 'Do you live in Bapu Khote Street?' was the favourite 'expletive' of our St Mary's school English teacher Mr Noronha, whenever he wished to express disgust at a student's lack of manners.

During winters in the northern hemisphere, the waters of the Atlantic Sea can be exceedingly choppy, and therefore, our journey was a nightmare, especially for pregnant Rukya. To say that Rukya was miserable would be a gross understatement, what with embryonic Tarique in her tummy. The cramped cattle class cabin my father could afford was most uncomfortable and, being in the lowermost deck, barely skimmed above the Plimsoll line over the icy, turbulent sea. The passengers were mostly southern European refugees seeking Valhalla in the so-called land of milk and honey, where the streets are said to be paved with gold. The food was anodyne and barely edible, the coffee, ersatz. Large number of passengers on board were seasick; the stench of unwashed human bodies commixed with pasta, wine and sickening vomitus, befouled the dining areas even as the hardier ones kept stuffing their mouths nonchalantly as if there was no *domani* (Italian for 'tomorrow').

The eight-hour stopover at Halifax, Canada, seemed to last for an eternity but all eyes lit up and many a tear shed as we sailed past the colossal neoclassical 93-metre copper Statue of Liberty, a gift from the French people to the Americans on their Independence Day in 1776.

School of Hard Knocks

Stanford University brought about a near-miraculous transformation in me not only as regards acquisition of professional knowledge but also the development of an evolved and balanced mindset.

The milieu almost surreptitiously bred logical thought processes. More importantly, the interactive participative discussions helped rid me of my reserve ingrained by the cram-and-regurgitate system endemic to Indian education. Leaving aside the constant striving for superior grades against fierce competition from the best minds from all over the world, the overall intellectual and cultural environment ipso facto made for self-confidence.

The interaction with fellow-students and the faculty, possessing outstanding intellect that one encountered everywhere—in the corridors, the lounges, at informal coffee and cocktail sessions—helped combat my deep-rooted reserve and lack of self-confidence. Our dean at the department of journalism was the wise, and wizened, Dr Chilton Bush, who had dedicated the best part of his life to teaching what was drummed into our psyche as 'responsible' journalism.

This was the time when tough-as-nails, cheap cigar chomping unshaven journos, in a hangover from the US Prohibition days, churned out and edited no-nonsense, no frills, circulation-driven but, at all times, scrupulously correct copy.

I had the distinct impression that Dr Bush initially singled me out for special sympathetic attention in the condescending belief that I needed it, coming as I did from a backward Third World country—as was, and continues to be, the popular perception in the US. He was frank enough to privately admit as much to me at the end of the first quarter, while adding that he had been delighted to be proven wrong.

◆

One of my courses entailed practical newspaper experience in San Francisco (which was half an hour's drive away from Stanford University) at *The Examiner*, the No. 2 newspaper to the leader, the *San Francisco Chronicle*, founded in 1865 by the de Young brothers and later bought by the hard-headed Hearst family.

We also had to work at the *News Call Bulletin* in the city, which published as many as four editions between 9 a.m. and 2 p.m. As can be imagined, the staff worked at frenetic assembly-line pace putting one edition to bed no sooner the previous one had gone to press.

As may also be expected, the routine took an extremely heavy toll on the health of the editorial staff. I worked under Harry Law, the city editor, a diminutive product of the old school that had convinced itself, for no rhyme or reason, that journalism could not be taught. Kids from fancy schools like me, were, by implication, unwelcome in their bailiwick. In their view, the only way to be a good journalist was to be lucky to be born one or by learning at the 'school of hard knocks,' namely experience, by getting your hands dirty with printer's ink.

Cynical at first, Harry warmed to me in due course and would insist I join him in drinking swigs of vodka from a bottle he kept in his top drawer after each of the four editions went to press, starting at 9 a.m.

I later learnt that this was the lot of many, devoted, but grossly underpaid news journalists across the US.

◆

There was a lesson to be relearnt from this regarding fair wages for editorial staff—one of my father's cherished principles—which I was taught at a very young age. Whatever I may have achieved, is very largely because of the dedication and hard work of my associates, which in turn would not have been possible without fair recompense. It is amazing how influences from one's younger days can last a lifetime.

Speaking of youthful influences: one morning, during my JWT days, my sons Tarique and Sharique, perhaps 11 and 9 then, when leaving for high school, bid my wife Rukya and me goodbye saying, 'Bye Mom, bye Dad.' Set in my fossilized norms of discipline, I sat them down next to me and said, 'Listen sons, in his household we don't say "Bye Mom, bye Dad," we say "Goodbye Mummy, goodbye Daddy" or respectful words to that effect.'

Looking back, I feel I was harsh in my dictatorial imposition of fuddy-duddy discipline (that's the way I'd been brought up), but I must, at the same time, say that I'm proud of my sons. To this day, they address their elders with utmost respect and are acclaimed in our circle of friends as being immaculate in the way they conduct themselves.

In the process of writing these remembrances, I was working out at my club's gymnasium where I bumped into Keshav Sanghi, the 50-plus-year-old son of my dear departed friend Krishna Sanghi. Seeing him after years, I went up to say hello. He happened to be in the middle of a bench press routine but seeing me approach him, dropped his weight, jumped up to his feet and wished me 'Good morning, sir.' When I told him how impressed I was with his manners and respect for elders, for a person of his generation, he replied, 'But, sir, that's the only way!'

Manners, like most things, change with the times. I have believed that what were considered impeccable manners in my days, have different manifestations today. But young Keshav has proved me wrong. And I'm delighted he's made me revise my opinion.

Prohibition

Coming back to Harry Law's insatiable need for alcohol: it was reminiscent of our own Prohibition in Mumbai during the 1960s, at numerous secretive, Chicago-type dives and speakeasies—'Aunty's Bars' or joints—small, grimy rooms where 'thirsty men furtively guzzled rotgut and moonshine behind dirty curtains.'[8]

It was at these convivial watering holes that we graduated from rotten fruit in battery water *tharra* (hooch) to Indian Made Foreign Liquor (IMFL, as it was grandiloquently called) by greedy excise officers, always on the lookout for palm-greasing *pyaase* (thirsty) pen-pushers like us. Half the excitement was derived from the fact that it was clandestine, a thrilling, even glamorous, 'robbers and police' type, hide-and-seek escapade. The accursed law, banning consumption and even buying of alcohol without a liquor permit, was introduced in 1960 when Gujarat separated from the erstwhile Bombay state.

The new law brought about a new wave of opportunism with one-time thugs and smugglers switching to bootlegging and spawning hundreds of underworld dons in the wake of Varadarajan Mudaliar, the Don Corleone of the Mumbai underworld.

---

[8]Abbey Perreault, 'Remembering the Clandestine 'Aunty Bars' of Prohibition-Era Bombay', *Atlas Obscura*, 3 September 2018, https://www.atlasobscura.com/articles/prohibition-in-bombay. Accessed on 2 November 2021.

The following is from the *Hindustan Times*[9]:

> The massive profits from the illicit liquor trade would act as the launchpad for a parallel economy with tentacles in everything, from prostitution and gambling to Bollywood and, eventually, gun-running and terror.
>
> Gangs formed and allied with one another to protect their territories. Their grip on the city, their ruthless wars and the deep inroads they made into local law enforcement, would last decades. It would take a special squad, the 'encounter specialists,' to break the back of the beast that was created as a by-product of Prohibition.

The Prohibition law still exists in Gujarat, birthplace of the Mahatma. It is understood that although alcohol has always been available there for permit holders on health grounds on a doctor's prescription, until quite recently applicants for a permit were required to fill in an application form which asked for information regarding: the *sharaabi's* (alcoholic's) name, *sharaabi's* address, *sharaabi's* father's name, *sharaabi's* mother's name and so on.

Following pressure from the state's sugarcane lobby, which saw potential profit in legalizing liquor, the Prohibition policy was abolished in 1972. In its place, a permit system (in keeping with the ubiquitous and evil 'licence raj') was introduced, and perfected, by the Congress party.

In a country inhabited by ingenious people who are past masters in the art and science of making money by, first enacting laws, then enforcing or breaking them with impunity for profit, the permit rules still exist for those in authority to enforce for personal profit and for politicians to avail of to blackmail and even incarcerate.

In retrospect, these gambits are no different from the Draconian laws enacted and used at will by our erstwhile lords and masters, the British, when they found it expedient. It's a matter of shame that

---

[9] Riddhi Doshi, 'In Bombay, Prohibition Didn't Just Fail. It Spawned the Underworld', *Hindustan Times*, 17 April 2016, https://www.hindustantimes.com/india/in-bombay-prohibition-didn-t-just-fail-it-spawned-the-underworld/story-PSLIEhNprWpbBYHk3ZeMZK.html. Accessed on 2 November 2021.

many of these laws still exist on our statute books for the benefit of those in positions of power and authority to extort, harm, harass and destroy.

'You Bloody Communist'

I was an 'abecedarian' (learning the letters of the journalism alphabet, in a manner of speaking) at the *San Francisco Chronicle* at the time of this incident. Having arrived at the City Hall a tad early for my initiation into the real world of journalism, I was killing time in the reporters' lounge during my student days at Stanford University.

Looking up from the newspaper I was reading, I noticed through a door that was ajar, a lady in the corridor outside, sizing me up in a rather strange manner. Attributing her seemingly inordinate interest in me to the fact that I was the only person of colour around at that time, I continued reading the newspaper.

A little later, (my subconscious may have prompted me to do it) I looked up in her direction again, to find the one I initially considered 'a sweet old lady,' now glaring at me in a not-so-friendly manner.

When it happened a third time, I walked towards her to find out if there was anything the matter. Seeing me rise, she scurried down the stairway. I was, however, much younger and faster than her. When I caught up with her, she shot back with a look laced, half-and-half, with terror and hate and yelled: 'Go away! Leave me alone, you bloody Communist.'

Quite a baptism by fire, that, in the harsh, ugly world of journalism!

◈

If I remember correctly, we were a total of 12 Indian students at Stanford in our first year, which Rukya, uncomfortably pregnant, attended as a part-time student in the first year, taking courses in sociology. Excluding myself from the reckoning, nine out of the remainder (all single males) were from a certain state and, therefore, spoke a common language.

When we arrived at Stanford, Rukya and I resolved to not get caught up exclusively in an Indian commune and to spend comparatively more time in the company of American students and those who were from other countries, for a more varied and meaningful learning experience. We shouldn't have bothered to even try since our fellow-Indians preferred to stick together, converse only in their provincial lingo, generally making it abundantly clear we were entirely unwanted in their scheme of things. This was Rukya's and my first experience of living abroad, and we were starved of the company of our compatriots. But our desi colleagues couldn't care less!

I'm ashamed to conclude that this proclivity towards separateness—linguistic, cultural, religious, provincial and other—in our society, fuelled not by votaries of apartness (as in apartheid) but by fire-breathing bigots, hatemongers and 'wolves in sheep's clothing' doctrinaires, has only worsened with the passage of time to the extent that it has now assumed frightening proportions.

'That Ansari—Let Him Live There, Die There'

After over four decades, I'm still struggling to come to terms with a vitriolic speech by a certain rabble-rousing, Hitler-like politician who had the audacity to rant at a public meeting in Mumbai before an audience of thousands: 'That Khalid Ansari—I'm told he's gone away to Dubai [this was when I was running the *Khaleej Times* newspaper]—let him live there, let him *die* there!'

At that stage I had totally relinquished control of my publications to my sons, who, in keeping with our belief in giving absolute editorial freedom to our editors, did not interfere with their authority in the day-to-day running of things.

I let the uncalled-for outburst pass, since responding to it would have served no constructive purpose and would have only made for an explosive situation. I only wish he, who had nothing at all to show for his own contributions in these regards, had remembered, when making that hate-driven statement, my father's services and sacrifices to our country during the freedom struggle. Also, I wish he had not forgotten my own unceasing efforts towards actively promoting the causes of peaceful coexistence, nationalism, secularism, in short, oneness at all times, through our various publications. But, in all probability, the putrid invective must have been greeted with near-unanimous acclaim by the ignorant *janta* (many of them, paid cheerleaders) who idolize the demonic *netas* (politicians) and consider every utterance of theirs, gospel truth.

It's that old Hitlerian gambit about conjuring up an enemy and shamefully capitalizing—behind their back—on the ignorance and credulity of the former's adoring followers. It hurts, and this hurt is increasing among responsible sections of the Indian Muslim community who pass the litmus test of Indianness by any yardstick. But they have to endure increasing hatred, surreptitiously spewed by the same biased elements—people they have always loved and respected as brothers and sisters. It is becoming extremely irksome, especially for those on social media, to have to prove their loyalty to their country every single day. Ignoring them is easier said than done, given the degree and persistence of the other side's vituperation.

As a God-fearing, but hardly orthodox Muslim, it breaks my heart to experience and hear about these clandestine manifestations of mistrust and suspicion regarding a certain people's loyalty to the motherland. This is particularly heart-rending when individuals one considers responsible, educated, trusted and respected to behave in this manner. Many either deny knowledge of the existence of this issue or, in turn, dismiss obvious instances of victimization as exaggeration. It would be unfair to say that this head-in-the-sand phenomenon is inherent, but it is certainly widespread and mushrooming.

Admittedly, there are any number of misguided and irresponsible elements in the Muslim community as well. They deserve to be put away and dealt with in the harshest possible manner under the law. But to suspect, and condemn, the entire community for the sins of a few, is grossly unjust and vitiates the time-honoured Indian ethos of ahimsa (not causing harm), of love, tolerance and peaceful coexistence.

In the words of former external affairs minister Natwar Singh in his autobiography *One Life Is Not Enough*, I write this 'not with fury, but certainly with exasperation and anger.'[10]

Since one's religion is an accident of birth, in a manner of speaking, and determined by the precepts followed by one's parents, and given my own cultural background (which I choose to call Anglo-Indian),

---

[10]K. Natwar-Singh, *One Life is Not Enough: An Autobiography*, Rupa Publications India, 2014.

I have no problem whatsoever with those who propagate the cause of Hindutva. After all, Hindus constitute the vast majority in our country. But, at the same time, I'm proud of the secular principles of our country's constitution, as also the teachings of our saints and sages of all faiths, who have unanimously advocated the universal religion of love, tolerance, mutual respect and peaceful coexistence.

Now that I'm retired and no longer have a family group of publications to spread my own message of peace, tolerance, secularism, oneness and Indianness, I find myself compelled to spend hours on social media waging an ongoing, one-man war against the sinister forces of communalism who preach hate and divisiveness among our people.

What is particularly distressing is to find 'friends,' people I always considered balanced and secular—wolves in sheep's clothing—show their true colours at this late stage of my life. With each passing day, it seems like an increasingly uphill climb, a waste of time unlikely to bear fruit. But the fight must continue, no matter what.

Flower Power

To come back to Stanford and our—Rukya's and mine—experiences in the US.

Sunny Gavaskar once joked to my son Tarique that I had the 'knack of always being where the action is.'

Stanford is in Palo Alto, California, and across the Golden Gate Bridge of San Francisco, less than an hour's drive away, lies Berkeley, where the term 'Flower Power' originated as a symbolic act of protest against the Vietnam War. In other words, Rukya and I were, in fact, just around the corner to where the action was.

The Flower Power movement, that was inspired by poet-writer Irwin Allen Ginsberg's essay, 'How to Make a March/Spectacle' and his Beat Generation's concept of non-violence, was then in its nascent stage but was rapidly burgeoning into a revolution. The movement captured the counterculture zeitgeist of the 1960s—symbolized and energized by the Flower children (hippies).

Flower-wearing protestors of the Vietnam War used marches, sit-downs, music, and, of course, flowers to represent love, peace and other anti-war sentiments. Slowly, as the movement grew, it became associated with the use of psychedelic drugs and the imagery of flowers became more abstract and vibrantly colourful. These predominantly young people who rejected conventional society, the norms of the 1950s, jingoism, hate and violence and instead advocated love, music, harmony and mysticism created the iconic hippie subculture of that era.

Unsurprisingly, the Beatles, who actually helped make the movement an international social phenomenon, gave it a decidedly Indian twist (given their own kinship with the Indian ethos) under the influence of Maharishi Mahesh Yogi. Mahesh Yogi, who was born Mahesh Prasad Varma, died at the age of 90 in Limburg, Netherlands, leaving behind a vast fortune (mostly in the form of landed property), estimated to be worth ₹60,000 crore, which sparked a bitter conflict between his heirs and followers.

In February 1968, the Beatles travelled to Rishikesh to take part in the Transcendental Meditation training course at the ashram of the yogi. The visit followed the group's denunciation of drugs in favour of the meditation course and received widespread media attention internationally.

Culturally, the Beatles took Liverpool (where they started their musical career), then the UK and, at raging fire pace, almost the entire world in the Swinging Sixties. They inspired a phenomenon that defined a generation, one that embraced a counterculture of drugs and sexual promiscuity.

Their record-topping album, *Sergeant Pepper's Lonely Hearts Club Band*, inspired awe and devotion on both sides of the Atlantic and was arguably the soundtrack of 1967's 'Summer of Love,' the period when the counterculture reached its peak.

The band's eventual break-up was the end of an era but not before making it one of the loudest and audacious decades in forms of art, music, culture, perhaps even the news, across the world.

Scott McKenzie's iconic single 'San Francisco (Be Sure to Wear Flowers in Your Hair)' became one of the most recognized songs associated with that era but, cloistered as we were at the university's married students' housing in Menlo Park, which went on to become among the most expensive residential areas in the country, we were cut off from the cultural tsunami that was sweeping the country.

Rukya's and my first abode at university was a decrepit one-bedroom apology for a home in downtown Palo Alto's seedy east end in which we almost froze. Classes were a miserable half-hour walk in the freezing cold, especially for pregnant Rukya; like me, she was ill-equipped for the weather. Salvation came in the form of a fellow Stanford student Trella Laughlin, who saw us trudging to college one morning and very kindly offered us a ride not only then, but every morning thereafter. Trella was from Jackson, Mississippi, and spoke in a most enchanting Southern drawl. Predictably, she found it hard to believe we didn't have snakes and tigers on the loose on our streets in India, and befriended us with extraordinary mindfulness.

In another manifestation of *jab upar wala meherbaan to gadha pehelwan*, in our very first week at Stanford, we wandered into International House, where sweet old ladies from the local community volunteered their time to welcome and make foreign students feel at home over piping hot cups of tea and coffee. That was the start of a relationship with the genial Maggie von Kempf who, perhaps taking pity on the hapless innocents from a 'poor country,' spontaneously adopted us, in a manner of speaking.

Maggie's husband Paul was of German ancestry and owned a botanical nursery in San Francisco. Maggie was of Austrian descent whose first love was genealogy, a glorious obsession which prompted her to spend long hours researching both her own and her husband's backgrounds at the local and San Francisco libraries.

Although we soon moved to the affordable, but comfortable Married Student Housing Complex of the university, we were encouraged by the von Kempfs to treat their comfortable four-bedroom suburban home as our own. They had two teenage sons, Paul, Jr and Peter, and two teenage daughters, Karen and Kris. It didn't take us much time to feel completely at home at their place, with keys to the front door and uninhibited access to their well-stocked fridge. Rukya, an excellent cook, won over the hearts of the family with her creative culinary creations ('Write a book and call it *Ruky's Cookies*,' they would often suggest).

And, although Paul Sr and I seemingly had no common interests, we struck an indefinable bond. He took delight in introducing me to the unfathomable complexities of baseball at San Francisco's Candlestick Park and American football at the Stanford University Stadium. He would drive me on weekends to the nearby world-renowned Mondavi Brothers Winery, where he was a consultant, and treat me at the innumerable waterfront eateries on San Francisco's Fisherman's Wharf. In turn, I would introduce him to the joys and mysteries of 'magical India' for which he would pay, since Rukya and I were in no pecuniary position to foot the bill.

Our favourite was Franciscan Crab House, Alioto's and the famous Di Maggio's Restaurant and Cocktail Lounge, named after legendary baseball player Joe DiMaggio, who was renowned as much for his baseball exploits, as for being the first husband of Marilyn Monroe, who later married playwright Arthur Miller and policeman James Dougherty.

In those days, a typical de luxe dinner at Di Maggio's started at $1.50, an abalone steak dinner at $2.25 and seafood plate at $1.60.

Lovers of the outdoors, the von Kempf family would periodically take Rukya and me to the impressive Yosemite National Park, famous for its waterfalls, towering granite monoliths, deep valleys and ancient giant Sequoia trees. Frequent trips were also made to Bass Lake, which was famous for its plentiful bass.

However, Rukya's and my abiding memory is of driving up in our Chevrolet jalopy to San Francisco one Saturday evening to listen to jazz at the Blue Note Jazz Club. On another occasion, we managed to save just enough, from the money my father sent me, to go dancing at the enchanting Top of the Mark rooftop bar in the Mark Hopkins Hotel on Nob Hill. Almost 60 years on, we still cherish memories of dancing to the velvety voice of Nat King Cole and the frenetic drumsticks of the legendary Gene Krupa.

◆

The danger in narrating jokes in any book is the likelihood that the reader may have read or heard a particular one a million times before and, therefore, is likely to be turned off upon coming across an old chestnut.

However, by and large, there are countless jokes doing the rounds of civilized societies in different parts of the world at any given time. It is, therefore, illogical to presume that *all* readers are familiar with *all* subjects, ideas, jokes, bon mots, quips, puns, witticisms doing the rounds in *all* societies. Therefore, I prefer not to deny a particular segment of one's readership the joy of an amusing incident, joke or anecdote on the presumption that they are familiar with it. Instead, I consider it preferable to presume that the majority have *not* come across it before. At worst, the reader will dismiss your masterpiece as a timeworn yarn and move on! After all, not *all* masterpieces of stand-up comedians are original—or even funny, for that matter!

◆

> Speaking of Marilyn Monroe, I'm reminded of the old story (move on, dear reader, if you've heard it a million times) concerning the iconic 'blonde bombshell' and Albert Einstein, developer of the Theory of Relativity.
>
> The seating plan at a VVIP dinner, at which they were both distinguished guests, was so devised that they were seated next to each other at the head table.
>
> Flushed with excitement, heightened by more than a few glasses of wine, Einstein spontaneously proposes marriage to Monroe.
>
> He buttresses his suggestion with the logic: 'Just imagine, Marilyn. If you agree, our child will be blessed with your looks and my brains,' to which Monroe replies, 'Yes, Albert—but what if it has my brain and *your* looks.'

◆

I might mention at this stage, in the interest of fluidity of narration that, when Tarique was born midway through my master's, at the Stanford Medical Centre on 11 June 1961, Paul and Maggie kindly offered to become his godparents, an offer Rukya and I were delighted to accept. Our friendship with the von Kempf family lasted a lifetime, in a manner of speaking, initially by proxy and later by personal contact, despite the distance between our two countries.

On one of my business trips to the US in connection with the purchase of printing machinery in 1963 (the year John F. Kennedy was assassinated, allegedly, by a Lee Harvey Oswald), I flew to San Francisco, then my favourite city, especially to meet Paul with whom I had a delightful lunch at the American Express rooftop lounge. During lunch, Paul asked me how his godson Tarique was. I sprang a surprise by saying that he was getting married a few months later.

Half in jest, I added 'Rukya and I hope you and Maggie will come to the wedding to bless your godson.'

I almost choked on my chop suey at his reply: 'We will come... come hell or high waters!'

And come they did to Tarique's wedding ceremony to the gorgeous Ayesha, daughter of Jamshed and Zareen Bilimoria, and the subsequent reception in Mumbai. Being extremely private individuals who detested pomp and circumstance, both partners opted for privacy and simplicity at the wedding.

Sadly though, they were too mismatched and immature for marriage and eventually decided to go their separate ways.

◆

Paul and Maggie fell absolutely in love with India and, a few years later, persuaded their friends to also come on a *Bharat darshan* (tour of India). Maggie passed away a few years later, followed by Paul who had been suffering from Alzheimer's.

Regrettably, Maggie could not complete the family genealogy endeavour she had pursued so devotedly. But at the 'young' age of 70, dear, dear friend Maggie, graduated from Stanford with a degree in French, fulfilling a promise she had made to me at my graduation—that she would follow in my footsteps and graduate from the university.

Upon graduation, I was offered an assignment with the Carnegie Foundation for the Advancement of Teaching centre, something I was compelled to turn down as we had to rush back to India because of my father's health issues. Had I accepted it, there's every possibility I would have decided to make the US my home. But it wasn't meant to be.

However, I did return to Stanford twice for summer courses to, hopefully, remove mental cobwebs and catch up with the latest innovations and also to experience life on campus which was very different from living in the Stanford Married Students Village.

No Bed of Roses

Tarique's birth made life at Stanford extremely difficult for us. Rukya, never the healthiest of people, found it difficult to cope with the newborn as well as household chores, especially with me having to bear a heavy burden at classes to graduate before the end of the academic year. This meant extraordinarily long hours at the library while I wrote my master's thesis.

My mother offered to fly across to the US to help but language and the lack of financial resources were major hurdles. Fortunately, Paul and Maggie were always only a phone call away. As for money, for my mother's airline ticket, I still do not know how my father managed, but I have a sneaking suspicion he must have had to take a loan which, knowing him, must have been a great embarrassment. Nevertheless, the brave lady managed to fly half across the world from Mumbai with the kind assistance of some friendly desi (Indian) passengers.

My scholarship covered my tuition fees but nothing else. The only way out to make ends meet was for me to squeeze in time for a part-time job as a salesman in the men's clothing department at a Macy's just outside campus. A part-time job as dogsbody at a Catholic community newspaper *The Monitor* in San Francisco helped, but only just!

◆

San Francisco is the cultural, commercial and financial centre of Northern California and the tenth most populous city in the US. Its iconic suspension Golden Gate bridge is one of the most internationally recognized symbols associated with the city, California and the US itself.

Until Sydney in Australia displaced it for purely personal reasons, 'Frisco' was my favourite city in the world for its romantic aura thanks to Hollywood films and the long-enduring tribute to it in the song *I Left My Heart in San Francisco* by the inimitable Frank Sinatra.

Frommer's Travel Guide describes the Bridge as 'possibly the most beautiful, certainly the most photographed bridge in the World.' At the time of its opening in 1937, it was both the longest and tallest suspension bridge in the world.

Known for its cool summers, steep rolling hills, eclectic mix of architecture, winding streets (one of them, Lombard Street, is said to be the world's crookedest), the former Alcatraz prison, Fisherman's Wharf, fabled cable cars and much more, San Francisco is among the most visited cities in the US.

But it also has an underbelly of crime going back to the notorious, alcohol-driven underworld of Prohibition of the 1920s that continues to this day in the form of ghettos overflowing with sleazy drug addicts, winos, criminals, prostitutes and other shady elements inhabiting its central districts.

Today, the city's spectacular economic growth, coupled with the boom in property values, have made for a housing crisis to the extent that only very highly paid corporate professionals in the city, peninsula and suburbs can afford decent housing. Stories abound of lower-level professors at Stanford and elsewhere in the Bay area being compelled to make cars their permanent abodes, so dire is the situation.

SIX

LAUT KE BUDDHU GHAR KO AAYE
(The Innocents Return Home)

A Son Disowned!

No sooner had I received my MA degree at a moving convocation ceremony at Stanford, when my mother, Rukya, Tarique (then under a year) and I headed home since my father's health had taken a turn for the worse. That said, his condition was no impediment for the raucous cheerleaders of the community—the ones who were ready to celebrate any and every occasion—to again turn up at the airport in large numbers and behave in a manner that almost prompted us to flee the place.

Since Rukya and I were going to live with my parents and also my stepfamily, my father disposed of the earlier accommodation and, now able to afford it, acquired a spacious four-bedroom flat in Abdul Kader Mansion near the Club Road YMCA at Mumbai Central, formerly a prestigious locality but which fast went to seed with the onset of the building boom.

Living in a joint-family situation with a stepmother and her four offspring was never going to be easy for my mother, Rukya or me. It turned out to be a living hell. In a cloistered home environment, the singular lack of respect, trust, even basic decency—forget cordiality—became unbearable to the extent that it even soured my relationship with my father, and it pushed us to the breaking point. It made for a volcanic situation waiting to explode.

On an irretrievable collision course for some time, a disenchanted father and his impetuous son clashed one evening, and it ended with him disowning his son in a moment of pique.

J. Walter Thompson

Thanks to the efforts of my Good Samaritan friend Amir Curmally (mentioned in an earlier chapter), I landed an interview with Nurjehan Swaminathan who, in turn, arranged an interview with the Managing Director of J. Walter Thompson, the leading advertising agency.

Edward J. Fielden (EJF), a patriarch of the Indian advertising business, who had steely, piercing blue eyes and a forbidding exterior, condescendingly made me a three-month probationary offer at the princely salary of ₹350 per month.

'Listen, young man,' he thundered, 'we mean business here,' or some words to that effect. 'As the No.1 agency in the world, we have extremely high standards. You will be under the scanner for three months, at the end of which we will evaluate your performance. If you come up to scratch, your probation will be extended for another three months for a second evaluation. If at the end of six months you are found to be incompetent, we will bid you goodbye, otherwise you will continue your probation until a year. If you meet our expectations, you will be confirmed at a monthly gross salary of ₹1,500. Think it over...you have a week to decide.'

'*So this is what a Hobson's Choice is*,' I told myself. Thinking of Rukya and Tarique, I replied in a flash, 'I'll take it, sir.'

◆

It just so happened that the ad agency, under its hard-driving MD,

Fielden, had just decided to recruit fresh young foreign university graduates for training to handle its rapidly growing client portfolio. This change of direction opened the doors for Murad Ali Baig, Janak Jhunjhunwala, Jayant Shah and yours truly to join the ad agency at about the same time as, what was misleadingly known as, Accounts Executives. The term 'accounts' involved not the handling of rupees and paise but advertising clients.

As was expected, our arrival caused unhappiness in certain quarters and we were deprecatingly referred to as 'The Fab Four' (after the Beatles) and 'The Young Turks.' According to one 'behind our back' joke: 'Two bright young JWT executives bump into each other. "Ansari," apologizes one, "I Baig your pardon," responds the other.'

It was all in good spirit, though. We soon became friends and worked together harmoniously until, because of his failing health, I had to return to my father and his beloved *Inquilab*.

Under Fielden, JWT had a strong, no-nonsense work ethic. Punctuality was non-negotiable no matter the excuse, and conservative attire, which was jacket and tie, and correct protocol de rigueur. His criterion for a worthy executive was an ability to 'confidently have tea with clients' who, in his opinion, were the be-all and end-all of our profession.

EJF must have been an alumnus of the school for scoundrels. He was past master of every trick in the art of one-upmanship, down to the arrangement of his resplendent office that had his capacious seat facing the door through which his two reverential, tiptoeing secretaries—then Vilma Fernandes and Hansa Rajaram—escorted wide-eyed callers. Visitors were made to sit on sunken uncomfortable chairs across the wide mahogany desk at a respectable distance from, and at an angle to, the gilded throne of the grand emperor. The entire setting was designed to enable EJF to glare down straight into the eyes of the by-then intimidated visitor who had to converse from an uncomfortable sideways angle with a crick in their neck. I have been an embarrassed witness to even major clients supinely surrendering Round 1 in their dealings with him no sooner were they ushered into his sanctum sanctorum.

So taken up were some of us by EJF's gambits, and also his impressive appellation, 'Edward J. Fielden,' that Murad Ali Baig became Murad 'MRA' Baig, our chief copywriter Roger Pereira, Roger C.B. Pereira and yours truly, Khalid A-H Ansari.

◆

Then there was the one and only Nurjehan (Nuru) Swaminathan, of the illustrious Chagla family, director of JWT.

In the course of an illustrious career, her father, M.C. Chagla, was the minister of education under Jawaharlal Nehru, the external affairs minister under Indira Gandhi, high commissioner to the UK, ambassador to the US and the first permanent Indian Chief Justice of the Bombay High Court.

His son Iqbal, went on to build a formidable legal practice and many senior lawyers have embarked on their careers from his chambers; his former understudies are now senior lawyers in high places.

Nuru's eye for beauty and make-up was so perspicacious that many of the glamourous models who featured in her Pond's and Bombay Dyeing advertising campaigns were girls who sold fruit and flowers in the Flora Fountain area near the Bombay High Court.

Speaking of Bombay Dyeing, I was once approached to model in a modish business suit for a print advertisement in the mainline newspapers of the country. JWT came up with a campaign that was approved by the client and released in the press with some fanfare. I'm still wondering why the campaign was pulled out in such an unholy hurry. Could it have been the concept, its execution or perhaps, the model?

There was also this Corona Sahu sports shoe press ad campaign, which featured me as a tennis player in action. Not being an actual player of tennis, I consulted the pros at the club to ensure that my swing was flawless; my footwork, impeccable; my head position, perfect. This campaign, too, was dumped in a hurry—leading me to conclude that it could only have been because of the blasted model!

Being the uber-sensitive sod that I am, I would be less than honest if I were to say that my male self-esteem did not take a massive hammering!

Queen Bee

Nurjehan Swaminathan was Queen Bee of the advertising profession. Regal in her bearing, she had immaculate dress sense, as evidenced by the range of her sarees. She is the only professional woman I have known who would change her sari daily when she went home for lunch and again in the evening if she had a social engagement.

The imperious Nuru was married to 'Suds' Swaminathan, director at Mahindra & Mahindra and her exact opposite; her explosive temper became almost legendary in the corridors of JWT.

As executive trainee under her (she was my director-in-charge), I was under strict written instructions that, under no circumstances, was I to deal with any of the accounts I was assigned without her prior clearance.

◆

As it so happened, I managed to develop a good rapport with two of my clients, Shunu Sen of Hindustan Lever and Denis Ridley of Goodlass Nerolac, and didn't feel the need to trouble Mrs Swaminathan with minor details.

One day my phone rang and her secretary, Flavia D'Souza, who later married Roger Pereira, was on the line saying, 'She (the regal "She") would like to see you.'

Wondering what the matter might be, I made my way to her office and saw her in a meeting with about eight people.

'Come in,' she commanded, ignoring my greeting. 'Sit down,' was the follow-up injunction.

I did as I was told, only to be deluged by a vitriolic attack: 'So you think you are very smart. You think you don't need to consult me...' and on and on, in the presence of her staff.

Having let off steam, she ordered, 'You may go now.'

I got up and, throwing caution to the wind given that I was utterly dependent on the job for my immediate family's bread and butter, walked up to the front door, opened it and while walking out of the room, banged it behind my back.

For almost a month after that, Nuru would haughtily turn her head from the direction of my office while walking to hers.

One morning, Flavia called again on the intercom. 'Mr Ansari, *"she"* would like to see you,' she announced, apparently aware of our little tiff during our last encounter.

As nervous as I could possibly be, I hurried to her office, greeted her and, this time, shut the door behind me as gently as I possibly could.

'Sit down,' she ordered, leaving me in a state of panic-stricken apprehension.

'You foul tempered Mussulman (Muslim). If I were your wife, I'd put you on a vegetarian diet and calm down your temper.' For the record, Nuru was herself a Muslim, although a non-practising one.

Getting up from her seat, she walked up, put her arms around me and hugged me tight.

'*Forgive but not forget.*' The gesture reminded me of those words.

'She,' Rukya and I became the best of friends after that and would socially meet up frequently for many years until her passing. We even named our daughter Tehzeeb, after Nuru and Suds's daughter.

A Visit by Chacha Nehru

Apart from my inborn shyness, my delicate financial situation induced in me a feeling of acute subordination, of which I was far from proud.

One day, Charles Moorhouse, another British director of JWT, called me at Bolton Printing Press at Tardeo (where I had been assigned to learn the ropes of offset printing) and summoned me to his office immediately.

He informed me that Ciba Geigy, whose account was then with JWT, had called to convey the news that Indian prime minister Jawaharlal Nehru was scheduled to visit the newly opened, ultra-modern Ciba Research Centre at Goregaon, outside Mumbai.

It didn't take long for the jigsaw puzzle to fall in place: one of the directors of the Switzerland-based Ciba Geigy pharmaceutical firm was a Saigal whose wife was related to the eminent writer Nayantara Saigal, a member of the Nehru-Gandhi family, the second of three sisters born to Jawaharlal Nehru's sister, Vijaya Laxmi Pandit.

Spelling out details of the VIP visit, Moorhouse informed me that this being a prestigious visit, EJF, our managing director, had ordained that we pull out all the stops and make sure to do a 'bloody good job' of it.

'We're short-staffed for an assignment like this one. Apart from the advertising aspects such as creative, production, etc., there will be a hell of a lot of donkey work involved: getting permissions, organizing press conferences, press handouts, getting contractors to put up loudspeakers, setting up the *shamiana* (tent or awning), making police *bandobast* (arrangements), emergency ambulances…the whole shebang. Everything down to ensuring the correct space between steps of the staircase for young Chacha (uncle) Nehru…' he said with a wink. 'It's every man to his station. Are you up for it?' he asked.

At the time, I hardly realized that these were the very 'positive forces' that Paulo Coelho talked about; it was a providential opportunity for the allegorical Donkey to believe he was King!

And given the situation with my family, this was a do-or-die opportunity. Was I 'up' for it?

'I'll give it my best shot, sir,' I replied.

The benevolent forces looked down kindly: the inauguration went off without a hitch, prompting Mr Saigal to send a warm letter of appreciation to Fielden in which he made a special mention of me. EJF summoned me to his durbar (court) a few days later and flashing his all-too-rare toothy smile, conveyed the joyous news that it had been decided that I was to be allotted the Kemp's Corner company flat, which had fallen vacant after the resignation of account executive John Stephen upon his migration to Australia.

The conjunction of the two events was nothing if not a manna from heaven for me. Although my father had forgiven me and allowed Rukya, Tarique and me to move back since our altercation, living with the rest of the extended family was no bed of roses.

The Ciba inauguration also led to my confirmation as full-fledged accounts executive at ₹1,500 per month (later raised to ₹3,000 per month) with perks in the form of a chauffeur-driven car and an expense account.

The Donkey was truly at work!

◆

At JWT, my favourite client was Shunu Sen, then product manager of Hindustan Lever Limited, who went on to become the marketing director and CEO of Quadra Advisory.

In a moving obituary on his death in 2003 at the age of 63, *The Times of India* wrote he was, 'India's premier marketing guru, a manager par excellence and a people's person to the core… A home-grown marketing pro, Sen has universally been acclaimed a whizz-kid, generally acknowledged as one of India's sharpest marketing minds. For someone who joined Hindustan Lever as trainee in 1960, Sen had come a long way to be identified as the icon of Indian marketing. Sen would always be remembered for ad campaigns like Liril, Lipton and Surf, which gave rise to household catchwords.'[11]

Shunu Sen started handling the marketing of Pepsodent about the same time I was given charge of their advertising account at JWT. The product's national market share at that time was four per cent, almost a poor last in a crowded toothpaste market, way behind market leader Colgate, which enjoyed a near monopoly.

The product's advertising was increased substantially and a two-year sales target set at double its then national market share. Our JWT creative teams got down to work in real earnest and we managed to exceed our target in the very first year.

Apart from Hindustan Lever, some of my other clients at JWT were Goodlass Nerolac, Larsen and Toubro, India Tobacco, Power Cables and Tata Sons.

◆

My contact at Goodlass Nerolac Paints was Denis Ridley, a taciturn Englishman from the Midlands with a predilection for prolonged elbow bending.

Always game for a chugalug, Denis underwent an amazing character transformation after a drink and more. His preferred time for meetings was noon or 5 p.m. at his office—a convenient time for a lunchtime beer or two—or an extended pre-dinner sundowner at one of the posh nosheries in the area.

I was more than happy to try and make time to suit Denis's convenience because he would become increasingly convivial with each drink and, consequently, inclined to approve ad budgets and creative submissions without being too pedantic.

---

[11]'Marketing Guru Shunu Sen Dies', *The Times of India*, 4 January 2003, https://timesofindia.indiatimes.com/business/india-business/marketing-guru-shunu-sen-dies/articleshow/33295123.cms. Accessed on 6 November 2021.

The Kiss

Fielden now had two personal secretaries: Vilma Fernandes and Vinoo Lalvani; the former (mentioned earlier) an established fixture in the company for quite some time, and the latter, a petite, chirpy young lady who became a good friend after I got her to model for Pepsodent toothpaste.

Vinoo's smiling advertisement photograph capturing her talking into a phone made her then, perhaps, the most recognizable model in India. She was, at that time, seeing former Test cricketer Abbas 'Buggy' Ali Baig, who played 10 Tests for India between 1959 and 1967 and coached the Indian cricket team on its Australia 1991–92 tour and later, the 1992 Cricket World Cup. Like most young couples, they would have occasional lovers' quarrels over which Vinoo would cry on my shoulder during the office's lunch time.

The two got married and moved to Delhi following 'Prince Charming' (as he was then called) Baig's retirement. Although short-statured, the good looking Baig was a great favourite among female cricket fans, as were his close friends of the Hyderabad Ranji Trophy cricket team 'Tiger' Mansoor Ali Khan Pataudi and M.L. Jaisimha.

Old-timers will recall the incident at the Brabourne Stadium when a young female fan of Buggy ran on to the wicket from the clubhouse and kissed him in full public view when he reached a milestone (50 or 100 runs—I do not recall which—against Australia in 1960, but I do recall watching the match as a student from the East stand).

Baig, now 81, said this of the incident: 'We were coming back for tea and suddenly this young lady comes out and sort of gives a kiss here and there. I withdrew. My main worry was my parents were watching in the stands, what will they think. 'We sent our boy to England, has he gone astray?'[12]

Many years after my resignation from JWT and after I had started *Mid-Day* in 1979, a veterans' cricket team comprising of former Pakistan Test players visited New Delhi and Mumbai to play 'friendly' matches against their Indian counterparts. Vinoo's niece, Hasina (now married to 'Tony' Jethmalani, renowned son of his legal luminary father Ram), happened to be an inseparable friend of my daughter Tehzeeb who too was born in 1971. Recalling Abbas's 1960 experience, I got Tehzeeb to stage-manage a 'Down Memory Lane' picture, along with Hasina, a picture of the kiss at the Brabourne Stadium during the second Veterans' cricket match. I remember the match was on a Saturday and I had arranged a *Sunday Mid-Day* reporter and photographer to be present from the start, in case the Indian side batted first. Not wishing to take any chances (in case Buggy got out early), we had conspired for Hasina to be ready and run on to the pitch as soon as Buggy scored 10 runs.

The plan worked to perfection: Buggy scored 10, at which point Hasina sprinted, with photographer in tow, on to the middle and planted a shower of kisses on her uncle's mouth, lips and forehead, to Buggy's great astonishment. The photograph appeared on the front page of *Sunday Mid-Day* the next morning under the headline 'Remember When?', catching even wife Vinoo, then back home in New Delhi, by surprise.

---

[12]Rohit Brijnath, 'Opinion: The Kissing of Abbas Ali Baig and Other Stories', *Mint*, 15 November 2019, https://www.livemint.com/mint-lounge/features/opinion-i-the-kissing-of-abbas-ali-baig-and-other-stories-11573803307992.html. Accessed on 6 November 2021.

The Yokel Returns Home

As mentioned in an earlier chapter, I resigned from JWT with tremendous regret, as also gratitude for the fact that my stint there had enabled me to look after my family in fairly reasonable manner. Apart from the professional expertise that I had acquired, it taught me many lessons that have lasted a lifetime.

I was also beholden to Rukya for being an outstanding mother to Tarique, and Sharique, who was born two years after Tarique to the day, on June 11.

The passage of time and experience of working in a well-oiled multinational corporate environment had taught me many valuable lessons. For one thing, my wings had been clipped: I was brought down to earth, suitably chastened over the manner in which I had behaved towards my father who had sacrificed so much for me, especially in giving me the most valuable gift a father can give his offspring—an education of the highest-possible order.

His increasingly poor state of health, as well as my maturity after working at JWT, led to a mellower approach on my part. Father's inability to work long hours left me with no option other than to take on not only the managerial and financial, but also the editorial responsibilities, even as he unfailingly continued to write his daily column with undiminished fire and zeal. His espousal of public causes also continued apace. That said, the patriarch kept a benign watch over my functioning, holding my hand at every step, unwittingly causing me to regret my enfant terrible behaviour all the more.

At the *Inquilab*, I was fortunate to have the unbridled assistance of a devoted staff that revered me, not so much because I was *phoren-returned* (person who spent some time abroad but was now back in the homeland) or that I knew a few monkey tricks about newspaper printing and publishing, but because of their fierce loyalty to my father, a legend in his lifetime.

For this reason, they made generous allowance for my lack of proficiency in the Urdu language (it was half-baked at best, certainly no match for the giants of the beautiful Urdu language, but barely enough not to let wool be pulled over my eyes!). As the result of my training and publishing experience at Stanford, I was able to bring to the table many modern editorial models, lessons and techniques which could be adapted for an Urdu newspaper. The comprehensive course had also embraced advertising (the lifeblood of newspaper publishing), marketing and production techniques.

Together, my father, staff and I could manage to bring about what readers termed an *inquilab* (revolution) in the Urdu newspaper business. I use the term advisedly, because, at the end of the day, it is essentially a business, irrespective of how public-spirited a particular newspaper may be.

◆

In short, we devised an attractive package: a modern, sexy look; clean, attractive calligraphy; sharp, clear, true-to-life photographs; succinct, informal style of writing and printing technology that did not smudge the reader's hands with ink.

Some of the major editorial changes were tightly-edited copy; focused, no-frills, unostentatious, informal style of writing and with it design innovations on the editorial front that appealed to the readers.

With all this we combined aggressive techniques at the marketplace (the *bhaiya*-newspaper vendor-level) and new production technology involving imported and the most modern printing machines, all of which made the paper's popularity, and consequently, circulation zoom.

◆

A word here about the technology involved in Urdu newspaper publishing may be in order: until the turn of the twenty-first century, Urdu newspapers in India and Pakistan were printed by the primitive lithography printing process, which involved *kitabat* (calligraphy) and printing on slow-as-snails flatbed machines.

Taking a leaf from the advanced technology of Middle-Eastern newspapers that use the Arabic script (also used by Urdu newspapers in India), we at *Inquilab*, liaised with typesetting and printing machine manufacturers in Europe and the US to innovate modern typesetting and printing machinery which were compatible with the Arabic script. Today, almost all Urdu newspapers in India have moved on from what was termed 'hot metal' to modern computer-based 'cold-type' typesetting, and from the obsolete flatbed lithography to rotary offset printing technology.

On a recent Danube cruise in Europe, our ship docked at Heidelberg in Germany which, for decades, had a monopoly on the old-style monotype and linotype composing machines. Upon disembarkation, I asked the tourist guide and many other people at the quay to show me the way to the world-renowned composing machine manufacturing factories. Nobody seemed able to help, until a wizened gentleman very kindly informed me that the manufacturing units had become dinosaurs and been consigned to the ages many years ago. Needless to say, all those involved in the joint effort to bring about the 'inquilab' in the *Inquilab*—especially my father—were thrilled at this news.

Press Institute of India

Yet another manifestation of Paulo Coelho's thesis about 'positive forces' around us—and the parable about the Donkey—was my introduction to Chanchal Sarkar, the founder director of the Press Institute of India, during one of my then frequent work trips to New Delhi. The institute was highly regarded internationally as representative of the Indian media (this was before the advent of television). Sarkar, a soft-spoken, true-blue newspaperman was its face.

One day, out of the blue, Chanchal sent me an invitation to a residential two-day press seminar to be held at the salubrious Maharashtra hill station, Mahabaleshwar, about 260 km away from Mumbai. At the delightful and productive conference, Chanchal, and another senior PII functionary, Tarzie Vittachi (a gruff, old-school-tie Sri Lankan newspaperman), and I got to know each other.

A few months later, we got a circular from the PII informing the *Inquilab* about a scholarship that the Canadian owner of the *Times* of London, Lord Roy Thomson, had instituted, for a two-week training programme for senior journalists from Commonwealth countries. With nothing to lose, I sent in my application and was duly asked to appear for an interview in New Delhi where journalists were to be selected for the course at the Thompson Foundation in Cardiff, Wales, in the UK.

In due course, I received intimation that I had been selected for the programme. Among those selected were active journalists from Commonwealth countries in Asia, Africa, South America and from the nation of Malta in Europe.

◆

The purpose of the foundation was 'the advancement of knowledge and enlightenment of all peoples enabling them to achieve closer understanding and to play an informed and responsible role in the affairs of their nation and the world.'

The hands-on experience at the *Western Mail* daily (our classes were held at the adjacent Thompson Foundation building) was invaluable, especially since we were asked to bring out our own newspaper. The staff consisted of former and current newspapermen, including Don Rowlands, former editor of the *Western Mail* in Cardiff and John Cardownie, a delightful Scottish native who previously worked on *The Scotsman* newspaper in Edinburgh.

Practical experience included working on the desk at the *Western Mail* and Thompson group newspapers in London and Reading. Our convocation was attended by Prince Philip, and among the distinguished speakers was the legendary Sir Harold Evans, editor of *The Sunday Times* and *The Times* newspapers. I remember listening to Evans, wide-eyed and completely gobsmacked, as he explained how his newspaper actually forecast an airplane crash almost down to the exact month by studying the history of crashes in Britain in relation to the type of aircraft (engine, model, etc.), mileage, the airline's record of crashes, turnaround as well as servicing and treatment of aircraft, all of which determine its fatigue factor.

While all the other members of our course opted to live in Cardiff, I asked for accommodation elsewhere, preferring the suburbs and the beautiful Welsh coast. The foundation agreed and allotted me a room in a university students' hostel overlooking the ocean in beautiful and cosmopolitan Penarth, a short, four-mile bus ride from the Cardiff city centre. After classes, I would take the bus home, find a seat on the front on the upper deck and make my way to my local.

Apart from having my close immigrant friends from South Africa—Moosa Kola, a Manchester-based businessman who I knew from Mumbai, and London magistrate 'Sunny' Kotwal—visit me on the weekends, I made many young friends at the student hostel where we spent many enjoyable and intellectually stimulating hours. I have always found interaction with young, receptive minds most refreshing.

The local Welsh were extremely friendly. On one occasion, I had just seated myself at the bar, as was my wont, when an elderly Welshman joined me and, while introducing himself, asked where I came from. When informed I came from India, he guffawed, extended his hand and exclaimed, 'Shake hands young man. We both have a common enemy, the (expletive deleted) Brits!'

◈

Our course members voted to select the editor and assistant editor of our For Private Circulation only newspaper. I was chosen as deputy to a Pakistani editor who, sadly and unnecessarily, injected religion and politics in the working of the newspaper. Not having the stomach for office politics, I resigned in disgust.

But all in all, it had been a tremendously enriching work experience. More importantly, it also enabled me to sow the seeds for what I had in mind for my next step in life.

SEVEN

AND HERE COMES *SPORTSWEEK*

Sportsweek

The Thompson Foundation experience was welcome twice over. Apart from providing me the opportunity to learn the latest newspaper editorial and production techniques, it also helped me pursue my proposed dream of creating a sports magazine.

Following the completion of the course, I stayed back a week in London to tentatively line up syndication arrangements, namely exclusive rights to reproduce material from the successful *Daily Express* newspaper, the personality and extensive sports coverage of which was best suited to the kind of magazine I had in mind.

To Peter Knight, syndication head at the *Daily Express*, I owe a huge debt of gratitude for making available to us all possible material for use, at extremely competitive rates, in *Sportsweek*, which I started in 1969.

◆

Another Paulo Coelho and Donkey parable phenomenon was made manifest to my father and my family soon after my return to Mumbai.

Before my departure for London for the Thompson Foundation course, I had joined the CCI as a life member on the urging of my father-in-law who, as a long-standing member and because of personal popularity, had friends in high places in the club's hierarchy. He found out from the grapevine that the club's life membership fees would be increased 'steeply' from ₹7,500 to ₹10,000. Prior to becoming aware of this information, I had no intention whatsoever of joining the club, content as I was in my simple 7 a.m. to 9 p.m. family-work-family routine.

Not only did the club's acceptance of my hurriedly submitted membership application change my family's lifestyle (with sons Tarique and Sharique being able to use the club's excellent sporting facilities), it also providentially paved the way for me to start *Sportsweek* magazine, which changed the sporting landscape of the country while also kick-starting a modest sports revolution.

It is now obvious, the kick of the poor silly Donkey in our fable is not always instantaneous, as will be seen in this chapter.

I happened to be at the CCI bar one Saturday afternoon to have lunch with a friend. As I awaited his arrival, the unmistakable portly figure of the renowned Aziz Currimbhoy, racing correspondent of Rusi Karaka's *Current* tabloid, with trademark cigar in the top pocket of his bush shirt, plonked himself on the nearest stool.

In the course of conversation, I asked Aziz what he did apart from writing his popular column. 'Nothing much, boss,' he replied, flashing an ear-to-ear smile across his cheery face. 'Why don't you start a sports magazine and I'll join as your editor.' We both laughed it off, and I left to join my friend for lunch.

That evening during dinner with the family, I mentioned what had transpired and the strange coincidence of Aziz Currimbhoy, most probably jocularly, offering to work for my sports magazine which, until then had been a crazy dream and closely guarded secret as far as the world at large was concerned. In any case, I had no money to spare, no decent office premises, no staff, no spare printing capacity, nothing except a syndication arrangement waiting to happen! And sure, I had a dream, a fond one at that, of 'flying to the moon to play among the stars'—to compete against an established sports magazine like the hugely successful *Sport and Pastime* from a resourceful group like *The Hindu*.

Rukya takes after her (now-deceased) mother. She is a great believer in strange occurrences, coincidences, signs, omens and phenomena, whereas I'm the exact opposite taking after my father as I do. I would often dismiss Rukya's interpretations as hocus-pocus, but she would often surprise me with proof of the abstruse. I would dismiss them as coincidences or, as in this case, counter her with facts that proved otherwise—such as Currimbhoy had possibly heard about my obsession and had put two and two together to bowl me a googly.

To continue with the pie in the sky narrative: Currimbhoy turned out to be almost as passionate about the new project as me. Having sensed my keenness, the very next day, he spoke to the legendary Ardeshir Furdorji Sohrabji 'Bobby' Talyarkhan (AFST) during their customary morning coffee session at the Brabourne Stadium, where AFST lived for many years with his English wife 'Jay.' Jay loved using the expression 'The older the fiddle, the better the tune' in relation to her husband.

AFST expressed a desire to meet me the next day.

One of the earliest cricket commentators in India, AFST, whose radio commentaries played an important role in popularizing the game of cricket, especially the Pentangular Tournament, and who refused to share the microphone with anybody, had a reputation for being acerbic. Until then, I had never met him, and following Aziz's mediation, went to meet him with more than a little trepidation.

Imagine my surprise when he turned out to be charm personified, with quaint, old-world English mannerisms, and an underpinning of stiff upper lip reserve. I failed to read him, felt he was searing my soul and was relieved to leave. He promised to mull over whatever Aziz and I had told him and get back to us.

And so he did—the very next day—and requested another meeting at the CCI at the usual time of 11 a.m., this time without the presence of Aziz. The meeting turned out to be an inquisition with me having to reply to all manner of searching questions, which were mostly financial in nature; this was understandable given the enormity of the project and AFST's own formidable reputation.

When he flashed his rare smile and said, 'In horse racing, risk-taking is the name of the game. You're a very brave man...and I like your passion. Count me in.'

To say that I was relieved would be the understatement of any year.

Sportsweek

Sheer Lunacy

*Go confidently in the direction of your dreams,
Live the life you have imagined.*

—Henry David Thoreau, American naturalist,
essayist, poet and philosopher

Making a commitment of this magnitude to the likes of AFST and Aziz Currimbhoy, without first getting my father to agree, since I was totally dependent on him financially, was sheer lunacy, but the dye had been cast. Deep down inside, I was convinced that father would not disappoint me this time, despite the state of his health and my neck-deep involvement in the *Inquilab*. However, it was not going to be an easy task considering that our earlier split had been caused entirely by my desire to break free and over my obsession to start a sports magazine in the first place.

Choosing what I considered to be a suitable opportunity, on a day that he was feeling better and appeared to be in a good mood, I broached the topic and was shocked out of my wits by his reply: 'I'm not the fool you think I am. I know very well what you've been up to—making all your plans for your sports magazine. I was waiting for this moment... What took you so long?' Then, putting his arms around me, he hugged me saying, with tears in his eyes, 'May God be with you,' adding 'let me know if you ever need my help.'

And help he certainly did: granting every request; making funds available; speaking to suppliers of newsprint, office and printing material; even requesting the three distributors of the *Inquilab* for advances to be adjusted against future sales of the embryonic magazine.

And, most touchingly (with his old-fashioned concept of advertising), after the launch of my baby magazine, despite his failing health, travelling up and down in a suburban train with the *Sportsweek* cover held at eye level for all the world to see! As a formally uneducated father, it may have been advertising at its most primitive, but for me it was paternal love of the purest kind, and something I shall *never* forget.

◆

For a product of my generation such as myself, who had been weaned on a regular diet of *Sport and Pastime* from a very young age, the very thought of competing with it bordered on the heretic.

Sport and Pastime, which is also the name of the novel *A Sport and a Pastime* by the American author James Salter, was the brainchild of S.K. Gurunathan, sports editor at the venerable *Hindu* newspaper, headquartered in the city of Chennai. Among its star writers was Bill O'Reilly, rated as one of the finest Australian spinners in the history of the game, who became a respected cricket writer and broadcaster.

With the financial backing of its parent newspaper, *Sport and Pastime* built up a huge and loyal all-India following, thanks to the booming popularity of sports during the period from 1947 till the time when it closed down in 1978. I was among the magazine's most loyal readers and seldom missed a copy, largely because of its sports photographs. Therefore, when I was toying with the idea of starting my very own publication, a sports magazine was what I first thought of.

In yet another exemplification of the parable about the Donkey (*jab upar wala meherban...*), I happened to meet the virtuoso sportswriter Ron Hendricks, a hard-punching pro from the school of hard knocks, at a hockey match at the Lloyd's Reclamation stadium in Mumbai, when I was scouting for a team of sports journalists. Hendricks was then the sports editor of the *The Free Press Journal*, the nursery of distinguished journalists such as cartoonists R.K. Laxman, Shankar and Bal Thackeray, as also an array of journalists such as Dom Moraes,

T.J.S. George, M.V. Mathew, M.V. Kamath, Rajat Sharma, M.J. Akbar, S. Sabavala and others who moved on to other publications.

Hendricks was involved with *Sportsweek* from its inception, as friend, guide and mentor for a number of years, during which he and I covered a number of international sports events in India and abroad. He later did a stint with *Mid-Day* when the paper was launched, but left because of incompatibility with one of his senior colleagues.

◆

With the help of friends in the profession, we managed to build a team of outstanding sports journalists who shared my passion for that form and genre of journalism, in addition to, well, sports. They were all imbued with a fire to help spread the magazine's gospel to improve health, develop character, build bridges and break barriers among people. The staff members, one and all, were disgusted with the disgraceful state of sports infrastructure in our country, the appalling manner in which things were being run, which, in turn, was largely responsible for our abysmal showing at the international level.

Apart from Hendricks and veteran Sharad Kotnis, who joined us from the *Free Press Journal* as editor, we had Gopi Baskaran, the modest-to-a-fault deputy editor, associate editor Ossie Manuel, Javed Akhtar Siddiqui and yours truly as head cook and bottle washer and designated managing editor.

Fired with youthful ambition and a fierce determination to take on the lion *Sports and Pastime*, in its den, our hand-picked team designed *Sportsweek* initially in tabloid form to distinguish it from our established competitor, which was in magazine format and was showing unmistakable signs of decrepitude.

In time, *Sport and Pastime* unfortunately lost its sparkle: its writing style became old-fangled; its reportage, bereft of zing; its subediting, shoddy and the quality of its action pictures, once its forte, humdrum. Sadly, founder of *Sport and Pastime*, Gurunathan was keeping poor health at this stage, which led to the magazine becoming rudderless. After 20 years of basking under monopolistic glory, it had become decidedly tired and vulnerable to a siege by a youthful competitor that made up in passion what it lacked in financial muscle.

In fact, starting the magazine when I did was sheer madness when you consider that I had, leave aside the means, neither the human resource, the premises nor the machinery to embark upon an ambitious venture of that magnitude (as well as taking on the giant Hindu Group!).

◆

The distribution network that we had built up for the *Inquilab* was focused and therefore inadequate for a specialized magazine with a much wider appeal not only in Mumbai but all over India.

I remember approaching the newspaper vendors outside the gates of the CCI and opposite the Churchgate station, magazine bundles on my shoulders, requesting them to stock copies of the magazine.

'Arre Bhai, itni purani sports magazine—Sports and Pastime— to rakhte hain, ek aur magazine kaun kharidega? Aur dekho, naiee magazine rakhne ki jagaah footpath pe kahaan hai?' (I already sell the established *Sport and Pastime* magazine. Who will buy another new one? Besides, take a look, where do I have space on the pavement to keep another magazine?)

Summoning all my powers of persuasion, I coaxed and cajoled one vendor to keep 10 copies of the magazine on a sale-or-return basis, saying I would come back at the same time the following week with copies of the new issue.

And thereby hangs a tale: all copies had been sold out, whereupon I increased the supply, again on a sale-or-return basis, to double and so on, week after week. The two vendors who occupy prime positions in the Churchgate area were amazed and, in time, became my friends and our biggest small-stall sellers in the city. Their sons and successors in business remain my friends to this day and I make it a point to stop by and shake their hands whenever I'm in their vicinity. After all, it was they who gave *Sportsweek* the jumpstart it needed at the time of its birth.

At the same time, I caught up with the formidable triumvirate of Ramnath Misra, Savla Ram and R.B. More who had a vice-like monopolistic control over almost the entire newspaper and magazine distribution network in the city, barring The Times Group publications.

In time, the three partners became our biggest distributors in Mumbai and the suburbs of not only *Sportsweek*, but also the *Inquilab* and later *Mid-Day*, Hindi *Mid-Day*, *Gujarati Mid-Day* and *Sunday Mid-Day*. In a manner of speaking, they were my biggest bankers—money lenders in my all-too-frequent times of need, and believe me, my needs were unceasing. They willingly opened their cavernous vaults stacked with currency notes to the very top since they did not believe in banking. In any case, their business of newspaper and magazine vending was strictly cash and their dealers, petty vendors and delivery boys.

I shall never forget the time I was seated at the congested office of one of the triad awaiting a loan. The good man opened his safe rather carelessly and was a tad slow to stem the torrent of notes which cascaded down on him. I couldn't contain my laughter, but he was a sport and joined me in my imprudent hilarity. For a moment there, I had been unsure whether to laugh or not. After all, it was *his* money that I desperately needed to borrow.

A Mission

When one looks at it from the perspective of cold logic, even the coming into being of *Sportsweek*, forget the successful run it had internationally for as many as 20 years, is an instance of the Donkey thinking he's King!

In another effort to be different, we endeavoured to make *Sportsweek* youthful, racy and frothy as regards content, style of writing and design with an emphasis on exciting action pictures. After all, sport is nothing if not action.

Our informal research had shown that the competition's readership profile consisted predominantly of male teenagers, school and college students and professionals between the ages of 20 and 40, with a major interest in cricket. Given the fact that male school and college students constituted the bulk of our readership, I often joked to friends that our fans were largely young and male, with nubile females showing conspicuous lack of interest in our labours.

Personalized, first person quotes were de rigueur. In our reportage, we endeavoured to put the reader in the heads, hearts and shoes of their sporting icons. Moreover, we took the important decision to not imitate the competition as regards 'pastime' and endeavoured to make *Sportsweek* exclusively sports-oriented sans frills and, more importantly, with a mission. Dropping the pastime element was a gamble but we did make token concession to sports crosswords, jokes, mindbenders, etc.

With Indian sport in a rut at home and international competitions, we started campaigning for reform if not revolution—as in the case of the *Inquilab*. We decided to christen the publication *Sportsweek* with the motto on the masthead reading 'the magazine that cares for Indian sport.'

We adopted a fearless, crusading—even strident—tone, calling a spade a shovel, and exposing the shortcomings and wrongdoings of the *pooh-bahs* (officials) of Indian sports who, in our opinion, were the prime culprits in dragging it into the quagmire.

By way of illustration: a dispatch from the 1970 Edinburgh Commonwealth Games attracted the following comment from *The Times of India*, in its issue dated 6 September 1986:

> That enterprising sportswriter Khalid Ansari, who edits the lively sports journal *Sportsweek*, has an interesting dossier to offer to any government-sponsored inquiry body. As he was on the spot, Ansari's observations are authentic and not picked up through a clairvoyant medium.
>
> Even before the contingent arrived in England, Sardul Singh, manager of the athletic team, gave clear notice of his intentions by deserting the team during its sojourn in West Germany for a fortnight's pleasure jaunt in London. He wasn't wasting any time in pursuit of a good time. Coach Siben Choudhary tried to do likewise but his attempts were foiled.
>
> Then it was Siben Choudhary's turn to return to London on the intervening Sunday during the Games (two days after commencement) leaving his contingent high and dry, without any instructions for training or reporting for events the next day.
>
> I met some of the boys that Sunday and found them totally demoralised. They complained of lack of coaching and guidance, of training facilities and of being left to their own devices.
>
> Only the powers that be can explain Choudhary's choice as coach. The athletes had no respect for him. According to them, his complete knowledge of athletics and of training methods can be written on a postage stamp.

So on and on.

The following headlines (because of space constraints) from

Edinburgh should suffice to indicate the campaign conducted by *Sportsweek* at the Edinburgh Games:

'Officials shame India's name.'

'Wrestlers retrieve prestige—despite official bungling.'

'Manager deserts athletes.'

'Punish the guilty.'

Our efforts were not in vain. The Arjan Singh Inquiry Commission of 1986 vindicated our stand against the footloose and fancy-free officials and recommended 'severe disciplinary action against them.'

◆

Lamenting India's disappointing performances at the Bangkok Asian Games, my first dispatch started: 'The doings and non-doings of officials accompanying our teams on foreign tours invariably provide a wealth of material for good copy. The Asian games are no exception.'

The dispatches were headlined 'MUST WE ALWAYS DEMONSTRATE WE ARE A POOR NATION,' with reference to our shoddy turnout at the Opening Ceremony march past.

The Arjan Singh Commission also stated: 'If we want to improve our standards in the international sphere, we must pay particular attention to keeping up-to-date in performing equipment even though it may involve import of such equipment.'

Vindicating *Sportsweek*'s expose, the Commission concluded: 'Arrangements for sending teams abroad are always made in great haste and there is not enough time left to make adequate preparations for such trips. If we expect better results from our teams, they must be selected well in advance and allowed time to attune themselves to such trips and to prepare properly.'

Sportsweek responded by stating: 'It is indeed gratifying to know that the time and money spent by us, a publication with not so vast resources, have not been wasted. And it is heartening to learn that the powers that be in our sports administration are at last beginning to take heed of what appears in the press. Perhaps there's still hope for Indian sport.'

◆

Sportsweek was among the only six publications invited to the Queens's annual garden party at Holyrood Palace, Edinburgh during the Commonwealth Games.

Prince Philip, while meeting guests, remarked to us, 'yours is a fairly large contingent and with such busy games schedules and the venues so scattered, it must be quite a rush'. We couldn't have agreed more. And it was just as well he wasn't aware of the shenanigans of our contingent's officials.

Notable Writers

Other unique sales propositions (USPs) that we introduced was getting big names from the world of sports journalism, not only from India but all over the world. Many of them, including past and present big-name sports people, had their contributions 'ghosted;' several professional journalists wrote under pseudonyms or their own names, or sometimes moonlighted for prestige or to augment their earnings. We owe a debt of gratitude to these eminent sportspeople and professional journalists who added immeasurably to the magazine's credibility and standing during its 20 years of existence.

The first *Sportsweek* Annual issue (a special once-in-a-year edition) that came out in 1970, featured Mansoor Ali Khan Pataudi and Australian captain Bill Lawry on its cover. The contributors and subjects list featured the names of K.S. Ranjitsinhji, Pataudi, Richie Benaud, A.F.S. Talyarkhan, Vinoo Mankad, Rusi Mankad, Farokh Engineer, Keki Tarapore, D.J.S. Rutnagar, Wilson Jones, A. Jasdanvala, R.S. Gentle, Dr Karni Singh, Dilip Sampat, Neville D'Souza, Rod Laver, Doug Walters, Graeme Pollock and Cassius Clay (Muhammad Ali).

The syndication arrangement with London's *Daily Express* newspaper, made available to us, week after week, many notable foreign journalists. Later, during tours of England as correspondent for *Sportsweek*, I managed to assemble a star-studded line-up of writers such as John Woodcock (*The Times,* London), E.W. Swanton (*The Telegraph*), Clive Taylor (*The Sun,* London) Alex Bannister (*Daily Mail,* who also ghosted Don Bradman's column), Michael Melford (*Daily*

Telegraph), Henry Blofeld (BBC radio), Tony Cozier (*Barbados Daily News*), R.T. Brittenden (*Christchurch Press*, New Zealand).

To this distinguished list we added in due course the names of Sunil Gavaskar, Viv Richards, Bishan Singh Bedi, Imran Khan, Asif Iqbal, N.S. Ramaswami, (*The Hindu*), Kishore Bhimani (*The Statesman*, Kolkata) and Rajan Bala (*The Hindu*).

Additionally, our list of writers included the original stalwarts—A.F.S. Talyarkhan and Aziz Currimbhoy, Sunder Rajan, Joe Crasto, Raju Bharatan, Arvind Lavakare, horse racing correspondent Cecil Hendricks (known by the noms de plume 'Pegasus' in *The Times of India* and 'Railbird' in *Sportsweek*).

(More about the English cricket correspondents in relation to the infamous John Lever 'Vaseline' incident in a later chapter.)

After his retirement, the GOAT (Greatest Of All Time) Sunny Gavaskar took over the reins of Sportsweek's *World of Cricket* in 1988, to which he brought the same degree of flair, grit, dedication and determination that he had to his splendiferous batting.

◆

Again, call it luck or providence or whatever you wish, *Sport and Pastime* shut shop following a labour dispute soon after the passing away of S.K. Gurunathan, just before the launch of *Sportsweek,* leaving the field wide open for the latter to establish itself.

Meanwhile, we were hard at work creating a nationwide and, later, international distribution network in neighbouring countries in the Middle East, Asia and Africa. Predictably, advertising support, which is the sine qua non of advertising media selection in an ever-expanding market, was not easy to come by for a magazine in its infancy that was trying to build readership with limited purchasing power. As we soon discovered, despite the large number of sports lovers in the ranks of client and agency firms who would welcome me into their offices to have a chat about their favourite sportsmen, there was discernible reluctance when it came to releasing their advertising in the magazine.

In the publishing scenario, large circulation levels, entailing increased corresponding cost of expensive newsprint, production and distribution expenses but *without* equivalent adequate advertising revenue, is a shortcut to disaster. In other words, the more the popularity of your publication but without corresponding returns from advertising, the more unprofitable the entire exercise, making it a calamity waiting to happen. Each additional copy without additional ad revenue equates to a greater loss situation.

As a former advertising professional, I should have known better: it is not enough to have a large circulation, which *Sportsweek* soon achieved—setting a new record for any Indian sports magazine, by far, of 1,25,000 copies sold. This was on the crest of India's delirium-inducing victorious performances in the 1971–72 West Indies cricket series, followed by the series win in England and the World Cup hockey win in the Kuala Lumpur World Hockey tournament in 1975.

I covered the last-named tournament for *Sportsweek* and was invited to write post-mortem cover stories for *The Illustrated Weekly of India* and the *Dharmyug* Hindi weekly belonging to the Times of India group, which later became a competitor group when I started *Mid-Day* to compete with the *Evening News of India*.

◆

> Apart from India's proud victory in Kuala Lumpur in 1975, among the other items of interest was what the Malaysian Hockey Association, organizers of the event, did out of caution because of the late afternoon rains that are endemic to Malaysia (and neighbouring Singapore). They summoned the services of the *bohmos*—a particular type of Malay shamans—who claimed to possess the ability to summon, and also keep away the rains.
>
> It just so happened that it rained cats and dogs on every *single* afternoon of the tournament. So much for *bohmos* and all their abracadabra!

Doing Our Bit for Sports

The seemingly unending dismal performances by our sportsmen at home and abroad through the 1960s aggravated by the ceaseless dirty tricks of our sports administrators, accentuated the need for us to try and live up to the slogan: 'The magazine that cares for Indian sport.' And we were delighted that the sportspersons, our entire reason for existing, embraced us as one of their own against the common enemy: an insouciant government as well as the parasitic administrators of our sports associations and federations at the central and state levels.

Cricket was fast becoming the rage in the length and breadth of our country, so it made sense for us to concentrate on that game by persuading former and current players of the sport to write pithy, albeit ghost-written, articles using the first-person POV.

I remember good friend Bishan Singh Bedi, whom we honoured with the *Sportsweek* Sportsman of the Year award at the CCI in 1976, publicly upbraiding us at the function for giving inordinate coverage to cricket at the expense of other games. It was a curious rap on the knuckle coming from a cricketing legend. At the same time, he also suggested we change the name of our magazine to 'Bombay Week' since we gave inordinate coverage to sport events in Mumbai and news concerning Mumbai cricketers. But then, Bishan-paji is in a class of his own!

There was also this journalist friend from Dubai who faulted us on the same score during the World Cup hockey tournament in Mumbai and to whom I had to explain that for my magazine to even survive and then promote other sports, I needed to willy-nilly depend on cricket.

◈

Friend Farokh Engineer—the debonair Brylcreem poster boy (along with Keith Miller and Dennis Compton)—very kindly agreed to do, gratis, a radio commercial on Radio Ceylon and elsewhere, which had him say: 'I read *Sportsweek*, do you? *Sportsweek*—the magazine that cares for Indian sport.'

The circulation zoomed to over a 100,000 copies per week within a month (and it crossed the 1,50,000 mark during the 1987 Reliance Cricket World Cup), which was way beyond our wildest dreams. Having reached that unprecedented sales figure in Indian sports publishing history, the next target became one of not surrendering the lead, as in a 100-metre race.

Most importantly, we had been able to sow the seeds of sports awareness in the country. This was slowly but surely leading to sport being increasingly acknowledged in schools, colleges and by the public at large, not only as a means to improve physical and mental health but also to develop character, positively channelize youthful energies and build bridges among people. Every single person on our minimal staff was energized beyond description, delighted that our efforts were being appreciated by sports lovers in the nation and abroad. We were seeing a ray of hope in that there was increasing pressure on the country's sports governing bodies to demonstrate greater accountability and better results.

We were on a high, an adrenalin rush!

As a result of the efforts of the energetic marketing team through direct contacts in the metro and major cities, as well as via the established national railway's newspaper-selling organizations such as A.H. Wheeler and Co. and Higginbotham's, *Sportsweek* acquired a nationwide footprint which, in time, was extended to neighbouring countries in Southeast Asia, Middle East and Africa.

Sportsweek Awards

In an endeavour to brand *Sportsweek* as 'the magazine that cares for Indian sport,' we pioneered the *Sportsweek* 'Man of the Match' awards at cricket Tests against visiting teams and offered cash incentives to the national hockey team which participated in the FIH 1973 Hockey World Cup in Amsterdam.

We also organized a football match between a *Sportsweek* XI for which five football internationals and 'Tiger' Pataudi played and a Bangladesh XI which included two international players. The entire proceeds of the match were donated to the Maharashtra governor's East Bengal Refugees Fund.

◆

In 1985 when the Swedish Davis Cup tennis team, which included Mats Wilander, Stefan Edberg and Anders Jarryd, passed through Mumbai en route to Bengaluru where they defeated India (4–1), *Sportsweek* sponsored a dinner at Mumbai's Oberoi Hotel for the benefit of the Spastics Society of India (now known as ADAPT—Able Disabled All People Together). The Swedes went on to beat West Germany in Munich in the final to give them their second successive title and third successive title overall. The visitors kindly gave their rackets for auction to A.F.S. Talyarkhan.

According to *Mid-Day* sports editor and cricket historian Clayton Murzello: 'In his meticulously researched book on Indian cricket, Dr Richard Cashman wrote that *Sportsweek* raised ₹18,000 for Bangladesh relief in 1971. The next year, a *Sportsweek*-conducted match boosted the National Defence Fund by ₹150,000.'

When Ajit Wadekar's all-conquering team returned from its historic triumphs in the West Indies (1970–71) and England (also 1971), *Sportsweek* announced a lifetime gift of subscriptions for all members and officials of the two teams, a commitment honoured until the magazine's closure in 1989.

By today's inflationary standards, the awards may seem niggardly but, on balance, they were in keeping with the living standards in those days, as evidenced by a menu (reproduced below) from the city's Willingdon Sports Club very kindly sent by my neighbour Dr Quresh Maskati, an ardent cricket lover.

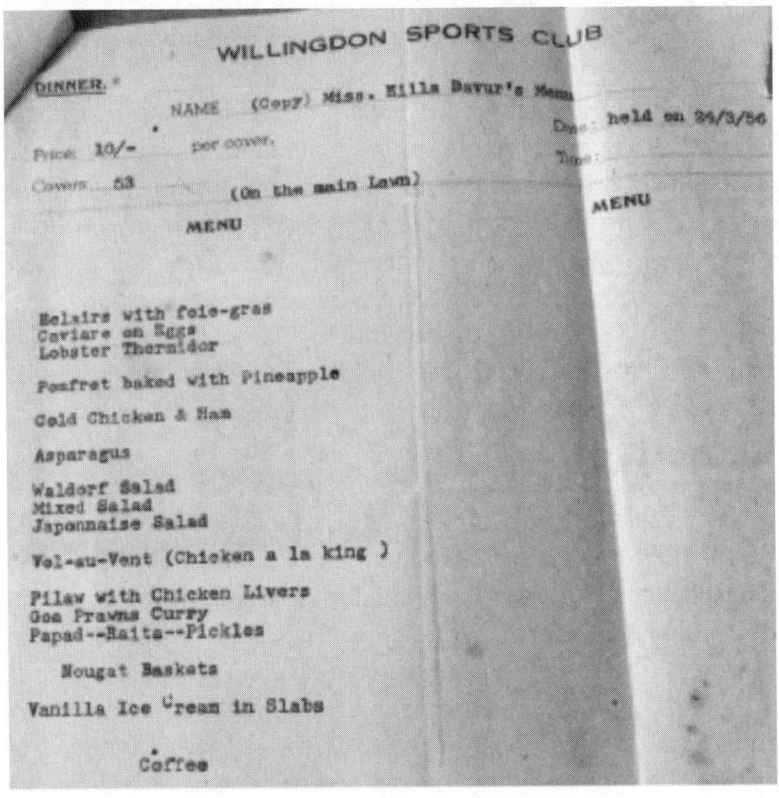

Sportsweek Awards

The 'Value for Money' Magazine

With *Sport and Pastime* rendered hors de combat a few months before our launch, *Sportsweek* had a clear run, an opportunity we fully capitalized upon.

The 20-year period between 1968 and 1988 was our golden age, during which we endeavoured to give our readers value for money (our slogan was VFM), by exclusive coverage of all major sporting events around the world, either from syndicated arrangements, special correspondents or stringers (part-time journalists). To the extent possible, I, too, helped by covering cricket, hockey and international events such as the Olympics, and the Asian and Commonwealth Games.

Burning My Candle at Both Ends

My candle burns at both ends;
It will not last the night;
But ah, my foes, and, oh, my friends—
It gives a lovely light!

—Edna St Vincent Millay

In Dubai one night, where I was running the *Khaleej Times* newspaper, son Tarique called from Mumbai to ask if I had the time to discuss a 'very important matter.' I replied that I did.

'Dad, I don't know how to say this but…'

'Go ahead, Tarique… Is it about *Sportsweek*?' I asked.

'Yes, Dad.'

'Do you think we should close it down?' I asked, catching the drift.

'Dad, we've been losing a lot of money for a long time now, and it's throwing the whole group's finances out of whack. We can't keep…'

'I understand Tarique. How much are we losing on *Sportsweek*?' I asked.

He mentioned figures—the previous and current year-to-date.

'Close it down, Tarique,' I replied, obviously failing to disguise my tremulous voice.

'But Dad…it's your baby and you've nursed and sustained it for 20 years.'

'Thanks, Tarique. I appreciate what you're saying...and I know you've wanted to say this for a long time. Thanks for trying to keep it afloat. But the odds were overwhelming from the start, and it was one hell of a ride... God bless you.'

And, that was it.

Even though *Sportsweek* was revamped in style and content, rechristened and relaunched as *Sportsweek and Lifestyle* with Sunil Gavaskar as the editor after the Little Master spelt 'finis' to his many-splendoured career.

The injection of the Lifestyle element into what was essentially a sports magazine was dictated by the objective to widen the readership base to a wider audience in a rapidly expanding consumer-oriented, aspirational environment driven by higher purchasing power. In keeping with everything he has done in his illustrious career, Gavaskar was no figurehead but applied himself to his new responsibility with sincerity—writing regularly, doing interviews, arranging cover stories and organizing photographs such as the celebrated one of Viv Richards dressed as a maharaja and a boxer.

But, alas, *India Today*'s description of sports magazines as waifs and television having become all the rage in the country captured the state of affairs to a tee. *Sportsweek* and *Lifestyle* breathed its last in 1989.

◆

In an article headlined 'Sudden Death—Lack of Advertisements Leads to *Sportsweek*'s Closure,' *India Today* magazine wrote: 'For many sportsmen and sports fans, the disappearance of Sports week (sic) was like the collapse of an institution. Like its predecessor *Sport & Pastime* in an earlier era, *Sportsweek* (sic) was closely identified with the thrills and trauma of Indian sport.'[13]

The article also quoted Tarique, the managing director, as saying, 'Everyone's losing money. I'm the guy who blinked,' adding that

---

[13]M. Rahman, 'Lack of Advertisements Leads to Sportsweek's Closure', *India Today*, 15 February 1989, https://www.indiatoday.in/magazine/society-the-arts/media/story/19890215-lack-of-advertisements-leads-to-sportsweeks-closure-815767-1989-02-15. Accessed on 8 November 2021.

following market research, his group was planning to relaunch the magazine in an altered avatar. Detailing reasons for the magazine's closure, *India Today* mentioned head honcho of Madison Advertising, Sam Balsara's response: 'For the advertiser, television is the primary medium, not a sports magazine, which only ensures duplication of the ad.'

◈

Clayton Murzello has co-authored two books (*Cricket at Fever Pitch* and *Sachin: Born to Bat*) with me. He has worked devotedly with our parent organization, the Mid-Day group, for 26 years now (in 2021). He is still with the new owners—the Jagran group. The following are some excerpts from an article he wrote for *Mid-Day* in 2014:[14]

> Historian and author Gulu Ezekiel informs me that it is 25 years this month (January 2014) of the shutting down of *Sportsweek*, the popular magazine which widely travelled journalist Khalid Ansari started way back in 1968.
>
> It's a pity *Sportsweek* failed to survive when it was renamed *Sportsweek and Lifestyle* and edited by then recently-retired Sunil Gavaskar.
>
> In pre-satellite television days, these magazines helped popularise the game immensely. In the early 1970s, Sportsweek 'covered' some of their issues with the latest update on Test matches featuring India. And as any collector will tell you, those issues are priceless. In the mid-1980s, a famous actor-cum-passionate sports fan visited my home to borrow a book, which had a collection of sports articles that included an extract from Jesse Owens' autobiography *My Life as Black Man and White Man*. He asked if he could see my modest collection and among the few bound volumes of Sportsweek, he spotted the one that contained issues of India's 1971 triumph in the West Indies. He asked if he could have that volume. I politely refused.

---

[14]Clayton Murzello, '25 Years On, We Still Miss Sportsweek', *Mid-Day*, 30 January 2014, https://www.mid-day.com/news/india-news/article/25-years-on--we-still-miss-sportsweek-15058025. Accessed on 8 November 2021.

Sportsweek's popularity gave rise to the need for a cricket quarterly magazine in 1974. In its 10-year existence, it gave cricket fans and statisticians much more than what Sportsweek could fit in their editions. I know of a collector whose complete set was broken when a bound volume containing 1979 issues was reduced to flames in his pathologist friend's laboratory that caught fire many years ago. The collector hasn't been able to set it right (pun intended) and the good doctor passed away.

Star columnists are a common sight in newspapers today, but Sportsweek was where it all started in India and Khalid Ansari must be credited for the concept. Getting the most famous name in Indian batting as editor was a big catch in itself. Gavaskar didn't just have his name printed as editor. He did justice to his role by writing editorials whenever available and even interviewed the most famous names in the sporting world for various cover stories.

Even a quarter century after its closure, some cricket lovers like me, miss the thrill of getting their hands on a new issue every Thursday morning. Well played, Sportsweek (1968-1989).

EIGHT

SPORTS IN MY INK

Olympic Games

I've had the good fortune to witness—and cover—nine Olympic Games between Munich 1972 and Beijing 2008 (barring the one in Barcelona, 1992): Montreal 1976, Moscow 1980, Montreal 1984, Seoul 1988, Atlanta 1996, Sydney 2000, Athens 2004 and Beijing 2008.

I've had the privilege of experiencing uncontrollable surges of excitement and unbearable tingles in my spine at the opening and closing ceremonies, at which I witnessed the spectacle of blood, tears, toil and sweat that is sports. I've shed tears of joy at the amazing deeds of valour and heroism of winners as much as I've empathized with the pangs of sorrow and heartaches over misfortunes and near misses, which are far too many to recount in these memoirs.

I've despaired at instances of jingoism, chauvinism, unprofessionalism and dishonest practices geared towards winning at all costs, but I've also marvelled at the touching displays of fair play and sportsmanship where an athlete has sacrificed a once-in-a-lifetime opportunity to become an Olympics winner at the altar of sportsmanship.

I was present at the 2008 Olympics in Beijing where American swimmer Michael Phelps took home an awesome eight gold medals, breaking Mark Spitz's 1972 feat of seven in one Olympics. (Phelps eventually became the athlete with the most number of Olympic gold medals ever—a staggering 23 in number.)

I've been blessed to witness Jamaican Usain Bolt set three Olympic and world records in Beijing where he won gold in the 100 metres,

200 metres and 4x100 metres relay, to become the first man to win three sprinting events at a single Olympics since Carl Lewis in 1984.

I've also been fortunate to see Michael Johnson take home two gold medals in the 1996 Atlanta Olympics while smashing two world records along the way (in the 400 metres and 200 metres races, with only a few days of rest in-between) to become the first person to win both races in the same Olympic Games.

Also at the 2008 Beijing Games, I witnessed German weightlifter Matthias Steiner win the super heavyweight category using the clean and jerk technique to lift a weight nearly 30 pounds over his previous best. This was arguably among the Games' most touching moments since it came only a year after his wife's death.

There was also Vasily Alexeev's hoist of 562 pounds overhead in his final clean and jerk attempt, which established him as the one of the most revered Olympians of the twentieth century.

And how can one forget India's hockey gold in the 1980 Olympics in Moscow? Although the feat was somewhat diminished by the absence of some of the hockey powerhouses due to a boycott by some of the leading Western nations.

There was also Nadia Comaneci's Perfect '10' at the 1976 Montreal Games where she won three gold medals to become the first female gymnast ever to be awarded a '10' in an Olympic gymnastics event.

I also happened to be at the Seoul 1988 Games where Canadian 100-metre sprinter Ben Johnson won an incredible race beating American titleholder Carl Lewis only to test positive for drugs and be banned for life.

As I said before, I've seen many instances of cheating, foul play, the bending of rules and such, but I've also borne witness to tear-inducing feats of sportsmanship, of gallant self-actualization and the pushing of human limits—all of which has made me marvel at the human capacity for extending mental and physical potential in the pursuit of the Olympic motto *Citius, Altius, Fortius* (Faster, Higher, Stronger).

The Olympic Games charter proclaims that the event 'celebrates the best of humanity.' The 1972 Games in September may have got together the best of humanity in terms of sporting prowess but it also ended up exhibiting its most inhuman traits.

That year's Games were organized by West Germany (before the historic fall of the German Wall, which heralded the unification of West and East Germany into the Federal Republic in 1990). In the words of *Time* magazine, the Games were meant to 'exalt its athletes, tout its democracy and purge the stench of Adolf Hitler's 1936 Berlin Games,'[15] when the legendary Jesse Owens of the US torpedoed the myth of Aryan and German supremacy by winning as many as four gold medals causing Hitler to storm out of the stadium. The Germans, who had almost conquered the world during World War II, just three decades earlier, lowered their guard and considerably reduced the security level as a public relations exercise.

Eight members of the Palestinian terrorist group Black September took nine persons from the Israeli Olympics team hostage, after killing two of them, at the Games Village. The ensuing massacre saw the deaths of all nine hostages (with a total of 11 Israeli casualties), five of the Palestinian attackers and one West German police officer.

The world was stunned as organizers scrambled to put the Games back on track—with awesome German efficiency, one might add.

The stentorian statement in five historic words 'the Games must go on' in a speech by didactic International Olympic Committee president Avery Brundage announcing the resumption of the Games still reverberate in my ears.[16]

---

[15]The Editors of TIME, *TIME 100 Influential Photographs*, Time Incorporated Books, 2018.
[16]David Binder, 'The Munich Massacre', the *New York Times*, 5 September 1972, http://archive.nytimes.com/www.nytimes.com/packages/html/sports/year_in_sports/09.05.html. Accessed on 8 November 2021.

1982 Asian Games, New Delhi

Apart from the nine Olympics there were the Commonwealth Games in Edinburgh (1970) and Kuala Lumpur (1998), the Asian Games in Bangkok (1970 and 1978)—events that I covered for *Sportsweek*.

In 1982 I was given the honour to publish, on behalf of the organizing committee, the official daily publication of the New Delhi Asian Games called the *Asiad Chronicle* in the capacity of managing editor.

The publisher was Sankaran Nair (Shankar), known as 'Colonel Shankar' among his colleagues, retired head of the Research and Analysis Division (RAW) of the Government of India which, like the FBI in the US, Federal Security Service (successor to the KGB in Russia) and Gestapo in Nazi Germany, was the apex intelligence agency of the country.

In the lead-up to the Games, after we had completed our considerable workload for the day, Shankar and I would routinely switch over to lighter topics of discussion over dinner, with the former 'spook,' as I would tease him, regaling me with his experiences—but with impressive circumspection!

Shankar, a product of Loyola College, Chennai, later served as high commissioner to Singapore from 1986 to 1988. He is reported to have played a crucial role in the formation of Bangladesh, through

RAW operations during the Bangladesh Liberation War.

His memoirs *Inside IB and RAW: A Rolling Stone that Gathered Moss* in 2008 made news for the insider details about two of the highest intelligence agencies in India. The Indian government awarded him the third highest civilian honour of the Padma Bhushan in 1983 for his contributions.

Shankar passed away in Bengaluru on 17 November 2015, aged 95. More about the *Asiad Chronicle* later.

The 'Hitting Out' Column

The cricket series covered personally by me included important Tests involving India at home, in England, Australia, Pakistan, Sri Lanka and the West Indies, as also the Champions Cricket Trophy in Australia and the Cricket World Cup in South Africa.

According to an article in *The Print*: 'With its graphics and detailed covers, *Sportsweek* covered some of the biggest events in the sports world such as American athlete Jesse Owens autobiography detailing his life as a black man and a white man, Indian badminton champion Prakash Padukone, tennis champion Steffi Graf eyeing a Wimbledon title, the story of Chris Evert and Jimmy Connors winning the Women's and Men's 1974 Wimbledon titles and their romance. And, of course, the world of cricket—from Mansoor Ali Khan Pataudi and Ajit Wadekar to Vivian Richards and many more.'[17]

Leaving cricket aside for the moment, our endeavour to expose malfeasance among our sports bodies gathered momentum after our widely applauded Edinburgh Commonwealth revelations mentioned in an earlier chapter of this book. These exposes resulted in the setting up of an inquiry commission to investigate my allegations, making me revise my earlier opinion that trying to improve Indian sport is akin to banging one's head against the wall of the insouciant

---

[17]Revathi Krishnan, 'Sportsweek, the Popular Sports Magazine with Star Columnists that was Edited by Sunil Gavaskar', *The Print*, 19 December 2020, https://theprint.in/features/brandma/sportsweek-the-popular-sports-magazine-with-star-columnists-that-was-edited-by-sunil-gavaskar/570029/. Accessed on 8 November 2021.

powers that be in New Delhi.

It inspired the birth of my regular column 'Hitting Out,' which continued through the lifespan of *Sportsweek* and was often reproduced or quoted in publications in different parts of the country. It also led to me being asked to contribute to some publications such as *India Today*, *The Illustrated Weekly of India*, *Dharmyug* and others.

◈

The exposes and other writings in *Sportsweek's* 'Hitting Out' column are too many to be accommodated in these memoirs. Therefore, I have picked a few, in no particular sequence or logical order, merely to illustrate the intensity we had to try and rectify the faults in our sports administration set-up and ensure that our teams and individual representatives at the international levels brought joy and inspiration to our sports *deewane* (aficionados).

K.N. Prabhu, the doyen of Indian cricket writers and sports editor of *The Times of India*, wrote in a signed column: 'That enterprising sportswriter Khalid Ansari who edits the lively journal *Sportsweek*, has an extensive dossier to offer to any government-sports inquiry body. As he was on the spot, Ansari's observations are authentic and not picked up through a clairvoyant medium.'

Leslie Wilson, sports editor of the *Bangalore Times Weekly*, in an editorial lambasting the efforts of Raja Bhalindra Singh, scion of the Patiala royal family and chef de mission of the India contingent at the 1972 Munich Olympics wrote: 'Bhalindra Singh is going to come out with some explanations (concerning my allegations regarding the official's 'sins of commission and omission).'

Quoting Bhalindra Singh as saying 'most of the allegations were uncharitable and distorted,' Wilson writes, 'I am sure he read what Khalid Ansari has written in a Mumbai daily. If that is so, it cannot be uncharitable and distorted. Khalid was an eyewitness to everything at Munich.'

◈

Bhalindra Singh was son of the late legendary Bhupinder Singh, Maharaja of Patiala, who is said to have had five wives, innumerable consorts and an estimated 88 children. According to legend, he was driven in a cavalcade of 20 Rolls Royce cars. He was the owner of the world famous 'Patiala Necklace,' manufactured by the famous brand Cartier, which his wife Maharani Bakhtawar Kaur presented to Queen Mary on behalf of the Ladies of India in 1911 to mark the first visit of a (British) Empress to India.

Bhupinder is perhaps the best-known maharaja of Patiala, famous for his extravagance and for being a cricketer and patron of sports. He was captain of the Indian team that visited England in 1911, played 27 first-class matches, including many for the MCC.

On a personal note, Raja Bhalindra was an epicure and outstanding cook and, when president of the Indian Olympic Association (IOA), personally cooked a memorable meal for me and his son Raja Randhir Singh at his New Delhi residence. Randhir Singh succeeded his father as secretary general of the IOA and the Asian Games Federation and was also an Asian shooting champion.

◆

To come back to my dispatches—in *Sportsweek*, there was this bylined article from Munich during the 1972 Olympic Games, which read:

> If the participants performed below par, our officials excelled themselves—in spoiling the country's image.
>
> Enough has been written by this columnist about the doings of our callous officials, about unauthorised people living in the Olympic Village inconveniencing the competitors, hapless souls who had no option but to share beds, sleep on floors and smuggle out food for inconsiderate, uninvited VIPs.
>
> Enough has also been written about ineligible people participating in the opening ceremony just so that they may see gratis the ceremony, for which tickets were being sold at a high premium. In doing so they deprived genuine competitors of a place in the march past which is an honour and to most a once-in-a-lifetime opportunity.
>
> I am absolutely amazed at the audacity of the officials who on their return to India, have refuted these allegations and challenged the press to prove them. I was on the spot. And I can say that all

manner of officials, who were not entitled to this privilege, DID stay in the village and took part in the march past.

I was also present when wrestler Premnath was injured and can state categorically that no Indian doctor was present to attend to him...

The charge regarding the unauthorised officials in the march past has been sought to be explained away by the assertion that some of the players had to be excluded because they were bad at marching and that officials had to be included to avoid making the contingent look small.

What utter nonsense...

◆

Addressing the oft-repeated question as to why a country as vast and with as large a population as ours cannot do better at sports, this writer, in a curtain raiser to the 1976 Montreal Olympic Games, observed in *The Illustrated Weekly of India* in its issue dated 11 July 1976:

The lament, although indicative of frustration, is not, one must confess, logically tenable. The obvious answer is absence of infrastructure, lack of financial resources and enough dedicated sports administrators with breadth of vision. The important criterion is that only a fraction out of the (then) 600 plus million (now 1.3 billion) people in our country are involved in sport.

Only out of quantity will come quality. One cannot dispute the fact that the task of organising sports in a country as large as ours, down to the grassroots, is a gargantuan one, calling for vast financial resources and having wide sociological ramifications. All of which means that we really have to make a beginning—NOW.

◆

Exposing the shocking state of affairs in our hockey, my article in *Sportsweek* read:

Our campaign for the Kuala Lumpur World Cup Hockey Tournament started in reverse gear. It took an ultimatum from the players to ensure that the team ultimately participated. Following that, when the gold trophy had been brought back, the country, understandably, went hysterical with joy. The very officials who put every obstacle they could to prevent India's participation in the tournament, were now exulting by bellowing, 'We did it!'

Were we able to repeat the performance next year at the Montreal Olympics?

In a wide-ranging analysis of the ills that afflict Indian sport and if we were a sporting nation, my lengthy article in *The Illustrated Weekly of India*, in its issue dated 14 August 1977, read in effect:

> After thirty years of Independence, our achievements in international sport are near cipher. But the dearth of medals is only a symptom of a deep-rooted malaise. Mass participation is necessary to make a nation really sporting. Equally important is the need to free sports from the stranglehold of self-seeking officials.

◈

The legendary Parsi-Gujarati theatre impresario, Adi Marzban, who also published and edited the *Jaam-e-Jamshed*, the beloved newspaper of the Parsi community, wrote the following piece in 1983:

> Really it is quite sickening to realise how hysterical (with joy) we Indians become whenever we win a cricket match. The recent jubilation over India winning the Prudential World Cup is a case in point. I was about to write on this subject when Khalid Ansari beat me to it. In one of his excellent front-page editorials *Hitting Out* (*Mid-Day* 4 July 1983), he gives some really thought-provoking advice. What he has said makes so much sense that I cannot resist quoting him. I hope he will not mind.
>
> I am quoting Khalid at some length because he has put into words much better than I can, exactly what I feel. Space in this column being limited I cannot reproduce the entire editorial which is a pity.

Khalid writes:

Even those who consider cricket a colossal waste of national time and energy will grudgingly acknowledge the exploits of the heroes if only because they have renewed the nation's faith in itself to succeed.

So let's, by all means, acknowledge and applaud. But in a gracious, dignified manner.

'We are known the world over to be very emotional people. Which in itself is not such a very bad thing after all. But need our display of emotion be VULGAR? Do we need to put our heroes—the few that we have—on pedestals and worship them? Do we REALLY have to lose our sense of proportion, go berserk, behave in frenzied fashion?

A member of the victorious team stated in London yesterday that the celebrations (organized by members of the Indian community in England) following the World Cup victory have been 'more taxing than the actual winning of the Cup.'

Bharat darshans, cavalcades, receptions, honours and erecting of statues in such situations are the work of people who do not understand the ESSENCE of sport. They do not know what winning and losing in sport is all about.

And the LAST concern of our sports VIPS (the officials) is the promotion of sport. Their ONLY interest is hogging the limelight. And basking in reflected glory. Such men are dangerous. They cause incalculable harm to the sportsmen themselves by inflating their egos, making them lose their sense of balance, distracting their attention. Public memory is notoriously short.

Khalid winds up his editorial with:

Without in any way meaning to sound a discordant note or to distract from the stupendous performance of Kapil Dev's team, we would like to gently remind all concerned that India are scheduled to play a Test series against Pakistan as early as September this year. The horrors of the last series against that country are still fresh in our minds.

And we shall play host to the West Indians later this year. Needless to say, they will be thirsting for revenge on our soil.

Let us, by all means, applaud our cricket heroes. They have done a great deal to deserve it. Honour si, worship NON.

And the team would be well-advised to remember that success, like public adulation, is fickle, harlot-like.

Thank you, Khalid.

The Unsporting Indian

The following is an excerpt from my piece titled 'The Unsporting Indian' that was published in an edition of *Sportsweek* in 1976:

From our sports 'lovers,' right up to our sports officials, our attitude towards sport is most unsportsmanlike. As for our sports administrators, their dedication is limited to lining their pockets, jetting off on foreign jaunts.'

One is sick, tired, fed-up of hearing the lament ad nauseam that India, merely because she is a nation of sixty-five crores plus (in 1975), MUST be able to produce a genuine fast bowler, a world-beating hockey team, a Wimbledon champion etcetera.

To argue that a nation, only because of its population must *ipso facto* win at least one bronze medal at the Olympics is to oversimplify the problem. The hypothesis is as naïve as it is illogical. The line of thinking, it must be granted, is indicative of frustration over our pathetic record in international sport, but it also suggests the intelligence of a rhesus in prime.

Consider: Are we really a sports minded nation? From the Centre downwards—the state governments, educational authorities, parents, the youth of the nation, how many among them are remotely involved or even interested in sport? How many of our people indulge in some form of physical recreational activity on weekends if not regularly?

Meanwhile Indian sport continues to languish in the doldrums at every level. Small wonder, then that every time our team participates in an international event, chances are rupee to a *rosogolla*, there will be nationwide mourning, with abuse, disenchantment and enquiry commissions to follow.

Any solution short of a complete overhaul of the present infrastructure is doomed to fail. The guidelines laid down by the Government are a commendable attempt in this direction. Whether or not they succeed in their objectives remains to be seen...

Only structural changes have been attempted in this critique. The task of organising sports at every level down to the grassroots is an enormous one, having wide sociological ramifications.

The objective should be not so much to produce world champions or a team to take on all-comers as to make more people take to sport, to make sport a way of life, to make the Unsporting Indian Sporting.

It is only when the youth of our nation is compelled to take to sport, either through the educational curriculum or as a desirable form of activity, favoured and encouraged by parents and society at large, it is only when the infrastructure in the form of playgrounds, scientific coaching, sports scholarships etc. is provided, that we can hope to produce champions commensurate with the population.

The stupendous task boggles the imagination. But a start has to be made. To begin with, changes should be made at the top. Once the right people are involved in sports administration, the desired far-reaching changes down the line can be brought about in time.

Our national priorities place sport—and rightly so—way below food, housing, education and others. Hungry stomachs must be fed, the homeless provided shelter, the illiterate taught to read and write before all else.

But the importance of sport as a healthy and character-building activity, one which constructively channelises youthful energies towards producing better citizens of India—Sporting Indians—should not be overlooked.

It's 'Do or Die' for Us

My report from Kuala Lumpur published in *The Illustrated Weekly of India* after India's victory in the 1975 Hockey World Cup in the city read:

'Now it's 'do or die' for us!' said he.

When asked after India's shock 1-2 defeat at the hands of Argentina, to comment on our pathetic performance which had put us in the unenviable position of being able to create history of a dubious nature—of being kicked out of an international hockey tournament at the qualifying stage—Ajit Pal Singh smiled that sad smile of his. He said in an emotion-choked, barely audible voice: 'We played badly, very badly. But we will do better.'

And true to word, 'do or die' it was for Ajit Pal and his gallant lads in the matches that followed: first, the relentless blitzkrieg on the beleaguered goal of 1972 Olympic Champions West Germany fetched a thoroughly deserved and workmanlike 3-1 win.

Then, in the semi-finals, after having outclassed Malaysia in all departments of the game save that of scoring—hardly a new shortcoming—India found herself 'Going, going' from the World Cup.

Then, three minutes from the end, Manager Balbir Singh, himself a battle-scarred great of the halcyon days of Indian hockey, tried a desperate gamble as Manager Gentle had attempted in the last World Cup at Amsterdam.

With Indian trailing 0-1, Gentle had brought on Baldev Singh five minutes from the end in place of Surjit Singh, who had been having atrocious luck with his penalty-corner hits. The phlegmatic, unflappable Baldev had then saved India in the dying minutes of the game with the very first penalty-corner hit taken by him.

Against Malaysia, the much-wronged Aslam Sher Khan, whose omission from the side of the earlier games could only have been due to reasons totally unconnected with merit, slammed in that equaliser, taking the match into extra time which brought victory. 'Do or die…'

And that memorable final which produced vintage hockey, the best of the tournament, showed to the world, in the words of the great veteran player and one of the founders of Indian hockey, A.B. Rosser, 'the creme de la creme: what hockey should be.'

'Do or die!' One goal down in the 18th minute of the final against Pakistan. Then that Surjit Singh equaliser of the penalty-corner in the 45th minute. And, finally, victory, glorious victory from a 51st minute goal.

The marvellous display which the team turned in, surprised even the most partisan supporters of the team.

Ours was superb, aggressive, vintage hockey: artistic stickwork, delectable body swerves and feints, uncanny understanding between the inside forwards, halves and full-backs which had hitherto been conspicuous by its absence.

Also accurate long passes, excellent trapping, the utilisation—for the first time—of the wingers who opened out the game to catch the opposition, which had been concentrating down the middle, unawares.

On the day preceding the final—a Friday—Manager Balbir had taken his team to a temple, mosque and a church. He and Coach Gurcharan Singh Bodhi had kept guard outside the players' rooms on the morning of the big battle to ensure that 'my boys' did not 'get up to any monkey business.'

On the way to the Merdeka Stadium for the final, the players had, as one man, chanted Sat Sri Akal Nara-e-Takbeer Allah-O-Akbar.

From Olympian Heights to Stygian Depths

But, alas, it was not to be.

In the very next tournament—the 1976 Montreal Olympics—India was knocked out of the reckoning for a medal for the first time ever and finished with an ignominious seventh rank.

Gone were the days when India, winning six consecutive Olympic Gold medals leading up to Rome, 1960, (when they surrendered supremacy to Pakistan but following which they won in Tokyo, 1964), didn't let the opposition score even a single goal, leave alone actually letting them win a match.

It has been a heart-breaking fall from Olympian heights to Stygian depths: India didn't win a single Olympic Games medal, of any colour, until finally the tide turned at the 2020 Tokyo Games with the team winning a Bronze medal. The historic win occurred after 41 years, with India having won its last medal (Gold) at Moscow, 1980.

The fond hopes of hockey lovers have surged before every Olympics and World Cup only to be dashed largely because of bad management of the sport, exemplified largely by infighting in the Indian Hockey Federation (IHF) and inability to retain outstanding foreign coaches, whom they find with attractive financial offers but fail to hold on to. That in a nutshell epitomizes the tragedy of Indian sports, the mess that it is in, its rock-bottom prestige in sports circles abroad. Neros, in the form of our hockey mandarins, have fiddled while Rome burnt.

Causes of India's Hockey Decline

An article in *Sportsweek* read:

Without oversimplifying the issue, we may briefly analyse the root causes of India's hockey decline from the Tokyo Asiad. In a nutshell, the more important ones are:

The emergence of Pakistan, who are, in a manner of speaking, after all a chip off the old block, playing the same brand of traditional, artistic but aggressive hockey. The important differences between the two neighbours stem out of better planning, organisation and greater dedication across the border.

The playing surfaces at the more important international hockey events—which have become oftentimes, not quite unwittingly, slower and slower, thereby curbing Indian (and Pakistani) artistry at top speed.

The changes in the laws of the game designed to suit European style, physique, conditions and temperament in callous disregard for the representations of Asian countries. Besides, many of our technical delegates have remained mute spectators at FIH (Federation Internationale de Hockey) meetings, pandering to the dictates of European delegates to ensure their own continuance in the FIH, while far-reaching changes have been brought about in the rules of the game.

The more blatant instances of fiddling with the rules of the game are the modified offside rule, laxity as regards dangerous and body play, undercutting the wide discretionary powers conferred on the umpires, who have now come to be VIPs in the matter of penalty-corners and strokes.

These have resulted in the placing of proficiency at conversion of penalty-strokes and penalty-corners at an absurd premium to the definite advantage of the European countries, who have transformed this into a fine art, it must be conceded, through application and hard work, whereas we continue to be woefully deficient in this all important match-winning department.

Then there was the renunciation, at the whims of our hockey bosses, of our fast, natural, artistic game. They decreed that we shall, instead, play "direct hockey", ape the robust hit-and run style of the Westerners, which in fact was evolved to counter our own traditional style. A case of the dog chasing the dog.

The idiocy of the policy is testified to by the results of the Olympics, the World Cup and the Asian Games from the Asian Games onwards.

The article concluded by stating:

But our obdurate all-knowing hockey pooh-bahs, in their infinite wisdom, refused to see reason for fear of losing face, while our hockey stock plummeted. I for one have no doubt that it was a reversal to our traditional style of hockey which won us a World Cup at Kuala Lumpur.

In the midst of all the delirious *wah-wahs*, we will have to set right at once the many deficiencies if we hope to add the Olympic title to our world crown.

For a start, we must put our hockey affairs in order, call an immediate halt to all toasting and backslapping and address ourselves to the task of ensuring that our hockey glory is not short lived, as it was in the case of our cricket.

Not All Fun and Games

Contrary to popular belief, covering any major international sports event, especially multidiscipline ones such as the Olympic, Asian or Commonwealth Games, is hardly fun and games.

Enjoyable though they may be for fans, they are mentally and physically draining for correspondents, with working hours extending from early morning to the early hours of the next morning for the entire duration of the Games, which normally last a fortnight.

Many of the venues are scattered at distant locations in the Games' complex. Since India normally sends a large contingent spanning many disciplines to most international games, it means making a dash from one venue to the next scheduled event. Although the media transport facilities are normally efficient, simultaneous events at scattered venues require fleet footedness, stamina and navigational skills.

Depending upon printing deadlines, one constantly has one eye on the clock to ensure strict adherence to schedules, the bugbear of all correspondents. To top it all, are the constant demands for exclusives or specials from headquarters since the sports editors, who have their hands on the readers' pulse, are in a much better position to evaluate readership response than the harried and harassed correspondent at the venue.

Then there is the constant worry as to whether one's dispatch has been received in time by headquarters. The mind-boggling technological and communications improvements over the past few years have made transmission infinitely faster and more reliable whereas before the advent of emails, transmission was a constant source of worry. Often after handing in copy to the telex or fax operator one had to wait anxiously for hours for confirmation of receipt from the headquarter's sports desk. There have been occasions when I have had to wait at the venue office until 2 a.m. to ensure receipt.

Following the late nights, one has to be back to the stations by early the next morning to make it in time for the next day's first event. Missing an event such as the 100-metres sprint, lasting under 11 seconds—much less when the likes of Usain Bolt were involved—made late arrival at the venue a cardinal sin.

Then there were accidents, crucial late arrivals of buses to the next venue, and the like.

For me, the worst accident occurred at the Tehran Asian Games, 1974 when I had, what Joe Crasto of *The Times of India* termed, a 'miraculous escape.'

In an article dated 7 September 1974, Crasto wrote in *The Times of India*:

> An ill wind blew across Tehran today. It quickly developed into a thunderstorm and such was its gale force that it disrupted the hockey and tennis fixtures and sent a huge television stand crashing down at the Aryamehr Sports Complex. Three of the 20-foot metal flag posts flew. At least two spectators were injured while several journalists and commentators covering the India-Sri Lanka hockey match had a miraculous escape.
>
> Soon after halftime in the India-Sri Lanka hockey match came a slight drizzle accompanied by gusty winds. I moved a row higher and protected myself under the radio commentators' desk.
>
> Surjit Sen had just handed over the mike to Melville de Mellow and as soon as de Mellow announced: 'It's a tornado', down came the television cameramen's platform. De Mellow was lucky to escape with abrasions on his hand. I threw myself on the floor and pressed myself against the side of the concrete steps, watching with fear and horror the mighty installation slide down over the commentators' desk and on the desk where only five minutes earlier, *Sportsweek*'s Khalid Ansari and myself had been. It was a miraculous escape for all.

A sports journalist's life isn't all fun and games, after all!

Sachin: Born to Bat

	Runs	Average	100's	50's	Highest Score	Wickets	Catches
Tests 200	15,921	53.78	51	68	248*	46	115 115
ODI's 463	18,426	44.83	49	96	200*	154	175 175

My semi-retirement stage enabled me to find the time to also write a biography of the all-time cricket great, Sachin Tendulkar, in collaboration with my friend and *Mid-Day* sports editor, cricket historian and wonderful human being, Clayton Murzello. He had edited my previous book *Cricket at Fever Pitch* on limited-overs cricket.

Sunil Gavaskar wrote the foreword and several cricketing luminaries, very kindly, wrote a few words by way of introduction to the book. They included Field Marshal Sam Manekshaw, Kapil Dev, Bishan Singh Bedi, Vivian Richards, Inderjit Bindra, Ajit Wadekar, Dilip Vengsarkar, Greg Chappell, Ian Chappell, Nari Contractor, Mike Coward, Jagmohan Dalmiya, Zaheer Abbas, Rahul Dravid, Raj Singh Dungarpur, Farokh Engineer, Ranjit Fernando, Karsan Ghavri, Michael Holding, Tunku Imran, Imran Khan, Air Marshal (Retd.) Idris Latif, Bob Merriman, A.C. Muttiah, K.N. Prabhu, Dicky Rutnagur, Dilip Sardesai, Roger Binny, Rusi Surti, Sachin Tendulkar, Polly Umrigar, Goolam Vahanvati, Bapu Nadkarni, and retired umpires David Shepherd and Billy Bowden.

My prologue to *Sachin: Born to Bat* read:[18]

> I have long been intrigued by the fascinating conundrum of what makes a champion a champion, not merely in sport but in any walk of life. In other words, what are the qualities that foster extraordinary, and at times, awesome achievement?
>
> For a long time, I have been fascinated by yin and yang, the opposing elements of our mindsets.
>
> As a passionate sportsman of rather limited physical, mental, emotional and, if you will, spiritual attributes, I have often marvelled at the single-minded, seemingly manic, dedication that has driven champion sportspersons to acts of epic and seemingly impossible achievement.
>
> This is the result of a rare mix—*mojo* 'of talent, courage, tenacity and a never-say-die mindset with extraordinary underpinnings of faith and confidence,' as defined by the University of Sydney's Centre for the Mind.
>
> I have been wonderstruck by the unbelievable physical and mental attributes, the matrix, 'that has powered champions to defy gravity, time and space and to drive themselves to near physical collapse for a mere abstraction,' in the words of Rich Franklin in *What Makes A Champion*.

---

[18] Khalid A. H. Ansari, *Sachin, Born to Bat: The Journey of Cricket's Ultimate Centurion*, Jaico Publishing House, 2012.

And, I have wondered how 'mindset', as defined by the Centre in its multidimensional research on the subject, is 'shaped by our genetic make-up, by our education, by our culture and the society we live in, and even by our ongoing emotional interactions.

Sachin: Born to Bat seeks to apply to Sachin Ramesh Tendulkar—India's pride and joy—in layman terms, some of the findings of scientists, sport psychologists and coaches in the ongoing and exhilarating attempts the world over to understand a 'champion mindset'.

Since this publication claims no pretensions to being a psycho-analytical treatise, I have supplemented some of the research findings with the understanding, experiences and impressions of some of Sachin's mentors, coaches, friends and teammates to help readers understand, for themselves, what makes the Little Champion the awesome champion he is.

After all, what is a champion mindset? Is it a triumph of mind over matter, a victory of will over skill—or the other way around? Or, perhaps, is it largely a matter of what is loosely referred to as 'good luck', the result, possibly, in Sachin's case, the conjunction of the planets at the precise moment when he was born in Mumbai on 24 April 1973?

In my endeavour to help understand what makes Sachin Tendulkar the great champion he is, I have tried to avoid the extremes of pseudo-abstruseness and condescending simplicity.

This is not intended to be a half-baked psycho-analytical, physiological or medical treatise, nor a mere pictorial essay for neophytes. While bearing in mind the paramount aspect of the discerning reader's love for the nuances of the game, I have tried to not foolishly rush in where angels fear to tread.

Sachin: Born to Bat is an attempt to impartially probe the crucial mental, physical and emotional ingredients of a cricketing 'god', an all-time great sportsman, a legend in his lifetime, an extraordinary role model and exemplary, sensitive human being.

In words reminiscent of Lord Alfred Tennyson in Ulysses— 'To strive, to seek, to find and not to yield'—Sachin, ever the perfectionist, recently told London's newspaper *The Guardian*:

'I'm really focusing now on how I can get to the next level as a batsman. How I can get even more consistent. How I can get better.'

'Crisp 'n' Crackling'

Reproduced below is an excerpt of a report of the book release event of *Sachin, Born to Bat* at the CCI published in *Mid-Day* on 22 November 2012.

The book *Sachin: Born to Bat* was officially released at a crisp 'n' crackling function at the Cricket Club of India's (CCI) C K Nayudu Hall last evening. With more than 100 books on Sachin Tendulkar, one can say that Tendulkar has become a 'genre' in literature.

The articles range from straight cricket reportage, opinions and analyses to lighter pieces bringing out different facets of Sachin's 'super bat' by Harsha Bhogle who began by saying that Sachin Tendulkar and Khalid Ansari were both in different ways, 'symbolic of Mumbai' and added that Clayton was an able lieutenant putting the book together.

Ansari said that he was always interested in exploring 'what are the qualities that foster such awesome achievements? What is the champion mindset?' He quoted Robert Browning about aspiration and achievement, to conclude a spirited address.

Dravid was short and punchy at the mike, like a T20 knock rather than The Wall-like innings, which was his trademark. Dravid said of Ansari and Clayton, that, 'they are two people that I have known for many years now. I recall how, when there was an article about me by Khalid Ansari, it would be there in an envelope underneath my hotel door early the next morning.'

About Clayton, 'he is a nice guy. I could sense that when things were not going well, Clayton would actually feel bad for you, when he was asking questions. Now, with me on the dark side (from cricketer to commentator) I count Khalid and Clayton as colleagues.'

Commentator and writer Ayaz Memon read a chapter from the book, a no pulling punches piece about Sachin as captain and the 'Monkeygate' scandal with Harbhajan Singh as central character.

NINE

SIGHTS, SMELLS AND SOUNDS

The Communicators

I consider myself tremendously fortunate for having met some very friendly, interesting and erudite people around the world in the course of my career as a sports journalist.

In England there was John Arlott, the world-renowned voice of radio broadcasting, cricket writer for *The Telegraph* and commentator for the BBC for over 30 years, E.W. Swanton (*Daily Telegraph*), John Woodcock (*The Times*, London), Michael Melford (*Daily Telegraph*), the acerbic former Australian captain-turned-TV commentator Richie Benaud, Henry Blofeld (nicknamed 'Blowers') of Test Match Special on BBC Radio, Brian Johnston (veteran commentator, author and television presenter) and my good friend, Andy Jalil (freelance correspondent and radio commentator, UK).

The Infamous Vaseline Incident

While the aforementioned senior journalists and broadcasters were dignified, knowledgeable and wrote impartially, some of their colleagues from the 'yellow' tabloids were sensation-mongers, chauvinistic anachronisms in a supposedly gentleman's sport.

One such person was 'Pat' Gibson, of the *Daily Express*, for whom the game was all about one team—England. A votary of 'Rule Britannia' whose sole purpose in life was to project his home team as the greatest ever, he was a disgrace to the game from which he made a living.

I had an unfortunate—and nasty—run-in with him during Keith Fletcher's England team's 1981–82 Test series against India in India. It was the aftermath of the 1976–77 visit by Tony Greig's team, which defeated India 3–1 under controversial circumstances; that series has since gone down in Indian cricket history for left-arm seam bowler John Lever's alleged chicanery. The left-arm swing bowler from Essex was reported by umpire Judah Reuben—in the third Test at Chepauk, Madras, with India down 0–2 in the series—for allegedly using a foreign substance (later said to be Vaseline-impregnated rough-woven gauze over his eyebrows) on one side of the ball to make it swing disconcertingly into right-handed batsmen.

Reuben, who first detected the wrongdoing, reportedly told cricket historian Gulu Ezekiel that a sticky substance had indeed been found on the rogue ball by a BCCI-appointed forensic laboratory, but the entire episode had been hushed up in order to not damage relations with England.

Indian captain Bishan Bedi was furious, but his complaints fell on deaf ears. He spoke to me, and I, as his friend, called an informal press conference in my Chennai hotel room. Unfortunately though, not one Indian journalist from among the numerous reporters (who quaffed the whisky and wolfed down the food) had the gumption to write about it.

Even as Pat Gibson played vituperative cheerleader for Greig's team via his column in the *Daily Express*, calling me all manner of names, I stepped up the campaign against Lever and his team in *Sportsweek*. The Board of Control for Cricket in India (BCCI), though, remained characteristically supine.

In the process, the entire English press corps, including Bill Swanton, John Woodcock, Michael Melford, Roger Bannister, Clive Taylor and others (mentioned in an earlier chapter) en masse stopped writing permanently for *Sportsweek* in a show of British solidarity. We stood firm and countered Gibson's rantings in the *Daily Express* in my *Sportsweek* column.

Forty-Seven Large Scotches

When Keith Fletcher's 1981–82 team landed in Mumbai for the first Test in the six-match Test series (which India won 1–0), a welcome reception was arranged at The Oberoi (now Trident) hotel poolside and to which my wife Rukya and I were invited. And lo and behold, my bête noire Pat Gibson was also present at the reception, along with some British journalists.

Civility demanded that, no matter what our differences, we should be courteous to our *mehmaan* (guests). Therefore, forgiving but not forgetting, I greeted him with a smile.

In due course, Gibson made his way to me, while my wife was engaged in conversation elsewhere, and asked if I knew 'any place close by where 'Gorilla' (Ian Botham) and some of the (English) players could go for a 'good time.' I was taken aback. The Vaseline episode, and all that had transpired with it, came rushing back to my mind's eye. 'I'm not in the business of getting people a good time, Pat,' I snapped, at which Gibson beat a hasty retreat.

Later, seeing Gibson by himself, standing alone in the shadows, I felt remorseful that I had been perhaps harsh, even vengeful, towards him. I approached him and told him in no uncertain terms, but as civilly as possible under the circumstances, that I knew nothing about having a 'good time' but would be happy to suggest a disco bar—Studio 29—just down the road and across from the CCI.

The disco belonged to friends Sabi and Chotu (now deceased) Merchant, who had very kindly given Rukya and me complimentary membership of their, what is now called, Resto Bar. I even foolishly, as it transpired, offered to introduce a few members of the team as Rukya's and my guests, since we were on our way out to a dinner and the disco was on our way.

Gibson and one of the team members got into our car and the others made their way to the disco where Rukya and I signed in the entire British party as our guests and left saying that they were thereafter on their own and stating very clearly that they would have to take care of the bill thereafter.

The next morning, the English team was at the nets at the Wankhede Stadium. I stopped by to see them practise and was disappointed to find that neither Gibson, nor Keith Fletcher nor any of the others whom we had dropped at the disco the previous night, recognized me and, in fact, chose to ignore me, without even the courtesy of a 'hello.' Nevertheless I let it pass, joking to Rukya later that I was now convinced it was the 'brown man's burden' and that in any case, 'All Indians look alike to Westerners.'

Imagine my surprise when, a few days later, I received a bill from the discotheque for around ₹30,000 for ostensibly downing 47 large scotches for which, according to Gibson in his column, 'Botham airily signed a piece of paper thrust before him.'

When I met Gibson at the Wankhede Stadium on the first morning of the Test (27 November–1 December), I handed him the bill. He responded by saying, 'F***ing hell, it must've been 'Gorilla'...knocking back those f***ing Blood Marys.'

I said I wasn't present, so didn't know what happened after Rukya and I had dropped them off. In any case, since I had signed him and his party in only because of him (Gibson), he should settle the bill.

Over the next few days, Gibson didn't recognize me in the press box and since we were all busy covering the Test, I let the matter be, believing that he would be a gentleman and arrange for its settlement after the Test ended. (India won the Mumbai Test by 138 runs to win the series, since the other matches were all draws).

But it wasn't to be.

Forty-Seven Large Scotches

The cricket merry-go-round moved on to Bengaluru for the second Test. I accosted Pat Gibson in a manner that didn't allow him to dodge me. This time his response was, 'Botham says he will not pay.' I then reminded Gibson, who by that time had started getting cocky and was beginning to fulminate against me in his London paper (as though his readers cared!), that he was morally responsible etc., but all my entreaties fell on deaf ears.

Next was the third Test at the Feroz Shah Kotla stadium in New Delhi (Ramprakash Mehra's bailiwick). And there came the same reminder and the same reply.

Not getting anywhere, I decided to change tactics and bring the matter to the notice of the English team management. Former English Test cricketer Raman Subba Row, ever the soft-spoken and courteous gentleman, was, at the time, the assistant manager of the team.

I explained to him in detail that it wasn't the amount involved but the principle for which I was approaching him as a last resort. He assured me he would 'have a word' with Gibson and Botham and get back to me.

Fourth Test at Eden Gardens, Kolkata: Subba Row said that he was 'awaiting Botham's reply.'

> (*Sportsweek* editor, the Late Sharad Kotnis, returned from the Test narrating the endearing story of this lovely middle-aged genteel bhadralok (literally means 'a polite, well-mannered person' in Bengali, but used to denote a certain class of people, or, the haute bourgeoisie) fan who was obviously more of a soccer than cricket fan.
>
> She was seated in the front row of the stand immediately behind the press box so we could hear the conversation distinctly. The batsman hits a four to the loud applause from the stands at which, the lady engrossed in her knitting, looks up and asks in all innocence: 'Who scored the goal?')

Fifth Test at M.A. Chidambaram Stadium, Chepauk, Madras: same reminder from me to Subba Rao. Same polite brush-off.

With time running out, I approached our legal firm to prepare for the worst. They devised a strategy to serve notice to the team via the British Deputy High Commission in Mumbai and, as a desperate last resort, to attach the team's cricket gear (not during the series so as not to disrupt it—but after).

Meanwhile, summons were issued requiring presence of skipper Keith Fletcher, Ian Botham, five other England cricketers and two reporters in court, causing William Hickey of the *Daily Express* (a newspaper that belonged to a nation that proclaims itself as being the 'fountainhead of the rule of law') to lament, 'such are the mysterious ways of the Orient.'

As an ultimate course of action, the intent was to prevent the team from leaving the country to return home to England after the sixth and last Test until redress.

Sharad Kotnis, editor of *Sportsweek*, covered the sixth Test at Kanpur (also drawn) and returned to Mumbai with a 'ditto' reply from Subba Row to the effect that Botham is 'refusing to pay.'

The solicitors then served notice to the British Deputy High Commission in Mumbai, which requested time to reply. Meanwhile the team was in Kerala playing a benefit match for a retiring groundsman. Even as the match was in progress, we received word—from the British Deputy High Commission—that the English team management had agreed to settle the bill and that the bill was to be shared equally by the players.

While thanking the legation, *Sportsweek* replied that the full amount would be donated to the Cheshire Home in Pune, of which England's Prince Philip was chief patron, stressing that the dispute was never over money but one involving a principle.

In a Lighter Vein

This reminds me of the gourmand who walks into a Spanish restaurant. He is seated next to a bullfighter gorging on luscious sweetbread (giant-sized bull testicles).

His mouth watering, he asks the waiter to get him a similar dish.

'It's finished, sir,' the waiter whispers into his ears, 'it's our signature dish...if you wish to order it, you must come at noon when we open. You see, this restaurant belongs to the matador sitting next to you. He fights the bulls every morning and brings in the testicles for lunch for our special guests.'

The customer returns promptly at noon the next day. With great gusto, he tells the waiter. 'Remember me? I was here yesterday and had ordered those delicious-looking testicles but they were finished. You asked me to come at noon, so here I am—at noon sharp. I'd like to order them now.'

'But señor, we do not have special meat balls today.'

'What? What do you mean you don't have special meat balls? You had promised them to me yesterday!' The gourmand is livid and implacable.

Unable to handle the diatribe any longer, the waiter asks the customer to wait, goes into the kitchen and returns.

'Here you are, señor, special meat balls *a la toreador* for you!' he exclaims with gusto while opening the serving dish with an exaggerated flourish.

Seeing the contents, the diner is livid. 'These are not the

> same meat balls, you nincompoop. The ones I saw yesterday were really large and juicy,' he cups his hands by way of demonstration. 'These are tiny.'
>
> 'You are right, señor", replies the waiter, 'but sometimes the bull wins!'

◆

Speaking of Henry Blofeld, the crazy-as-a-coot radio commentator of BBC's Test Match Special fame: I was covering an Ashes series match at the scenic Adelaide Oval—arguably one of the most gorgeous grounds in Australia—set in the midst of beautiful jacaranda trees along the River Torrens that dissects the Adelaide city centre from North Adelaide. It was the thrilling last day of an Ashes Test with England. At the end of the previous fourth day, Australia was poised to score an upset win.

The irrepressible 'Blowers,' as he was called, an inveterate England supporter, had said on air that he would 'eat his hat' if Australia won. As it so happened, the England batting crumbled on the last morning to hand Australia a narrow win.

At lunchtime after the match was over, Blofeld moved up to the front row of the press box, pulled out a black jacket, top hat, plate, fork and knife from his bag, put on the jacket, placed the hat on the plate and, with fork and knife in hand, grinned into the television and press cameras for a memorable photo-op.

Blofeld, now retired, was a great favourite of cricket fans (one of the stands at the Adelaide ground is named the 'Blowfly Stand' after him) for his mention of inconsequential details in his commentary such as ladies' ear rings, dresses, hairdos and the number of pink shirts in the crowd, as well as pigeons, buses, aeroplanes and helicopters over the ground. His *takia-kalaam* (catchphrase) was 'my dear old thing.'

He was awarded an OBE (Order of the British Empire), despite his indiscretion (the curse of spontaneous, stop-me-if-you-can commentators!) in 1995 when he was censored for an allegedly anti-Semitic comment live, on-air during a commentary.

On the subject of indiscretions, Blowers was guilty of committing a major one when, in one of his books, he portrayed me uncharitably for allegedly not paying him on time for some freelance work he did for *Sportsweek*.

Those were the days of strict foreign exchange regulations when Indian publications had to seek red tape-ridden permissions for even small foreign remittances.

I wasn't aware of this until I happened to chance upon the unkind reference in his book during an assignment in Australia. Upon checking with my office, *Sportsweek* editor Sharad Kotnis explained that the remittance had been caught up in bureaucratic formalities but was settled long since.

Being a 'Brown Saheb' myself (as some of my friends affectionately called me at college) I was, admittedly, browned off(!) but decided to ignore it, the only option being the legal one which just wasn't worth the time, effort, energy and expenditure involved in any litigation in our, or any other, country.

Besides, it was quite possible that the 'dear old thing' had fallen on bad times and needed the money desperately, given the hand-to-mouth existence of even celebrity freelancers such as Blofeld.

Forgive—but never forget!

Parsi-Monious

The unfailing cordiality and hospitality which we Indian cricket writers showed towards our English counterparts was never reciprocated for reasons I have never been able to fathom.

Barring a few notable journalists and occasions, we were never offered a meal or a drink, leave aside being invited to their homes.

I joked to Farokh Engineer, a Parsi himself but one who laughs uproariously at jokes about the foibles of his brethren, that the Brit journos were 'Parsi-monious.' He also cracked up at the corny suggestion that 'Adi-das' is a Parsi-Bengali joint venture between an Adi and a Das.

Speaking of which, 'Rookie' is the biggest 'leg-pull artiste' I have ever known. At Ravi Shastri's fiftieth birthday party in Mumbai, Farokh and I were having a quiet chinwag when this IPL windbag intruded magisterially, whereupon Farokh politely introduced him to me.

'Who doesn't know him,' the windbag replied referring to me and shaking my hand vigorously, 'he's a leggend (pronouncing the 'g' as in 'leg').

To this day, when Farokh and I meet, he always pulls my leg, greeting me aloud in public with, 'So how's the 'leggend'?' by way of imitating the bumptious official, even as he boisterously cracks up at my discomfiture.

Incidentally, 'Rooky' Engineer calls me his 'better looking twin brother' since some British cricket writers who covered the tour of Tony Lewis's team to India were convinced we were twin brothers.

While we have never expected from the English journos and photographers the *mehmaan nawazi* (hospitality)—as we in India know it and shower upon our journalist friends from abroad—one has always been struck by the general lack of affability, cheer, companionship and, hospitableness among our stiff upper lip counterparts in England.

This is in sharp contrast to the hail-fellow-well-met warmth experienced from journalists in the Caribbean especially, as also in Australia, New Zealand, South Africa, even Pakistan.

And to think that players and commentators from England, their own country, earn fortunes—even by their own English standards—plying their trade in India, a 'third world' country.

◈

During the Cricket World Cup in the West Indies in 2003, I was staying at the same beachfront hotel in Barbados as was Patrick Eagar, the Cambridge educated, renowned cricket photographer who is said to have covered 325 Test matches between 1965 and 2011.

We would see each other frequently at the hotel during the tournament, but Eagar would manage, at best, a constipated, condescending, half-hearted smile by way of greeting, even though *Sportsweek* was his client of long standing and from which he earned a decent income.

After returning to the Barbados hotel one evening after a game, I saw Eagar seated at the bar with some of his English friends, to be greeted again in his characteristic patronizing manner. His demeanour sparked unpleasant thoughts of victims of history, of defiant heroes, of General Dyer and Jallianwala Bagh, of Uncle Tom and helpless slaves, of 'the sun never sets on the British empire,' and of 'Rule Britannia:'

> When Britain first, at Heaven's command,
> Arose from out the azure main,
> Arose from, arose from out the azure main;
> This was the charter of the land, the charter of the Land
> And Guardian Angels sang this strain:
> Rule Britannia, rule the waves!
> Britons never, ever, ever shall be slaves.

Something snapped inside me. Enough was enough. I walked up to Eagar and his friends and—softly but firmly—gave him a piece of my mind, reminding him of what we were taught at school, about the so-called exemplary English manners, etc.

The effect was magical. Eagar was a changed man thereafter. It took just one 'boo' to put the arrogant snob in his place!

Unlike some of the uncouth cricket writers of Britain's 'gutter' press was the suave Ben Brocklehurst of the respected *The Cricketer* magazine, which thrived during his ownership and later merged with *Playfair Cricket Monthly* in 1973 before going online in 1996 and amalgamated with *Wisden Cricket Monthly* to form the *Wisden Cricketer*.

Brocklehurst was a fairly average County cricketer who went on to captain Somerset. He was an Indophile and served as an officer in the Royal Berkshire Regiment before transferring to the Indian Army. Posted to the North West Frontier, he was attacked by a bear in Kashmir and later volunteered for service in Burma where he commanded a Pashtun company and took charge of thousands of Japanese prisoners.

Rukya and I met Ben and his gracious second wife Belinda at Lord's and struck up an immediate friendship. Ben was interested in some form of association with *Sportsweek*, to discuss which we were invited to their tastefully designed home in pastoral Tunbridge Wells, Kent.

Incidentally, the picturesque rhododendron-lined ground on the periphery of Ben's home is the one at which Kapil Dev, the greatest all-rounder India has produced, scored his hurricane 175, a feat described by *Sportstar* (from the publishers of *The Hindu*) as 'almost above human possibility.'[19]

But for this hurricane knock which lifted India from an abysmal 17 for five to 266, and of which, unfortunately, no television record is available for posterity, India's historic win in the 1983 World Cup

---

[19] "On this day: Kapil Dev special at Tunbridge Wells", *Sportstar*, 18 June 2020. https://sportstar.thehindu.com/cricket/on-this-day-kapil-dev-175-india-zimbabwe-tunbridge-wells-1983-world-cup/article31854805.ece. Accessed on 10 November 2021.

would not have been possible.

The Brocklehursts linger in memory for their gentility, their gracious English old-world charm that one might have read about in English literature. They were very unlike larrikins such as Pat Gibson and his cronies, exemplifying the cliched aphorism that human beings are generally the same everywhere; what make the all-important difference are genes, upbringing and education.

◆

Then there's the peripatetic, veteran gentleman-freelancer Andy Jalil, who works for the BBC and other radio and television platforms. For many years, Andy—he comes from a mixed Indian, Pakistani and Bangladeshi background—divided his time following the sun, between the northern (UK and Ireland) and southern (Australia and New Zealand) hemispheres.

A bon vivant, Andy has covered and commented on cricket all over the world. Now semi-retired, he commentates on cricket and football and writes regular political columns for newspapers in the UK and the Middle East. He and his Irish wife Ann are good friends of ours. Zeyna and I have spent many delightful times together at their homes in London, St Neots (Cambridgeshire) and County Mayo (Ireland).

Speaking of the Irish, their prime minister is called 'Tánaiste.' Leo Varadkar, the current Tánaiste, is head of the government of Ireland and is the first Irish government leader of Indian origin. Varadkar completed his internship at KEM Hospital in Mumbai. His father, Ashok, is a medical practitioner who was born in Mumbai and moved to Leicester (UK) before settling in Ireland. His mother, Miriam Varadkar, is Irish. Leo, his parents and family moved back to India before settling in Dublin in 1973. He continues to reside there with his partner, Matthew Barrett, a doctor.

It is known that the prime minister also goes by the name 'de Varad' meaning 'of Varad.'

A Vast Wasteland

By contrast, Australia with its sparse, dispersed population (2.57 crore), is a vast wasteland where quality cricket writing is concerned; its rich cricketing culture does not translate to excellence in writing, although its cricket writers are congenial to a degree that is antithetical to many of their pretentious English counterparts.

Ray Robinson (not to be confused with boxer 'Sugar' Ray Robinson) is known as the man who changed the state of Australian cricket writing. A syndicated *Sportsweek* columnist, he ruled the roost until his retirement and the advent of Gideon Haigh, the England-born Aussie upstart who shot to fame during the Packer Revolution and laid claim to being a worthy successor, followed by Mike Coward of the old school who makes up with sincerity of purpose, what he lacks as regards turn of phrase.

Mike is among my favourite people in the Australian press boxes: warm and caring, he studied geology at the Imperial College, London, and is arguably the most erudite of all Australian cricket writers and is considered an international authority on the sport.

Mike's tribute to Peter Roebuck (who, as a writer, was perhaps in the same league as Ray Robinson and Gideon Haig) at the latter's memorial service at the Sydney Cricket Ground (SCG) remains etched in my memory. He described Roebuck as a 'humanist, social justice crusader, cricketer, cricket captain, cricket coach, mentor, writer, broadcaster, educationist and polemicist.'

I never had the pleasure of meeting Jack Fingleton, the legendary Don Bradman's batting partner and fiercest critic, who became a celebrated cricket writer after his retirement. In the 1936–37 Ashes series, he became the first batsman ever to score Test centuries in four successive innings.

According to Rohit Bhaskar of the *Hindustan Times*, the two (Bradman and Fingleton) never saw eye-to-eye and disapproved of the other's methods. Fingleton was particularly critical of Bradman for his supposed inability to counter the Bodyline tactic. However, for all his flaws, Bradman still averaged 56.57, but it wasn't good enough for Fingleton who, in his World XI, included Bradman but only as 12th man.

◆

Like England, Australia too has had its jaundiced tabloids for whom there is no greater joy than seeing the home team win at all cost.

Ask Bishan Bedi and his contemporaries and they will narrate horror stories of how the Australian players of their time would form an unholy alliance with the umpires (there were no so-called neutral umpires in those days), media and spectators to whip up a jingoistic frenzy to put pressure on visiting teams.

There are many reports of unsporting behaviour of larrikinism by boisterous local fans who, out of over enthusiasm to see their team win no matter what, would at times overstep the limits of sporting behaviour.

One such incident concerned South African opening batsman Hashim Amla, among the most sporting and gifted but, underrated, Proteas batsman in South African cricket history. Not only was he barracked by rowdy fans who termed him 'kaffir' (meaning 'heathen' and which, along with 'coolie' is the most offensive racist word for a non-white in South Africa), he was termed a 'terrorist'—for his flowing black beard—by intemperate former Australian cricketer-turned commentator Dean Jones, now deceased.

Dean Jones is best remembered for his 210 in Chennai (then Madras) in 1986, scored despite suffering from dehydration in the oppressively hot and humid conditions and as the result of which he was frequently vomiting on the pitch. This score remains the highest Test score by an Australian in India. After the match, Jones was reportedly put on an intravenous drip.

Legendary Sri Lankan off-spinner Muttiah Muralitharan, too, was given the whole enchilada of racist taunts and jibes on two tours of Australia, prompting him to announce that he would never tour Australia again, a decision he afterwards reconsidered.

Of Two-Fingered Salutes Down Under

Despite being an old cricket chestnut, the Aussie 'two finger salute' story concerning the jovial spin bowler Bhagwat Chandrasekhar and raffish Australian crowds bears repetition even though it has been around international cricket grounds a few times over.

I covered the 1977–78 series played by Bishan Bedi's team in Australia against a home Test side debilitated by the migration of its leading players to Kerry Packer's World Series Cricket competition. Bobby Simpson, at age 41, was recalled from retirement to reinforce the Australian team and, by squeaking a narrow 3–2 victory, denied India its best chance ever to beat Australia in Australia.

According to the Indian camp, the 'Dirty Tricks Department' of the Australian Board, in an attempt to destabilize and demoralize, had spread the canard through the tabloid press that ace Indian spinner Chandrasekhar's bowling action was suspect and that a hawk's eye was being kept on it.

In a match of fluctuating fortunes, the Indians had a chance of winning, with Australia needing 339 in the fourth innings after Bedi had snared opening batsman John Dyson late on the fourth evening.

Tony Mann, the Australian leg break and googly wrist spinner from Perth (he batted left-handed), who played only four Tests in his all-too-brief Test career, was sent out to bat at number three as nightwatchman and steered Australia to a thrilling two-wicket victory, with a doughty knock of 105. He was only the second man in history to score a century in a Test match after being sent in as lower-order batsman.

Imagine the tension when play resumed with the *jadugar* (magician) Indian spin trio comprising Bishan Bedi, Bhagwat Chandrasekhar and Erapalli Prasanna sniffing victory and bowling with their tails up.

If one were to go by the version of the Indian team, there were at least three instances of Tony Mann being out because of plumb leg before wicket (LBW), which Australian umpires Robin Bailhache and Dick French nixed despite the vociferous protestations of the Indian fielders. After his third—sanguine—appeal was turned down, a visibly furious Chandrashekhar snatched his cap from umpire Bailhache's hands and went to field at his customary third leg/fine leg position. Seeing this *natak* (drama), the Aussie cheerleaders started chanting on cue 'Chandra Chucker, Chandra Chucker' to which the normally timid Chandra angrily responded with the internationally recognized two-finger salute.

The sizeable Indian contingent included a vernacular radio commentator: an innocent abroad, who was unschooled in the crude local mannerisms, this being his first trip Down Under.

I have it on good authority from colleagues in the commentators' box that the then novice, desi commentator described the incident thus:

'*Ab Chandrasekhar fielding karne jaa rahe hain...aur darshak naare laga rahe hain, "Chandra chucker Chandra chucker."* (Chandrasekhar is now going to field and the crowd is chanting, "Chandra chucker, Chandra chucker.")

'*Aur Chandra jawaab de rahe hain: woh ek baar nahin, do baar out the.*' (And Chandra, with two fingers pointing upwards, is responding: he was out, not just once, but twice.)

When the Indian team arrived in Sydney for the fourth Test, the irrepressible Bishan Bedi narrated the incident in typical uproarious manner to a friend from the press who passed it on for publication. In those days, *The Sydney Morning Herald* newspaper would carry a sudsy daily front-page column called 'Column 8.' On that particular day, the leak featured in the eighth column of the front page and was a variant of the 'fifth column,' a term that signifies 'betrayal' or activities that belie a quality reminiscent of 'backstabbing.' Needless to say, the published story caused much amusement wherever the Indian team played on that tour. It was easily the crème de la crème of all cricket yarns in Australia that year!

◆

The Western Australia Cricket Association (WACA) ground is located close to the scenic Swan River and is known for the fruit flies that can be discomfiting to the players.

I recall Chandrasekhar telling me of the time he was facing the ferocious Jeff 'Thommo' Thompson at the ground when a fly decided to settle on his nose. *'Main to bhaag gaya,'* (I ran away) Chandra said, stressing that his life was more precious than scoring runs which, in any event, was an impossibility given the fact that the freak spin bowler was the butt of many jokes concerning his timorous batting.

Chandra's innumerable Australian fans presented him an oversized bat with a large round hole where the sweet spot should have been and which the ever-smiling Chandra, good sport that he was, accepted graciously.

The WACA ground is also famous for the Freemantle Doctor or Freo Doctor—the Australian vernacular term for the wafts of cooling afternoon wind that blows from the sea during the summer months and is known to assist pace bowlers bowling into the breeze.

Four Seasons in a Day

Traditionally, the Melbourne Test starts on Boxing Day, the day after Christmas which is celebrated on 25 December. Incidentally, the day has nothing to do with the sport of boxing as we know it and originated as a holiday to give gifts to the poor (in boxes). Today it is known primarily as a shopping holiday.

Boxing Day has its own special significance in the Australian cricketing calendar, and the Melbourne Cricket ground has its own folklore and traditions connected with it. The Boxing Day Test is played in a unique holiday atmosphere but with all the gravity of a solemn occasion.

The Melbourne Cricket Ground (also known colloquially as 'MCG' or 'The G'), which was established in 1853, has a capacity of 90,000 seats (down from its original capacity of 125,000), and also hosts Australian rules football, soccer, the Rugby Union League, lawn bowls and my favourite sport, squash.

The press box has efficient air conditioning units as well as heaters to keep the fastidious journos comfortable in a city that is notorious for often dishing up four climates on any given day. Once, after trudging through the lawns surrounding the stadium in the pouring rain, I took my seat in the heated box at 10 a.m., at which point the heaters were turned on. Then, as the temperature soared soon after lunch for an hour or two, they switched to air conditioners, only to make way, again, for the heaters in the evening. Such is the notoriously inclement Melbourne weather.

◆

Various versions of the Gavaskar 'walkout' incident during the Melbourne Test of 1981 have been doing the rounds over the years, but I have it on good authority from the legend himself that he is truly contrite for his aberrant behaviour in the heat of the moment as expressed by him to a TV channel then, even though he faulted Dennis Lillee, the bowler, for his 'extremely provocative and unsportsmanlike behaviour.'

Gavaskar was given out LBW at 80 to Lillee by rookie Australian umpire Rex Whitehead, standing in only his third Test. The decision riled the Indian captain who was in the middle of a rough patch form-wise and already smarting from a series of unfair decisions. According to Gavaskar, it was aggravating all the more because of the bowler's uncouth behaviour, which prompted him to prod batting partner Chetan Chauhan to walk off in protest, a move which, had it succeeded, would have triggered off a situation of seismic proportions akin to the 'Monkeygate' argy-bargy in 2008.

Almost 40 years later to the day, Gavaskar cleared the air on the infamous walkout telling a Melbourne television channel that it was Lillee's 'get lost' call and not his LBW dismissal that prompted him to storm off.

'The misconception is that I was upset at the LBW decision,' said Gavaskar. 'Yes, it was upsetting. But the walk-off happened only because as I had gone past Chetan (Chauhan) on the way to the change-rooms, the Australians gave me a spray. They told me to get lost which is when I went back and asked Chetan to walk off with me.'[20]

I have seen replays of the incident during the writing of these memoirs, and it is obvious from hindsight and slow-motion replays that the Indian captain had indeed played the ball. Also, there was blatant provocation from the combative Lillee who later became a great friend of India during his 25-year stint with the MRF Pace

---

[20]'Jibe from Australian Player, Not LBW Decision Caused Walkout in 1981 Melbourne Test: Sunil Gavaskar', *Scroll.in*, 1 Jan 2021, https://scroll.in/field/982905/jibe-from-australian-player-not-lbw-decision-caused-walkout-in-1981-melbourne-test-sunil-gavaskar. Accessed on 10 November 2021.

Bowling Academy in Chennai. 'Yes, I was disappointed,' said Lillee when asked about whether he would have liked to work with the BCCI, in an article that announced the news of him stepping down from the MRF post, 'I like to do things my way and sometimes that frightens people.'[21]

In his tour report to the BCCI, team manager Shahid Ali Khan Durrani said he was worried when he saw the attempted walkout. He said: 'Fortunately for India, a very ugly situation was averted which could have caused India and the BCCI a great deal of embarrassment.'[22] For his deft handling of some volatile situations that had arisen in the course of his career involving the Indian High Commissions and the Indian and foreign press, Durrani was awarded the Vishisht Seva Medal by President Neelam Sanjiva Reddy in 1982.

> **MORE SHEEP THAN HUMANS**
>
> There's this other story, also time-worn, from Bhagwat Chandrasekhar (and I have no reason to disbelieve him), which concerns the New Zealand umpire who believed he would be considered not worth his salt if he ever adjudged a compatriot batsman out LBW.
>
> Chandra speaks of this series in New Zealand, wherein both umpires, as per the practice in those days, were Kiwis. The subject of this narrative was at his patriotic best, with appeal after appeal against the batsmen, his fellow countrymen, disallowed.
>
> Finally, the batsman is clean bowled at which Chandra bellows a loud 'Howzat?' The umpire is bemused and says, 'He's bowled', to which Chandra retorts, 'But is he out?'

---

[21]'Lillee to End Association with MRF Pace Foundation', ESPNcricinfo, 26 June 2012, https://www.espncricinfo.com/story/india-news-dennis-lillee-to-end-association-with-mrf-pace-foundation-570048. Accessed on 10 November 2021.
[22]Santosh Suri, 'My Stand Vindicated: Durrani on Gavaskar Walkout', *The Times of India*, 29 December 2014, https://timesofindia.indiatimes.com/sports/new-zealand-in-india-2016/top-stories/my-stand-vindicated-durrani-on-gavaskar-walkout/articleshow/45674208.cms. Accessed on 10 November 2021.

My 'outlaws'—that's how I tease my in-laws—come from New Zealand, but I'm an unabashed admirer of their picturesque country and gentle, compassionate people. I've often felt that their admirable traits as good and exemplary people must have something to do with the fact that they live far removed from the vast majority of the flawed human beings that inhabit this planet.

An outstanding example of this is the respectful and cordial manner in which they coexist with their Māori brethren. Another demonstration of this was the extreme tact and compassion with which their prime minister Jacinda Ardern handled the insane and inhuman gunning down of 51 innocent people and the attempted murder of 40 others at two mosques in Christchurch by a terrorist on 15 March 2019.

On a lighter note, there was the exemplary spirit of sportsmanship, in the highest tradition of the game, shown by their cricket captain Kane Williamson when asinine interpretation of the rules of the game denied them a well-deserved victory over England in the 'tied' final of the Cricket World Cup at Lord's in 2019. The Kiwis were shattered emotionally but remained magnanimous in defeat.

A popular tweet that was making the rounds in the aftermath of that match described Williamson as someone who 'Never sledges opposition, never shouts at his own players, never fights with umpires, never gives up. The most respected captain of WC.' Another widely shared post on Twitter said, 'When the going gets tough; when the storm takes over uprooting everyone, you'll see a tiny warrior standing still, fearless. That's Kane Williamson for you.'

Regarding the upsetting result match, the ever-graceful Kane Williamson said, 'It was an amazing game to be a part of and the aftermath of the game was very difficult to understand. You sign up and play by rules and you move on and look forward to next challenges and our focus is on that only.'[23] This is so reminiscent of

---

[23]'T20 World Cup: Kane Williamson Says New Zealand Have "Moved On" from 2019 World Cup Heartbreak', *Hindustan Times*, 9 November 2021, https://www.hindustantimes.com/cricket/t20-world-cup-kane-williamson-says-new-zealand-have-moved-on-from-2019-world-cup-heartbreak-101636450873314.html. Accessed on 10 November 2021.

the other indomitable Kiwi, Edmund Hillary of Mount Everest fame, who was said to be full of worldly wisdom. He spent much of his life to support the Sherpa community, the unsung heroes of Himalayan climbing.

New Zealand also had the prolific Dick Brittenden, as fair a writer as you could hope to meet, and the West Indies the incomparable Tony Cozier whose dulcet voice and honeyed Caribbean intonations became the voice of cricket all over the world.

Cozier too was a fecund cricket writer and regular contributor to *Sportsweek*. A generous host, he often invited me to his Barbados home where he never tired of singing the praises of Indian rum, something he considered infinitely superior to its Jamaican counterpart, which he considered grossly over-rated.

Then there was the unassuming and soft-spoken Tony Becca, sports editor of the *Jamaica Observer* who covered cricket for more than 40 years. He covered the remarkable exploits of the all-conquering West Indies cricket team and was inducted into the Cricket Hall of Fame for his contribution to the development of the game in the United States.

◆

> **ANIMAL LOVERS**
>
> It would be grossly unfair to suggest that all English cricket writers—or, for that matter, most, if not all English people—are colour conscious. In fact, one has come across any number of kind, refined, tolerant, compassionate people in Old Blighty.
>
> (I have often wondered if the epithet is derived from the hobson-jobson 'Vilayati' meaning 'of or from Vilayat', or its corrupt version 'Bilayat,' meaning 'England.')
>
> If one were to apply the theory that animal lovers are kinder, gentler and more caring specimens of Homo sapiens, the fact that Britain is one of the most animal-friendly countries and has one of the strictest animal welfare laws in the world, much more so than other so-called civilized countries, tells its own tale.

The Chappells

Adelaide is home to the legendary cricketing brothers—Ian, who captained Australia with distinction (and has been a *Sportsweek* columnist since the last millennium), Greg, former controversial Indian Test coach, arguably among the most stylish batsmen Australia has produced, and Trevor.

In 1981, Greg had ordered younger brother Trevor to bowl that infamous underhand delivery, the 'Mullygrubber,'—it was an event that has since then gone down in cricketing history as a matter of shame and disgrace. The gambit prevented New Zealand batsman Brian McKechnie from getting under the delivery with sufficient power and elevation to hit the six off the last ball of the match against Australia and winning that one-day international.

I was present during the incident, which took place in the final of the Benson and Hedges World Series Cup at the Melbourne Cricket Ground.

New Zealand required six runs off the last ball to win the match and, being a traditionalist, I was horrified to see the display of utterly unsportsmanlike conduct that denied the visiting team a chance to score a thrilling win.

Underarm bowling was banned by the ICC as a result, as it was thereafter deemed to be against the spirit of the game. However, the technique is allowed if it has been agreed to by both teams before commencement of the match. A delivery bowled is deemed a no-ball if it rolls before reaching the popping crease as mentioned in Law 24 of the Laws of the Cricket.

Lord's—among the Best

Of all the cricket grounds in the world, according to me, Lord's would have to rank among the best for its old-world charm, its iconic Long Room and the 'noblesse oblige' decorum of its dignified Members' enclosure, although the space-age design of its new press box is incongruous with the rest of its charming Victorian architecture.

At the risk of sounding sentimental, the historic Brabourne Stadium at the CCI in Mumbai, ranks, for old stagers like me, among the best in the world, if only for warm memories of being a wide-eyed child in its East stand during the Pentangular tournament.

And, of course, for later abiding memories of the West Indian greats such as the three Ws—Worrell, Weekes, Walcott—Wes Hall and Roy Gilchrist, Sonny Ramadhin, Alfred Valentine, Pakistanis Mohammed Hanif and Fazal Mahmood, not to mention C.K. Nayudu, D.B. Deodhar, the Vijays—Merchant and Hazare—Lala Amarnath, Vinoo Mankad, Rusi Modi, Polly Umrigar, Datoo Phadkar, Hemu Adhikari and others too many to name.

Unsavoury incidents from well-known cricket grounds are also too numerous to narrate. Unfortunately, the world-renowned Brabourne Stadium lost its sheen on 5 November 1969, when off-spinner Srinivas Venkataraghavan was given out caught behind by umpire Shambhu Pan in response to a half-hearted appeal by Brian Taber, the Australian wicketkeeper.

All hell broke loose with Ajit Wadekar at the non-striker's end demanding an explanation from the umpire. Devraj Puri, the Delhi based commentator criticized the decision in the strongest terms with thousands in the 20,000-capacity stadium listening on their transistor radios (this was before the days of mass ownership of television; the advent of national telecasts and colour televisions happened around the 1982 Asian Games).

With India facing imminent defeat, it was the spark that ignited shameful behaviour from the spectators who hurled bottles, chairs and bricks and lit fires. The ground was littered with glass and stones while the police chased the crowd off the field.

The scorers refused to continue after even covering their heads did not work. The fire brigade was called in and a riot squad formed a line between the dressing rooms and the pitch. The reputation of the Brabourne Stadium lay in tatters.

London's *The Spin*, *The Guardian's* weekly cricket email, reported the following on the incident:[24]

> Through it all the Australia captain Bill Lawry refused to go anywhere. Play continued as seats and stones rained down on the outfield, and the fires in the stands started to spread thick, dark smoke across the field. At one point Graham McKenzie aborted his run-up after a large rock whistled just past his head. A Test that had already featured two crowd fatalities–a 50-year-old on the first day and a 35-year-old on day three, both apparently of natural causes – had taken an unexpectedly violent turn. Play ended soon afterwards, but the Australians stayed on the field for another 20 minutes while police cleared the area, clutching stumps for self-defence, before being ushered to the dressing rooms through an improvised tunnel formed of police shields.

The bad blood between the sides continued during the series, climaxing at the Eden Gardens, Kolkata, where an approximate 25,000 people

---

[24] Simon Burnton, 'How Umpire Sparked Riot in India V Australia Series of Deadly Disorder', *The Spin*, 5 November 2019, https://www.theguardian.com/sport/2019/nov/05/india-australia-disputed-decision-deadly-disorder-the-spin. Accessed on 10 November 2021.

had camped overnight in group in expectation of seeing the fourth day's play. By the time the police arrived and brought the situation under control with the aid of repeated lathi charges and tear gas, six people were dead, around 100 injured.

> The game still continued, and Australia romped to a 10-wicket win. The next day, as their players travelled to the airport by coach, they came under attack. "Before we had time to collect ourselves, rocks the size of half house-bricks were smashing into both sides of the bus, shattering nearly all the windows," wrote Lawry. "The driver tried to accelerate up the hill while all members of the team flung themselves to the floor, wondering whether they would be dragged out and stoned to death if the bus stalled. As we reached the top of the hill we regained our seats with as much dignity as possible. Looking back, we could see a group of about 100 Indians waving their arms angrily at us."[25]

---

[25]Ibid.

Sydney Cricket Ground

The cricket ground at Sydney, where I lived sporadically for a decade at the start of this millennium has hosted Test matches between Australia and England since the dawn of the Ashes in 1882.

The Sydney Cricket Ground (SCG) Museum is a wonderful repository of sporting activities that occurred on the historic grounds since the mid-1880s. It also provides an incredible insight into the history of the Ashes, its greatest moments and the way the series has always been linked to the SCG.

The ground is undistinguished for the most part. Apart from its familiarity to me stemming out of frequent visits to the beautiful city of Sydney during Test matches, it lingers in memory for rather trivial reasons.

There are the convivial meetings of the Primary Club, founded in 1974 by Richie Benaud and other cricket lovers, an organization whose fundamental aim is to give those with disabilities, the opportunity to engage in physical activities. Traditionally, the club meets over breakfast before the commencement of Test matches at the SCG premises. A distinguished cricketing personality from the country of the visiting team playing in that particular Test is invited to speak, after which members proceed to the adjacent cricket ground for the Test. The meetings are held in an atmosphere of typical Australian bonhomie among people from different backgrounds, and passion for the game is palpable in all its proceedings.

I was invited as guest of friend Raj Singh Dungarpur, former BCCI president, to attend a Primary Club meeting, and later, to join the club. Membership is far from exclusive in the sense that anybody who has scored a 'duck' in his cricketing career at any level is eligible. And I certainly was qualified!

My other reason is the ground's famous 'Hill', now demolished, originally one of two spectator mounds on opposite sides of the ground, which became known as the 'Bob' Stand during the Depression years, because it cost one shilling (a bob) to enter.

In time, the Hill gained international renown, or shall we say, notoriety, for its fiercely partisan, raucous, beer-swilling crowds, the cacophony from which increased in direct proportion to the proceedings under the oppressive Antipodean sun. Pleasurable consumption of the amber brew inevitably brought pressure upon bladders necessitating frequent visits to the toilets that were nowhere in the vicinity of the open enclosure.

Solution? Use the empties. Disposal? Toss them in the air and hard luck if it results in a shower of sickening, malodorous rain shower on someone's head!

Quite a 'heady' experience—if idiotic pun be excused!

A Many Splendoured Game

I have no hesitation in saying that, of all cricket spectators in the world—with the exception of the Barmy Army, the raucous latter-day phenomenon—the English are, by far, the most knowledgeable, appreciative and sporting in the world.

The British fans' understanding of the nuances, tactics, subtleties, ebb and flow of the game as well as the traditional spectators' grasp of its history and traditions, is unparalleled. However, English cricketers at the top level are almost universally considered moaners and bad losers, if not downright cheats (observe the 'Vaseline,' 'sand-paper in pocket' incidents and the like!). Cricket writers of the quality press, on the other hand, are generally acknowledged as being the most balanced and accomplished, but its tabloid press, the most partisan, if not outright jingoistic.

Sydney Cricket Ground

Following the blitzkrieg of Kerry Packer's World Series Cricket, the Australian Board was quick to make up with the media mogul and adopt, for unabashed financial reasons, what former Australian greats derisively termed the 'pajama game.'

Be that as it may, as poignantly pointed out in The Guardian, the 'World Series Cricket wasn't just a cricket story; it was one of the great untold stories in modern Australian history, a revolution which fundamentally changed the way that cricket was watched, played and sold in a nation whose national cricket team predates the nation itself by some 23 years.'[26]

The cash-rich BCCI was characteristically quick off the mark to seize the money-making opportunity which came its way from the opening of financial floodgates of Limited Overs, Twenty20 and, now, Pink Ball cricket.

Its English counterpart, however, initially stuck to its guns, sacrificing filthy lucre for tradition until its recent avarice-driven capitulation.

Apart from being a tongue-twister, the Indian cricket Board's nomenclature—Board of Control for Cricket in India—is toffee-nosed in these egalitarian times, especially given the efforts of its world body to globalize the game. Worse, the organization betrays its overweening reluctance to relinquish its vice-like 'Control' in cricketing affairs—both in letter and spirit! Why not just call it 'Cricket India,' like Cricket Australia, New Zealand Cricket, Cricket South Africa, Sri Lanka Cricket, Bangladesh Cricket Board and the like?

One of the most appropriate distinctions that I have heard drawn between the traditional five-day game and its slam-bang progeny is: 'Limited overs cricket is like a Britney Spears pop number; Test cricket a Beethoven symphony.'

---

[26]S.B. Tang, 'Why Gideon Haigh is So Important for Cricket Writing', *The Guardian*, 19 January 2014, https://www.theguardian.com/sport/blog/2014/jan/20/gideon-haigh-cricket-writer. Accessed on 11 November 2021.

Wanderers

Cricket spectators in South Africa are rather staid and their grounds, nondescript, barring the Wanderers Stadium in Johannesburg, known as the 'Bull Ring' (for its intimidating atmosphere for visiting teams).

In the florid words of Daniel Gallan in quarterly cricket magazine *The Nightwatchman*: 'This is the Bull Ring. Not merely a cricket stadium but an ode to the elements. A cathedral that pays homage to the full fury of nature's brilliance. All that is thrilling about this meandering sport is condensed here. This ground has grown up in the City of Gold and now embodies the impatience of its people, never missing a chance to hit the fast-forward button on a stagnant day's play. No other venue in the world can match the firework of a breathless showstopper at the Wanderers.'[27]

I was fortunate to have witnessed the 2003 ICC Cricket World Cup—the eighth of the international championship, co-hosted by South Africa, Zimbabwe and Kenya, and the first to be played in Africa. It was my first and only cricketing experience at the Wanderers. India, who had toured New Zealand before this World Cup and been subjected to a torrential barrage of short-pitched Kiwi bowling on fast, bouncy wickets, had reached the final against Australia by drawing upon

---

[27] Daniel Gallan, 'The Bull Ring: An intimate portrait of The Wanderers Stadium', *Wisden* (originally published *in The Nightwatchman*, 25 January 2020. https://wisden.com/the-nightwatchman/the-bull-ring-an-intimate-portrait-of-the-wanderers-stadium. Accessed on 11 November 2021.

deep inner reserves of blood and toil. But the rampaging Australians, astutely led by Ricky Ponting, subjected India to a crushing defeat in what turned out to be a hopelessly one-sided final.

Put in to bat by Sourav Ganguly on a damp wicket as the result of overnight rain, Australian batsmen Matthew Hayden and Roy Gilchrist, followed by Ponting and Damien Martyn, lost no time in going on the rampage, targeting Zaheer Khan, in particular, and Javagal Srinath who were on a hiding to nothing.

Gilchrist scored 57, Hayden, 37 and Martyn, 88. Ponting remained unbeaten on 140 and Australia finished their 50 overs on 359 for two and dismissed India for 234 in 39.2 overs to register a convincing 125-run win, their third victory overall in the World Cup.

Sehwag scored 82, but Sachin Tendulkar, who was named Man of the Tournament with a total of 669 runs at an average of 66.90, could manage only four off five balls, an early setback from which India never recovered despite a doughty 47 from Rahul Dravid.

◆

Speaking of Tendulkar, another GOAT (along with Gavaskar, Kapil Dev and, in my opinion, Rahul Dravid), would have to be counted among the most modest, gentle, soft-spoken cricketers of worth that India has ever produced.

Whereas Sunil Gavaskar, who studied at Mumbai's St Xavier's High School and, later, College, was quick-witted and gifted with a felicitous turn of phrase, he could be acerbic whenever his national and/or personal pride were concerned.

On the other hand, of that particular generation, Tendulkar, Rahul Dravid, V.V.S Laxman, Anil Kumble and even Sourav Ganguly to a lesser extent (barring his shirt-removing episode at the Lord's balcony in 2002 after India won the Natwest Trophy) were the epitome of grace, modesty and sportsmanship.

Sourav Ganguly's shirt-swirling incident at the Lord's balcony has become a part of Indian cricketing folklore. Psychologists have different interpretations of it, as do social scientists (in terms of contemporary Indian youth manifesting pride and self-confidence). On his part, Ganguly ('Dada'), the affable former Indian captain has revealed—

rather simplistically—that it was a spontaneous retaliation to England all-rounder Andrew Flintoff's similar reaction at the Wankhede Stadium field on an earlier occasion to celebrate his team's victory over India to draw the 2002 one-day series 3–3.

'Bada Rona Aata Hai'
(Feel Like Shedding Tears)

Speaking of decorum, people management skills and flair for public affairs, these came naturally to Fatehsinghrao Gaekwad, who was to the manor born.

The former ruler of Baroda went as manager of the Indian cricket team to England in 1959 at the age of only 29 (many members of the team were older than him) and although the performance of Dattaji Gaekwad team's was less than distinguished, it won innumerable friends for Indian cricket if only for its conduct and bearing.

The captain was Datta Gaekwad, father of Test cricketer Anshuman Gaekwad who played for India as opening batsman and was later appointed Test coach.

The manager was nicknamed 'Jackie Baroda' by the *gora sahibs* (white men) who found his august name (another example of the Britishers' ridiculous penchant for giving us natives absurd nicknames)—Lieutenant-Colonel Farzand-i-Khas-i-Daulat-i-Inglishia, Shrimant Maharaja Fatehsinghrao Prataprao Gaekwad, Sena Khas Khel Shamsher Bahadur, Maharaja of Baroda—quite a mouthful!

Here's how Pradip Dhole, medical practitioner and life-long cricket lover describes Fatehsinghrao Gaekwad:[28]

---

[28]Pradip Dhole, 'Fatehsinghrao Gaekwad (Jackie Baroda): Youngest BCCI President', Cricket Country, 28 July 2016, https://www.cricketcountry.com/articles/fatehsinghrao-gaekwad-jackie-baroda-youngest-bcci-president-477006. Accessed on 11 November 2021.

When the Indian tours of Pakistan for 1978–79 and 1982–83 were planned, given the sensitive issues pertaining to the long-standing political rivalry between the two countries, it was felt that the manager for these tours would have to be a man of unimpeachable integrity and proven skills as far as public dealings were concerned, and a man who would be able to carry off the difficult assignments with the requisite aplomb.

As the members of the touring parties would later testify again and again, Fatehsinghrao had carried out these difficult assignments in an exemplary fashion. That both the series passed off amicably and without any untoward incidents was as much a tribute to the sporting skills of the players as to the diplomatic skills of the manager, who had to work very hard at ensuring that the players could concentrate solely on the job at hand without having to concern themselves with affairs off the pitch.

As one who covered the two cricket tours of Pakistan, I can testify to Dhole's assessment. The affection and respect, bordering on reverence, that people across the border showed towards 'Jackie' had to be seen to be believed. Many of them, some his former subjects from Baroda, who emigrated to Pakistan, would fall at his feet out of reverence.

I got to know Jackie rather well on tour, and we would spend many delightful evenings conducting a post mortem of the day's play in Urdu, a language he loved and was fairly proficient in. I would be unfailingly enchanted by the opening lines of his addresses to local Pakistani audiences. After being introduced to the invariably fawning audience, he would smile beatifically and proclaim solemnly: *'As-salaam alaikum'* (May God's grace be upon you). Then, stroking his designer beard, and after a practised, prolonged pause: *'Bada rona aata hai'* (Tears come to my eyes).

Round One would unvariably go to Jackie. The audience would be eating out of his hand thereafter.

◆

Fatehsinghrao Gaekwad's achievements as a right-handed batsman were rather modest: he played 28 first-class matches, scoring 831 runs with a highest of 99 at an average of 21.30 that included five 50s.

He held eight catches and took a solitary wicket.

Fatehsinghrao cut his cricketing teeth at a young age; his contemporaries in the Ranji Trophy were D.B. Deodhar, C.K. Nayudu, C.S. Nayudu, Gogumal Kishenchand, Vijay Hazare, Vijay Merchant, Ghulam Ahmed and Amir Elahi (who emigrated to Pakistan).

After retirement from cricket and following the abolition of titular state rulers, Fatehsingh served in public office as Member of Parliament, parliamentary secretary of the defence ministry, chancellor of the Maharaja Sayajirao University of Baroda, and chairman of the board of governors of the National Institute of Sports (NIS, Patiala).

At the age of 33, he became the youngest president of the BCCI from 1963 to 1966.

'Jackie' spent the last years of his life engaged in conservation of natural resources, particularly the native fauna of India, which led to enactment of legislations such as of the Wildlife (Protection) Act and the Forest Conservation Act. Despite his preoccupations, he seldom missed our *Sportsweek* and *Mid-Day* soirees.

A wildlife hunter in his younger days (as for me I have never approved of the cowardly, one-sided sport, which I consider cruel), Baroda switched over to photography and would often joke that he had made the civilized jump to 'shooting with his camera'.

Bon vivant 'Jackie' passed away at Mumbai's Breach Candy Hospital in 1988 at the young age of 58. Being away on assignment in Dubai, I could not attend the funeral of a dear friend and exemplary human being from whom I learnt poise and finesse.

His regal but affectionate demeanour remains ever fresh in memory and his sonorous *'bohot rona aata hai'* still rings in my ears.

We Came Down from the Trees for the Booze

There are no cricketing venues in the world as enjoyable as those in the Caribbean: Kensington Oval (Bridgetown), Queens Park Oval (Port of Spain), Bourda (Georgetown), Sabina Park (Kingston), St Johns (Antigua) and Sir Vivian Richards Stadium (North Sound). And fans none as friendly, fun-loving, rambunctious, sporting, even discerning as the West Indian cricket lovers.

It is said that we, Homo sapiens 'came down from the trees for booze.' This is nowhere else as demonstrable as at a cricket match featuring the West Indies team in the Caribbean.

According to Andrew Curry, a Berlin-based journalist who writes for a variety of publications including the *National Geographic*, 'The story of humanity's love affair with alcohol goes back to a time before farming—to a time before humans, in fact. Our taste for tipple may be a hardwired evolutionary trait that distinguishes us from most other animals.' He adds that, 'Alcohol isn't just a mind-altering drink: It has been a prime mover of human culture from the beginning, fueling the development of arts, language, and religion'[29]—and, one might even add, sport.

---

[29] Andrew Curry, 'A 9,000-Year Love Affair: How a Passion for Alcohol May Be Part of Our DNA', *National Geographic Traveller India*, 1 March 2017, https://natgeotraveller.in/a-9000-year-love-affair-how-a-love-for-alcohol-maybe-part-of-our-dna/. Accessed on 12 November 2021.

It is Curry's belief that ethanol, the ingredient in alcohol, 'makes us feel good. Ethanol helps release serotonin, dopamine, and endorphins in the brain, chemicals that make us happy and less anxious.'

So it is with the average uninhibited West Indian cricket fan (and fans of other sports, I dare say!).

Although, as a pampered member of the press corps who write on cricket, I was, during my working days, eligible for entry to press boxes. In the Caribbean, however, I refused to watch a match from the comfortable confines of the box, preferring instead the sights, smells and sounds of the spectator stands. In the stands, I have quaffed rum, sung Calypso songs, and shaken a leg with wild abandon to the most primordial beats imaginable with the friendliest, ingenuous, fun-loving people.

They are the salt of the earth, even though, at times, their support for their team takes extreme form, as when they bayed for the blood of the Indian batsmen of an earlier era, when facing the fearsome West Indian fast bowlers of the '70s and '80s.

My father, Justice of the Peace and founder of the *Inquilab*, Abdul Hamid Nizamuddin Ansari.

My mother Amina Begum Ansari.

Lofty aspirations.

Graduating with a Master of Arts and Bachelor of Laws degree.

At the Epsom Derby in the UK.

Top: With Rukya at our wedding in June 1960.
Bottom: (Fifth from left) With Pandit Jawaharlal Nehru at a Ciba Geigy inaugural function at Goregaon, Mumbai, during my tenure at the advertising firm of J. Walter Thompson.

Top: With Mansoor Ali Khan Pataudi and Rukya.
Bottom: With Rukya and West Indies Test cricket captain Clive Lloyd at a *Sportsweek* award ceremony at the Cricket Club of India.

Top: With Imran Khan at a New Year's function at the Willingdon Sports Club, Mumbai.
Bottom: With Vivian Richards at a hotel in Kolkata.

Top: With West Indian Test cricketers Jeff Dujon (left) and Michael Holding.
Bottom: With politician and cricket administrator Seshrao Wankhede after whom Mumbai's international cricket stadium is named.

Top: With Tony Greig in Sydney, Australia.
Bottom: At the Ansari home with the Indian cricket team with their wives before their departure to Australia in 1976: (left to right) Brijesh Patel, G.R. Vishwanath, Sunil Gavaskar, Bishan Singh Bedi, Anshuman Gaekwad and myself.

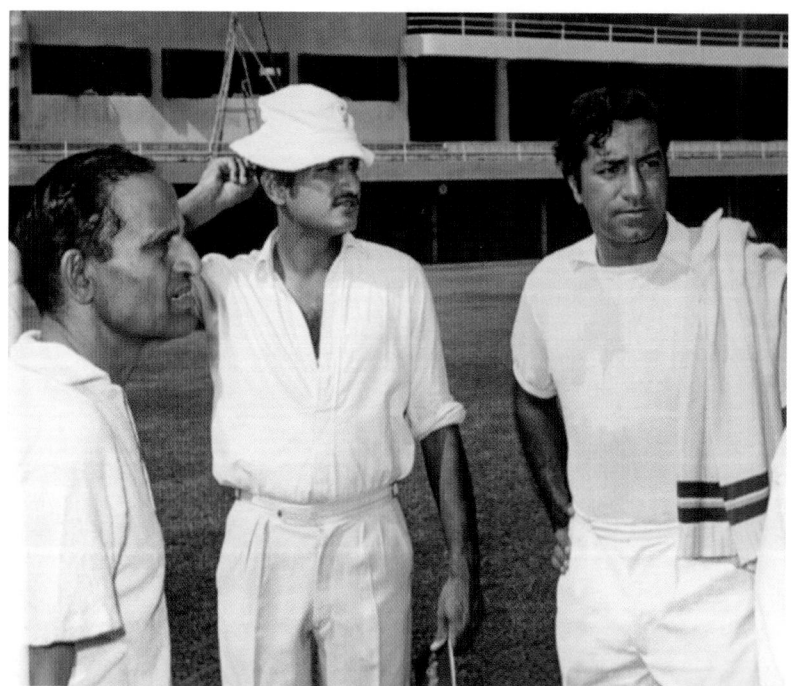

Top: At the Brabourne Stadium with (left to right) former Test captain and coach Hemu Adhikari and former India captain Ajit Wadekar.

Bottom: At the premier of film *Shalimar*: Seated at the table is Rukya (second from left) and Gina Lollobrigida (on right). Standing behind them is friend and entrepreneur Krishna Sanghi.

The first issue of *Mid-Day* dated 27 June 1979.

Top: With former cricket captain Bishan Singh Bedi.
Bottom: 'That was funny!' With Sunil Gavaskar and Dilip Vengsarkar.

Top: Speaking at a hockey function before departure for Moscow.
Bottom: With the gold medal winning Indian hockey Olympic team at the Ansari home prior to their departure for the 1980 Moscow Olympic Games: Ashok Kumar (extreme left), Behram Contractor (second from left), hockey legend R.S. Gentle (third from left), editor of *Sportsweek* Sharad Kotnis (fourth from right), assistant editor of *Sportsweek* Gopi Baskaran (third from right), sports editor of *The Times of India* Sundar Rajan (second from right) and racing correspondent of *The Times of India* Cecil Hendricks (extreme right). Daughter Tehzeeb and son Tarique seated on floor.

Top: Touring journalists at the Adelaide Oval during India's 1980–81 tour of Australia: (left to right) commentator Narottam Puri; correspondent of *The Telegraph* Dickie Rutnagur; R. Mohan, cricket writer at *The Hindu*; Raj Singh Dungarpur; K.N. Prabhu, cricket writer at *The Times of India*; radio commentator Jasdev Singh Soin; cricket correspondent of *The Statesman* Kishore Bimani, journalist Narayan Thakkar and Ravi Chaturvedi from All India Radio.
Bottom: With Vijay Amritraj at the tennis court of Cricket Club of India after he became the first Indian to enter the Wimbledon semi-finals in 1981.

Top: Going out to bat at the Brabourne Stadium during Sunil Gavaskar's charity match under the auspices of his charity Foundation, CHAMPS. Vivian Richards and members of the World Cup 1983 champion Indian team took part in the limited-overs match.
Bottom: With President of India Giani Zail Singh and son Tarique at Rashtrapati Bhavan, New Delhi.

KHALID ANSARI *giornalista*
Due lauree: una a Bombay, l'altra a Stanford. Due Master, sempre a Stanford: uno in Scienze Politiche, l'altro in Giornalismo. Khalid Ansari, 47 anni, è tornato in India nel 1962. Oggi dirige *Inquileb*, il quotidiano in lingua urdu fondato dal padre, *Sportsweek*, il settimanale sportivo più diffuso in India, *Mid-Day*, quotidiano tabloid del pomeriggio (ma la domenica diventa quotidiano del mattino e tocca le 200 mila copie) e il *News-Day*, altro quotidiano del mattino, formato standard, fondato da appena due mesi e con una tiratura che ha già raggiunto le 100 mila copie. «Ma forse la maggiore soddisfazione della mia carriera è venuta con l'*Act*, Action by Citizen Today, un movimento popolare che ha trovato nel *Mid-Day* il suo catalizzatore» dice Ansari. «Ho cercato di insegnare alla gente di Bombay a tenere moralmente pulita la propria città, impegnandosi a rispondere in maniera positiva e legale agli amministratori pubblici qualora questi non facciano il loro dovere. E la gente si è svegliata: gli studenti, le organizzazioni dei lavoratori, la Camera del Commercio insieme ai club privati e a semplici cittadini si sono organizzati. Oggi, dopo un anno passato a scrivere tre-quattro volte alla settimana per aiutare l'*Act*, ho preferito tirarmi indietro: ormai il movimento è forte, continua a crescere e sa andare avanti da solo».

A portrait from *Vogue Italia*.

Top: With Field Marshal S.H.F.J. Manekshaw and athletics coach Jal Pardiwala (centre) at an All India Council of Sport event.
Bottom: With Dilip Kumar and Saira Banu at a press inaugural function of the *Inquilab*.

Top: With former police commissioner and ambassador to Romania, Julio Ribeiro at *Sportsweek*'s 'Run for Fun' event at Mumbai's Marine Drive.
Bottom: Receiving Field Marshal S.H.F.J. Manekshaw at the Rotary District Conference: (left to right) Tarique Ansari, Fatehsinghrao Baroda, Begum Bilkees Latif (wife of Air Marshal Idris Latif, former governor of Maharashtra), the field marshal, Rukya Ansari and Air Marshal Idris Latif.

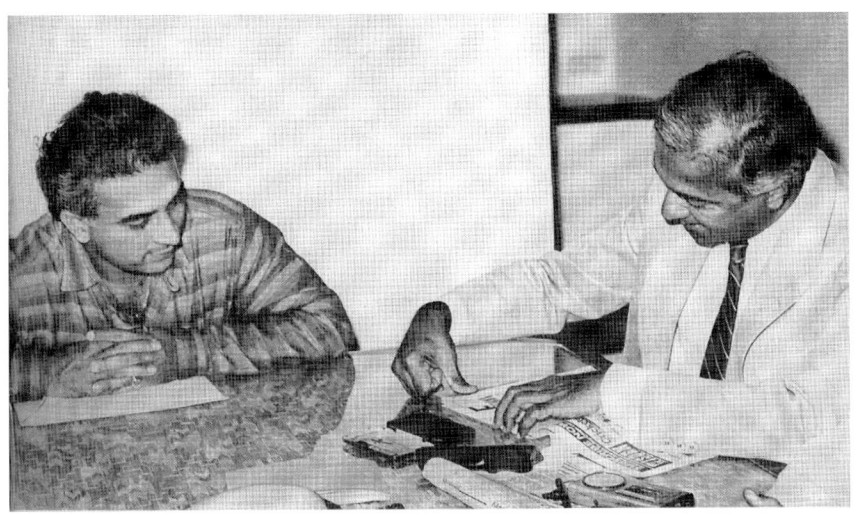

Top: In a lighter mood with Sunil Gavaskar, while giving my thumb impression after signing him on as editor of *Sportsweek*.
Bottom: Addressing the United Nations General Assembly on human rights in 1989.

Article by father Abdul Hamid Nizamuddin Ansari reproduced from a book on him published in *Mid-Day*.

Top: With John Major, former prime minister of Britain (left) and Sarosh Zaiwalla, UK solicitor at a Conservative Party function in London.
Bottom: Receiving former Indian president Shankar Dayal Sharma with daughter Tehzeeb and son Sharique.

Top: At the Padma Shri function in New Delhi, 2001. Prime Minister Atal Bihari Vajpayee is seated on the left. Former Deputy Prime Minister L.K. Advani is seated third from left.
Bottom: Receiving the Padma Shri award from President K.R. Narayanan.

Top: Padma Shri awardees 2001 with President K.R. Narayanan, Prime Minister A.B. Vajpayee and former Deputy Prime Minister L.K. Advani: Tennis champions Mahesh Bhupathi and Leander Paes (standing, middle row, second and third from left), former India hockey captain Dhanraj Pillai (standing, middle row, seventh from left) and squash champion Bhuveneshwari Kumari (seated third from right). *Bottom*: With actor and squash aficionado Aamir Khan who inaugurated the A-H Ansari Squash Academy in Mumbai.

Top: With Rajmata Gayatri at her home in Jaipur and Rukya (left).
Bottom: With legendary fast bowler-turned commentator Michael Holding at Sabina Park, Jamaica.

Top: Being presented the distinguished alumni award at a St Xavier's College function by founder-editor of *Upper Crust* magazine Farzana Contractor in Mumbai.
Bottom: With friend Tunku 'Pete' Imran of Malaysia, member of the International Cricket Council and former president of the International Squash Federation; industrialist and squash patron Mahendra Kumar Sanghi (second from left) and renowned squash writer Raju Chainani at the Bombay Gymkhana.

Top: With former Australian cricket captain, Ian Chappell.
Bottom: With president A.P.J. Abdul Kalam on a four-nation tour of Europe.

Top: With Chief Justice of India Yogesh Kumar Sabharwal at a function organized by the Government Law College, Mumbai, to honour distinguished alumni in 2006.
Bottom: With tennis ace Leander Paes, winner of 18 doubles Grand Slam titles, men's singles quarterfinalist at the Atlanta Olympics in 1996 and one of the greatest doubles players in tennis history.

Top: With V.V.S. Laxman, batsman extraordinaire turned commentator.
Bottom: Receiving the Junior Chamber of Commerce Outstanding Citizen's award from Renuka Chowdhury, former Union minister and Member of Rajya Sabha as Jaycees founder-chairman Nana Chudasama looks on.

Wedding with Mattie Tomasevich (Zeyna) in Rotorua, New Zealand.

Top: Wedding ceremony with Zeyna at the home of friends Abbas and Madhurani Jasdanwalla in Mahabaleshwar, Mumbai.
Bottom: At the launch of of my book *Cricket at Fever Pitch* at the Cricket Club of India.

Top: At an event promoting *Sachin Tendulkar: Born to Bat* at the Cricket Club of India: (left to right) cricket commentator Harsha Bhogle, director of Jaico Publishing Co. Ashwin Shah, sports editor of *Mid-Day* Clayton Murzello, myself, Rahul Dravid and Farokh Engineer.

Bottom: At Farokh Engineer's seventy-fifth birthday at the Ansari residence in Mumbai: (left to right) laparoscopic/bariatric surgeon Dr Muffazil Lakdawala, myself, Farokh Engineer, Sunil Gavaskar, former UN Under-Secretary General Prakash Shah, Zeyna and Dilip Vengsarkar.

Top: At a private reception hosted by Arvind Singh Mewar and his wife Vijayaraj at their Udaipur Palace: (left to right) Lakshyaraj Singh Mewar, his wife Nivritti, Vijayaraj, Zeyna, Arvind Singh Mewar and myself.
Bottom: With children and grandchildren: (left to right) son Sharique, granddaughter Safiya, grandson Noah, grandson Emraan and daughter Tehzeeb.

Top: Family photograph at my eightieth birthday: (left to right) Tarique, Rukya, unknown, Zeyna and Sharique.
Bottom: With former India cricket captain Kapil Dev at Bishan Singh Bedi's seventy-fifth birthday celebrations and book release in New Delhi.

With Zeyna on a cruise.

'...Make it Fish and Chips'

This is a story from the days when cricketers from the subcontinent had to make do with a very meagre food allowance while on tour.

Like any other touring team, members of a touring Pakistani team, consisting of nubile young 'Casanovas,' desperate for a bit of fun but without the means to afford it, would gaze longingly from the outside at the beautiful young ladies inside the pubs in the St John's Wood area near London's Lord's cricket ground. Apart from money, inability to converse in English was a major obstacle in 'scoring' with the ladies.

One evening, a particularly venturesome member of the team—an opening batsman—borrowed money from his teammates, mustered enough courage and found himself a place at the popular pub's bar counter.

As luck would have it, a gorgeous young thing came in and sat next to the dashing *Majnu* (Romeo). The swashbuckling opener made bold to strike up a conversation but language proved to be a huge barrier. Pointing at a glass of beer, he offered her a drink, which she accepted but that proved to be the end of the exchange.

Not one to give up easily, he confided his frustrating experience to the team manager who happened to be young and a good sport.

'Forget the usual cheap takeaway and fish and chips joints where you guys like to eat,' the manager advised him. 'There's this romantic restaurant down the road with soft lights and music. Go there the next time, ask for a table for two and take a seat. When the place gets busy, chances are some young lady will ask if she may occupy the spare seat at your table. Welcome her and ask her if she'd like to have a beer with you. If she accepts, it will be Round One to you. Then ask her if she'd like to have another beer and join you in eating a steak. Hopefully she'll agree. Order the steaks...and take it from there. You're on your own now, Charlie Boy...dance with her and enjoy yourself. Good luck.'

The ambitious lover boy followed the instructions to a tee. Things went as planned. The beers were ordered and quaffed. Then came the time to order the steaks.

'We'll have two steaks,' said our Don Juan with great aplomb.

The waiter then asked, 'And how would you like your steaks, sir?'

End of education. Befuddled, the Lothario broke out into a sweat, and replied: 'Make it fish and chips!'

This joke seems to have become a classic in the cricket-playing world. I've heard it from England to Australia, India to Pakistan, New Zealand to South Africa and in-between—in Sri Lanka, Zimbabwe and Ireland, too.

Interestingly, the name of the poor batsman—as also where he is now working—is the same wherever in the cricketing world the story is recounted.

Makes one wonder if it is, in fact, a true story. If not, one can only feel sorry for the poor Casanova.

◆

Then there's the unsubstantiated story concerning the illustrious Pakistani captain whose proficiency in the English language is not the best and whose wife gave birth to a son on the last day of a Test match which his team had just won impressively.

It's no secret that many, if not most, cricketers from his country are not known to be fluent in the English language and that successive captains of Test teams have learnt to reply to stock questions about their team's victories with standard replies which pass muster.

During the Man of the Match ceremony, the commentator congratulates the captain on the new arrival in English and asks how it feels to be a father.

Flushed with his team's victory and only half catching the drift of the question in the din of the victory ceremony, the skipper presumes the question to be the routine one pertaining to his team's victory and replies by rote:

'Yes, you see, it was a great achievement: it was a great team effort, with every player contributing his share, especially Shahid Afridi who made a great single-handed contribution.'

◆

Since one good joke deserves another: when the dictatorial General Ayub Khan assumed office as president of Pakistan, he releases a diktat that a postage bearing his picture be issued in his honour.

'If Pakistan can have a Jinnah stamp, so can we have an Ayub Khan one as well,' he decrees.

So with much fanfare, creative people are selected, designs chosen and, with great ceremony, the stamp is released to the nation of Pakistan at a public function in the capital, Islamabad.

A month later, Ayub summons the post master general and, stroking his moustache proudly, asks: 'Tell me how are the stamps selling?'

There is no reply from the PMG.

'Tell me, you idiot, you nincompoop! How are those stamps selling?' thunders Ayub.

The dejected PMG answers, 'I'm sorry, sir. I'm told they're not selling too well.'

Flying into a rage, Ayub roars, 'It's such a beautiful stamp! What do you mean it's not selling well? If the Jinnah stamp could sell well, mine should break all records.'

'I'm sorry, sir, but it's reported that they don't stick well,' explains the trembling PMG.

'Rubbish!' the prez rages, 'what do you mean they don't stick well? Show me a stamp.'

A stamp is duly produced. Ayub admires it, licks it and sticks it on his wrist. 'What do you mean, it doesn't stick well? It sticks perfectly.'

Replies the PMG: 'I'm sorry, sir—but it's said they spit on the *wrong* side.'

'...Make it Fish and Chips'

All-Time Cricketing Greats

It's always fun to meet cricket aficionados, put on one's selectorial hat and indulge in the absorbing pastime of picking all-time great players and teams, either of one's own country or the world, in the different formats—Tests, ODIs and Twenty20s

For the present, I take pleasure in reminiscing about the cricketers I have been privileged to see in action in different countries, against varying opposition, under diverse and evolving playing conditions, changing rules, etc. I thank my cricketing stars that many, if not most, of the all-time greats in the acknowledged knowledgeable lists were products of the 1970s and thereafter.

Lest this be misunderstood: let me hasten to stress that it is almost impossible to make comparisons over different eras.

There were, indeed, innumerable great batsmen, bowlers, wicket keepers (and all-rounders) before my time starting in the 1970s. It must be borne in mind that India did not play a Test until 1932, and that its successes have coincided with the nation's rise as a global power.

Off the top of one's head, the names of the following Test GOATs immediately stand out (in no particular order). From among those I have seen in action: Garfield Sobers, Viv Richards, Sunil Gavaskar, Sachin Tendulkar, Virat Kohli, Brian Lara, Ricky Ponting, Steve Smith, Kapil Dev, Ian Botham, M.S. Dhoni, Imran Khan, Richard Hadlee, Graeme Smith, A.B. de Villiers, Jacques Kallis, Rahul Dravid, Adam Gilchrist, Mark Waugh, Kane Williamson, Hashim Amla, Malcolm Marshal, Matthew Hayden, Bishan Bedi, Wasim Akram, Zaheer Abbas,

Shane Warne, Glenn McGrath, Muttiah Muralitharan, Dennis Lillee and Shaun Pollock merit inclusion.

I have not watched Don Bradman, who must figure somewhere near the very top of any World XI list, nor Jack Hobbs, Graeme Pollock, Keith Miller, Mike Proctor, South African wicket-keeper batsman Dennis Lindsay and Andy Flower, captain and wicketkeeper- batsman of Zimbabwe), so shall refrain from commenting on their merits.

◆

To celebrate the ICC World Cup 2019, the BBC Asian Network asked fans to vote for the Greatest Cricketer of All Time from a short list of 30.[30]

For what it's worth, the below-mentioned made it to the list in the following order:

(My personal list differs from the selection above in many respects. For one thing I would like to place Sunil Gavaskar near the top but that's another matter.)

---

[30] 'The Greatest Cricketer of All Time—your votes revealed!', BBC Radio Asian Network, May 2019. https://www.bbc.co.uk/programmes/articles/2V6BjFgdJ5KcfVHhR3bwBLz/the-greatest-cricketer-of-all-time-your-votes-revealed. Accessed on 12 November 2021.

1. Don Bradman (Australia)	16. Kumar Sangakkara (Sri Lanka)
2. Sachin Tendulkar (India)	17. Kapil Dev (India)
3. Garfield Sobers (West Indies)	18. Richard Hadlee (New Zealand)
4. Imran Khan (Pakistan)	19. Adam Gilchrist (Australia)
5. Ian Botham (England)	20. Chris Gayle (West Indies)
6. Shane Warne (Australia)	21. Glenn McGrath (Australia)
7. Viv Richards (West Indies)	22. Ricky Ponting (Australia)
8. Brian Lara (West Indies)	23. Steve Waugh (Australia)
9. Jacques Kallis (South Africa)	24. Rahul Dravid (India)
10. M.S. Dhoni (India)	25. Sunil Gavaskar (India)
11. Wasim Akram (Pakistan)	26. Shoaib Akhtar (Pakistan)
12. Virat Kohli (India)	27. Curtly Ambrose (West Indies)
13. James Anderson (England)	28. Mahela Jayawardene (Sri Lanka)
14. Alastair Cook (England)	29. Dale Steyn (South Africa)
15. Muttiah Muralitharan (Sri Lanka)	

Invited by 'Mr Dependable' Rahul Dravid to his traditional (but strictly no-media) wedding reception to Vijeta (née Pendharkar of Nagpur), a surgeon, in Bangalore in 2003, I decided to be naughty. While congratulating the couple, I took the liberty of saying to the bride that she was an extremely lucky lady for marrying such a decent human being as Rahul, and that if I had a daughter of marriageable age, I would have pushed her to pursue him.

Without batting an eyelid, Vijeta replied, 'She wouldn't have stood a chance, sir.'

Touché—a charming combination of brains and beauty. They now have two sons Samit, aged 16 and Anvay, 12.

It's a Wonderful World

Hockey Despair

Much as I enjoyed covering cricket events, I was irresistibly drawn towards hockey at a time when the game was undergoing rapid transformation as regards rules, playing surface, technique and balance of power.

Apart from covering Hockey at the Olympics, Commonwealth and Asian Games, I also covered less-important tournaments namely the Esanda Hockey Tournament in Perth (Australia) and the Champions Trophy in Pakistan.

After India exhilaratingly lifted the FIH Hockey World Cup in 1975 in Kuala Lumpur, (followed by a miserable exit from the 1976 Montreal Olympics), I travelled halfway across the world to cover the 1978 Hockey World Cup in Buenos Aires, Argentina. Pakistan lifted the trophy but India finished a dismal sixth, scoring barely eight goals in the entire tournament as against 12 conceded.

I was the only Indian correspondent covering the tournament and was disgusted at some of the behind the scenes goings on. One of my dispatches from the tournament read:

> What went wrong? What were the causes of India's ignominious performance in the hockey World Cup at Buenos Aires. The bitter truth must be told in its entirety—not as a witch-hunt, nor an exercise in excuse-making, but to properly appreciate the reasons for our disgraceful show and the plummeting of

our hockey stock from world champions to a miserable sixth.'[31]

In another piece I wrote:

> The coach and manager were too busy doing their own thing to have time for the team. There was no contact whatsoever between them and the players were left to their own devices.
>
> So callous were the two officials that neither was on hand when Syed Ali and Lakra were injured during the tournament. They were too 'busy' to even accompany them to the hospital. That was left to the players and the female interpreter.
>
> The faults of this team have existed for a long time but nothing has been done about them. Unless these problems are addressed, and a total overhaul of the entire system undertaken, Indian sportsmen and sports lovers will continue to be disillusioned and disenchanted.

As for me, so disgusted was I with Indian hockey that I made enchanting Buenos Aires my last hockey stop for good.

Be that as it may, I was delighted when the characteristically somnolent Government of India awoke from its slumber and ordered an inquiry into India's miserable performance.

◆

In a guest column in *The Times of India*, I wrote the following:

> If our participants performed below par in the Bangkok Asian Games, our performance at the Munich Olympics, '72, was "pathetic", as I remarked during a speech to the Rotary Club of Bombay, 'except at hockey (in which we retained third place, and boxing and wrestling in which our representatives put up at least the semblance of a fight.
>
> Even worse was the behaviour of the officials who showed

---

[31] Khalid Ansari, 'India Display Humiliating Performance in Hockey World Cup at Buenos Aires', India Today, 30 April 1978, https://www.indiatoday.in/magazine/sport/story/19780430-india-display-humiliating-performance-in-hockey-world-cup-at-buenos-aires-822946-2014-04-17. Accessed on 12 November 2021.

scant respect for their responsibilities towards their charges or the country they represented.

India has the talent to excel at the top international level but that will not mature as long as the present crop of incompetent and irresponsible officials rule the country's sport.

In a piece in *Sportsweek* on the Buenos Aires debacle, my piece faulted R.S. Gentle, a good friend:

Come off it Mr Gentle, let's not start it all over again. On your return home you have passed the buck and taken the easy way out by attributing our inability to win the 'gold' to 'Fate.'

Our hockey enthusiasts have the utmost respect for your knowledge of the game, but aren't you indulging in an exercise in over-simplification, thereby insulting the intelligence of lovers of the game?

Hard-luck stories in Indian sport are beginning to pall. We were told we were 'unlucky' at Mexico City in 1968, at Bangkok in 1970, at Barcelona in 1971, and now in Munich in 1972.

Are we doomed to eternal 'BAD LUCK?'

Asiad Chronicle

Having made a successful bid for the ninth Asian Games in New Delhi, the government set up an organizing committee, under the chairmanship of Rajiv Gandhi with Union Home Minister Buta Singh, to conduct the Games in conjunction with the Indian Olympic Association (IOA).

Buta Singh flew down to Mumbai and informed me that it had been decided to publish, from scratch, an afternoon daily newspaper, the *Asiad Chronicle*, with me as editor and, as I discovered later, head cook and bottle washer.

The editorial board consisted of: Shankaran Nair, head of RAW, who was designated secretary general of the special organizing committee; Fatehsinghrao Gaekwad (former Maharaja of Baroda) and Ranjit Bhatia (professor at Delhi University and national long distance running champion, incidentally also a friend and *Sportsweek* correspondent).

When accepting the assignment, which I considered an honour, I was sprung a surprise later in New Delhi: I would myself have to set up headquarters in the dingy bowels of the Jawaharlal Nehru Stadium, which measured a total of 1,500 square feet, with an additional space for a 200-square-feet dark room and also a section for photo composition!

I'm no Euclid, nor Archimedes, nor designer or architect, but this appeared to be a task that seemed not only impossible in terms of the space being allotted but Herculean given the lead time of under a month. Moreover, my letter of appointment (LOA) stated: 'You may contact the Stadium authorities for putting up partitions and also for setting up the dark room and photo composition section. For the requirement of an air conditioner for the darkroom, you are authorised to hire a suitable air conditioner for use up to 10th of December [the Games' duration was 19 November–4 December 1982], payment for which will be made by the SOC.'

The LOA went on to say, 'You may hire the necessary furniture and fixtures in consultation with me,' etc. Then there was the *small* matter of getting typewriters, telex machines and teleprinter and telephone lines from various government agencies and authorities—all of which are notorious for red tape and lack of understanding as to what time is all about—all under a month!

Whereas eight double rooms at the government's two-and-a-half-star hotel Ashok Yatri Niwas were allocated for my staff and me, they had no beds but only mattresses on stone slabs in the Delhi winter, prompting the fiercely independent Behram Contractor to take a swipe at them in his *Mid-Day* column in Mumbai.

◆

Incidentally, this was the same Yatri Niwas hotel of Delhi's 1995 infamous 'tandoor murder case' in which Naina Sahni, a former functionary of a political party, was murdered by her husband Sushil Sharma, who tried to dispose of the body by burning it in a tandoor (oven) at the hotel.

◆

And, 'two cars and one Jeep on minimum tariff' were allotted on government expense, but, as though all the above-mentioned non-editorial responsibilities thrust on to us were not enough, *we* were required to liaise with the authorities, as also with suppliers of newsprint and the government's corrupt advertising agency for support. My first reaction upon being informed of all these conditions and requirements was to say, 'To hell with it!' but it was, after all, a *huge* honour for me to be awarded the assignment.

Looking back, my acceptance of the terms of the contract was sheer idiocy brought on by a confused salmagundi of nationalism, youthful derring-do and foolishness.

It was the Donkey of this narrative at work again. However, when I took on the seeming absurdities of the above-mentioned conditions with various authorities, I found New Delhi's babus (white-collar government workers) refreshingly amenable to change. After all, we were on the same side—with the prime minister and home minister in charge and, most importantly, national prestige at stake.

◆

The personal involvement of Prime Minister Rajiv Gandhi in ensuring the success of the Asian Games was an undeniable boon for me, but it also injected a large dollop of red tape in the proceedings which often was the source of much mirth.

> For instance, there was this senior, but fawning, minister, whom the prime minister would telephone frequently. He was in and out of my office periodically and calls to him would be directed to my extension.
>
> Each time the prime minister called for him he would jump to his feet respectfully while talking to the august personage, making it extremely difficult for me to suppress my laughter at the frequent display of ludicrous *chamchagiri* (servitude).

◆

New Delhi's *Hindustan Times* reported:

> The Asiad has gingered people up. Almost overnight not only new restaurants and shops but even journals have sprung up in the capital. The Bombay paper *Mid-Day* was given a plot in Okhla Industrial estate by the SOC just five weeks before the show began and asked to bring out Asiad's official newspaper. It's Chief Editor, Khalid Ansari says he borrowed a brand-new offset machine, pulled out over a dozen journalists from *Mid-Day* units in Bangalore and Bombay, flew out a production man

It's a Wonderful World

posted in New York and a bunch of press workers from elsewhere and brought out an edition running into 40,000 copies daily of *Asiad Chronicle* several days before the deadline. He hopes to break even.

But 'producing the journal is giving the team a feel of the place. Delhi is where the action is' says Mr Ansari and he is likely to give the capital yet another journal, probably a tabloid which will ultimately be a daily with a difference—more human-interest stories, more humour.

◆

Sportsweek and *Mid-Day* staff numbering about 30, from Mumbai—including Behram Contractor ('Busybee')—Kolkata and Bengaluru, were taken to New Delhi and did us proud by bringing out, against tremendous publishing odds, day after day, a newspaper of international standard for a fortnight, which was greatly appreciated by journalists from all over Asia. Many of them thanked us profusely for permitting them to lift exclusive material from the *Asiad Chronicle* for their own self-styled 'exclusive' dispatches.

In his syndicated column 'View from the Gallery,' Arvind Lavakare wrote in the *Sunday Observer*: 'It is learnt that many leading newspapers were interested in publishing the official newspaper of the Games but ASGOC (the Asian Games Organising Committee) chose the *Sportsweek* group because in its 14 years of existence, the magazine has generally lived up to its claim of being 'the magazine that cares for Indian sport.'

◆

Incidentally, India fared exceptionally well at these 1982 New Delhi Asian Games—for a change—finishing fifth on the medals table with 13 gold medals, 19 silver and 25 bronze medals for an overall total of 57.

TEN

A MAD DREAM TO START A DAILY NEWSPAPER

Advertising, Advertising

Sport and Pastime's closure in 1968 had left *Sportsweek* in a monopolistic situation for 10 years, until 1978. It was relaunched by the prosperous and respected Hindu Group of Chennai in the new razzle-dazzle avatar of *Sportstar*.

The new incarnation, now a fortnightly, was craftily strategized replete with glossy paper, attractive colour, action pictures and was printed on ultra-modern printing machinery, none of which we could afford because we had neither the wherewithal nor economies of scale that the Hindu Group did.

It was clear, the gambit by the Brobdingnagians was to annihilate Lilliputian *Sportsweek* with unmatchable financial muscle, which we certainly were incapable of even withstanding, leave aside countering.

To add to our woes, the Ananda Patrika Bazar (ABP) Group of Kolkata decided to jump into the fray in 1978 with the launch of the magazine *Sportsworld*, of which Mansoor Ali Khan 'Tiger' Pataudi was the titular editor. His editorial inputs were, at best, infrequent, but the mere association of his name with the magazine was a coup of sorts and helped propel the magazine's take off. The magazine was professionally produced by outstanding young talents like Rohit Brijnath, Mudar Patherya and quizmaster Derek O'Brien who later opted for a career in politics.

Although he had long since retired, Pataudi still retained his charisma and his association, indubitably attracted a starry-eyed readership, especially in eastern Indian, because of the *Ananda Bazar*'s established newspaper distribution network in that region, which neither *Sportsweek* nor *Sportstar* were able to penetrate with any degree of success.

I would be guilty of being economical with the truth if I denied that the new kid made a dent in the circulations of its two established rivals. I'm not aware of the extent to which *Sportsworld* cannibalized the readership of *Sportstar*, but its impact on *Sportsweek*, now the entrenched market leader, was not insignificant.

Sportsworld ceased publication in 1994, leaving *Sportstar* the only survivor. But to deny that the latter exists today with the same degree of professionalism and devotion to sports as it did in its previous avatar of *Sport and Pastime* would be churlish. One could chalk that up to aspects like its financial muscle and monopolistic situation. But what the new entrant *did* succeed in doing was play the role of spoiler, in a manner of speaking, poaching on the already diminutive advertising cake.

Sportsweek, for 20 years the monopolistic beneficiary of the total advertising spending in the sports magazine segment in the country, now found itself having to share the prized advertising treasure with two new competitors, without any corresponding increase in size of the lolly. Moreover, we were both unable to match the excellent paper and print quality of *Sportstar*.

To be fair, the competition from the two newcomers was exemplarily fair and sporting, with dirty tricks conspicuous by their absence. Readers of sports magazines were now spoilt for choice with three where previously there was only one. But the matter of advertising, the lifeblood of newspaper and magazine publishing, was another story.

I'm not aware of the financial fallout of this altered matrix on the other two magazines, but the division of advertising spoils grievously hurt *Sportsweek*, which had been bleeding for some time. Try as we did, advertising revenue was just not commensurate with the impressive wide and loyal readership of the publication. The signs were ominous—and I accept full responsibility for this—but I was on such an adrenaline high that I failed to comprehend their seriousness. With an abysmally low financial base and astronomically increasing costs under various heads to sustain the growth, we were a runaway train, a disaster waiting to happen.

While singing the praises of *Sportsweek*'s editorial quality and impressive readership, advertisers and advertising agencies kept citing the magazine's readership profile: its acknowledged popularity, but predominantly among students and young male sports-loving professionals with low (if not zero, in the case of students) purchasing power. More importantly, they pointed to the low percentage in its readership of a large and eminently desirable universe of women with purchasing power, of vast numbers of people with significant discretionary income.

In short: good magazine, but no good as advertising medium! Thanks, but no thanks!

To be honest, entrapped as I was, in an all-consuming obsession with sport and an irresponsible (as I now see it) missionary zeal to reform, I got sucked up in the nirvana of success, the fickle bitch goddess. I was grossly remiss even as I lost balance, focus and financial prudence.

The fact that I was away from the headquarters for prolonged periods, covering sport in all corners of the globe and VIP visits with political dignitaries and the like, didn't help matters.

◆

This reminds me of the story of the worried mother who takes her six-year-old son to the psychiatrist.

'Doctor, doctor, I'm very concerned. Every time I take young Willie to the department store, he picks up things and puts them into his pocket. What could the problem be, doctor?'

'There's nothing the matter, ma'am. Your son's a thief.'

No excuses, plain and simple. I, as head cook and bottle-washer, am to blame, entirely, for getting too complacent, failing to take adequate disaster management measures, for refusing to see the woods for the trees, for not being prescient.

It would be facile to argue that the shortcomings of *Sportsweek* as a worthwhile advertising medium for most advertisers—other than those in consumer and sports goods—are endemic to the very essence of a sports magazine. In the history of Indian sports magazine publishing, no sports magazine starting with *Sport and Pastime*, down to its reincarnated *Sportstar*, or *Sportsworld* have been profitable.

As far as I'm concerned: if *Sportsweek* could break all-time circulation records—set by the pioneering *Sport and Pastime*—there's no reason why I could not come up with innovative space-selling and creative marketing means to attract much more advertising revenue to help balance our books.

Looking back, our ad sales infrastructure was pathetic with most of our energies devoted to editorial excellence and circulation building. We were simply not creative and aggressive enough in our space-selling efforts.

I'm delighted *Sportstar* is alive and, seemingly, in robust health. They were, after all the pioneers of Indian sports magazine publishing and I know Indian sport is in safe and good hands under their watch! More power to their elbow in the cause they have espoused!

Mid-Day

In hindsight, the decision to start an afternoon paper was another exemplification of the allegory about the donkey thinking he's a wrestler.

In the early '70s, the unassuming Behram Contractor was fast becoming a legend of sorts among readers of Mumbai's afternoon newspaper, the *Evening News of India* of the Times of India group because of his sharp wit and formulaic name-dropping of the city's haute monde.

I recall a chance meeting with Behram at a press conference. We soon struck a warm friendship to the extent that I would be invited to all his parties and vice versa. And he would mention me in his column to an embarrassing degree.

On such an occasion, many hours into the night, I was invited to a dinner at his Churchgate flat and, as was our normal practice at each other's home, stayed back after all guests had departed, solving the world's problems, as we would jokingly term it.

Many hours into the night I realized Behram's light in the balcony facing the suburban railway station was on. I mentioned this to Behram who went 'blink-blink' (as was his distinctive peculiarity), stepped out and returned to inform me that it wasn't his balcony light but the sun that was rising. Such was our enjoyment of each other's company.

In fact, even after Behram left *Mid-Day* to branch out on his own and start the rival *Afternoon Despatch and Courier*, we resumed this practice at his Harkness Road flat without objection from his indulgent wife Farzana.

At one such dinner at my home for some international cricketers at which Farokh Engineer, Imran Khan and Rohan Kanhai were present, Behram stayed back after my wife Rukya had gone to bed. For some reason our conversation veered to his job at the *Evening News of India*.

Since we were now close friends, I thought nothing of asking Behram if he was happy with his job to which he replied categorically: 'If you start a daily newspaper, I'll chuck up my present job and join you tomorrow,' in a manner that reminded me of Aziz Currimbhoy and *Sportsweek*.

We both laughed it off and Behram made his way home.

Ruminating over the previous evening's conversation over my morning cup of tea the next day, an epiphany of sorts struck, I picked up the phone and invited Behram to lunch to ask if he was serious about what he had said the previous evening.

To my astonishment he, stone-cold sober, confirmed that he had. And thereby hangs a tale!

◆

To be absolutely honest, I was shocked out of my wits. Although I had long nursed the desire to start a daily newspaper, it had always been a fond hope—and nothing else—for the simple reason that I just didn't possess or have access to any resources worth talking about. My father had repeatedly warned me about the perils of partnership.

After *Mid-Day* had established itself, I was privileged to be invited by the likes of the feisty Ramnath Goenka, owner of the multiple-edition *Indian Express*, the self-made Dhirubhai Ambani whose spectacular rise from humble beginnings as a mere clerk in Aden, Yemen, to the richest man in India is the stuff of legend.

Also, by S.P. and Gopichand Hinduja of the multifaceted Hinduja empire and Vijay Mallya, the high-flying entrepreneur who later in life ran afoul of the law—for discussions over lunch or tea, which were inevitably infructuous because of my father's conviction about partnerships.

In my moments of idle conjecture, I sometimes wonder what might have been had I decided to merge my family's humble publishing endeavours with any of those giants, only to realize that that is a futile exercise.

Nor did I have a proper roof over my head: no office premises, printing capacity beyond what was required for the *Inquilab*, human resource, admin, marketing, production personnel, editorial staff versed in the English language, stock of newsprint worth talking about, nothing; nothing except fond hope on a wing and a prayer!

Even dreaming of starting an English newspaper under the circumstances was imbecility of the most egregious sort.

It must be said to Behram's credit that he took my casual suggestion seriously, promptly speaking to many of his colleagues, as also friends and acquaintances in the profession and managing to rally the troops, in a manner of speaking.

Malavika Sangghvi, who put her hand up when Behram mooted the idea to her, recalls: 'Behram had NO idea about Khalid Ansari's financial resources nor his management expertise—all he knew was that "he was a nice young man with a pleasant personality."'

In an interview to *Society*, Behram Contractor said: 'In January 1979 the blueprint for *Mid-Day* was prepared, in March we had set a date for kick off and on 27th July the first edition of *Mid-Day* hit the stands. Four of my colleagues and myself resigned from our jobs at *The Times of India* and consequently lost our leave and other allowances for not giving adequate notice.'

In its issue of 12–25 July 1979, *Businessworld* wrote:

> If an enthusiastic staff was Ansari's greatest asset, *Mid-Day*'s working environment and infrastructure were far from satisfactory.

It also quoted me as saying:

> I was a little mad, to put it mildly, to attempt to bring out a daily newspaper and weekly magazine (*Sportsweek*) on our eight year-old antiquated *Newsking* two-unit web offset equipment, and there were several breakdowns. And to add to the frustration of periodic machine breakdowns, Ron Hendricks, the deputy editor, left after two months because he reportedly could not see eye to

eye with Behram Contractor. But despite these setbacks, within six months *Mid-Day* had managed to break even and, since its launch, doubled its price from the initial 20 paise to 40 paise and revised its advertising rates from Rs 6 per column centimetre (contract) and Rs 8 (casual) to Rs 26 and Rs 29 respectively.

Behram said the following about his initial thoughts on the publication:

> Brought up as I was—journalistically speaking—in a somewhat uppity newspaper atmosphere, *Sunday Mid-Day*'s curious product mix of some well-known and not-so-well know names in different spheres was a little difficult for me to stomach in the beginning. Yet, despite my scepticism the formula proved to be right, as was evident from the sales in the market.

The article went on:

> Spurred by its success, the *Mid-Day* team embarked upon on their next venture—*Sunday Mid-Day*, a weekly that claims to give 'value for money' with regular columns on investments, astrology, homeopathy, a beauty guide and even a true confessions column.
>
> Since its launch, *Sunday Mid-Day's* sales graph has moved in one direction—upwards. On 13th July 1980 when it hit the newsstand 50,000 copies of the Sunday paper were printed of which 40,000 copies were sold.
>
> Since then, despite revising its prices from 40 paise to 60 paise in a year, *Sunday Mid-Day* commands a circulation of 84,000 and a Thursday 'dak' (early) edition of 20,000 which is sent to the country's major metropolitan cities.
>
> What accounts for the spectacular success of *Mid-Day* and its Sunday edition? 'Readability and objective reporting,' says Contractor. 'We don't believe in fighting for causes or carrying out campaigns on our pages. We report the news and let the reader judge for himself. We also believe in pictorial stories and therefore have three fulltime photographers on our staff.'
>
> Not that it has been smooth sailing all the way. Until 1979 *Sportsweek* and *Mid-Day* were being printed on machinery that even Ansari admits is obsolescent.

'The tension was too much,' reminisces Ansari. 'when the machines broke down, which they did frequently, the printing was held up and timeliness is very important in this business. Even today, colour pages have to be farmed out and until we acquired our own phototypesetting machines in 1980, typesetting had to be done elsewhere.

It required enormous patience and coordination to make sure everything went right. In late 1979, we acquired one Orient Press unit manufactured indigenously and another one of the same brand last month. And although this has helped our printing capacity, lack of infrastructure has hampered our growth considerably.

The working conditions too are far from perfect, though *Mid-Day's* staff which brought out the first edition of the paper despite a leaking roof and puddles, bravely soldier on with promises of a brand new Nariman Point office on the horizon (Incidentally, we did move our Ad Sales department to Nariman Point a few years later.)

But whatever other problems that he may have been confronted with, recurrent labour agitation as is the norm in the newspaper industry, has not been one of Ansari's major headaches.

Not that Ansari has not had his share of troubles. In July 1979 for the first time ever in the history of the company, 6 members of the *Inquilab* staff struck work for a week demanding a revision of pay scales.

Recently on 29th July 1981, on *Mid-Day's* second anniversary, except for the editorial teams, all production personnel of *Inquilab*, *Mid-Day* and *Sportsweek* struck work for a day.

'Though slightly taken aback by the first ever labour agitation on our hands, we managed to devise a wage policy that was acceptable to both sides and within a week all employees were back at work,' says Ansari who is however reluctant to comment on the reasons that prompted *Inquilab* and *Mid-Day* publication employees to resort to strike action. 'Negotiations for demands such as sickness leave, etc. are still going on,' admits Ansari.

His trials and tribulations notwithstanding, Ansari has a number of new projects up his sleeve. Already working on the launch of an edition of *Mid-Day* from Bangalore and Delhi, the journalistic grapevine is humming with rumours of Ansari's attempts to acquire Bombay's ailing morning daily—the Free Press Journal (circulation: 40,000).

'My dream is to start a morning daily,' says Ansari enigmatically and adds, 'I hope to retire at the age of 50 and do something quite different—farming for instance.'

With seven years to go, the chances are that the man who has surprised the press barons with his smooth entry into the big league of Indian journalism may do it again—launch a successful morning daily before he makes for the green fields.

Strike

Coming back to the subject of strikes, my father had never faced a strike by his employees. Therefore, I was deeply hurt when, at the instigation of a labour leader who had managed to get workers to form a union and influence some of his members to make demands for ridiculous increases in emoluments, threatened to go on strike.

My father had always taught me to be fair to the staff and pay them even more than what the law stipulated. I was distraught when a strike notice was sent to me, especially since I had, of my own accord, started the practice of serving every press worker a mid-morning glass of milk. What hurt even more was the fact that the threat came soon after I had, for the first time, invited my managerial staff to my home for an evening of food, music and revelry.

About 30 members of the press staff—two of whom had physical disablities and whom I had employed at the request of the then retired Test cricket captain Vijay Merchant, who did sterling work persons with disabilities, struck work.

As was normal practice in those days of irresponsible trade unionism, they would collect outside our premises and raise slogans. One afternoon, I was going home for lunch along with sons Tarique and Sharique when a demonstrator shouted *'Khalid Ansari Murdabad!'* (Death to Khalid Ansari!) I stopped in my tracks and asked, 'I want to see the person who said that.'

Upon not receiving a reply, I held my sons close and told the demonstrators, 'See these sons of mine. Even though they've returned after studies in the US, they dirty their hands working on the printing presses. I'm telling you here and now in their presence: if you do not behave yourselves and instead, make unfair demands, you'll have to leave. Behave yourselves and you will get more from me than what the law provides.'

I was delighted when AFST, Aziz Currimbhoy and senior members of the *Sportsweek* editorial staff—Ron Hendricks, Sharad Kotnis, Ossie Manuel, Gopi Baskaran, Javed Akhtar Siddiqui, Sunder Mani et al. offered to help in the continuity of *Mid-Day* during the strike even though it was way beyond their call of duty and meant working for inordinately long—and punishing—hours.

The strike ended the very next day; that was the first and last time we had one in the history of the organization.

Going back, even weeks near the scheduled *Mid-Day* launch date, several well-meaning friends tried their best to dissuade me from the seemingly insane venture.

Shunu Sen, the marketing wunderkind and my former JWT client at Hindustan Lever, summoned all his persuasive powers to dissuade me from my 'folly.'

But a few friends, and fellow Rotarians such as Sadanand Shetty, founder of Fouress Corporation and Firoz Baldiwala of Tayabi Bucket Factory, treated my magnificent obsession as their own and helped no end in my attempts at getting bank loans for the acquisition of imported printing and typesetting machinery.

I owe Mihir Bose—bhadralok of the illustrious Bose family of Calcutta that manufactured the renowned Duckback raincoats and gum boots, and who has won renown in England as a distinguished journalist—a huge debt of gratitude for his invaluable guidance and editorial inputs at that stage of *Mid-Day*.

As an aside: Mihir and I were wetting our whistles on the balcony of the Patiala Pavilion at the Brabourne Stadium at the time I was planning the paper. I happened to mention to Mihir that work on the under-construction revolving tower atop the Ambassador Hotel, opposite the stadium, had been suspended because of alleged unlawful activities indulged in by the owners under the Maintenance of Internal Security Act (MISA).

Always quick on the draw, Mihir retorted, 'You should rename it the "Leaning Tower of MISA!"'

Ye Hai Bambai Meri Jaan
(This is Bombay, My Dear)

In our editorial planning, the *Mid-Day* staff and I endeavoured to be supra-local, sons and daughters of the city—after all, good journalism is all about addressing and championing the needs of the community to which one belongs.

We endeavoured to be young at heart, cheeky and not afraid to take on government, politicians and vested interests. This prompted then chief minister A.R. Antulay (who secretly enjoyed being addressed as 'Aurangzeb') to point a finger at me at a public meeting and thunder, 'My friend Mr Ansari is here. Mr Ansari, I'm not afraid of you...you and your paper can write whatever you like against me.'

All manner of inducements were made by politicians, consulates, business houses and vested interests to influence and pressure. I'm proud to say that our staff was steadfast in its integrity and commitment to what I may term 'honest' journalism with deep allegiance to our profession and readers.

◆

After being in existence for 11 years, *Sportsweek* was well established as regards circulation but within a limited distribution and marketing universe in metropolitan Mumbai. Setting up an effective, efficient network in the suburbs and beyond to compete against established giants such as *The Times of India* and *Free Press Journal* groups, which published our competitive newspapers, was no mean task.

But for some strange reason, both our rival groups continued to treat their afternoon offerings, the *Evening News of India* and the *Free Press Bulletin*, indifferently as regards content and marketing even after we launched our campaign announcing commencement of publication from 20 June 1979.

In yet another strange occurrence in keeping with the theme of the benevolence of the One Above and the Donkey, a terrible twin tragedy in the form of a fire at the offices of the *Free Press Bulletin* and a strike at *The Times of India* prompted closure of both publications in June 1979. Our senior staff members, as well as my family, instantaneously and unanimously decided that it would be grossly improper to launch *Mid-Day* keeping in mind the recent calamities that had befallen our competitors.

There is a very apposite German word 'schadenfreude' (meaning pleasure or advantage derived from someone else's misfortune). We decided to postpone our launch by a week to provide a level playing field for what we expected to be a war of attrition.

In an analytical article on Mumbai's afternoon newspaper scene, *Society* magazine wrote:

> The birth of *Mid-Day*, four years ago was in the most fortuitous circumstances. *Evening News of India*, the leading eveninger was off the market because of a strike at *The Times of India*, *Free Press Bulletin*, the second runner, was off the stands too due to a fire in the '*Free Press*' building. *Mid-Day* naturally became an instant hit. The first two hurriedly put things in order, but to their dismay realised that the market had eloped with a new lover.
>
> A team of dedicated reporters, headed by the self-effacing Behram Contractor, worked night and day to build the paper into another of Bombay's daily habits.
>
> Khalid Ansari, its managing editor, till then known for his sports publication *Sportsweek*, suddenly became one of the most successful publisher-editors in India.
>
> As the paper grew from strength, leaving its competition behind, it suddenly began adopting a more strident attitude towards politics and civic affairs.

Ye Hai Bambai Meri Jaan(This is Bombay, My Dear)

The attractive glossy eveninger with its foreign titbits and city ads and large headlines became a forum where exasperated citizens could vent their venom at public officials and others.

A consumer action soon took shape with tremendous success and probably created a situation wherein germs of the concept of accountability came in. ACT (Action by Citizens Today), *Mid-Day's a*ctivist project launched in 1983, was only a small step from there on.

Elaborating on the mass movement, *Society* magazine went on:

> Khalid Ansari is, perhaps, the city's highest profile editors. Almost every day, his columns in bold lettering on the top left-hand corner of the front page, have been exhorting the people to ACT.
>
> The language used is rhetorical, similar to the one used during times of war. Perhaps, it is an emergency. Ansari earnestly feels that Bombay (he calls it 'Slum-bay') has had it unless we ACT now. The slogan is 'help yourself, don't depend on others to help you.'

◆

It took a herculean effort, toil and sweat from our committed team and me to establish, from scratch, a newspaper distribution network in the far-flung corners, nooks and crannies of our metropolis in order to effectively compete against established rival channels. We set about to achieve these goals through personal contacts with individual shopkeepers, hawkers and delivery boys.

The task was all the more daunting since, although the delivery channels for the numerous English and Indian language morning newspapers were well-established, that was not the case with the afternoon/evening papers. Most of the part time delivery boys were already settled in their full-time day jobs. With no office or home delivery system in place during the day, it initially took immense coaxing and cajoling to convince general shopkeepers and hawkers to give the new kid on the block a fair trial.

I have a hunch: the sight of the newspaper publisher personally approaching the vendors ('*bhaiyyas*')—with bundles on his shoulders, as had happened in the case of the *Sportsweek* launch, and pleading with them to stock copies, made them pity me.

Whatever the reason, it served my purpose since I learnt fairly early in life to not let false pride come in the way of achieving what I have set my mind on.

◆

If establishing a distribution and circulation network for the new entrant in the afternoon (and later, Sunday morning for *Sunday Mid-Day*) market was fraught with problems, getting advertising support from major advertisers in the commercial capital of the country, was relatively much easier.

As advertising guru Alyque Padamsee remarked to me at the *Mid-Day* launch function, the tabloid eveningers then in existence in Mumbai were considered dispensable 'rags' or scandal sheets. But the *Mid-Day* concept was 'an idea whose time had come… it has come like a breath of fresh air in an otherwise turgid market,' he said. It was certainly high praise from an ad professional who knew his onions, soon vindicated by the flood of advertising that flowed in from almost the paper's inception.

As far as I was concerned, a tabloid's personality should be judged not only by its size and format but by content of relevance to readers in terms of important, interesting, useful, illuminating and entertaining news and features presented *honestly* in simple, racy, and at times even saucy, style.

For me, the dimensions of a newspaper did not matter. There are newspapers of all shapes, sizes and personalities in the world.

As popular English poet William Cowper (1731–1800) wrote in the poem 'The Progress of Error' about the good, the bad and evil influence of the press:

> Thou god of our idolatry, the Press?
> By thee religion, liberty, and laws,
> Exert their influence and advance their cause:
> By thee worse plagues than Pharaoh's land befell,
> Diffused, make Earth the vestibule of Hell;
> Thou fountain, at which drink the good and wise,

Ye Hai Bambai Meri Jaan(This is Bombay, My Dear)

Thou ever-bubbling spring of endless lies;
Like Eden's dread probationary tree,
Knowledge of good and evil is from thee!

◆

Speaking of tabloids, in a wide-ranging tête-à-tête in *Celebrity* magazine between the illustrious Russi Karanjia, founder of *Blitz* and *The Daily* newspaper and me, we discussed the scurrilous campaign launched by the established morning dailies of that time against his and my so-called 'dirty tabloids,' to stunt our development and growth. 'All kinds of impediments were placed in our way,' Russi averred, 'I am eternally grateful to you for your help in distributing *The Daily*. You called at my office in person, Khalid, that's the most important thing, a presence in time of need.'

When the *Celebrity* magazine reporter pointed out that we were competitors, Russi interjected, 'So what? We live in a competitive world,' at which I reminded him, 'When we started *Sunday Mid-Day*, we were in the same slot as you—Sunday morning tabloid—yet this did not come in the way of helping each other out. You Russy were kind enough to print my paper when my machines broke down.'

◆

My earlier analysis of the content and readership of the competitors, the *Evening News of India* and the *Free Press Bulletin*, had made it clear as daylight that in the bustling *urbs prima in Indis* (premier city of India) there was a crying need for an afternoon newspaper of substance, which would *inform, educate, entertain and enlighten, even titillate,* the commuter on his way back home from work.

It was vital to enlarge the paper's appeal to the *entire* family and thereby compel the working person to carry the copy home to family, children and grandchildren. It raised my hackles to see a discarded copy on the streets. Therefore, the motto 'The Complete Family Newspaper' on the paper's masthead. In other words, unlike the other afternoon/evening dailies, the challenge was to produce, day after day, a substantial, unputdownable, sexy tabloid (for its ease of handling in a train or bus). A tabloid that would captivate tired, working people of both sexes who were, otherwise, bored while commuting long distances between their offices and homes.

Furthermore, also unlike other Indian metro cities, the Mumbai commuter was privileged to be able to commute in relative comfort but who had nothing inexpensive—and with pizzazz—to engross, amuse and entertain them on the trip back home.

Ye Hai Bambai Meri Jaan(This is Bombay, My Dear)

'Call It Bloody "Midnight"'

Among some superstitious people in India, there is a belief that rain on an important occasion can portend either extreme calamity or unmitigated good luck! Be that as it may, in the case of *Mid-Day*, it rained torrentially from the previous night, right through the day and into the next night.

On the morning of the launch, to the flash of lightning and clap of thunder, we made our way to our office/printing press premises at a low-lying Tardeo junction, which is prone to knee-deep flooding, to be greeted by the heart-breaking sight of our drenched newsprint rolls, stacked in the passageway for lack of indoor space. The makeshift ceiling below the porous roof of the leaking, dilapidated super-structure was drip, drip, dripping as editorial and other staff took their seats above their typewriters, umbrellas in hand.

If all that wasn't bad enough: the antiquated studio and pre-press departments were ankle-deep in water with staff valiantly trying to drain the water out. At around press-time (11.30 a.m.), the electric supply failed and came back only at around 1 p.m. when word came in that the obsolescent printing press was refusing to respond to the print foreman's commands.

The edition had been 'put to bed' according to schedule at 12 noon, but there was no sign of the press starting. Precious minutes turned to agonizing hours and the hawkers, in anticipation of the new paper, touted as 'bright, new, exciting' were getting resigned to seeing a stillborn.

With witless optimism—and bravado, as I see it in hindsight—I had decided to be installed the same day as president of the Rotary Club of Bombay Mid-Town at 7 p.m. at the Taj Mahal Hotel Ballroom at which Field Marshal Manekshaw had very kindly agreed to be chief guest.

Apologizing profusely to my staff at a hurriedly called meeting, I rushed off home at 4 p.m.—egg all over my face—to try and look respectable, and unfazed, for the inaugural function. I had left word at the press for the first copy of the newspaper to be rushed to the function in a sealed envelope for my eyes only. With one eye at the entrance, I was getting increasingly apprehensive as the function got under way with no envelope in sight at 8.30 p.m.

Imagine my mixed emotions when the envelope was finally at hand. I slipped it under the head table at which we were seated, sneaked a surreptitious look at the contents to ensure it wasn't blank or totally black and, hands trembling, handed the copy to the field marshal.

'Here we are, sir—my first copy of *Mid-Day*.'

The field marshal, unmindful of the large audience, unfolded the copy, looked at his watch, then at me, smiled and said with an expression that I can only describe as one expressing beatitude, 'Call it bloody "Midnight," Khalid.'

◆

In its issue dated August 1979, three weeks after the launch of *Mid-Day*, *Business India* magazine quoted me as saying:

> To be honest, I am overwhelmed by the response of the public.
>
> By any yardstick, the paper has proved to be a success with sales spurting dramatically from an initial circulation of 21,700 to 100,000 on 17th July, i.e. within a short span of 21 days.'
>
> We have been very lucky that just as we launched *Mid-Day*, events that would gladden any newsman's heart followed one after another with astonishing rapidity.'
>
> First it was the fear of *Skylab,* the 78-tonne monster that was hurtling through space and which could have crashed down

on anyone's head. Then there was the excitement generated by the Wimbledon tennis tournament and now the political crisis in Delhi (fall of the Janata government). All these events generated a lot of interest and they were covered intensively by *Mid-Day*.

Be that as it may, I was perplexed at the insouciance shown by the larger, well-established groups at the shifting sands, the changing dynamics, in the afternoon/evening newspaper segment.

◆

Even as the *Free Press Bulletin* remained surprisingly unconcerned, the *Evening News*, finally, roped in poet-turned-journalist Pritish Nandy, then the flavour of the month and editor of *The Illustrated Weekly of India*, as its editor to stem the tide and resuscitate the paper in a new avatar as editor.

Around that time, there was this invitation for a cup of tea from The Times Group vice-chairman Sameer Jain at his headquarters, followed by another at the Willingdon Sports Club. As I waited, for a takeover bid from the affectionately-nicknamed Old Lady of Bori Bunder (*The Times of India*), it just didn't materialize.

I'm still perplexed as to what it was all about: had the Jains of the gargantuan Times Group so desired, they could have easily devoured the comparatively miniscule *Mid-Day* and *Inquilab* papers—small fish swimming in vast oceans and in which we were way out of their depth—for breakfast.

Mid-Day's Plan For Citizens (ACT), 1983

ACT—Action by Citizens Today—was really Tarique's brainchild but he made me believe it was mine. Recognizing its awesome potential through *Mid-Day*, I embraced it passionately, penning daily front page editorials calling upon the citizens of Mumbai to shed their apathy and reliance upon others and ACT to help themselves.

Limitations of space in these memoirs come in the way of reproducing too many of the ACT articles here. Just one, below, should suffice to convey the intent and—if I may say so myself—sincerity of purpose, which sadly came to nought for a variety of reasons and my own faulty judgement.

The inaugural front-page editorial read:

> Here it is. ACT—'Action by Citizens Today'.
>
> *Mid-Day's* long-awaited plan to help improve the quality of life in this wretched toilet city of Slumbay. It's an ACTION-orientated plan to make elected representatives and public servants responsible, answerable, accountable to the people.
>
> ACT is of the people, for the people.
>
> The PEOPLE: the fountainhead of all power and authority. The raison d'être of our public *servants* who have become our *masters*, entirely because of our own indifference and unconcern.
>
> It has, therefore become *Mid-Day's* responsibility to come up with a well-reasoned, carefully worked out plan which will

be accepted by the people and which will succeed, given the people's disgust with the state of affairs and their impatience to do something about it immediately.

We are grateful to our public servants such as the RTO, The Bombay Telephones GM, the municipal and police commissioners, the BEST chairman and the Regional Transport Officer who have assured us all cooperation in the public interest. They have welcomed our move to strengthen their hands in the service of the people.

At the outset we would like to emphasise that ACT calls for ORGANISED action by the PEOPLE themselves who have to learn that the best form of help is self-help.

Mid-Day's role in ACT will be that of a catalyst. It will, while remaining in the background, actively perform the role of friend, guide, adviser.

It will NOT project itself or any personalities associated with it. It will hopefully inspire, guide, show the way.

Today Mid-Day is publishing a map showing the zone-wise breakdown of the city for ACT-ion calling upon people to organize themselves into informal working groups in their respective zones.

It is imperative that politics be kept out, that there be no hankering after position and power, and that NO money be collected from the public.

If these zone-wise ACT-ion groups do decide to raise money at any time, they will have to ensure prudence as regards spending, as also proper audit procedures and complete accountability to their zonal committees.

Confrontation, which can be counterproductive, will have to be avoided as far as possible.

Most importantly, ACT will be uncompromisingly scrupulous and law-abiding in its methods at all times. It will respect authority and the rule of law. It will, under no circumstances, take the law into its own hands for that can only lead to anarchy and chaos.

Now the objectives.

The problems confronting the hapless citizens of this metropolis are, alas, so numerous that any attempt at solving all or most of them will only result in dissipation of energies and, therefore, be unproductive.

ACT will, therefore, concentrate on 12 problem areas which call for urgent attention and which affect a vast majority of the population.

The problem of overpopulation, congestion and corruption will, therefore, NOT be the immediate concern of ACT although they will not be lost sight of.

What then, will the short-term objectives, the immediate concern of ACT be?

Having defined the problems and geographical area of operation, ACT will zero in to the TARGET or PRESSURE points for concentrated attack.

One of the prime factors responsible for peoples' frustration is insufficient knowledge as regards avenues for redress of grievances.

Only because we have not yet created a culture of telling our public servants that they occupy their high and mighty positions for us, the people, who pay for their jobs. And that they should jolly well deliver the goods or else...

Tolerant and patient as we are as a people, we do not, in our resignation to destiny, raise hell in organized fashion and make it clear in no uncertain terms to our elected representatives in parliament, the legislative assembly and council and the municipal corporation that we are concerned NOT with excuses and promises, promises and more sickening promises – but only with RESULTS.

Because, bluntly put, we do not tell them that if they want our votes, they must, absolutely MUST, produce RESULTS.

Mid-Day will therefore publish every Saturday a zone-wise list of members of parliament (MPs), MLA's, MLC's and municipal councillors and more importantly, deputy municipal commissioners, ward officers, executive engineers, complaints officers and the like in the Bombay Municipal Corporation, Bombay Telephones, the police administration, the regional transport office, the BEST and the Western and Central railways.

Individuals and citizens groups will thus know who to

approach and whose necks to catch hold of, who to pester, whose life to make miserable until their problem is solved.

The task, therefore, before the various zone-wise groups which we see coming up under the ACT banner, is arduous.

Only ORGANISED, CONCERTED action on the part of these zone-wise groups will bear fruit and help create a climate in which accountability to the public will be of paramount importance.

There can be no panacea for the city's ills. The cure will come only from the hard work of its residents.

ACT can only show the way. The rest is up to the people themselves.

Let's, therefore, ACT—NOW.

'Will You Accept Bombay's Challenge, Madam PM?'

In another ACT column on top of page 1, headlined 'Will You Accept Bombay's challenge, Madam PM?' written on the day of prime minister Indira Gandhi's arrival in Mumbai, I wrote:

Welcome, madam prime minister, to Bombay, the city of which your father was so proud.

Swagatam to Urbs Prima in Indis, as it was known in days gone by.

Khushamdeed, to slum-bay, toilet metropolis gutter city—as it is becoming known the world over.

The problems the city, as you are aware, are gigantic, incapable of solution in the near future. But, as is well known, the ills have been caused by members of your own party.

Your responsibility, madam prime minister, is therefore that much greater. Bombay, after all, is the acknowledged financial capital of the country. The cancer afflicting the city, therefore, should be the concern of the whole country and your prime concern, madam prime minister. Viewed dispassionately, the problems of the megapolis stem out of congestion and its concomitant, overpopulation, a national malaise. Disperse the population and most of the city's problems will be solved expeditiously, if not, *ipso facto.*

The intention of those who advocate slum improvement is not what it is termed, but their REMOVAL in a planned, phased-out and, MOST IMPORTANTLY, humane manner. Followed by the provision, for half the city's population which lives in squalid, inhuman conditions in 'jhopadpattis', decent accommodation OUTSIDE (but close to) the city with provision for good commuting facilities.

Unfortunately, vested interests are doing their best to prevent this from happening for reasons well known to you. The paradox of the situation is that the more Bombay is made beautiful, habitable, liveable, the greater the influx.

And, therefore, the more acute its problems caused by migrants who have to be provided for from the limited resources of the state government and the municipal corporation but whose contribution to the exchequer is negligible if anything at all.

The influx from the villages into the metropolis is caused, as you are aware madam prime minister, not for any love for the city on the part of those who flock to it at the average rate of 500 families per day. It is caused because of job opportunities, which the bursting-at-the-seams city provides.

Since it is not possible in a democracy to restrict the movement of people from one part of the country to another, it is important to demagnetise the city as provider of jobs and feeder of hungry stomachs."

Calling for central and state government offices, wholesale markets and textile mills to be shifted to the hinterland and to (then) stillborn New Bombay, as a means to decongest the metropolis and disperse the population, the appeal to Indira Gandhi said:

In the process, the hapless inhabitants of the city who are compelled to live in conditions unfit for beasts and which are an affront to human dignity, will find an attractive alternative—provided, of course, the entire infrastructure for the Good Life is set up by government and the textile mills, some of which your government took over yesterday.

The article goes on to conclude:

> What is called for, essentially, is POLITICAL WILL—of the variety demonstrated by us when we enabled our people to hold heads high by impeccably organising the Asian Games in New Delhi against tremendous odds.
>
> And the Non-Aligned Summit (NAM) thereafter. 'These two major events proclaimed in unmistakable terms to the world at large that 'India can do it', as you term it.

◈

A full page called 'Action Mail' was devoted to readers' woes. A few sample headlines:
'Manhole Hazard'
'Clean Up'
'Don't make us wait for the Rajdhani'
'Whose side are you on, BEST?'
'Start a rowboat and pedal service in the Bandra Talao'
'Why not a ropeway between Mankhurd and Navi Mumbai?'

'Will You Accept Bombay's Challenge, Madam PM?'

JRD and Palkhivala

Mid-Day's crusading style struck a chord with the Mumbaikars and the circulation figures of the paper zoomed beyond expectation.

The response to ACT was overwhelming. Readers flooded us with offers of help. They wished to stop by at our office to make suggestions, volunteer their time, even offer money. But accepting even a paisa was an absolute no no. Our informal manifesto made it clear that neither we, nor any of our well-wishers would touch even a paisa. And politicians were anathema.

The revered JRD Tata invited me to tea at his office in Bombay House and while expressing disappointment that the Eastern Express Highway project, his brainchild, was gathering dust in some musty government office, offered help in its execution. (Note: the 16.8 km long freeway connecting P D'Mello Road in South Mumbai to the Eastern Express Highway at Chembur was, at long last, completed on 16 June 2014, long after JRD's demise).

The scholarly Nani Palkhivala, who, while dissecting the annual Finance Bill dazzled thousands of us with his amazing memory, oratorical fluency and analytical brilliance at the capacious Brabourne Stadium lawns, very graciously invited my wife Rukya and me to his Commonwealth Building home at Nariman Point to offer help. Air Marshal Idris Hasan Latif and his charming lady Bilkees also befriended us.

The Latifs very kindly included Rukya and me in their guest list (as a result of which we were invited to informal lunches and dinners as also VVIP banquets with H.H. Prince Karim Aga Khan IV—the Imam and spiritual leader of the world's approximately 15 million Ismaili Muslims, and Prince Charles of England) at Raj Bhavan, their official residence at Mumbai's southern tip.

It was because of ACT and it was all very heady. It opened my eyes to the enormity of the task I had taken on without realizing the burden.

WEIGHING THE AGA KHAN IN DIAMONDS

On the topic of the Aga Khan, I remember, in 1946, my uncle Abdul Rehman taking me, then all of nine years old to see the weighing-in ceremony, from the North Stand of the Brabourne Stadium, on the Diamond Jubilee of the 48th Imam, Sultan Sir Mohammed Shah (Aga Khan III), head of the Ismaili community of that time. I remember being very impressed when informed that the funds from sale of the diamonds bought from community members' donations would be utilized worldwide for the education and social welfare of the community.

According to witnesses alive today, the Aga Khan was seated on one scale, and a stockpile of diamonds were placed in a casket 'with a flourish,' on the other. Given that, although only 5 feet 5 inches in height, he was amply endowed as regards avoirdupois—243 pounds—the value of the diamonds at that time was estimated at £640,000.

A similar function was held in Dar es Salaam, Tanzania the same year, where his loyal followers were said to have made generous donations as well.

I shall never forget the *mehmaan nawazi* (hospitality) of my idol Nani Palkhivala and his lovely wife Nergish at a buffet dinner referred to above and from which I learnt valuable lessons.

We were a group of eight altogether. Although domestics were in attendance, periodically bringing beverages and mixers to the lounge and dining table, the humble genius insisted—absolutely insisted—on serving us all with his own hands. Such was the humility of the great man.

Jugaad

There is this unsophisticated but versatile colloquial Hindi-Urdu word called 'jugaad' that has been officially accepted by the world's most acknowledged English dictionary, the *Oxford English Dictionary*. According to that, jugaad means 'a flexible approach to problem-solving, that uses limited resources in an innovative way' (in other words, by craftily bending the rules!).

Some latter-day linguists would have us believe that the closest English translation you can have is 'lifehack' or 'hack' for short. For instance: 'Lifehacks become the solutions when the actual ones are too arduous or laborious' or 'I really must think of a lifehack, else there's no way I can get this work done on time'.

And so it was with ACT.

As explained, ACT was conceived as a people's movement—of, by and for the people—with the sole objective of improving the quality of lives of the people of Mumbai.

While I was adamant that politicians should have no part in the movement, in my naivete—call it guilelessness, if you like—I had reckoned without the ingenuity of the self-seeking, publicity-coveting *jugaadis*. Here was a golden opportunity for hucksters, hustlers, fixers, to masquerade as social workers, for NGOs, self-proclaimed activists and for all manner of pretentious wannabes and opportunists to feather their nests, promote themselves and their nefarious interests and even cosy up to the powers that be in the city's public services for *waasta* (Arabic word meaning 'gain').

Moreover, there was gross misunderstanding of the basic concept of the entire people's movement: ACT certainly wasn't meant to be an agency to solve—that too, gratis—the personal civic problems of residents of the city; it was intended as a guidepost for aggrieved people to know which door to knock, where to go and whom to meet for redress.

The response was overwhelming. Although, innumerable groups of people from various wards and areas were formed, we at *Mid-Day* were deluged by requests from people who weren't prepared to lift their own little finger to solve their own problems (viz. garbage collection etc.,) but expected us to get it done on their behalf.

Then there was the usual unscrupulous lot which saw in ACT a stepladder and an opportunity to fulfil their fond hopes and aspirations of self-centred leadership and who resorted to ingenious forms of jugaad.

There was also this 'social worker' celebrity who once tried to persuade a keen social service-minded young lady to disassociate herself from ACT and switch over to his own moneymaking organization only because—'Khalid Ansari is a Muslim.'

In any event, soon after the launch of ACT, I had moved to Dubai on the *Khaleej Times* assignment in the belief, more out of wishful thinking than hard-headed reality, that the movement would snowball, as it had shown promise of doing, gather momentum and carry on in pursuit of its objectives.

If wishes were horses...

◆

The movement did take off, but not in the manner it was meant to. It was certainly *not* meant to be for the benefit of the *jugaadis*. Most importantly the people, its raison d'être, were not prepared to help themselves. Surely we could not possibly solve everybody's problems. We had grossly underestimated Mumbaikars' deep-rooted tendency of refusing to help themselves.

My hopes dashed, we were compelled to discontinue ACT, despite entreaties from the *jugaadis*.

◆

However, there was some small comfort to be gained from the experiment: our dream of making ACT a people's mass movement, that would rid the metropolis of at least some of its many problems and continue in the long run for the good of the people by the people themselves, had taken root.

Many of the area-wise citizens' groups formed during its existence by well-meaning people who were in tune with the fundamentals of ACT, are doing outstanding work to this day, although not on the scale we envisaged.

The seeds of the mass movement seem to have taken root, just as *Sportsweek's* 'Run for Fun' mission was to introduce the undoubted health benefits of running and walking to the masses. It's a wonderful feeling: every time I see people of all ages 'running for their lives' in the streets and open spaces of Mumbai, and read about citizen's groups helping themselves.

ELEVEN

THE BOLD(S) AND THE BEAUTIFUL(S)

Field Marshal 'Sam Bahadur' Manekshaw

As for my persistent advocacy through *Sportsweek* that sports be made compulsory in schools all over the country, I must admit it was a non-starter. My campaign got mired in centre-state politics, with both governments passing the buck to the other saying it was not their 'subject' (meaning jurisdiction).

Having flopped in efforts through *Sportsweek* to convince the powers-that-be not only of the benign physical, mental and emotional but also character-building attributes of sport, I decided to pursue this agenda through the nation's premier sports advisory body, the All India Council of Sport (AICS), of which I was appointed member, first under General P.P. Kumaramangalam, then Field Marshal Sam Manekshaw.

Week after week I tried to hammer home the point that sports should be made compulsory in schools, but I must admit my efforts were again a colossal failure. I should have known better. I was taking on the slothful and devil-may-care bureaucratic machinery of the central government's then leviathan Ministry of Sports, for members of which the good of Indian sport, forget the physical well-being of their fellow Indians, was consistently the last item on their agendas.

General Kumaramangalam was a cultured soldier of distinction but, sadly naïve in knowing how to tackle the devious gargantuan government machinery. The bureaucrats in New Delhi knew precisely how to manipulate him.

Working under him was a most frustrating experience. I was about to resign when word got around that the charismatic Field Marshal Manekshaw (India's second field marshal after Kodandera Madappa Cariappa) would succeed General Kumaramangalam.

I delayed submitting my resignation in the hope that I would be renominated to the country's august body, believing naively that under the field marshal we could breathe life into Indian sport which, was then in a pathetic state to say the least.

It so transpired that I was renominated. I vividly remember the inauguration of the AICS at Shastri Bhavan, headquarters of the Ministry of Information and Broadcasting in New Delhi by some joker-turned-minister.

No sooner had he departed after the inauguration (whoever heard of a committee inauguration!), chairman Field Marshal Manekshaw rubbed his hands derisively and thundered: 'Well, lady (there was one woman on the council) and gentlemen, now that we've finished with the rubbish, let's get on with brass tacks...let's do something about Indian sport. We all know where the problems of Indian sport begin... around this bloody table!'

Before he knew what hit him, the same government officials seated around that table—secretaries, including under/joint/additional secretaries and sundry other 'babus'—had clipped the wings of the redoubtable hero of the 1971 Bangladesh War, a legend in his own lifetime.

Impartial, well-considered decisions taken by the council were overruled with impunity. If we (AICS) decided that any individual or team recommended by the particular discipline's national body should not be cleared for participation in an international event for sound and valid reason, they would be cleared and vice-versa.

The devoted but, at times, breviloquent attempts of Sam Manekshaw to reform the pompous, Machiavellian pooh-bahs who presided over the destinies of Indian sport, to make them abandon their obsessive pursuit of the fishes and loaves of office: the leeches were just too devious and bloodthirsty for the guileless soldier in matters of sport administration—or, more aptly, maladministration!

On a personal level, however, my association with the field marshal in the AICS enabled me to learn some valuable life lessons for which I shall remain grateful. Despite his abject failure in his dealings with the mandarins of Indian sports, I was an unashamed admirer of Sam Manekshaw, who was my hero and who I always addressed as 'Sir,' despite his repeated admonishments that I address him by his first name. Much more than any other individual whom I came in contact with, except my father, he was my role model not only for his exploits as soldier, but more so for the manner in which he conducted himself, his demeanour, his patriotism, humility, egalitarianism, secularism, transparent honesty and sincerity and, above all, charm and humour.

In the words of William Shakespeare (in *Julius Caesar*), Antony says of Julius Caesar:

His life was gentle, and the elements
So mix'd in him that Nature might stand up
And say to all the world, 'This was a man!'

Unlike some of our hypocritical public life figures who are notorious for leading duplicitous lives, with the field marshal, you got what you saw.

There were no smoke and mirrors where he was concerned. A

Field Marshal 'Sam Bahadur' Manekshaw

quintessential bon vivant and engaging raconteur, he liked the good things in life: attractive ladies who could converse intelligently, good whisky poured in generous measure. 'I'm a Patiala Parsi, pour me a double,' he would say unapologetically.

Sam, affectionately addressed as 'Sam Bahadur' by his Gurkha regiment, also loved music. When upbraided by then Prime Minister Indira Gandhi for reportedly being seen dancing in public late one night at a five-star New Delhi hotel discotheque, he retorted, 'Your information is absolutely correct, Madam Prime Minister, I was out until late last night...dancing with my daughters.'

AICS meetings were held in different parts of the country to coincide with important events, training camps and the like. After a while, the field marshal settled into a meeting routine:

- Meeting commencement at 9 a.m. sharp (no excuses)
- Tight, disciplined, no-nonsense conduct of meetings to ensure culmination between two to three hours, irrespective of number of items on the agenda
- Lunch at 1 p.m. sharp
- 'Me-time' in hotel suite
- 7 p.m. drinks and dinner for the two of us in his hotel suite (or my home, if in Mumbai), solving the world's problems until the cows come home

Arjuna Awards

I can say in all honesty that these evening sessions with the legend rate among the most educational, edifying, entertaining experiences of my life.

Tragically, they were all too short-lived, since the AICS was disbanded for political compulsions (and to be honest, since it served no real constructive purpose) and the two of us went our different ways: the field marshal on his multifarious post-retirement military and corporate involvements and I on mine.

The exchange between him and Prime Minister Indira Gandhi in which he reportedly asked her 'to mind her own business and leave the business of war to him' is well-known. But before changing gears, I must narrate an amusing lesser-known real-life incident that proclaimed the admirable, but misunderstood, human being he was.

Having attended an Arjuna Awards ceremony at Rashtrapati Bhavan, New Delhi, he and I were making our way back to our hotel. Upon seeing Manekshaw, the liveried chowkidar (watchman), caught somewhat unawares by our unannounced arrival, bent low in an impromptu gesture of comical servility, that was neither salute, nor namaste. The field marshal went up to the embarrassed watchman, put an arm around his shoulders with a smile, saying, '*Beta, kabhi kisi ke samne mat jhuko, siwai apne biwi ke*' (Son, never bow before anybody—except your wife).

◆

Having watched field marshal's dedication, his no-nonsense can-do demeanour at close quarters, I was deeply saddened that the iconic son of India was not allowed by the parasites who control Indian sport to clear the filth that had entered the soul of Indian sport.

Sam Manekshaw died of pneumonia at age 94. He did not really 'retire.' The first Indian Army officer to be promoted to the rank of field marshal with a career spanning four decades and five wars, 'faded away' as all soldiers are said to do.

He was given a 17-gun salute at a state funeral and laid to rest with full military honours in a Parsi graveyard in Udhagamandalam (Ootacamund) adjacent to the place where his late wife Silloo lies buried, after the last rites were performed according to Zoroastrian custom.

After his death, there was anger in many quarters that the farewell given to Manekshaw was not befitting his services to his country: that the last rites were held in Tamil Nadu and not the country's capital and that neither the President of India, the Prime Minister or the Army Chief were present at the funeral.

It is said that the field marshal incurred the wrath of some political elements in New Delhi because of his candid remarks that were construed as being 'unpatriotic.' He was charged with alleged sedition—the new buzz word which seems to be fast becoming the staple for people with a demented vindictive agenda in our country.

Rajmata Gayatri Devi of Jaipur

Age cannot wither her, nor custom stale
Her infinite variety.

—*Antony and Cleopatra*, William Shakespeare

I was introduced to the indescribably beautiful Rajmata Gayatri Devi at a party in Kolkata after which, with cricket our mutual magnificent obsession, we became good friends.

She would graciously come home, for tea or cocktails in the course of her prolonged dental treatment in Mumbai. She also did me the honour of having me, as guest, at Lillypool, her *kothi* (cottage) behind Jaipur's Rambagh Palace. The latter was subsequently converted into a hotel for the Taj group. Rajmata continued living at the *kothi* after her release from imprisonment during the infamous Emergency, a shameful blot on our democracy, until her death.

On one occasion during my stay at Lillypool, she presided over an elephant polo match and, on the other, a prize distribution event at the local school named after her and, at which she insisted that I too give away some of the trophies. Playing tennis ball cricket with the 'nippers' (children of the domestics) as she affectionately referred to them, in her backyard was an enchanting experience I shall never forget.

When I was president of the Bombay Midtown Rotary Club, I invited her to a reception for the Pakistan cricket team at the Taj, Mumbai which she kindly accepted. The adulation showered upon her by Imran Khan and his team had to be seen to be believed.

I requested Rajmata Saheba to be the chief guest at the release function of my book *Sachin: Born to Bat* at the CCI by Sunil Gavaskar, which she accepted provisionally, her fragile health permitting. Unfortunately, she couldn't make it but her profuse apologies, before and after the event, were embarrassing.

Rajmata's beauty was ethereal: her skin almost impossibly translucent, her features perfect beyond description: her nose classically aquiline, her doe-like eyes limpid with a hint of coyness. What made her absolutely ravishing was her comportment, elegance and civility which far exceeded mere stunning beauty and for which *Vogue* magazine is said to have voted her among the 10 most beautiful women in the world.

That said, like Cleopatra in Shakespeare's *Antony and Cleopatra*, Gayatri Devi was overwhelmingly attractive to men not so much because of beauty alone but because of her fascinating unpredictability and range of moods.

La Lollo: the Most Beautiful Woman in the World

'I am very spoiled. All my life, I've had too many admirers,' Gina Lollobrigida is quoted as having said.

The reclusive Lollobrigida, who has not allowed visitors to her home since 2013 and now spends her time between Rome (where she has an Indian den) and Monte Carlo, was far from reclusive when she came to Mumbai in 1978 for the premiere of the film *Shalimar*. She was the life of the party at the film's reception at Mumbai's Mahalaxmi racecourse hosted by Krishna Shah, writer and director of the film.

The living legend was called the 'most beautiful woman in the world.' Humphrey Bogart said of her: 'Gina makes Marilyn Monroe look like Shirley Temple.'

I remember her for her gift of smiling at every man she was introduced to in a manner that made him believe he was the only man in her world.

Apart from being a successful actor, 'La Lollo,' now 94, is also a photojournalist and sculptor, and is reported to have a net worth of $50 million She owns a series of properties in Italy and Monte Carlo.

In 2014, she won a bitter legal battle with her son Milko Skofic Jr who wanted to wrest control of her fortune, saying she was under the sway of young admirers, and was therefore incapable of handling her affairs.

In the process of writing these memoirs, I chanced upon some memorable old photographs of the erstwhile international sex symbol. I regret unearthing them: she had aged and certainly didn't conform to Shakespeare's memorable words (above) about a woman's 'infinite variety.' Sad!

'Lasting Beauty' Goldie Hawn

Then there was the meeting with the iconic 75-year-old Goldie Hawn who doesn't look a day older than half her age.

The Oscar and Golden Globe award-winning American actress, an Indophile, and producer, dancer and singer had just flown in to Mumbai with Sally Field for the star-studded premiere of her friend and my college-mate the late Ismail Merchant's feature film directorial debut of the Urdu movie *Muhafiz* ('In Custody').

As she spoke of her closeness to her family in Austin, Texas, I was struck by her limpid blue eyes which reflected her transparent persona and sincerity of purpose. More than her physical appearance she is also a woman of substance, involved in a virtual COVID-19 health and medicine endeavour with Dr Sanjay Gupta of CNN.

TWELVE

'PHOREN' JAUNTS

UK, Bahamas, Cuba

I often joked to people I was introduced to, that I started *Sportsweek* and *Mid-Day* because ownership was the only way to ensure that the 'garbage' I write is published. 'Who else will publish the rubbish I write?' I would deadpan, often leaving the listener confused.

But the fact remains that being able to push my pen for guaranteed publication opened many avenues to cover sport and other events, as also to travel the world, at times in the company of VIPS.

Again, space limitations, and the nature of these memoirs, prevent reproduction of too many of my dispatches from the trips abroad. A few should suffice to convey the flavour of the coverage.

For example, I was invited, as a representative of the *Inquilab* daily, to be a member of the press party accompanying former president Fakhruddin Ali Ahmed on a five-day visit to Singapore, Malaysia and Myanmar. A few hours after we landed at Singapore and checked into our hotels, we were informed that the president had taken ill and had to be rushed back to New Delhi. There has been much conjecture concerning this but not long after his return, the President signed the order declaring the abhorrent, draconian Emergency.

Among the memorable foreign VIP trips was the one in 1985 with Rajiv Gandhi, made possible for me by the maverick Mani Shankar Aiyar to whom I was casually introduced during one of my then frequent trips to the capital in connection with government work and advertising sales.

Mani was, at that time, finalizing the list of journalists for a rather extended trip to Britain, the Netherlands, the US, Bahamas and Cuba and was trying to fill the slot reserved for an Urdu representative. Now if that isn't being at the right place at the right time, I don't know what is. The 15-day trip on board Air India's 'Trishul' started with a day's halt in London where British Prime Minister Margaret Thatcher breached two protocols to receive our PM: she received Rajiv and wife Sonia on the tarmac (which is never done) and, with a guard of honour, a privilege normally reserved only for heads of state.

Rusi Karanjia of *Blitz* was a member of our press party and carried his story with the banner headline: 'Britannia Waives the Rules.' Brilliant! *Aapro* Rustomji (our Rusi) did have a way with words!

Boris Johnson, then mayor of London, hosted a lunch for the prime minister to which the media was also invited. Speculation lingers among Indian media persons to this day as to how a person who, by common consensus, was seemingly a buffoon, could occupy the high office he did in a city like London!

◆

This was followed by a brief stop at Stockholm, a meeting with the Swedish prime minister and a PR visit to the burial place of late Swedish Prime Minister Olof Palme who had a special equation with the Gandhi family and was assassinated on a Stockholm street, a murder that is said to have taken 34 years, 10,000 interviews and 134 murder confessions to solve.

Commonwealth Heads of Government Meeting (CHOGM)

Then there was the Commonwealth Heads of Government Meeting (CHOGM) 1985 hosted by the prime minister of the Bahamas, Sir Lynden Pindling in Nassau with whistle-stops by Prime Minister Rajiv Gandhi in London, Amsterdam, New York, Havana (Cuba) and an unscheduled last-minute halt at Moscow.

At the CHOGM conference, the Nassau Accord was agreed to, which called upon the government of South Africa to dismantle its apartheid policy (Britain's Margaret Thatcher was a stout opponent), enter into negotiations with the country's black majority and end its occupation of Namibia.

A Commonwealth Eminent Persons Group was established with Rajiv Gandhi, who played a major role in the proceedings concerning South Africa, as member, to investigate the South African issue and report back with recommendations ahead of the next CHOGM in London.

My report concluded: 'The harsh reality however is that many CHOGM members have an axe to grind, dependent as they are upon South Africa for profit and gain. And, at the end of the day, the dollar, pound sterling and krugerrand determine the course of action.'

New York

Followed a three-day layover in New York, where Rajiv Gandhi had innumerable meetings with heads of various governments and, in a greatly hyped event, addressed the UN General Assembly in what turned out to be a damp squib as regards both content and delivery.

In bilateral talks, Gandhi expressed the deep concern and disquiet of the people of India regarding Pakistan's nuclear policy to US president Ronald Reagan. However, during discussions with Pakistan's President General Zia-ul-Haq, described by an official as 'very cordial,' when Gandhi articulated India's great concern over that country's nuclear weapons programme, Zia repeated ad nauseam his earlier assertion that his country did not have any such programme.

At the start of the meeting held in the US president's suite at the Waldorf Astoria hotel, Reagan had made an appreciative reference to Gandhi's role as peacemaker. And, as detailed in one of my dispatches for *Mid-Day*, 'during a confab with Chinese prime minister Zhao Ziyang, the two leaders agreed to give a push to efforts to find a solution to the long-standing border issue that has come in the way of closer ties between the two countries…'

Diplomatic drivel! The 'long-standing border issue' between the two countries remains unresolved with prospects of outbreak of hostilities real and imminent, even as the scourge of pandemic COVID-19 continues to take a heavy toll around the world.

Havana, Cuba

Next stop on the trip was Havana, Cuba, the highlight of which was a banquet hosted by the charismatic Fidel Castro. Twenty-five minutes had been set aside for his interaction with the Indian media, 20 of which were consumed by the soft-spoken dictator singing the praises of his 'old flame,' Indira Gandhi. The remaining five minutes were taken up by unnecessary introductions which left no time for meaningful questions which was an annoyingly transparent gambit by the Cubans to dodge embarrassing issues.

The trip to Havana was fascinating in the context of India's rather nebulous relationship with the host country and Cuba's combustive imbroglio with the US.

For me, one of the highlights of the trip was seeing, at first hand, Cuba's impressive healthcare system with its emphasis on free medicine.

◆

We were scheduled to fly back to New Delhi but were informed, upon boarding at New York, that there had been a last-minute change of plans and that we were instead heading for Moscow on a hush-hush overnight visit amid all manner of speculation among the media.

Such are the devious ways of international diplomacy. There was no point in pushing too many questions since, from experience, straightforward answers are seldom forthcoming! One must arrive at one's own conclusions which can often be, way off the mark.

NAM Summit, Harare, 1986

Whereas Prime Minister Rajiv Gandhi had come in for a great deal of criticism at home for his overall performance, his foreign trips, which his detractors considered excessive, didn't help matters any.

However, viewed objectively, the balance sheet of his achievements in building India's image, taking unequivocal stands on major issues and generally advocating the cause of non-alignment, as envisaged by the founding fathers, makes for some impressive reading.

As mentioned in one of my dispatches from Harare, this was particularly conspicuous at the NAM summit, on the occasion of the twenty-fifth anniversary of the movement where 'Gandhi pledged the movement anew to its central objective of coexistence and co-development in peace, honour and equality.' At the end of the summit, the consensus among delegates was that India's contribution to NAM had been invaluable.

The movement represents two-thirds of the human race and was founded in 1961 by Jawaharlal Nehru, Josip Broz Tito (Yugoslavia), Gamal Abdel Nasser (Egypt), Kwame Nkrumah (Ghana) and Ahmad Sukarno (Indonesia).

I reported from Harare, 'Addressing the packed assembly hall before heads of state and government of the 101 member nations, Gandhi said: "We are drawn together by a shared view of the world. We come from a hundred nations but we belong to one family. We want our family to live better, we want it not to be half affluent, half deprived, but vivified by a sense of equality. We want all to have access to knowledge, growth and fulfilment. We want to live not in fear but in freedom, not in the shadow of war but in peace...'

NAM Summit, Harare, 1986

'The Most Hated Man in Africa'

During the 1986 NAM conference in Harare, a colleague from Kerala's multi-edition *Malayala Manorama* newspaper (founded 1888) and I conspired to try and get an exclusive interview with Ian Smith, who had recently stepped down as prime minister of Rhodesia. The man was, for 16 years until 1980, considered by some to be 'the most hated man in all of Africa' until Rhodesia gained independence and the new nation was renamed Zimbabwe. We hailed a taxi and asked to be taken to the former dictator's home on the outskirts of Harare (formerly known as Salisbury).

In my dispatch to *Mid-Day*, I wrote:

> Ian Smith had unshakeable faith in the racial and technological superiority of the white man. He believed that Africa's blacks were mentally inferior, if not animals, and that providence had chosen him to rule over them for their own good.
>
> Whatever happened to the man who once strode the African political scene like a Colossus and who, in a manner of speaking, was the original practitioner of Rhodesia's abhorrent doctrine of *apartheid* or apartness?
>
> Ian is now bronzed and physically fit at 67, according to his wife. They live in an exquisitely appointed villa in Harare.
>
> Surprisingly there are no wire fences, the front door is wide open, no dogs bark, no security guards police the entrance. We

ring the doorbell and, after what seems like an eternity, a high-pitched female voice responds: 'Coming, coming, I'm drying my hair.' We certainly did not expect such a reception.

After a long and agonizing wait, a genial lady opens the door and after initial preliminaries and introductions, says in an unexpected friendly manner, 'Oh, Ian has gone to the farm and won't be back until tonight…but I'll be happy to answer your questions if you don't mind asking me.'

Escorting us into the drawing room, Janet Smith asks if we would 'like a cuppa tea' in such a friendly and disarming manner that it makes me feel like an impostor for having clandestinely hidden a recording device in my trouser pocket. Repenting my treachery, I switch it off.

In a wide-ranging 90-minute state of the nation conversation, Janet informs us that the law-and-order situation in Zimbabwe is fast deteriorating, inflation is rampant, the economy grossly mismanaged.

The value of the Zimbabwe dollar is dipping alarmingly, and there is no opposition worth the name because the government is obsessed with the concept of one-party rule. That is a frightening prospect, she says, showing no signs she wants us to leave.

As we bid adieu, the lady with the benign smile but tough-as-nails convictions, jokes about her husband. 'Ian's very kind, very reasonable. In fact, he's so reasonable that I sometimes think he's unreasonable.'

Clasping my hand firmly, she says 'By the way don't forget to mention in your report that he's no racist…he's always believed the blacks in Rhodesia aren't ready yet to rule themselves…as Indians are not, just yet.'

Abel Muzorewa succeeded Smith to become Zimbabwe's first black prime minister. Smith was stripped of his Rhodesian citizenship by the new dispensation.

In 1965, he had defied the world and led 270,000 white Rhodesians in a unilateral declaration of independence from Britain rather than accept moves to black majority rule. Because of ill health, he moved to South Africa where he died, aged 88.

Greece, Yugoslavia, Poland, 1986

Then, there was the VVIP visit by President Zail Singh to Greece, Yugoslavia and Poland.

Intended essentially to foster goodwill, foreign visits by Indian presidents are strictly non-political. Largely ceremonial, they seldom provide scope for good copy for the dyed in the wool newshound journalist. This one was no exception, but rather conspicuous for Gianiji's warm accessibility and unfailing son-of-the-soil bonhomie.

To be honest, there was nothing memorable from his visit to Europe. The only thing that remains etched in my memory were the dictator's cold steely eyes and the lavish banquet which Poland's former communist and military leader Wojciech Jaruzelski, de facto dictator of the Polish People's Republic from 1981 until 1989, hosted for our president at his presidential palace.

To this day I remember the 'banquet fit for a king' at which a countless variety of dishes on the most ornate Czech crockery and cutlery were served on an elegantly carved table that extended seemingly interminably from one end of communist Poland to the other.

Many years later when Zeyna and I were resident at Hyderabad's opulent Falaqnuma Palace Hotel, we were amazed by the awesome prolix table (at which guests seated at one end of the table can, by all accounts, be heard by guests at the other.) We came away unconvinced but would love to revisit the global award-winning hotel if only ostensibly to ascertain the veracity of the claim!

It brought back youthful memories of being the guest of a ruthless dictator who acted on instructions from the Kremlin but insisted he was a 'Polish patriot who had always tried to do the best for his country.'[32]

The rise of the Solidarity movement spelt the end for Communist rule in Poland. Calling the event 'shameful,' the former communist and military leader apologised 37 years later for his role in the Kremlin's invasion of what was then Czechoslovakia.

Gianiji and I developed an excellent rapport which continued for many years and led to his accepting my invitation to be chief guest at the Rotary International District Conference in Mumbai, of which I was district chairman in 1984.

So gracious was the president that, despite his age and state of health, he made time to leave New Delhi by his special aircraft in the morning, eat lunch, rest briefly at Mumbai's Raj Bhavan (the Governor's residence), come to the conference for an hour and a half and fly back to Delhi at 5:30 p.m.

To revert to General Jaruzelski's piercing eyes, I have come across people from some Communist countries who, at first sight, strike you as being harsh, perhaps even unfeeling.

Generalizations can be grossly inaccurate, even unfair, and I have also met any number of people from those very countries who are exceedingly warm, friendly, caring, and even possessed of a sense of humour contrary to popular perception.

> The following risqué joke (with apologies to the squeamish, narrated to me by a Russian is a case in point):
>
> There was a time when the Russian Republic had an acute shortage of male contraceptives, as a result of which the country's population was galloping alarmingly out of control.
>
> Out of desperation president Putin frantically phones Margaret Thatcher, who was then prime minister of England asking for urgent help.

---

[32]'Obituary: Wojciech Jaruzelski', BBC News, 25 May 2014, https://www.bbc.com/news/world-europe-15575663. Accessed on 13 November 2021.

Greece, Yugoslavia, Poland, 1986

> 'And, don't forget Baroness, please make sure the condoms are large in size. As you know, we Russians are large in size!'
>
> Baroness Thatcher summons the Minister of State for Health and, emphasizing the then cordial climate of rapprochement between the UK and Russia, instructs him to rush to Moscow, as soon as possible, a very large consignment of condoms.
>
> 'Make absolutely sure,' she instructs sternly, 'the size is extra large—and stamp the consignment: "Made in the United Kingdom—SMALL SIZE."'

There's another one concerning British prime ministers Winston Churchill and Clement Attlee and their respective political parties, which are somewhat over the top and may offend refined sensibilities, so have decided to leave it out after my embarrassing experience with the eminently charming and dignified Begum Bilquis Latif of Hyderabad, wife of Air Marshal (Retd) Idris Latif, former governor of Maharashtra, of whom mention has been made earlier in these memoirs.

The French have an expression 'l'esprit de l'escalier' —the Merriam-Webster dictionary describes it as 'A witty remark thought of too late, on the way home (on the staircase); the clever comment you wish you had made.'

This personal experience was just the opposite and looking back, I squirm even today and regret having made it for being gross and most inappropriate, considering that Begum Saheba, incidentally a good friend, was the epitome of grace and rectitude.

The governor and his good lady were hosting a reception some years ago for Prince Charles of England during his visit to Mumbai on the verdant lawns of Raj Bhavan, the governor's official residence (the parties, were invariably genteel occasions and greatly looked forward to).

While receiving the guests, when I was chatting with the late Soli Godrej of the respected Godrej family, the Begum graciously made a complimentary remark about the suit I was wearing for which I expressed thanks spontaneously—and in imbecilic manner: 'Thank you Begum Saheba. The packaging may be good, how about the product?'

No sooner I had made the unforgivably inappropriate remark, I wished the garden would swallow me, but the damage had been done, as the hostess moved on nonchalantly.

Greece, Yugoslavia, Poland, 1986

John Major

Sir John Major succeeded Margaret Thatcher as prime minister of the UK and was leader of the Conservative Party from 1990 to 1997. He oversaw Britain's longest period of continuous economic growth and the beginning of the Northern Ireland peace process. He was also the last of eight British prime ministers who did not attend university after leaving school.

A cricket enthusiast, Major was elected to the Committee of the Marylebone Cricket Club (MCC) and, despite his lack of erudition, was a popular after-dinner speaker.

On a private visit to Britain, I was invited as guest at a black-tie Conservative party fundraising dinner by high-profile London lawyer and Government Law College classmate Sarosh Zaiwalla, where I met John Major and his wife Norma and where the British prime minister had the guests in splits with his dry wit. After the dinner, Sarosh introduced me to him: I found the prime minister to be extremely affable, crazy about cricket and a true admirer of India.

Sarosh is the founder of Zaiwalla and Co., a law firm in London. Over the years he has been involved in over 1,200 arbitrations in London and across the globe and has acted for many prestigious clients including an Indian President, the governments of China and Iran, the Gandhis and Amitabh Bachchan in the Bofors gun deal.

With President Abdul Kalam, 2005

For me, being invited to accompany former president A.P.J. Abdul Kalam on a four-nation trip to Germany, Switzerland, Russia and Ukraine was a dream come true.

Before departing, one had heard about the respect and regard in which Kalam Saheb was held abroad but what we saw with our own eyes on the trip defied belief.

The fact that Switzerland declared a national holiday during his visit tells its own story, but the love, respect, even reverence that people showed for the humble intellectual giant wherever he went was heart-warming and made one proud to be Indian.

Unlike his successor, who has gone down in history as an undistinguished functionary and who allegedly had put government funds to questionable use for self, family and country cousins, the aerospace scientist Avul Pakir Jainulabdeen Abdul Kalam, a strict vegetarian and teetotaller, was spartan and a person of unimpeachable integrity.

As compared to the freeloaders who accompanied some of the previous presidents on foreign state visits, Abdul Kalam had, in his personal party, just a scientist-friend and a personal cook. The humble cook had access to kitchens at VIP residences where the president stayed. But he always dished up for exclusive consumption by the president, his spartan desi favourites.

We *baraatis* ('wedding party members' in a manner of speaking) from the media were also invited to the incredibly lavish banquet at the Kremlin's regal, chandeliered ballroom hosted by president Vladimir Putin. And we were all treated to Beluga caviar and Russian Standard vodka, the latter of which is considered Russia's best by hard-drinking Russian journalists, who certainly know a thing or two, and more, about their vodka.

However, our humble president's menu was crafted around just his favourite daal, chawal and sabzi (lentils, rice and veggies).

'Sedition' Charge

Much as I enjoyed the foreign assignments for *Inquilab*, *Sportsweek* and *Mid-Day*, I failed to realize that my frequent absence from headquarters, exacerbated by the monster that was the perpetual lack of liquidity and our group's new start-ups in Delhi and Bengaluru without adequate seed capital, inflicted monumental stress on my sons Tarique and Sharique, who had joined me in the business after graduating from universities in the US.

But for the devoted and hard-working staff, it would never have been possible for us to even imagine starting an edition of the *Inquilab* in Delhi and *Sunday Mid-Day* in Bengaluru. I must accept full blame insofar as although my journalistic instincts regarding *Sportsweek* and *Mid-Day* being spot-on, they were way off the mark where the aforementioned two new ventures were concerned.

For one thing, although the potential in Delhi for an Urdu daily 'with a difference' (as I saw the Mumbai *Inquilab*) was tempting given the history and pervasive Urdu culture of the capital city, I had underestimated the rigor mortis condition of the Urdu media, and in fact of the language itself, in the north of India, where it had flourished in pre-Partition times.

Then there was the major obstacle of absence of an established newspaper distribution network in Old Delhi, where the majority of Urdu literates reside, its rapidly changing demographics notwithstanding.

◆

To make matters worse, an interview with the self-styled Khalistan leader Ganga Singh Dhillon for the English *Mid-Day* on the Khalistan movement by noted writer and our Washington correspondent Satinder Singh, reproduced in the Delhi edition of *Inquilab*, incurred the wrath of the authorities for its allegedly 'seditious' content. But the fact that the original version in the English publication passed muster with the vigilant authorities when the Khalistan agitation was at its peak, but not the *Inquilab* translation, tells its own story!

In my letter to then Prime Minister Rajiv Gandhi on Christmas Day, 1985, I wrote:

> Our group has been engaged in nationalistic and responsible journalism for the past 49 years. In very difficult times, the *Mid-Day* group has always consciously endeavoured to play a role in enhancing national harmony and integration.
>
> Day after day, week after week, the columns of all *Mid-Day* publications have spoken eloquently about this commitment and this fact is very clearly reflected in the nature of our readership which is secular, nationalistic and consists of proud Indians. And there has never been an occasion for anyone to question our record or motives.
>
> *Mid-Day* would never contemplate giving direct or indirect encouragement to any group or individual who questions the very basis of our nation and our national aspirations.

Nothing came of the complaint finally, but it made life hell for Tarique, me, my family and Urdu *Inquilab* (Delhi) staff for over a year, but which seemed like an eternity!

The incident was all the more traumatic since, in all my years as publisher, editor and writer in India and abroad, I have never ever been accused of breaching the law—civil or criminal—in the slightest manner.

◆

If I failed to recognize decay and degeneration in Delhi, I was a generation too early in launching *Sunday Mid-Day* in Bengaluru, which although seemingly ripe as regards having potential for a modern, swinging, new-age tabloid, wasn't quite as ready for it as I had imagined prior to becoming the IT hub of India.

Despite its outwardly signs of change, the 'Retirees City' still had an underbelly of venerated tradition and culture that I had failed to identify. Looking back, I was a decade too early in launching the edition, although I wasn't too wrong in assessing that it was better suited to a product like *Sunday Mid-Day*, rather than *Mid-Day* (an afternoon daily), the latter of which calls for an altogether unique readership mindset, work culture and distribution network conducive to reading during commuter travel.

THIRTEEN

KHALEEJ TIMES

The 'Indian Butcher' in Dubai

The hopelessly restless individual that I have always been, the PhD bug which had always been in the deep recesses of my mind since my graduation from Stanford University, prompted me to return to my alma mater in 2008, along with Rukya, to pursue my unfulfilled, but as yet burning ambition.

To my disappointment, the syllabus for a doctorate in journalism had undergone a sea change beyond recognition and many of the new courses had a completely new emphasis on digital communication and teaching methods. There was no way I could have fit the bill to be worthy of a doctorate in the new scheme of things. Prudence dictated that I accepted reality and abandoned what was almost a lifelong ambition. It would have been a different matter had I stayed on at Stanford in 1961, when I graduated, and pursued the degree.

I had missed the opportunity, and there was no point in wondering what might have been, and 'had my uncle been a woman, she would have been my aunt' as its colloquial equivalent goes. Tail firmly between my legs, I left for home not knowing in the slightest that fate—or whatever you choose to call it—had other plans.

Rukya and I had planned to return home to Mumbai (hopefully after getting admission for the PhD programme) via Dubai where we had plans to shop for a bit and then return to the university. During our stopover in Dubai, our friends Shyam and Vimla Bhatia, long-term residents of the city, hosted a dinner for us at which Syed Khalil, financial controller of the multi-dimensional Galadari Brothers conglomerate, was also present.

When Khalil asked what I did, I replied in jest: 'I'm *be-kaar*,' meant to signify that, of course, I had been '*bekaar*,' that is, completely idle, but also, literally without a car, shamelessly punning on the 'kaar' for 'car,' since a major component of the Galadari business was the dealership of Ford and Mazda cars. Pun and games aside, I was totally oblivious that the impish Donkey who thinks he's a wrestler was lurking in the shadows.

Khalil's persistent questioning about my present activities and future plans seemed somewhat odd, but he soon relieved me of my curiosity by asking in deadpan manner if I would consider relocating to Dubai and taking charge of the *Khaleej Times* newspaper.

As I discovered later, in 1978, *Khaleej Times* became the first English newspaper to be launched in the UAE, about a year before I started *Mid-Day* in Mumbai. The *Gulf News*, arch competitor of *Khaleej Times*, was launched in the same year as well but as a tabloid and it barely survived. The broadsheet *Khaleej Times*, however, carved a niche for itself and built up a loyal readership.

On New Years Day, 1980, the format of the *Gulf News* was changed from tabloid to broadsheet under the new ownership of Abdul Wahab Galadari, brother of Abdul Rahim and Abdul Latif Galadari (owners of the *Khaleej Times*). On the verge of closure, the fate of *Gulf News*, its circulation now down to 3,000 copies, changed dramatically as three visionary businessmen, Obaid Humaid Al Tayer, Abdullah Hassan Rostami and Juma Al Majid, bought it in 1984 from the receivers of Abdul Wahab Galadari. They relaunched it with a new look and vision on 10 December 1985 under the banner of Al Nisr Publishing LLC. Within a few months, *Gulf News* had new premises, new printing technology and revitalized editorial marketing and circulation teams to harness the new technology.

The new, energetic and financially flushed *Gulf News* started distribution in Gulf Cooperation Council (GCC) countries and relaunched its antiquated weekly *Al Juma'a* as a youthful, sophisticated weekend read.

While the *Khaleej Times* was left reeling in a state of stupefied impotence under the multipronged blitz, *Gulf News* introduced separate business and sports sections and even started the Gulf News Fun Drive, a fun and exciting initiative that included an off-road trip via large numbers of amateur vehicle drives through the desert. It also sponsored the first Dubai Desert Classic golf tournament and launched its annual Gulf Business Awards of which the annual Gala Dinner was a red-letter day in Dubai, the holy grail of Indian worshippers of Mammon.

A brilliantly multifaceted marketing strategy hit the target, advertising revenues soared by over 40 per cent in the first three months and subscriptions took a gigantic leap, all at the expense of the outdated and vulnerable *Khaleej Times*, which had become not only morbidly obese and incurably infirm, but dangerously bereft of chutzpah and professional expertise.

In effect, I was being asked to treat a terminally ill patient who was on the verge of rigor mortis.

◆

I returned to Mumbai saying the assignment seemed like an exciting professional challenge and that I would give it the consideration it deserved. A few days later the phone didn't stop ringing with Khalil repeatedly calling to ask if I had decided to join.

It seemed like an opportunity too good to refuse, so I went back to Dubai for further discussions and negotiation of terms, all of which seemed attractive enough. The intention was to spend just two days there but, so keen were *Khaleej Times* founder-chairman Abdul Rahim Galadari, and his son, Mohammed, that I joined immediately. I acquired a new wardrobe and stayed back for three months at a hotel that the multifarious group owned.

My primary pre-condition for joining was that I be given an absolutely free hand in the day-to-day running of the business under the designations of managing editor and executive editor, which the owners accepted without hesitation, so precarious was their financial situation.

As I saw it, the company's condition could not get any worse, so I suggested to the chairman that we agree to a six-month probationary period at the end of which we would both be at liberty to decide whether to continue the arrangement or not. As an additional responsibility, Abdul Rahim requested me to consider his (only) son Mohammed, then 23, as my own and groom him as his 'Prince of Wales', especially given his own rather indifferent health.

Father and son were true to their word and initially steered scrupulously clear of any form of interference enabling me to pare the human resource bill down to the bone. Over the years, the unprofessionally run, intrigue-ridden, favouritism-infested organization had collected a colossal amount of dead wood and professional detritus: blue-eyed, exorbitantly paid, high-living but low on productivity expatriate managers and editors.

The brief to me from the owners was unequivocal: turn the company around asap—'the bloodletting is insufferable.'

I had no option other than to go against my essential nature and ruthlessly ask the unproductive staff to return where they came from—whether it was India, Pakistan, the UK, Bangladesh, the Philippines—earning me the nickname 'Indian Butcher.'

As far as the financial health of the two rivals was concerned, it was a no contest, with the owners of my organization not a patch on the formidable trio of deep pocketed, well-connected owners of the competition.

Uneven Playing Field

Nevertheless, while competing with *Gulf News* on a woefully uneven playing field, at my level, I initiated moves to build bridges in order to bring about fair business practices, all the while convincing my rivals of the futility of trying to crush us in a manic manner. This brought about some sanity in our competitors' approach: for example, when they weighed the enormous saving to be made by doing away with the exorbitantly priced glazed newsprint (that we just could not afford) and reducing the number and frequency of colour pages per week. In any country governed by democratic norms this would have got us into deep trouble under Monopolies Commission regulations but it wasn't so in the UAE at the time.

Our purchases were rationalized, middlemen eliminated, waste in any form—be it at the staffing level or overtime in the production process—was closely monitored on pain of dismissal. After all, we were at war! At the same time, our advertising sales' thrust was strengthened with the appointment of more and aggressive ad sales representatives, innovative sales pitches, imaginative sales promotions (as regards both advertising and sales revenues) and placement of institutional advertising on a reciprocal basis. This enabled us to place free-for-free advertising that announced our readership benefits and editorial improvements.

And we streamlined our hitherto antiquated and woefully inadequate circulation network which had not kept pace with the meteoric growth of Dubai from somnolent village to urban agglomeration to futuristic metropolis.

Personally, I was repelled by the cupidity and crass materialism of affluent Indian and British expatriates that resided in the Emirates and their exploitation of Indian, Pakistani, Bangladeshi and Filipino labour that built castles in the desert with their blood, toil, tears and sweat, but that's a different story!

On the positive side, Dubai's proximity to Mumbai made for ease of travel for me from one city to the other, as also for VIPs to hop over or transit through. A case in point: former Indian ambassador Inder Kumar Gujral stopped over on his return from Baghdad to New Delhi for a confab on the Middle East situation.

And, after I had resigned from the *Khaleej Times* to set up my own ad agency, Kanz Communications, the legendary Dilip Kumar flew over for lunch to discuss the teething problems of his nephew who was, at the time, working with me.

At the *Khaleej Times*, we buttressed our channels of distribution with more point of purchase material which gave our title far better visibility in all seven emirates of the UAE and into neighbouring countries such as Oman, Qatar, Bahrain and Saudi Arabia. At the same time, we reinforced our push for circulation in the blooming emirate of Abu Dhabi, capital of the UAE, which was riding on the crest of its bountiful oil production.

Incidentally, the *Khaleej Times*'s general manager for Abu Dhabi was Arshad Sami Khan, a Pashtun married to Naureen Khan from Jammu.

I remember Arshad, father of popular Bollywood singer Adnan Sami, who as a Flight Lieutenant in the Pakistan Air Force was part of the Air Force attack on the Pathankot air base during the 1965 Indo-Pakistan war.

Arshad Sami Khan was a suave, articulate, soft-spoken subordinate who would drive down to Dubai from Abu Dhabi every Monday morning for my weekly managers' meeting at which he spoke most intelligently and constructively. I understand he was later sent as the Pakistani ambassador to various countries around the world, appointed federal secretary and conferred with the third highest civilian award of his country.

After battling pancreatic cancer for 20 years, Arshad passed away in 2009 at Mumbai's Kokilaben Dhirubhai Ambani hospital. He was buried in Islamabad with multiple military honours, including a 21-gun salute.

◆

Surprisingly, the previous dispensation had not taken the trouble to conduct a regional demographics survey or content analysis, things that should have been unquestionable givens. A methodical analysis helped us fine tune *Khaleej Times*'s personality and our understanding of its present and target audience.

I visited India a few times to recruit senior staff, notably, Magsaysay award winner and retired editor of *The Statesman* (Kolkata), S. Nihal Singh (now deceased), and Burjor Patel as Senior Ad Sales Manager, as also advertising, circulation and production department personnel.

A syndication arrangement with *Mid-Day* and *Sunday Mid-Day* made available to *Khaleej Times* readers popular circulation-building columnists such as the incomparable Khushwant Singh; communications guru Sabira Merchant, who has groomed innumerable Indian girls for Miss Universe and Miss World pageants; popular Bollywood actress Nutan; the immensely popular astrologer Bejan Daruwala and others. The syndication also brought the readers a star-studded list of high-profile sports writers from the two Mumbai publications.

◆

When I took charge of the *Khaleej Times*, I was distressed, given my liberal educational background, to find that the editorial staff was petrified when taking decisions concerning what could and/or could not be published in the newspaper for fear of retribution under the Emirate's censorship laws.

After testing the waters cautiously, I learnt that many of the existing 'can't dos' because of religion in an orthodox Islamic country exacerbated by imagined sensibilities of ruling family members and prickly government officials were more imagined than real.

One had heard harrowing stories of the fate that befell foreign journalists in some Middle Eastern countries because of so-called indiscretion that caused offence to local sensibilities.

One such tale concerned a former European editor who had been jailed for being 'irresponsible' in okaying a comic strip featuring a 'The Adventures of Legionnaire Beau Peep' cartoon.

Tired of routinely publishing only government press handouts which said only the nicest things about those in authority, I issued a diktat that I wished to see every day on page one at least one 'hard,' meticulously researched local story, which if need be was critical of local officials. Sensing shock and some resistance, I mustered all my powers of persuasion to convince my senior editorial colleagues that, in the event of any problem, it will be I who will 'sing the Jailhouse Rock.' The staff wasn't completely convinced but cautiously started getting newsworthy local stories about civic issues. These were well-received and started a trend although, on occasions, the chairman called to caution that some of the reports had 'crossed the red line'.

But nudity, even semi-nudity (the boundaries about this tend to be rather nebulous in the Middle East) and interpretations as to what is publishable can be extremely subjective. In 1988, as I was at Dubai airport awaiting departure of a flight to Atlanta to cover the drug-tainted 1988 Seoul Olympics, I received a call from the office to say that they had just received a 'rather revealing but beautiful' photograph of American sprinter Florence 'Flo Jo' Joyner during training. The sports editor was nervous about carrying the photograph to illustrate a news agency curtain-raiser about the champion sprinter and wanted me to take an immediate call about publishing it.

In the absence of modern technology, which would have enabled transmission of the photograph to me by phone, I asked the editor just one question: 'Will your wife be shocked when she sees the picture in the newspaper?' The reply was in the negative, so I told him to go ahead, which he did, rather nervously.

As expected, there were no repercussions, thus raising the bar for the entire UAE print media.

For the information of readers, 'Flo Jo' is the fastest woman 100 and 200-metre runner of all time, although doubts still linger as to whether or not she took performance-enhancing drugs. She is equally famous for her startling outfits and beautifully manicured colourful nails. She tragically passed away in her sleep in 1998 at the young age of 38.

Working to Plan

At *Khaleej Times*, things worked to plan and in under a year, we succeeded in turning the newspaper around, from a seemingly hopeless business venture to a profitable one.

I felt I had done my bit and wished to return home to Mumbai where son Tarique was successfully, but single-handedly and without demur, managing the family business following younger brother Sharique's decision to settle in Buffalo, New York. But chairman Abdul Rahim Galadari pleaded with me to stay on if only to continue mentoring his son Mohammed who, handicapped by the lack of higher education, would have found it impossible to take over the business, as was his fond hope.

I agreed to a six-month extension, which turned out to be a huge blunder since, with the company's tribulations now past, the heir apparent started believing he was the cat's whiskers and that running a newspaper was child's play. Mohammed had thus far worked under me as apprentice at the *Khaleej Times* when he suddenly started believing he had learnt everything there was to know. He started asserting his authority in matters which were far beyond his competence, working at cross purposes, overriding my decisions and generally making life at work an intolerable hell for me to the detriment of the newspaper.

I had no option other than to bring the state of affairs to the attention of his father, the chairman, who flew into a rage and said he would transfer his son to the automobile division to prevent him from interfering. I tried to dissuade Abdul Rahim, pointing out that

I was only a bird of passage and that, ultimately, Mohammed, the 'Prince of Wales' and only male heir of the family, would have to take over the business.

But matters went from bad to worse, with the young man refusing to mend his ways. I'm not given to squealing, so I went to the father and handed in my papers saying I had decided to return home to my business in India, which was not altogether untrue, and possibly, also set up an advertising agency in Dubai with a partner. Abdul Rahim tried his best to dissuade me, even offering to partner me in whatever new venture I might have been thinking about and assuring me that his son would not be part of the new scheme of things. But my mind was made up, so regretfully, it was time to bid farewell to the *Khaleej Times,* although I did stay back in Dubai, which had grown on wife Rukya and me, until after the Gulf War in 1991.

At a farewell lunch hosted by him, Mohammed Galadari was embarrassingly lavish in his praise and expressed the hope that the paper would benefit from my continued presence in Dubai.

'Mr Ansari will continue to be a member of the KT family,' he said, ending a chapter in my life from which I learnt many lessons.

Kanz Communications, Dubai

At the *Khaleej Times*, my advertising contact person was Nazli Shah, client services manager at the Lebanon-based Intermarkets and Test cricketer Imran Khan's contemporary at Oxford University. She moved on to Lintas Middle East and then to Publicis Graphics (the leading ad agency of the Middle East). After a total of 15 years of experience with different agencies in various capacities, she decided to start off on her own.

Shah's decision coincided with my resignation from the *Khaleej Times* and it made sense for me, given my own ad agency background in Mumbai, to consider setting up an advertising business in Dubai, a short flight away from home. The more I thought about it, the more feasible it seemed for me to run the business from Mumbai, with Nazli Shah in Dubai as partner in the exponentially growing advertising industry in the Middle East.

Besides, I was keen to let Tarique look after the newspaper business in Mumbai without, in the words of Field Marshal Manekshaw, 'poking my dirty nose' in it.

◆

Initially it seemed the benevolence of the One Above towards the Gadha would continue.

Nazli Shah's UAE contacts, coupled with her varied experience of the Dubai market, with me as backstop, enabled Kanz Advertising to get off to a fairly promising start.

It was probably an alignment of the stars that brought us a windfall in the form of a modest portion of the advertising account of the Galadari Motor Company (which belonged to the same group as the *Khaleej Times* from which I had recently resigned). This was followed, fairly quickly, by Jumbo Electronics, which belonged to self-made Indian whiz-kid expatriate Manu Chhabria (he had named his venture after the aircraft that flew him from Mumbai, where he was a retailer). He happened to be a fan of *Mid-Day* which, to some extent, made him gravitate towards us initially.

In the beginning, we were looked down upon not only by the established international advertising 'big boys' of the US and UK but also the johnny-come-lately Middle Easterners whose business ethics were unique and beyond our ability to match.

In keeping with our resolve to produce 'advertising that works', our motto, we recruited talented staff to provide our clients with unique marketing, creative and media strategies, backed up by research and development, and also set up our own film production unit. In time, we expanded our activities to the full gamut of communications activities such as media representation, corporate communications, promotions, marketing, merchandising and syndication of news, features, articles and cartoons from *The New York Times*, *Daily Telegraph*, *Daily Express* as also *Knight Features* and Marjorie Orr horoscopes in the UK. We syndicated the works of award-winning writer Phillip Knightley from the UK, Khushwant Singh, R.K. Laxman, Mani Shankar Aiyar and Imran Khan.

We also organized exhibitions of the works of the renowned R.K. Laxman and Abdul Ismail Gulgee, as also a stage presentation of Mumbai's acclaimed diva Sharon Prabhakar of *Evita* fame.

The competition started taking us seriously, but then the inevitable happened.

The dark clouds of turmoil in the Middle East were hovering, the eagles encircling. The last straw was the 1990–91 Gulf War which crippled the economy of the region, in general, and all but destroyed the advertising industry, in particular. Unlike the big boys, we just didn't have the staying power, the financial stamina to withstand the tremors.

Closing down Kanz, which had just attained cruising altitude, became a Hobson's choice.

There was no question of doing what many businessmen from India, Pakistan, Bangladesh and elsewhere were doing under stress in the Gulf: drive to the nearest airport, abandon the car, board a plane and flee to where they came from, leaving creditors to bid goodbye to their money.

I'm grateful to my creditors who negotiated and greatly reduced settlement of my dues. They were extremely sympathetic given the circumstances.

FOURTEEN

BONDS OF FRIENDSHIP

The Little Master

Sunil Gavaskar
born 10 July 1949
Tests 125
10,122 Test Runs
Average 51.12
34 Hundreds, 45 Fifties
Highest Score 236*
Catches 108

Sunil Manohar Gavaskar is a particularly good friend going back to 1971, when I interviewed him at his former Dadar Hindu Colony home soon after his return from his heroic exploits in the West Indies in 1971.

Since he is a good friend, it may be in order for me to reproduce an unbiased assessment of a cricketer who, in my opinion is, arguably thus far, one of the greatest batsmen and one of the best opening batsmen in the history of Test cricket.

Gavaskar set world records during his career for the most Test runs and most Test centuries scored by any batsman. He held the record of 34 Test centuries for almost two decades before it was broken by Sachin Tendulkar in December 2005.

Apart from Gavaskar and Tendulkar, technically, temperamentally, and even in terms of style, Indian batting maestros Rahul Dravid, Dilip Vengsarkar, Virat Kohli, Virender Sehwag, V.V.S. Laxman, Sourav Ganguly and Mohammad Azharuddin (who unfortunately lost his way at the peak of his career), inspirational captain and wicket-keeper batsman Mahendra Singh Dhoni and Anil Kumble, Zaheer Khan and Ravichandran Ashwin among bowlers must rank among the greatest modern-day Indian cricketers I have had the pleasure of seeing in action. In fact, they rate undoubtedly among the finest practitioners of their craft in world cricket and to whom Indian cricket aficionados are indebted.

Gavaskar was the first batsman to score 10,000 Test runs in a career and now stands at number 12 in the group of Test players with 10,000-plus Test runs. Nephew of Indian wicket-keeper Madhav Mantri, 'Sunny' or 'Little Master' is father of Rohan (who also played for India in both Tests and ODIs) and brother-in-law of the supremely elegant, the peerless Gundappa Vishwanath.

I shall not dwell upon his achievements (since they are now the stuff of legend). Gavaskar was widely admired for his technique against fast bowling, with a particularly high average of 65.45 against the West Indies—a team that possessed a four-pronged fast-bowling attack regarded the most vicious in Test history.

Gavaskar was named by *Wisden* (as also *Sportsweek* later) as the Indian Cricketer of the Century in 2002.

At a time when helmets were unknown and body guards not half as effective as the ones that are in use in present times, Gavaskar's memorable innings were 220 vs West Indies (Port of Spain, 1971),

102 vs West Indies (Port of Spain, 1976), 113 vs Australia (Brisbane, 1977), 221 vs England (the Oval, 1979—arguably the greatest knock of his career), 236 not out vs West Indies (Chennai, 1983), 127 vs Pakistan (Faisalabad, 1983), 103 vs New Zealand (Nagpur, 1987) and 96 vs Pakistan (Bengaluru, 1987).

Despite all his exploits at the world's famous cricket grounds, there had been one lacuna in Gavaskar's illustrious career: he had never scored a century at Lord's in any format of the game. Lord's was also the place where, in 1975, he had achieved the dubious distinction of batting out 60 overs in a World Cup match with only one boundary. During that particular match, I must admit that sitting in the press box, I couldn't help but cringe at the unkind and barely disguised sniggering of a section of the English press, but SMG was as yet wet behind his ears in that format of the game.

On 22 August 1987, however, Gavaskar scored his first first-class hundred at Lord's in its bicentenary match, playing for the Rest of the World XI captained by Allan Border against the Marylebone Cricket Club (MCC) led by Mike Gatting.

In a feature on the website Cricket Country that detailed the momentous point in history that was that particular match, Abhishek Mukherjee wrote the following: [33]

> As *Wisden* had pointed out, the only 'titans' the match missed were Ian Botham, Martin Crowe—and perhaps the biggest of them all—Viv Richards. Even the umpires were Dickie Bird and David Shepherd, the best in contemporary cricket.
>
> Whatever rifts might have separated Gavaskar and Vengsarkar in the past did not reflect on that day at Lord's in a match that *Wisden* called 'a game rather than a contest.' They batted for an hour adding 47 before speed demon Malcolm Marshall had Vengsarkar caught by Gooch. "He [Vengsarkar] is the one cricketer I have ever disliked and the only one I

---

[33] Abhishek Mukherjee, 'MCC Bicentennial Match: Gavaskar Signs off with a Hundred at Lord's', *Cricket Country*, 20 August 2014, https://www.cricketcountry.com/articles/mcc-bicentennial-match-gavaskar-signs-off-with-a-hundred-at-lords-30182. Accessed on 14 November 2021.

have felt consistently hostile towards,' Marshall had said in his autobiography *Marshall Arts*.

Strong words from Malcolm Marshall! They could be attributed to personal factors. On the other hand, they could also be a backhanded compliment to the tenacious batsmanship of the Mumbai stalwart. Mumbai cricketers are known for their *khadoos* (never-say-die) mental attributes.

Mukherjee continued in the article:

> He [Gavaskar] remained unbeaten on 80: it was already his highest score at the Headquarter of Cricket, and he was only 20 runs away from the landmark he had so craved for. Gavaskar announced his retirement from First-Class cricket that evening, despite being in complete knowledge that he might not reach the magic figure. 'My appetite for top cricket and plenty of fans has disappeared. I am not hungry, just like someone who has eaten a good meal,' said the great man.
>
> 'He [Gavaskar] seemed absolutely certain he would mark the occasion with a hundred', wrote *The Indian Express* the next morning. He lost Dujon early, caught by Gooch off Marshall, but carried on with Imran for company.
>
> He soon placed one from Shastri and ran for a single to bring up the hundred in 214 balls and 246 minutes.
>
> It is difficult to say whether Shastri was happy or not to dismiss his mentor 12 runs short of a double-hundred. The last 88 had taken Gavaskar only 137 balls, and had included 12 fours, as opposed to the first phase of his batting. The entire ground stood up in a thunderous ovation as he walked out.

Mukherjee could have added 'many a tear was shed, and there was a lump in many a throat.' It was certainly true of me as I watched the Little Master return to the Lord's pavilion in glory for the last time ever.

◆

It's a Wonderful World

> On a lighter note, with acknowledgement to Abhishek Mukherjee: a few years later, Sunil Gavaskar was denied entry to Lord's by an officious steward for not having his ID. Furious at the slight, Gavaskar turned down an invitation to become an honorary member of the august body.
>
> A few years later, when invited to deliver the Colin Cowdrey lecture at Lord's, Gavaskar began with a rather caustic retort: 'There may be some among you who, on receiving the invitation to this evening's lecture and seeing who was going to speak, must have said, 'Oh, yeah! If only he is allowed through the gate!' There must have been a question in your mind whether the lecture would take place at all. It's a bit like getting an invitation to a party on 1 April; you don't know whether if it's for real or if it's an April fool joke.'

'Rooky' Engineer

The most ebullient of all my cricketing friends, one whose love for *la vie en rose* (life in all its rosy hues) matches his gastronomic appetite, is the larger-than-life Farokh Maneksha Engineer.

In a Test career spanning 46 matches and 87 innings, 'Rooky,' 'Bawa,' 'Dikra Farookh' or 'Brylcreem Boy' as he is known, scored 2,611 runs at an average of 31.08 (16 fifties and two centuries). Farokh played five ODIs for India aggregating 114 runs at an average of 38.0 and altogether tallied 13,436 runs in 335 first class matches at an average of 29.5.

A resident of the Dadar Parsi Colony, as a schoolboy, Farokh would smash windowpanes of the area by his ferocious hitting while playing street cricket, for which he was bundled off to the Shivaji Military School, Pune. After graduating from high school, he joined Mumbai's R.A. Podar College, where Dilip Vengsarkar, Ravi Shastri and Sanjay Manjrekar also studied later.

Despite his lumbering and seemingly inflexible physique, Farokh had razor-sharp reflexes and brought off some unbelievable diving catches behind the wickets, especially with India's famed spin quartet in action.

He played some match-winning, as well as match-saving, Test innings during the period of 1967–70 when he was a member of the playing eleven in all matches that India played. Farokh also played a pivotal role in India's first ever Test victory away from home in New Zealand and was among the few Indian batsmen who did not flinch against the fast-bowling duo of Wes Hall and Charlie Griffith in 1967.

Unfortunately, Farokh's career was blighted by injuries and illnesses. His decision to move residence to Lancashire which prevented him from playing in Indian domestic cricket didn't help matters, nor did the politicking that characterized BCCI in those days.

He was embroiled in selection controversies involving his worthy rival Budhi Kunderan, his peer both as a dashing opening batsman and wicketkeeper, (and who was decidedly unlucky and ahead of his times) and also P. Krishnamurthy who was earnest, but not in the same league as the player.

◆

Farokh Engineer is best remembered for his whirlwind knock at Chepauk, Chennai, in 1967 against the visiting West Indians, who had in their ranks the fearsome Wes Hall, Charlie Griffith, the legendary Gary Sobers who could bowl pace and spin with equal felicity and the skillful Lance Gibbs. Engineer opened the Indian batting with Dilip Sardesai, the illustrious batsman from Mumbai whose services to Indian cricket are unforgettable, after Mansoor Ali Khan Pataudi won the toss and decided to bat. Overcoming 'first day, first bat' nerves and with disdain for the fresh wicket, he put the fearsome bowling to the sword and was 94 at the lunch break, just six short of the coveted century, and that too on the first morning of a Test.

In a recent interview, Farokh reminisced that his 94 had come off only 46 deliveries, which was the fastest ever, adding the tongue-in-cheek remark that in those days nobody kept records of number of balls faced and that, in any case, 'Wisden didn't have the 'wisdom' to do so!'

Referring to India's historic 1971 maiden Test victory over England, in England—at the Oval, no less—in which he was also instrumental, Engineer talked sportingly about how he had largely engineered the win towards the end, but the stampeding Indian fans had instead cheered Abid Ali after the win.

'What about me?' exclaimed 'Rooky' Engineer in characteristic jest in an interview with Richard Edwards of London's *Daily Mail* on the eve of the fiftieth anniversary of the win.[34]

(India scored a memorable 76-run come from behind win over Joe Root's England in the landmark 2021 edition at the Oval, prompting Australian legend Shane Warne to exclaim on Twitter: 'Congratulations Virat Kohli and the entire Indian team on another terrific win. What you guys have achieved over the last 12 months is absolutely magnificent! Clearly the best team in the world and that title is thoroughly deserved too! Long live Test cricket.'

Inevitably, Warne's comment caused New Zealand fans to take umbrage and point to the fact that India have not defeated the Kiwis in Tests in five years, including the inaugural World Championship final less than three months ago.

Farokh played five ODIs for India, aggregating 114 runs at an average of 38.0 and altogether tallied 13,436 runs in 335 first class matches at an average of 29.5. He also played for Lancashire in English county cricket (the first Indian to play in the league) alongside West Indian great Clive Lloyd from 1968 to 1976. When he made his debut, Lancashire had not won a major honour since 1950. After India's 1967 tour of England, John Arlott wanted him to play for his own home county of Hampshire. At the same time, Worcestershire and Somerset were also interested in him, but he decided on Lancashire for its history and gorgeous ground.

By the time he left Lancashire in 1976, the team had won the Gillette Cup four times and the John Player League twice. Lancashire were the undisputed one-day kings in the 1970s and Farokh was a massive contributory factor in those precious wins.

Farokh was among the most liked cricketers in the league. He received an amount of £26,000—a mind-boggling, unheard-of sum in those days—at a benefit match in Lancaster.

I recall leaving his home ground (Old Trafford) with him some years ago to go out for dinner. Without exaggeration, it took us

---

[34]Richard Edwards, 'Farokh Engineer recalls his side's amazing maiden Test win in England at the Oval in 1971', *Daily Mail Online*, 1 September 2021, https://www.dailymail.co.uk/sport/cricket/article-9948169/India-legend-Farokh-Engineer-recalls-sides-amazing-maiden-Test-win-England-Oval-71.html. Accessed on 14 November 2021.

almost three quarters of an hour to walk the short distance from the pavilion to the members' car park, such was the adulation of fans and autograph hunters.

It is said that a traffic policeman once stopped him for speeding on the streets of Manchester but let him off, saying, 'My father would kill me if I booked you.'

In *Farokh: The Cricketing Cavalier*, author Colin Evans included John Arlott's evocative words: 'I watched many of his performances from 1968 to 1976 and he had the ability to lighten up the gloomiest Manchester day, whether on the pitch or off it. Nowadays, 40 years after his retirement from the game, he is still warmly welcomed all over the world as speaker and an ambassador for cricket.'[35]

'Rooky' now lives in Cheshire with his English wife Julie. He has four daughters, Minnie, Tina, Roxanne Bianca and Scarlett Zia.

---

[35] Colin Evans, *Farokh: The Cricketing Cavalier: The Authorised Biography of Farokh Engineer*, Max Books, 2017.

Bishan Bedi

Slow left-arm orthodox bowler Bishan Singh Bedi played Test cricket for India between 1966 and 1979 and formed part of the famous Indian spin quartet along with Bhagwat Chandrasekhar, Erapalli Prasanna and Srinivas Venkataraghavan (nicknamed Rent-a-Caravan by his Derbyshire county teammates).

He played a total of 67 Tests and took 266 wickets. He also captained the national side in 22 Test matches during a tempestuous career in which he preferred to call a spade a shovel, as the expression goes.

Unlike Gavaskar and Vengsarkar, who live in Mumbai and are more in personal contact, my meetings with Engineer and Bedi are infrequent but our relationship remains constant courtesy social media, (even though, generally, I find WhatsApp and SMS increasingly difficult to cope with because of inanity, not to mention their overwhelmingly demanding characteristics).

An email exchange between 'Pa-ji' (Bishan) and me in the aftermath of the ball tampering controversy involving Steve Smith's 2018 touring team in South Africa might be of interest to readers.

As reported by Malavika Sangghvi in her weekly column in the *Hindustan Times*:[36]

---

[36]Malavika Sangghvi, 'Malavika's Mumbaistan: That's cricket!', *Hindustan Times*, 28 March 2018, https://www.hindustantimes.com/mumbai-news/malavika-s-mumbaistan-that-s-cricket/story-Jf9IV6ysHWWqEqAe7tjj7L.html. Accessed on 14 November 2021.

Even as the Australian ball tampering row snowballs into a major scandal, we are privy to an exchange between two stalwarts, legendary Test cricketer Bishan Singh Bedi and Khalid Ansari, journalist and former publisher of the sports magazine Sportsweek. 'Greetings from the Arctic, Bish pa-ji,' wrote the avid traveller Ansari, on Sunday 'I have just read about the Turnbull episode and am filled with tearful memories of you and your brave and honourable exposure of the contemptible behaviour of England's John Lever (of Vaseline ill-fame), his disgraceful captain, manager and the then dishonourable England cricket establishment.'

'You paid a very heavy price, because of which, you have gone down in the annals of the game as a man of honour, principle and conviction. Good on ya, mate – proud of you!' Ansari had written.

'What happened in the 'Vaseline' episode then was not quite cricket; and what happened in Cape Town is not cricket either..!!' replied Bedi. 'During the 'Vaseline' saga only I was vulnerable... with the BCCI literally bowing before the Imperial Cricket Conference... Indian Board officials were mere crumb pickers then... right? Well KA... let's leave it at that 'cos I'm not enjoying digging graves...!! Suffice it to say that I may have lost a few bob, but I managed to keep some friendships alive... as your wonderful mail would suggest..!!'

However faraway in the Artic, Ansari still fulminated. 'The more I think about the Vaseline brouhaha, the more incensed do I feel over the chicken-hearted approach of the BCCI when confronting the then imperialist International Cricket Conference (ICC) burra sahibs from England, Australia, and New Zealand backed by the brown noses from the West Indies,' he said later.

Bish's contract with Northamptonshire was not renewed and, if reports are to be believed, he was not given a benefit match, either, which is in effect a token of appreciation (and worth much more than 'a few bob,' if I may add) to overseas cricketers who dignify English county cricket with their wonderful exploits.

Bedi underwent heart bypass surgery following a stroke and subsequently underwent a procedure to remove blood clotting. Ever the doughty warrior, he bounced back under the loving care of wife

Anju, Bollywood actor son Angad, daughter Neha and daughter-in-law Neha Dhupia Bedi.

I met Bishan at his book launch and birthday celebrations organized by former Indian cricket captain Kapil Dev and his Punjab teammates in Delhi. Bishan looked good as gold, laughing and joking and generally 'in good nick' in a manner reminiscent of his days of glory.

In a florid tribute to Bishan Singh on his seventy-fifth birthday when Bishan's biography[37] was released, *The Times of India* correspondent Siddharth Saxena wrote: 'A former colleague once facing him in a festival game, spoke wide-eyed of the whirring hiss the ball made in flight and how it hung in the air, simply refusing to descend. Bishan Singh Bedi was 54 then, his playing days long over and he was still having a good laugh.'[38]

Describing Bedi as 'Indian sport's original rebel and romantic,' Saxena writes, 'the man has reemerged as a moral centre that our sport so badly needs. But his greatness lay beyond. It lay in his straddling both worlds with a progressiveness that was both educated and pushed by an earthy honesty. There was a forward-looking temper not necessarily in the way the world has eventually turned out but how it ideally should have. Till date, he steadfastly lives by that dictum, even if it may have cost him his share of the pie. In a largely transformed world, he fiercely holds on to a forgotten socialist ethos.'

As 2020—annus horribilis—year of the life-changing COVID-19 pandemic drew to a close, Bishan Singh Bedi caused seismic waves by writing to the Delhi and District Cricket Association (DDCA) asking his name be removed from the stands at the Feroz Shah Kotla ground. He also renounced his DDCA membership with immediate effect.

---

[37]Neha Bedi, *The Sardar of Spin: A Celebration of the Life and Art of Bishan Singh Bedi*, Roli Books, 2021.
[38]Siddharth Saxena, 'Bishan Singh Bedi, 75, Outspoken Moral Centre of Our Times', *The Times of India*, 25 September 2021, https://timesofindia.indiatimes.com/sports/cricket/news/bishan-singh-bedi-75-outspoken-moral-centre-of-our-times/articleshow/86500860.cms. Accessed on 22 November 2021.

Bedi was miffed at DDCA's decision to build a statue of their former president Arun Jaitley whose long tenure (1999–2013) was said to have been riddled with numerous corruption allegations and controversies. Five days later, Home Minister Amit Shah, in the presence of BCCI president Sourav Ganguly (who, incidentally had suffered a heart attack in Kolkata the following week and another one a little later), unveiled the six-foot, 800-kilogram statue of the late finance minister, near the Virender Sehwag Gate.

Shantanu Srivastava of *Firstpost* eloquently wrote: 'It was a moment of poignant shame and sorry disregard; a forgettable picture that said a thousand unfortunate words, and an apt reflection of the stifling conundrum that cricket administration in India has become.'[39]

Bishan, after whom the stand at the venue was named in 2017, referred to what he called the 'unsavoury past' and nepotism of Jaitley's reign as DDCA president as the reason for his decision.

In an email to Rohan Jaitley, Arun Jaitley's son and president of the DDCA on 22 December 2020, Bedi wrote:[40]

> I write this letter with a heavy heart & a deep sense of embarrassment. I'm old enough to know that one doesn't talk ill of the dead.
>
> My reservations about the choice of people he handpicked to run the day to day affairs of DDCA is well known.
>
> I think I was too headstrong ... too old school ... & too proud an Indian cricketer to be co-opted into the corrupt darbar of sycophants Arun Jaitley mustered at the Kotla during his stewardship.
>
> I'm not prone to disregard the honour that was bestowed upon me. My gratitude to Justice Sen & the Committee of M/s Dr ND

---

[39] Shantanu Srivastava, 'Bishan Singh Bedi-DDCA Saga a Reminder of India's Non-existent Sports Culture', *Firstpost*, 30 December 2020, https://www.firstpost.com/sports/bishan-singh-bedi-ddca-saga-a-reminder-of-indias-non-existent-sports-culture-9157471.html. Accessed on 14 November 2021.

[40] 'Full text of Bishan Singh Bedi's Email to DDCA President', *Sportstar*, 23 December 2020, https://sportstar.thehindu.com/cricket/bishan-singh-bedi-letter-full-text-ddca-president-arun-jaitley-rohan-jaitley-ferozeshah-kotla/article33403624.ece. Accessed on 14 November 2021.

Puri, Dr Ravi Chaturvedi, Vijay Lokapally & Neeru Bhatia ... all people of social & professional eminence, who extended the warm gesture to Mohinder Amarnath & me, will never fade.

But as we all know with honour comes responsibility. They feted me for the total respect & integrity with which I played the game.

Sporting arenas need sporting role models.

The place of the administrators is in their glass cabins. Since DDCA doesn't understand this Universal cricket culture, I need to walk out of it. I can't be part of a stadium which has got its priorities so grossly wrong & where administrators get precedence over the cricketers.

Please bring down my name from the stand with immediate effect. You needn't worry about me or my legacy. God Almighty has been very kind to me to keep me alive with my cricketing convictions. I don't wish my strength of character to be maligned by my silence or association with this unsporting act.

That's Bishan Bedi for you: man with the puckish laugh, of old-school-tie principles (as he confesses), even dogmas.

For me, he's a likeable hail-fellow-well-met scamp—but, most of all, a sincere friend and an undoubted spin wizard, irrespective of whether a stadium is named after him or not!

Kapil Dev Nikhanj

	Runs	Average	100's	50's	Highest Score	Wickets	Best Bowling
Tests 131	5,248	31.05	8	27	163	434	9/83
ODI's 225	3,783	23.79	1	14	175 *	253	5/43

The incomparable Kapil Dev Nikhanj is one of the finest human beings I have known in any sphere of life. Soft-spoken, gentle (despite the fire in his belly on the playing field), respectful of his elders, the Punjabi Jat, like many of his kin, is salt of the earth from whom I would buy a used car at any time.

Hailed as one of the finest all-rounders ever, Kapil is also regarded as one of the greatest captains in the history of cricket, as attested by the fact that he led a fairly pedestrian India XI to victory in the third Cricket World Cup in England in 1983.

He is also a successful businessman. His ventures include a restaurant called Kaptain's Retreat, Dev Musco Lighting, a stadium-lighting manufacturing outfit, and he holds a stake in and sits on the board of several firms.

'Kaps' retired in 1994, holding the world record for the greatest number of wickets taken in Test cricket, a record subsequently broken by Courtney Walsh in 2000. At the time, he was also India's highest wicket-taker in both Tests and ODIs.

Kapil's unbeaten—and immortal—175 against Zimbabwe in the 1983 World Cup changed Indian cricket forever. According to Atreyo Mukhopadhyay of the *The New Indian Express*, 'Other than being a part of modern cricket folklore, the knock which lifted India to victory from 17/5 has assumed mythical character because there is no video recording of that game.'[41] That India-Zimbabwe 1983 World Cup match between India and Zimbabwe remains the only international match held there.

If I missed Kapil's epic feat at Tunbridge Wells (Ian Chappell described his innings as 'the one which took India from the brink of defeat to the world title'), I was fortunate to witness an incredible batting display by him at Lord's.

He slammed Eddie Hemmings of the England team for four consecutive sixes to take India to relative safety. India were nine wickets down and needed 24 runs to avoid the follow-on. Earlier, England had piled on 653 for four declared, Graham Gooch scoring an imperious 333.

This was much before the days of slam-bang Twenty20 cricket and prompted Sunil Gavaskar, who was doing the match commentary, to

---

[41]'Tunbridge Wells Da Jawab Nahin: Where Kapil Dev Changed Indian Cricket Forever', *The New Indian Express*, 7 June 2019. https://www.newindianexpress.com/specials/2019/jun/07/tunbridge-wells-da-jawab-nahin-where-kapil-dev-changed-indian-cricket-forever-1987246.html.

remark 'Only Kapil Dev could have done it.'

Former Australian captain Richie Benaud remarked tongue-in-cheek: 'I suppose it's only logical. If you need 24 to save the follow on why wouldn't you get it in four hits?'

Kapil Dev, the legend, is the first player to take 200 Test wickets. He is also the only player in the history of cricket to have taken more than 400 wickets (434) and scored more than 5000 runs in Tests making him one of the greatest all-rounders to have played the game.

In my opinion, Kapil was a notch ahead of Imran Khan, Ian Botham and Richard Hadlee, his redoubtable contemporaries, and the fact that we are both Indians has nothing to do with this assessment!

Kapil Dev was inducted into the ICC Hall of Fame in 2010. His rough-hewn punchline on a television commercial 'Palmolive *da jawab nahin*' (there is no match for Palmolive) can veritably be applied to himself in the cricketing context.

Dilip Vengsarkar

One of India's most accomplished batsmen, Dilip Vengsarkar was just in his teens when he stormed into the limelight with a majestic century for Mumbai against Rest of India in an Irani Trophy match in 1975.

After a tentative start to his international career, 'Colonel' (Lala Amarnath's epithet for him after C.K. Nayudu), Vengsarkar became India's most consistent batsman over the next two decades, one of his most memorable knocks being against Pakistan in Delhi in 1979. With India needing 390 runs on the final day, the elegant batsman's 146 brought India to within sight of victory only to fall short by just 26 runs of what would have been an enthralling victory.

Along with Sunil Gavaskar and Gundappa Vishwanath, he was a key player in the batting line up in the late '70s and early '80s.

Vengsarkar was part of the 1983 World Cup winning team and was rated as the best batsman in the Coopers and Lybrand rating in 1986–87. He has the unique distinction of scoring three centuries at Lord's.

Dilip scored six centuries against the formidable West Indies bowling line-up of Michael Holding (nicknamed 'Whispering Death' by eccentric but respected umpire Dickie Bird for his fluxional bowling run-up), Malcolm Marshall and Andy Roberts. Holding, the mildest of human beings you can hope to meet—but the most principled—is generally acclaimed as the Rolls Royce of fast bowlers for his smooth run-up and rhythmic action. He was a Dr Jekyll and Mr

Hyde prototype: the height of gentle, soft-spoken grace off the field, but a demon with the ball in his hand.

Vengsarkar replaced Kapil Dev as captain after the 1987 World Cup but soon faded away and retired in 1992 when he was only behind Sunil Gavaskar in Test runs and centuries.

Vengsarkar, who is part of Farokh Engineer's Mumbai 'mafia' and his regular companion on the city's social circuit along with wife Manali, is also a regular at our Mumbai home. He is a great fan of the Bohri fare which my wife Zeyna organizes.

Dilip Vengsarkar

Squash Exchange with Malaysia

Dilip continues to run the Elf Vengsarkar Cricket Academy with which *Mid-Day* was involved between 1999 and 2002 in a squash and cricket coaching exchange programme. Under the scheme, Mumbai's promising squash youngsters were coached, among others, by former world No. 7 K.H. Ong, father of world junior champion Ong Beng Hee. In turn, promising Under-15 Malaysian cricketers were trained at Vengsarkar's cricket academy at the Oval ground in Mumbai.

To give him his due, the innovative exchange programme was the brainchild of the internationally respected and *Mid-Day* squash correspondent Raju Chainani. Many of Mumbai's players, who went on to achieve distinction abroad, owe a debt of gratitude to Chainani who single-handedly, and from his private funds, also published *Simply Squash*, a labour of love.

Malaysian women's squash champion Nicol David (who also trained at Malaysia's Petra Foundation) was anointed in 2001 as the 'World Games Greatest Athlete of All Time.'

Mid-Day A-H Ansari Squash Academy

Raju Chainani's passion to spread the game outside the confines of the five-star clubs of Mumbai, especially among youngsters, was an inspiration for us to set up a public squash complex, the Mid-Day A-H Ansari Squash Academy, at the Andheri Sports Complex in memory of my late father.

Typically, getting permission from the high and mighty Mumbai Municipal Corporation bigwigs who do nothing positive for the city nor let others do anything, was a monumental task. But after pulling a thousand strings and spending hours on the project, permission was granted most reluctantly, and Bollywood idol Aamir Khan inaugurated the academy.

When Malaysia's Tunku Imran came to Mumbai along with Datuk Vinod Sekhar, they visited the academy and were highly impressed with the facilities as well as the free training that was being imparted by coaches of Mahendra Agarwal's Indian Squash Professionals (ISP).

The academy attracted budding squash players from the locality as well as Mumbai's distant suburbs. But the recalcitrant powers that be, who were never happy that we had been able to go over their heads and get permission for the public service, scuttled it citing chapter-and-verse from Mumbai's archaic and senseless municipal laws.

Sad! But that's the way the cookie crumbles in our once-beautiful metropolis.

Raju Chainani

Unfortunately, the dedicated and indefatigable Raju Chainani, to whom Indian squash owes a huge debt, passed away prematurely, during a coaching assignment in Hong Kong, prompting me to write in *Mid-Day*:

> The widespread expression of grief in the world squash community—from the United Kingdom to Australia—over the sudden passing away of renowned squash writer Raju Chainani is a barometer of the regard and affection which he enjoyed in the fraternity.
>
> In his death, the game of squash has been bereaved not only in Mumbai and the rest of India but all over the world. RIP, Raju—they don't make them that way anymore!

Tunku 'Pete' Imran

The association with Malaysia through squash, the game I have played regularly since my college days, gave me the opportunity to befriend Tunku Tan Sri Dato' Seri Imran ibni Almarhum Tuanku Ja'afar al-Haj, prince of Negeri Sembilan, one of the 13 states of Malaysia.

His father was king of Malaysia between 1994 and 1999 when Malaysia took giant leaps forward in the form of the creation of Kuala Lumpur International Airport, the landmark Petronas Twin Towers, the Multimedia Super Corridor and the new administrative capital of Putrajaya.

'Pete,' as he is known in the sports fraternity the world over, has been a part of the top brass in the international squash, cricket, hockey and Olympics bodies. He was also president of the Commonwealth Games Federation and is as knowledgeable about matters concerning sport as he is the embodiment of good taste, charm and refinement; he is a connoisseur of good wines who enjoys good cigars and belts out Tom Jones ballads almost like the Welshman himself.

Pete has a Bachelor of Laws (LLB) degree from the University of Nottingham, UK, was barrister-at-law at Gray's Inn and has many honorary doctorates from universities in UK. and the US.

A gracious host, Pete invited Rukya and me to a lavish Eid banquet at his family palace in Negri Sembilan at which we were privileged be the only non-family members present. Later, when he turned 50, Zeyna and I were among Pete's select list of guests in Sydney, as also last year on his seventieth in Kuala Lumpur.

In 2019 when we were on a cruise that briefly transited Port Klang near Kuala Lumpur, Pete, good friend that he is, took time off from work, drove down especially from KL to take us to lunch and back. He is a special friend (as is his young son Tarrant) and we have in common a passionate interest in sports.

The Grand Prix

How can I ever forget Pete's invitation to witness the Malaysian Grand Prix the only time I have seen the thrilling event? Michael Schumacher, one of motor racing's greatest champions, driving for Ferrari amid rain and thunderstorms at the start, won the 55-lap event from pole position in Sepang, Selangor, in front of a crowd of 75,000 spectators. His teammate Rubens Barrichello finished second with McLaren's David Coulthard, third.

My report from Kuala Lumpur read:

> Take it from me, you haven't really lived if you haven't witnessed a Formula 1 car race from a sponsor's hospitality box.
>
> A Silver Arrow car parade: a spectacular, eardrum-bursting aerobatics display by the Malaysian Air Force and the chance to see at close quarters, the ultimate driving machines, their crew and drivers during a pit walkabout.
>
> Followed by a mind-boggling display of conquest of space by man-made machines, driven to their fullest potential by men whose reflexes, agility, strength, fitness and resilience compel the greatest admiration.
>
> Add to this the most lavish luncheon service provided by an international caterer *par excellence,* and you, dear reader, have every reason to feel envious!
>
> Known for his aggressive and unrelenting driving, the late, then 32-year old, German Schumacher was on record as saying: 'I do not do it for the glory... I go out there in my red rod to enjoy the race.'

The seven-time F1 World Champion had been on holiday in the French Alps in 2013 when he was involved in a devastating skiing accident that left him with severe brain injuries. Almost eight years later, he has not been seen in public with few details released about his current state. In 2020, lead Swiss neurologist Erich Riederer said the following about his condition: 'He's awake but not responding. He is breathing, his heart is beating, he can probably sit up and take baby steps with help, but no more. I think that's the maximum for him.'[42]

What a tragic end to a distinguished career!

Breaking her eight-year silence since Schumacher's accident, his wife Corinna, 52, said in a heartbreaking interview to Netflix: 'I miss Michael every day. But Michael is here—different, but here. He still shows me how strong he is every day.'[43]

She revealed how Michael complained about the snow conditions in the Alps and suggested flying to Dubai shortly before the tragic accident.

---

[42]'He is Awake but Not Responding': Leading Neurosurgeon Gives Update on Michael Schumacher's Condition', News 18, 23 September 2020, https://www.news18.com/news/sports/he-is-awake-but-not-responding-leading-neurosurgeon-gives-update-on-michael-schumachers-condition-2902441.html. Accessed on 15 November 2021.

[43]Emmanuella Ngimbi, '"He still shows me how strong he is every day" Michael Schumacher's wife's tearful update', *Express*, 14 September 2021, https://www.express.co.uk/showbiz/tv-radio/1490772/Michael-Schumacher-health-strong-wife-crying. Accessed on 15 November 2021.

My Dear Friend, Behram—RIP

Whereas spectacular progress in the fields of science and medicine has made unimagined longevity possible for our species, it has, sadly, also brought about greater sorrow for the larger number of unfortunate ones who survive their near and dear ones.

Utopian predictions of humans surviving up to age 150 in the not-too-distant future may be exciting to the medical community, but the amateur social scientist in me makes me wonder if life will be worth living for those surviving until that age without their loved ones!

Like most of us, I have been devastated by the loss of my dear parents. I have been inconsolable at the deaths of my many friends over the years going back to my school and college days.

I have plumbed the depths of despair upon the premature passing away of friends 'Sam' Manekshaw, Jaffer Durazi, Krishna Sanghi, Rajnikant Kilachand, Virenchee Sagar, Mohan Anand, Shashikant Morjaria, Sadanand Shetty, Anil Dharker, Farokh Hansotia, Gautam Thakkar, Firoz Baldiwala, Moosa Kola and 'Sunny' Kotwal in the UK, and others too numerous to mention.

I have been honoured to be singled out by families such as the Sanghis, the Shettys, the Anands, the Bhimanis (in Kolkata), the Harkirat Singhs and Farzana Contractor in Mumbai to deliver eulogies to my dear departed *bhais* (brothers) and *behens* (sisters). The list grows longer with the passage of time, as is the *zaamane ka dastoor* (way of the world).

But for me, the passing of Behram ('Busybee') Contractor has been perhaps the most poignant.

Contrary to the evil intent of nasty rumour mongers who spread all manner of vicious versions of our parting of ways, Farzana truly understood the depth of friendship and mutual personal and professional respect her husband and I had for each other.

Therefore, I considered it a special privilege to be asked by her to say my final goodbye to Behram at his largely attended condolence meeting.

In October 2001, when Farzana decided to launch a collection of Behram's published articles titled *Busybee-The Millennium Man,* she did me the honour of asking me to release it on what would have been his seventy-first birthday at their Harkness Road residence in Mumbai.

FIFTEEN

THE WAR AND THE MOUNTAINS

Kargil Indo-Pak War, 1999

India was in a state of shock when the Pakistan Army Chief General Pervez Musharraf orchestrated the Kargil War, purportedly without the knowledge of the Pakistani prime minister of the time, Nawaz Sharif.

In May 1999, I was in Australia covering cricket when hostilities broke out. Upon my return home, I was greatly distressed at the daily reports in the media of dead and wounded Indian soldiers. I felt I should have been in Kargil alongside our country's soldiers who were risking their lives for the country rather than enjoying a cricket series abroad from cushy air-conditioned press boxes.

Upon my return home, I dashed off a front-page editorial in *Mid-Day* addressed to prime minister Atal Bihari Vajpayee that read:

Dear Prime Minister:

As heart-rending reports of casualties among innocent civilians and brave *jawans* (soldiers) on our border come in, one question continues to haunt me day after day.

As hair-raising accounts of barbarism, brutality and bestiality filter in, an inner voice taunts me constantly.

The refrain, dear PM is: 'How can I help?'

Not having had the good fortune of being trained in the science of defence of my country, I do not have even a rudimentary understanding of how a humble individual like myself can help ward off an inhumane, nay satanic, marauder who stops at nothing in his evil designs.

But I do know that there must be *some* way in which someone like myself can be of some little help somewhere, somehow in the defence of his Motherland.

Show me how, Prime Minister.

Send me to Kargil, Drass or Batalik. Let me be of help.

Yours in the service of the Nation,

Khalid A-H Ansari

◆

And, almost as if a magic wand had been waved, I soon received intimation that the Government of India would be happy to arrange for me and two colleagues from my newspaper to go to Kargil to cover the war.

Unfortunately, newspaper clippings of my dispatches to *Inquilab* and *Mid-Day* have fallen prey to the ravages of ravenous termites, but I would like to say that my experience, along with Delhi *Mid-Day* correspondent Vitusha Oberoi and photographer K.K. Suresh shall forever remain etched in memory.

In the absence of physical published records of the war, I have been able to piece together some pertinent highlights of what took place between May and July of 1999 in Jammu and Kashmir's Kargil district along the Line of Control (LOC).

Let me begin by saying that my experience—and I know it was

the same for my two colleagues—was professionally the most satisfying but, at the same time, incredibly frightening, personally.

To begin with, our army escort which was meant to ferry us from Srinagar to Dras via the Zojila Pass (altitude 11,649 feet) in the Ladakh region of which Leh and Kargil are districts, somehow went missing.

Dras is the coldest place in India, with average lows of around -20°C (-4°F) and as low as -23°C (-9.4°F) at the height of winter, which lasts from mid-October to mid-May. It may be noted the Kargil War started in May 1999.

My dispatch from Srinagar read:

> Thanks to a monumental blunder by a particularly avuncular gentleman in New Delhi who just forgot to send word about our arrival to Srinagar and other forward areas, Team *Mid-Day* has had to fend for itself.
>
> Whereas in the normal course, the team would have been provided armed convoy escort, the cock-up has resulted in our having to navigate the treacherous conflict zone on our own in civilian transport.
>
> No hard feelings, though. Our tribe of newshounds always prefers to hunt on its own.
>
> Believe this, dear reader, there is humour even in this life-and-death business of war news coverage.

Kargil Indo-Pak War, 1999

If There Be Heaven on Earth...

My first dispatch on the Kargil War sent from Srinagar, Kashmir was headlined 'One's heart bleeds for Kashmir' and started with a Farsi (Persian) couplet by poet Amir Khusrau:

> 'Agar firdaus bar roo-e-zaminast
> Hameen ast-o, hameen ast-o, hameen ast

(If there be a heaven on earth, this is it, this is it, this is it!)

Thus spoke Mughal Emperor Shah Jahan, he who ordained that a fitting, eternal tribute be built to commemorate his undying love for his dear beloved wife, Noor Jahan (Light of the World) upon seeing Srinagar's Nishat Gardens.

Today, Srinagar is almost a ghost town. Hotel reception clerks just cannot remove their gaze from the front door in desperate anticipation of the next walk-in guest.

The expansive, lovingly crafted Chinar wooden houseboats on the placid waters of the Dal and Nagin lakes sing a dirge for what might have been.

Conspicuous by their absence are the hail-fellow-well-met *shikarawallahs* (boatmen) and the unscrupulous carpetbaggers so perspicaciously and eloquently described by wayward Kashmiri son of the soil Salman Rushdie.

Taxi drivers even at 'super *deluxe*' category hotels—call

it a day at 6 p.m. anxiously spending their evenings at home, transfixedly following the fortunes of a war which, by unanimous consent, is not of their own making but which is making their lives in this so-called paradise a *dozakh* (hell).

The water level in the Jhelum river which runs through the city is alarmingly low because of unusually inadequate rainfall last winter.

Even the muezzin's call to prayer seems to lack conviction.

There is a sad premonition of decay in a city which, until the 25th of last month, preceding the brief, panic-inducing closure of its airport seemed to be on an unwavering course to Valhalla.

Sad, sad, sad.

◆

So determined were we to push on, we decided to proceed, nevertheless at our own cost and in civilian transport without army escort. As we made our way through the valley below, we were veritable sitting ducks for enemy troops perched advantageously in the surrounding mountain peaks.

The conflict began with the infiltration of both Pakistani troops and terrorists into Indian territory. The intruders positioned themselves in key locations at higher altitudes that gave them a strategic advantage. However, based on information from local shepherds, the Indian army could ascertain the points of incursion and launch 'Operation Vijay.'

Having to live in exposed and vulnerable (also nauseatingly unhygienic) quarters—as evidenced by the fact that a mortar shell landed in our hotel courtyard in the dead of night (so close were we to the enemy on the ridge across)—tells its own story.

On 26 July 1999, the Indian Army recaptured all eight Indian posts in Kargil that had been occupied by Pakistan's army. Since then, that date has been observed annually as Kargil Vijay Diwas (Kargil Victory Day) to commemorate the victory and sacrifices made by Indian soldiers.

The victory came at a high price. The official death toll on the Indian side was 527.

Call to Paes, Bhupathi to Dedicate Win to Kargil Jawans

After the Kargil victory, my column on 5 July 1999, headlined 'Dedicate this win to our jawans (Bhupathi and Paes)' read:

Even with the entire nation's undivided attention focused on Kargil, heartiest congratulations are in order for Mahesh Bhupathi and Leander Paes for their historic men's doubles victory at Wimbledon yesterday, the day the Indian tricolour flew again over Tiger Hill.

Coming on the heels of their unprecedented win by any Indian in the French Open last month, this and Leander Paes' mixed doubles victory should serve as a colossal morale booster not only to the *jawans* now laying their lives on the line for the nation, but to all our countrymen everywhere.

After all, it is not very often that glory at the loftiest sporting summit comes our way—and back-to-back, at that!

It would be in the fitness of things if Paes and Bhupathi—who have brought sporting glory to the nation in the recent past—were to dedicate their victory to our armed forces presently defending the country.

And, it would be decidedly appropriate for all our commercial houses who milked the recent Cricket World Cup to the last drop for unabashed mercantile reasons to now come forward and demonstrate their largesse to the paramount national cause and, in smaller measure, to Paes and Bhupathi.

On the subject of cricket: whereas Mohammed Azharuddin magnanimously donated ₹5 lakh to the war effort, what are the other cricket millionaires doing?

The nation is proud of you Mahesh and Leander.

◈

The suggestion was heeded. On 11 July 1999 my column read:

Khalidoscope takes particular pride in thanking Wimbledon doubles crown winner Leander Paes for dedicating his victories to the valiant jawans in Kargil, as suggested in this column (*Mid-Day* 5 July).

A copy of *Mid-Day* making the appeal for dedication had been forwarded to Leander's father, Dr Vece Paes, in Kolkata.

And, hey presto, one gets the news on television in Srinagar on Friday night that Leander has thought it fit to pay heed our advice.

Game, set and match, Leander.

The Mountains Beckon Again

After the Kargil experience, the allure of the mountains beckoned and I returned to the Himalayas on an unforgettable trek in June 2004. I discovered that the vistas in the Khumbu Valley, land of the Sherpas, within sight of Mount Everest, are truly enchanting and the views of the Himalayas verily awesome.

Being there is a humbling experience in the sense of making one realize just how insignificant we conceited humans really are as compared to the grandeur and majesty of nature's remarkable creations. I experienced similar feelings of humility, of smallness, insignificance, utter irrelevance if you will, at the Hubbard Glacier that is in Alaska, US and Yukon Territory, Canada and the spectacular Northern Lights (Aurora Borealis) in Norway.

◆

The Gokyo Kang peak (5,360 metres) has a panoramic vantage point that is even more enchanting than Kala Patthar. The names Namche Bazaar and Tenzing Norgay, Edmund Hillary, John Hunt (the leader of the successful 1953 British expedition to Mount Everest) bring evocative echoes from the distant memories from one's schooldays. For this writer, when he was a romantic 15-year-old schoolboy with all the stars of the galaxy in his eyes, the name Namche Bazaar and related events, evoked orgasmic wanderlust.

The trail from Lukla continues through pines and rhododendrons through gorges on to Namche Bazaar, then on through the most indescribably beautiful forests, meadows, bridges, glaciers, moraines, plateaus, villages and monasteries in the shadow of the Everest and its satellite peaks to Kala Patthar, my destination.

Sad to say, insouciant but intrepid climbers and wannabe trekkers such as me stand charged on the count of polluting the pristine cleanliness and pure atmosphere of the region. The ubiquitous garbage dumps are as much a blot on the authorities as it is on the devil-may-care trekkers.

As though polluting the planet that we inhabit was not enough, we now seem to be focusing on outer space as well, if television reports of the amount of floating garbage and debris are to be believed!

Being a neophyte and certainly not fit enough at my then age of 57, I had no pretensions of being able to ascend to the holy grail of mountain climbing. I had gone unprepared in terms of oxygen, clothing and other essentials. In any event, some members of our group, including me, suffered from altitude sickness and had to fly back to Kathmandu. Although most cases of altitude sickness are mild, some can be life-threatening. The reasonably fit, who can withstand altitude sickness, can complete the trek in about 13 days, which can be increased to 18–20 days at a leisurely pace.

Total cost (excluding airfare to Kathmandu): an eminently reasonable US$1,000

If I may suggest to you, dear reader: walk. Just do it—health and physical fitness permitting. Go on a trek in the Himalayas, where nine of the planet's 10 tallest peaks stand. You will thank me for it.

Namche Bazaar is an enchanting trading post 11,300 feet up in the remote Khumbu region of the Himalayas in Nepal from where, 51 years ago, legendary mountaineers Tenzing Norgay and Sir Edmund Hillary launched their epic climb to the top of the world in May 1953.

The historic feat ('Ah, but a man's reach should exceed his grasp, Or what's a Heaven for?' as Robert Browning wrote) that took place at 11.30 a.m., to be precise, on 29 May 1953 came, almost as if by design, on the eve of the coronation of Queen Elizabeth II of Britain.

It was dedicated to her who, later, knighted Hillary and awarded Norgay a medal.

◆

It's not given to everybody to emulate the kind of historic glory that Norgay and Hillary achieved.

'Well George, we knocked the bastard off,' Hillary is reported to have said to teammate George Lowe, as the two descended from the summit of 'The Big E' via the Western Col and the South Col route they had taken.

In addition to Everest, Hillary, the unassuming, self-styled, poor country boy beekeeper from Papakura, New Zealand has also stood at both the North and South Poles. Now, if that isn't awesome, what is?

Notorious for its inclement weather, Everest is worshipped as a deity by the Sherpas, many of whom still consider attempts at ascending the peak disrespectful, if not downright heretical.

For this reason, Tenzing Norgay was virtually ostracized by many of his fellow Sherpas of an earlier generation, who were convinced that the arrogant attempt act would incur the wrath of the deity Sagarmatha.

◆

Needless to say, having congenial company on any expedition makes all the difference to its enjoyment.

I was fortunate to have been invited on the trek by the delightful Jain family of New Delhi. There was the personable and erudite Ajay Jain, a former tea company executive and businessman from Kolkata, his ebullient wife Jayshree and fun-loving son Chirag, who has an MBA from Oxford.

After a career as a management consultant in London, Chirag has gone on to carve a niche as stand-up comedian in the West End under the pseudonym of Papa CJ. His forte is to self-deprecatingly imitate the mannerisms of his fellow-Indians while cheekily 'taking the mickey' of Westerners, especially the British. Winner of the 'Asia's Best Stand-Up Comedian' award by *Top 10* magazine in Kuala Lumpur, Chirag (Papa CJ) has put on sell-out shows across five continents. He has also worked as an executive coach and motivational speaker and has trained executives from blue-chip companies all over the world.

There was never a dull moment with Chirag around and he and his jovial yet cerebral cousins, Dhruv and Vidur, made our trek a most hilarious and memorable one.

Then we had our genial and indefatigable Sirdar Sherpa, Mingma Lama, cook Pushkur Thakuri and their team of 13 helpers—including a yak rider and four (unchristened) yaks. They were simply superb.

Hand on my heart—it was an experience I shall always cherish.

SIXTEEN

AND THEN WE MET...

Bringing in the New Millennium Down Under

I was in Australia at the end of the last millennium covering Sachin Tendulkar's team's disappointing tour of Australia, which the home side, captained by the phlegmatic Steve Waugh, swept 3–0. Ricky Ponting scored the most runs in the series (375) and Tendulkar, for India (278), whereas Glenn McGrath (18) and Ajit Agarkar (11) bagged the highest number of wickets.

Sydney welcomed the third millennium with a kaleidoscopic extravaganza of light and sound, colour and celebration, the likes of which one has never seen. The theme for the memorable event depicted the arrival in 1778 of British convicts to the city's beautiful and world-famous harbour. The celebrations were on a breathtakingly lavish scale. At the stroke of midnight, church bells rang, technicolour fireworks that had cost the equivalent of approximately ₹15 crore lit up the sky from the iconic Opera House. Sirens hooted as the word 'Eternity' emblazoned on the Harbour Bridge in an incandescent burst of colour, while a soulful rendition of 'Auld Lang Syne' wafted into the night. It was easily the biggest celebration the metropolis has ever seen, reconfirming Sydney's reputation of a hedonistic city that knows how to party.

Passing judgement on the cerebral aspects of fun-loving Sydney apart, one can conclude after having watched the television coverage of the celebrations in different capitals of the world that the millennium eve pageant here was second to none, barring Paris perhaps.

As the dazzling fireworks colours painted the sky, an estimated 6,000 boats with over 100,000 guests from all over the world bobbed on the choppy waters, while close to 1.5 million revellers milled around on a night of unbridled cheer and bonhomie.

After the Kiribati Islands in the South Pacific and Chatham Islands in New Zealand, Sydney was among the first on Mother Earth to celebrate the historic event, five and a half hours ahead of India.

After the multitudes had returned home, a children's choral group greeted the millennium's first sunrise with a stirring version of 'Breath of the Spirit' to the mellifluous accompaniment of aboriginal music rendered by musicians perched atop the shell-like contours of the famed Opera House. The excellent arrangements enabled the clearing of 1.5 million people from the harbour area in less than half an hour.

Traffic snarls were non-existent, pedestrian movement amazingly smooth, drunken and unruly behaviour conspicuous by its absence, all thanks to meticulous planning, effective implementation and, above all, disciplined crowds, barring a few incidents of alcohol-induced larrikinism. By 7 a.m. on New Year's Day, streets had been swept clean of all the filth and rubbish of the previous boisterous night.

It was mere happenstance for me to be invited to witness the celebrations by the late Deepak Malhotra, a Sydney medical practitioner and occasional *Mid-Day* contributor, to witness the fireworks as guest at the residence of Rajan Parhawk, physician and bon viveur. At the time, Rajan resided on the 18th floor of a building that had an awesome view of the world's most beautiful harbour.

One couldn't have wished for a better ringside balcony seat to witness the festivities, to remember family and friends and, on the momentous occasion, to reflect on the majesty of the Maker and his wondrous creation.

Zeyna, Zeynasan

Speaking of wondrous creations, my presence at the splendiferous millennium bringing-in party turned out to be a godsend, which makes me marvel at the boundless ability of the Donkey to shower me with fortuitous pennies from Heaven.

In the words of the seminal 1936 lyrics popularized by Bing Crosby:

> Every time it rains, it rains pennies from heaven
> Don't you know each cloud contains pennies from heaven?
> You'll find your fortune's fallin' all over the town
> Be sure that your umbrella is upside down
> Trade them for a package of sunshine and flowers
> If you want the things you love, you must have showers
> So, when you hear it thunder, don't run under a tree
> There'll be pennies from heaven for you and me

It just so happened that I had no inkling of the Millennium Eve party, nor did Mattie Tomasevich, (my wife-to-be Zeyna's maiden name), a qualified accountant born in London to Yugoslav refugee parents who fled their Communist country to go to Rotorua, New Zealand.

I had just arrived in Sydney from Melbourne after covering the Boxing Day Test match, which the home side had won by a resounding 180 runs. I promptly accepted Deepak's invitation, being desperately in need of succour after the shellacking that had been dished out to us.

Mattie, on the other hand, had no intention of accepting host Rajan's invitation because of anticipated traffic and logistics problems after the midnight party, but his persuasive skills prevailed, and she decided to attend.

And thereby hangs a life-changing tale for both of us, a prodigious *sliding doors moment*.

At the party, as inebriated party revellers, showering lucullan benediction on all and sundry, took centre stage, I happened to set eyes on this empyrean being who, at first sight, was gentle as a lamb. She spoke in a mellifluous voice that was barely audible in the high voltage festivities and had a downward gaze that was reminiscent of my mother. Mattie came across as shy, but cerebral, without any trace of pretentiousness. She had worked with the world-renowned management consultancy firm, McKinsey & Company, in London and Australia and was modest to a fault.

Most importantly, as I discovered later, she was an animal lover, which I knew was a sign of a compassionate nature and had a heart of gold as evidenced by her numerous charitable involvements, about which she spoke passionately. She now partners me—with exemplary ardour and admirable compassion for girls from underprivileged communities, our primary focus, in our strictly private foundation—the Khalid & Zeyna Ansari Foundation.

◆

Mattie's Croatian ancestry went back to Split, close to the home of Marshal Josip Broz Tito who became president of Yugoslavia and co-founder of the NAM along with Jawaharlal Nehru.

We would meet in Sydney later, where I covered the 2000 Olympic Games, and visited periodically to cover cricket matches for my group publications.

Mattie and I decided to marry in 2011 in Rotorua, her hometown near Auckland, New Zealand, renowned for its sulphur springs that are a huge tourist attraction despite their malodorous effluvium. After marriage, she changed her name to Zeyna, meaning 'excellence' in Arabic. I address her as Zeyna-san (the honorific 'san' being a Japanese term of respect)—or affectionately, Mother Teresa!

We remarried—twice under Muslim law—first at the home of dear friends Abbas and Madhu Jasdanwala in Mahabaleshwar (a hill station near Pune) and later in Mumbai, not to make sure thrice over (!) but because of imbecilic interpretations of Islam by half-baked mullahs.

Zeyna, Zeynasan

SEVENTEEN

YOU WIN SOME, YOU LOSE SOME

The Asian Age

Mobashar Jawed 'M.J.' Akbar is the editorial wunderkind who signified overvaulting political ambition, a quality that catapulted him into the Union Council of Ministers as minister of state for external affairs under Narendra Modi. He had switched political affiliation to the BJP after many years in the Congress party.

A prominent journalist and writer revered by many in the industry, M.J. was a master craftsman as a journalist (given his background of English literature studies), impressive grasp of Indian and Islamic history and sharp political instincts. My favourite description of him can be summed up by the word 'polemicist.'

'Mubi,' as I called him, started his career as a trainee journalist at the Times Group's *The Illustrated Weekly of India* under Khushwant Singh. He then took charge of the *Onlooker* magazine, before moving to Kolkata, his native state, where he started the trailblazing *The Telegraph*. During his long career in journalism, M.J. also launched and/or edited some of India's finest political news periodicals such as *The Illustrated Weekly of India, The Sunday Guardian, India Today* and *The Asian Age*. He is also a best-selling author.

In 1998, M.J., along with T. Venkattram Reddy of the established *Deccan Chronicle* newspaper of Hyderabad, approached me with a proposal to start together an upmarket English morning daily newspaper in Mumbai, a project I had dreamt of all my working life. We discovered we were in sync in our thinking regarding most aspects of the project. M.J., Reddy and I had many brainstorming sessions, even fine-tuned its personality but differed on the price of the paper.

M.J. was insistent that the price be ₹5 per copy given the desired upscale readership image that he thought would attract the requisite level of advertising. Reddy was undecided, and I was of the firm opinion that the paper should take off at a respectable circulation base level, for which a reasonable cover price was essential.

M.J. argued that he was not looking at a hundred thousand copies to begin with and that he would be content with a figure of around 70,000. I was convinced that his expectation was unrealistic given the unprecedented price of ₹5 (the competition was then priced at between ₹2 and ₹3 per copy). I then suggested a price of ₹3, giving the analogy of an airplane take-off, arguing that for a newspaper launch, it is vital to price it in keeping with the competition, failing which the paper would not have the requisite thrust to attain cruising altitude. I was convinced that, in failing to do so, the result would be a 'splutter,' an inability to even take off, leave aside gaining cruising altitude.

We agreed to disagree: I wished M.J. and Reddy the very best, offered to print the paper at my press and even help distribute it through my regular *Inquilab* and *Mid-Day* networks. Since I had relocated to Dubai by then, my son Tarique implemented my offer for many years.

◆

Unfortunately, although *The Asian Age* was outstanding editorially—decidedly a cut above the competition—the initial damage because of its exorbitant original cover price of ₹5 has proven to be disastrous, as was my trepidation. The paper's steep cover price prevented it from taking off in terms of circulation and corresponding readership which, in turn, scuttled its advertising revenues from Day 1. In the ultimate analysis, the dictum about advertising being the lifeblood of the newspaper industry was vindicated.

Well-connected M.J. and Reddy roped in many financiers over the years to keep the project alive and, against conventional wisdom, kept the newspaper going without much advertising response. On the contrary, they even started ambitious editions in New Delhi, Kolkata and London.

But, sadly, buffeting by the electronic media, followed by the effects of the COVID-19 pandemic, took its toll on *The Asian Age,* although the time-honoured *Deccan Chronicle* is being kept afloat by its founders, the Reddy family.

Reddy and M.J. parted ways some years ago. M.J. migrated to politics but got embroiled in a #MeToo complaint and defamation case brought by Delhi journalist Priya Ramani.

But that's another story—and doesn't fall within the ambit of these memoirs.

Special Executive Magistrate

I accepted an invitation from the Maharashtra state government to work as what was described as a special executive magistrate (SEM) to assist the government in a quasi-judicial capacity in relieving the high courts and other courts in Maharashtra of their burden of a large number of cases.

As enunciated by Mr Justice K. Madhava Reddy, Chief Justice of the Bombay High Court, at a function where he was awarding shields of merit to SEMs, Lok Nyayalaya courts (people's courts) would constitute of 'persons of high integrity and independence to dispense justice in their honorary capacity.' I, however, had to regretfully resign without doing justice since a more challenging prospect from Dubai, to run the *Khaleej Times* daily newspaper, came along and it was an offer I just couldn't refuse.

> Intrigued by the strange certification norms of the Central Board of Film Certification, I had earlier accepted an invitation to work on the board. So asinine was the thinking of the members and so ridiculous the decision-making process that I resigned in double quick time, instead accepting an invitation to function as vice-chairman of the Maharashtra State Press Consultative Committee and also as vice president of the Sports Journalists' Association of Mumbai.

Ambassadorship

A humorous saying that I came across during my student days was: 'An ambassador is an honest man sent to lie abroad for the good of his country.'

As mentioned in an earlier chapter, Natwar Singh, who as external affairs minister wielded considerable influence in the corridors of power in New Delhi when the Congress party was in power, was keen that I get a suitable ambassadorial assignment. After being asked to meet a number of senior party functionaries in the capital, I was informed by more than one reliable source that 'my papers were in the final stages' and that it was only a matter of time before I would receive the good news.

I was in Muscat, Oman, during my stint with the *Khaleej Times* in the UAE, when we received news of Rajiv Gandhi's assassination—the result of a suicide bombing in Sriperumbudur, Tamil Nadu, on 21 May 1991 in which 14 others were also killed.

In all honesty, if there was one achievement I was aspiring to, it was an ambassadorship, especially since it was being offered without my initiative, something I know would have made my parents extremely happy and proud.

As it turned out, the tragic incident also shot whatever hopes I had entertained of being appointed ambassador. The efforts were revived when the Congress party formed the central government alliance (the United Progressive Alliance in 2009), but it was not meant to be. I would be dishonest if I were to say I was not acutely disappointed, but c'est la vie.

Padma Shri

Strange are the ways of destiny, if you believe in it.

The Congress big cheeses must have had their reasons for not considering me worthy of an ambassadorship. I was later informed that the practice of appointing non-Foreign Service (IFS) people to diplomatic posts was being discontinued because of the purported indiscretions of a diplomat in Europe, but I cannot swear by it. It was probably a lame excuse to not appoint me.

However, out of the blue, the BJP government, with Atal Bihari Vajpayee as prime minister, thought it fit to confer on me the honour of Padma Shri in 2001. The citation read 'for literature and journalism.'

The nomination was extremely surprising since our parent publication, the *Inquilab*, had been a dedicated supporter of the Congress party ever since the Independence movement.

Not being one to look a gift horse in the mouth, I accepted the totally unexpected honour at the hands of President K.R. Narayanan at a dignified ceremony redolent of old-world pageantry. Prime Minister Atal Bihari Vajpayee, L.K. Advani and senior members of the cabinet were present at the function at New Delhi's Rashtrapati Bhavan, at which sportsmen Dhanraj Pillai, Leander Paes, Mahesh Bhupathi and squash champion Bhuvaneshwari Kumari were also awarded Padma Shri awards.

On a lighter note, it made me wonder if this was a gambit from the jurisprudence of the rascally Donkey of this narrative to make amends for my disappointment at missing out on an ambassadorial appointment.

◆

On the subject of ministers, there are any number of jokes—some funny, others irreverent, tasteless and some plain humourless PJs (poor jokes)—concerning some ministers we have had in recent years.

According to a true story to which I was witness: when asked facetiously by an insolent foreign journalist if he was allowed to 'play squash' following his recent heart procedure, a country-bumpkin minister, ignorant of the game of squash and mistaking it for 'scotch' replies: *'ek waqt tha jab shauq tha, ab doctor ke kehne par band kar diya hai'* (there was a time when I was fond of it, but have had to give it up on medical advice).

On the other hand, there was also the refined, scholarly and kindly former prime minister Manmohan Singh, who was totally out of his depth in the cesspool of sharks and barracudas in the murky world of New Delhi politics.

Although he injected some sanity in the halls of Parliament with his sincerity of purpose and capacity for civilized debate, his enlightened submissions couched in soft, measured, civilized manner was fodder for the rowdy roughnecks who routinely shouted him down.

A conspicuous misfit in politics, Manmohan Singh belonged to the world of academia—to planning, business and finance. His considerable talent could have been of immeasurable value to the country but he rather unwisely chose to get involved in dynastic politics and hitch his wagon to a coterie without due regard for the larger national interest.

I was impressed when I met him on a few occasions but was greatly disappointed that the country was deprived of his true worth.

Whereas there's no doubting his laudable intent it is sad that, in all likelihood, posterity will not do justice to his true greatness.

◆

On the subject of members of the cabinet, but in a lighter vein: I was with a very senior minister of the Congress party (who later became prime minister) at his New Delhi residence on a Sunday afternoon due to my request for an interview.

The minister was in a rather relaxed but, at the same time, reflective mood even as he listened to what I had to say when his attention suddenly drifted away and he, believe it or not, started 'digging for gold' (picking his nose)!

That was the end of the conversation as far as I was concerned. My flow of conversation rudely interrupted, my sole concern thereafter was centred on how I could depart from the meeting without having to shake the worthy man's hand.

Taking my leave of the honourable minister reflexively, I jumped to my feet, thanked him, bid him 'namaste' with hands tightly folded before he could extend his and was off in a flash as fast as my feet could carry me!

You do need sharp reflexes in the company of our beloved netas. You never know what lies in store!

Sheriff of Mumbai

Around that time, some Rotary friends at the instance of Mr Y.A. Fazalbhoy, himself a former sheriff, proposed my name for the honorary and largely ceremonial British-era post of sheriff. Along with Kolkata, Mumbai was the only city in India to continue the meaningless tradition.

Essentially, the sheriff of Mumbai is an apolitical titular position of authority bestowed for one year on a prominent citizen. The most important social function of the sheriff is to receive foreign dignitaries at the airport on behalf of the city and to call condolence meetings on the demise of its prominent citizens. In government legalese, the duties of the office 'are to serve and execute processes such as Writ of Summons, Notices, Warrants issued by the High Court and the City Civil Court through Bailiffs'[44] and a multiplicity of legal functions.

The entire development was unbeknownst to me and came as a huge surprise when a senior government functionary at Mantralaya (the admin headquarters of the state government of Maharashtra) called to say that there would be some good news for me the following day but which he was honour-bound to keep confidential.

I didn't have the faintest idea what the post of sheriff was all about but discovered that luminaries such as Dinshaw Maneckji Petit, Fazal I. Rahimtoola, David J. Sassoon, Sir Jamsetjee Jejeebhoy, S.P. Godrej,

---

[44]'Sheriff of Mumbai', uploaded at: https://lj.maharashtra.gov.in/Site/Upload/Pdf/SHERIFF%20OF%20MUMBAI.pdf. Accessed on 13 November 2021.

Frank Moraes, Adamjee Peerbhoy, Dr K.A. Hamied, Sunil Dutt, Dilip Kumar, Nana Chudasama and Sunil Gavaskar had occupied the office.

I also had the impression that many Mumbaikars considered the post a waste of public money, which served to alleviate any disappointment I may have felt deep down inside, when the friend who had given me that first whiff of the 'surprise,' called the next morning expressing his sympathies. He said he was shocked—since my appointment as sheriff of Mumbai had been finalized and was about to be released to the press at 7 p.m. when he left for home the previous day.

You win some, you lose some—c'est la vie! That said, this was the least of my many disappointments in life, if one may call them that. Some things are not meant to be—irrespective of the ambitious cravings of the Donkey in our parable!

But, as things panned out, there were many compensations to follow.

TV? Thank You, But No TV

Apart from the spiels enumerated earlier, there was also, on a personal and lighter note, the one about my term as president of the Bombay Gymkhana that I shall never forget.

A soft drinks manufacturer via their ad agency, Trikaya, approached me to host a weekly television sports programme. TV had just taken off in India, and sports programmes were all the rage.

I need not go into my innate shyness on stage and in front of cameras again as I have dealt with them in an earlier chapter. Suffice it to say, I was a miserable failure: a tongue-tied, blundering, blustering, stuttering, nincompoop who just couldn't wait to *flee* from the ordeal of the screen test.

And which I did—to the clients', crew's and my own indescribable relief! Never again, I swore, and that's the way it has remained!

EIGHTEEN

LIFE IS BEAUTIFUL AND FULL OF SURPRISES

Think Big, Think Presidential

*Wo aaye ghar mein hamare Khuda ki qudrat hai Kabhi hum un ko
Kabhi apne ghar ko dekhte hain*

(It is the divine power that brings my beloved to my abode.
In disbelief, I look at her now—now at my abode.)

—Mirza Ghalib

It's an ineluctable certainty that if you ask senior Rotarians of Mumbai and neighbouring districts as to which, in their opinion, was the best district conference they have ever attended, a dollar to a doughnut the answer will be: the annual conference of District 314 at the Mumbai's Oberoi Hotel on January 21 and 22, 1984.

I say this with hand on my heart that even though 36 years have elapsed, I still come across people from all over Maharashtra who remember that event not so much in awe for the galaxy of distinguished speakers who were present there but for the warmth and fellowship exuded by the occasion.

For members of the Rotary organization, the annual district conference is the Holy Grail of its humanitarian activities, and the host club (for which bids are made) spares no time, energy or effort in making its own the best.

The club to which I then belonged and of which I was made

president in 1977–78—the Rotary Club of Bombay Mid-Town—made a successful bid to host the conference in 1984. The district governor that year was Dr Shirish Sheth, a distinguished gynaecologist and past president of our club whose geniality disguised his sincerity of purpose where the ideals of Rotary were concerned.

I was elated when Shirish asked me to be the conference programme committee chairman because, by then, I had made a number of good friends in the club who were as passionate about the opportunity to do some public good, as they were for enjoying 'fellowship'—a cornerstone of our club and for which we were objects of envy. To Shirish's credit it must be said that he gave me a completely free hand to pick my own team for the organizing committee and to do pretty much anything we decided.

I recall the first meeting of the committee: we met at the offices of dear friend, and now deceased, Sadanand Shetty at Mahalaxmi. Taking a cue from my experience of working with Field Marshal Manekshaw, I commenced proceedings by saying that I had absolute confidence in my team to organize the best conference ever and for which we would be remembered for posterity.

When I invited suggestions for the chief guest of the function, names of several mediocre personalities (the usual suspects—politicians and their ilk) were put forth.

'Come on, gentlemen, you can surely do better—think big, think laterally, think out of the box. This one has to be the *best district conference ever*!' I remonstrated.

Some more names were suggested but it all came to naught.

'Gentlemen, this will just not do. You *must think big*!'

Not getting much joy out of the whole thing, I closed the discussion by saying: 'If you agree, I'll write to Coretta King, widow of the late Martin Luther King Jr, the assassinated American civil rights legend, and invite her. At the most, she'll refuse us.'

The stunned silence was broken by incredulous giggles!

And write to Ms King I did and, as expected, she politely refused citing prior commitments.

At the next meeting, I began by informing members of Ms King's refusal but adding, 'However, gentlemen, I've taking the liberty of initiating a process whereby, with a little bit of luck, we may have the honour of having our Rashtrapati as chief guest.'

My observation was, understandably, taken as a joke until I disclosed that I had fortuitously made the acquaintance of Inderjit Bindra, president of the Punjab Cricket Association (PCA) and ADC to President Giani Zail Singh at a recent cricket match, and had taken the liberty of inviting the latter as chief guest at the district conference.

Not wishing to raise false hopes, I stressed that never before in the history of Rotary has the president of any country attended a district conference and that, in any event, the dates of our conference (21 and 22 January) were inconveniently close to our Republic Day (26 January) when the president's presence in New Delhi is obligatory at the parade.

◈

The mischievous Gadha's stars must have been perfectly aligned with mine: what started as a shot in the dark, at the hospitable Inderjit Bindra's lavish lunch at Mohali cricket stadium, became a reality in the form of a note confirming that Gyaniji would indeed grace our function by his presence; he could, however, only spare an hour, at most!

I, for one, would have been over the moon had the president been able to come for even five minutes. It was entirely the doing of Inderjit and for which I remain extremely grateful to him.

◈

As may be expected, the acceptance of the invitation set a zillion alarm bells ringing as we set about getting organized for the big event, made even bigger with the news that Rotary International president-elect Carlos Canseco, decorated physician and philanthropist from Mexico, had accepted our invitation to attend, as had John Spragge, public speaker and consultant from Toronto, Canada.

Having received confirmation from such notable people, I was encouraged to try and enlarge the list of luminaries and managed to get friend Sam Manekshaw and legal luminary Nani Palkhivala to agree to speak—which they both did with characteristic aplomb.

The legendary 'Nightingale of India' Lata Mangeshkar, who consented to participate courtesy Raj Singh Dungarpur, brought the house down with her final-curtain rendition of the heart-rending 1963 patriotic song 'Aye Mere Watan ke Logon.'

On a personal note, my welcome address started with a quote from the legendary Urdu poet Mirza Ghalib. I recited the memorable *'wo aae ghar mein hamare...'* lines (mentioned at the beginning of the chapter), which struck the right note and put the Urdu-loving president and the audience in a *wah-wah* (positive) frame of mind. They even induced President Zail Singh to say, in his address, that he was enjoying the afternoon so much, he had decided to delay his departure to Delhi by half an hour! Which he did!

Bada mazaa aaya (we had a lot of fun)—as they as say in Jhumri Telaiya!

Referring to the elaborate 'bandobast' (arrangements) that had to be made for the president's visit, when we went to see the chief guest off at the airport, Maharashtra governor Idris Latif and police commissioner Julio Ribeiro remarked: 'Khalid, don't put us through this ever again!'

Mid-Day Anniversary Celebrations

Over the years, we had established a unique tradition in our own 'city that never sleeps', to celebrate the newspaper's anniversary (during the monsoons, on the last Saturday of June) with a brunch at the rooftop of the Oberoi Hotel at Nariman Point.

In my opinion, it is easily the most enchanting and romantic of all venues in Mumbai, with its sweeping westerly view overlooking the harbour around Marine Drive (the Queen's Necklace) on one side and the Maharashtra Vidhan Sabha (Legislative Assembly), on the other.

The event soon became a red-letter day in the city's social calendar with regular invitees blocking it well in advance in their social diary, some ensuring their presence in the city on that day and some enterprising ladies even unabashedly crashing the party. We took it all in good spirit—after all it denoted the overweening desire of our 'friends' to be with us on our special day!

For the hotel's meticulous managers, chefs and service staff no trouble was too great, no request impossible to grant in their earnest endeavour to better their standard in every little respect year after year.

Be that as it may, our anniversaries were meant, essentially, to express our humble and sincere thanks to the One Above and to our associates, and to rededicate ourselves to the task we had undertaken.

The following piece written by Malavika Sangghvi in the Mumbai edition of *Mid-Day* illustrates the above:

SUNSHINE AND SPARKLE

Swashbuckling publisher, philanthropist, wordsmith and world traveller Khalid Ansari's Saturday champagne brunch at a five-star sun filled rooftop banquet hall was a sparkling affair.

After all, it was Ansari who had more or less set the bubbly brunch ball rolling with the iconic *Mid-Day* parties at the same venue and was celebrated for their guest list and its sumptuous table.

Yesterday's table was no different. From Eggs Benedict, to burrata topped with caviar, to juicy asparagus stalks in hollandaise, to risotto served out of a parmigiana oregano wheel, to an amazing fish molee, to tawa roasted leg of lamb with Malabari paratha, and desserts served on an antique cabinet, there were dozens of things to choose from.

But of course, it was the cake which was the piece de resistance. Especially crafted by Chef Joy, it was a replica of the first front page of the newspaper you are holding. Yes, if not for Ansari there might have been no *Mid-Day*. Put that in your pipe and smoke it, gentle reader. [45]

---

[45] Malavika Sangghvi, 'Licking the Food off Their Plates', *Mid-Day*, 11 September 2017, https://www.mid-day.com/amp/news/india-news/article/malavika-malavikas-mumbai-malavika-column-mumbai-news-malavika-sangghvi-18570168. Accessed on 13 November 2021.

A New Year in the Air

During one of my frequent trips Down Under while covering sports events, in 2004, Zeyna and I came across an airline newspaper advertisement for a trip to the Antarctica to bring in the New Year.

Out of abundant caution, I ran the ad by former Australian cricket captain and *Sportsweek* and *Mid-Day* correspondent, Ian Chappell (he continues to be a regular contributor to the latter to this day), who tried to dissuade me, reminding me of a horrific crash of a similar flight that took place a few years back. However, Zeyna and I decided the idea was too exciting to resist and opted to go ahead, the risk notwithstanding. The experience turned out to be one to cherish. Below is my record of the flight, which appeared in *Mid-Day*:

> Looking for a different and exciting way to bring in the New Year in the future?
>
> Consider a 12-hour Antarctica flight that will enable you to be among the first to see the sun rise in the New Year over New Zealand, then celebrate New Year a second time over the breathtaking and indescribably beautiful mountain ranges, glaciers and icebergs of the 12,000,000 square km Ice Continent.
>
> Over 23,000 ecstatic passengers have so far taken the unforgettable flight on 67 Qantas Boeing 747–400 flights to the Antarctica out of Sydney and Melbourne between November and February, including New Year's Eve.
>
> The New Year's flight has all the revelry associated with New

Year, including a jazz band.

The distance from Sydney to Antarctica and return is 10,160 km and flying time approximately 13 hours (11 1/2 hours from Melbourne). All flights have approximately three to four hours of viewing time over the stunning Antarctic region.

The aircraft flies figure 8's over various points of interest to allow viewing of the spectacular sights on both sides of the aircraft, and business and economy class passengers are made to rotate seats to allow all passengers to have a clear view.

I had the opportunity to take this flight on New Year's Eve and can attest to the fact that it is an unforgettable experience.

Inquilab Golden Jubilee

On 3 April 1988 we celebrated the golden jubilee of the *Inquilab* at a function at the Birla Matushri Sabhaghar which was presided over by Governor of Maharashtra, K. Brahmananda Reddy.

Among those present were K. Natwar Singh, minister of external affairs; eminent scholar-historian Dr Rafiq Zakaria, who was chairman of the celebrations committee; Ghulam Nabi Azad, general secretary of the All India Congress Committee (AICC); film industry legend Dilip Kumar; Sunil Dutt, Bollywood actor and MP; reputed Urdu poet Ali Sardar Jafri; R.K. Karanjia, founder of Blitz Publications; distinguished columnist Anil Dharker and Ayub Syed, editor of the tabloid, *Current*.

Paying tribute to the memory of the great patriot and nationalist, Abdul Hamid Ansari, founder of the *Inquilab*, the governor expressed confidence that, having completed its golden jubilee, '*Inquilab* will march towards its centenary with the mission of serving the cause of the people and of helping to build a new society, where all can live in amity and with dignity and honour.'

After the celebrations, Natwar Singh took me aside to tell me that our country 'needed young people to project our image' and asked if I would be interested in being appointed ambassador. The suggestion came like the proverbial thunder from a cloudless blue sky. I requested time to consider but said that if at all I accepted, it would have to be a posting in an English-speaking country and, preferably, one like Australia with its rich sports culture. And then, by now, you all know my ambassador story!

A PROVIDENTIAL ESCAPE, PHEW!

Later in life, when Zeyna and I were on a brief holiday in Sri Lanka (Serendib is among our favourite getaway destinations—and not only for its proximity to home!), we had a providential escape which brought to mind our friend, the Gadha (Donkey)—the leitmotif of these reminisces.

On Easter Sunday, 21 April 2019, eight 'Islamic' suicide bombers carried out a series of coordinated blasts on three hotels, a housing complex, and a guest house in Colombo, killing 269 people, the alleged motive being retaliation for the mosque shootings in Christchurch, New Zealand, earlier that year.

One of the affected hotels in the bomb blasts was the Shangri-La at the One Galle Face area, our favourite in Colombo. The attack took place at around 8.30 a.m., at a time when the first-floor restaurant (where hotel guests eat breakfast) is usually packed, especially on Sundays.

As luck would have it, we were staying at that hotel the *previous* Sunday and would have been in that very restaurant at the same time—since that was our usual time and place for breakfast at that hotel—had we been there a week later!

There Once Was...Squash

On the subject of squash: the 1970s and 1980s were the halcyon days of Mumbai's state-level squash association when legendary coach Yusuf Khan mentored the likes of Anil Nayar, Fali Madon and Dinshaw Pundole at the CCI. M.K. Sanghi and his nephews Krishna, Arun and Ranjan Sanghi, were its munificent benefactors, but the association fell on bad times with infighting rampant among its office-bearers.

As a regular player at the CCI and Willingdon courts, I was approached by squash sponsor Mahendra Agarwal (I refer to him as 'the Kerry Packer of Indian squash') to contest the committee elections, which I did and won along with him and like-minded players who had the interest of the game at heart.

We inducted Ranjan Sanghi, Gautam Thakkar (former Asian junior badminton champion), Vinita Agarwal, Ashish Gupta and other regular players on the executive committee to fight the ambitions of the dictatorial president of the all-India body Squash Rackets Federation of India (SRFI) that was trying to take over our state association, the Squash Racquets Association of Maharashtra (SRAM).

Ambitious to the core, the Chennai-based president of the SRFI had set his eyes on becoming president of the sport's international body, the World Squash Federation, which he did many years later. We at SRAM had no quarrel with that but were determined to not let the national parent body ride roughshod over us in running the sport in our state.

The imbroglio continues to this day. We remain autonomous and conduct our affairs in the best interest of our members in Maharashtra. The all-India body has stopped interfering in our affairs, with no seeming need to dictate, now that its ambitious president has achieved his goal of heading squash's international federation.

The national president had proclaimed from rooftops his resolve to get squash included in the Olympics. Four Games have gone by, and squash is nowhere near attaining Olympic status. Meanwhile, disciplines such as skate boarding, break dancing, softball, baseball, golf, curling and cricket have become Olympic disciplines. Ridiculous! Strange are the ways of the Lausanne-based International Olympic Committee. Makes you wonder if the high priests of the Olympics have taken leave of their senses. Or if there is more to this than meets the eye!

SRAM, in the meantime, continues to conduct prize money tournaments in major towns and cities in our state of Maharashtra. The one sponsored by Captain Jamshed Appoo of Herald Maritime Services offered a hitherto undreamt prize money of ₹75,000 in the men's singles category, ₹50,000, to the boys' Under-19 category and ₹30,000 to women's singles.

SRAM has built a squash complex—funded by Arun and Ranjan Sanghi of Sah & Sanghi Auto Agencies in memory of their departed brother Krishna—at the Police Gymkhana on Mumbai's Marine Drive. Many new housing societies in the state now have squash courts as the result of our efforts and the number of people now playing the game has increased by leaps and bounds.

Mahendra Agarwal, Ranjan Sanghi and I have stepped down to make way for new blood, but Ranjan and I—we have both been appointed chairman emeritus of SRAM—continue to fulfil our responsibilities.

ANIL NAYAR

Being, at best, a squash player of mediocre ability, I have always looked up to squash champions, for it is a sport that must indubitably rank high among those that demand awesome levels of fitness.

One such athlete was Anil 'Lucky' Nayar, undoubtedly India's greatest squash player of all time, and of whom I was an unabashed admirer. I would often observe him at the CCI squash courts of Mumbai, a place where I became acquainted with the game during my college days.

Squash has been an important part of my life and this is important for many of my readers: Anil was a protégé of the legendary Yusuf Khan, born in 1931 in what is now Pakistan in 1931 and notable coach to thousands of players, including his daughters Shabana Khan and Latasha Khan, both of whom won US National Singles titles and were ranked among the top 25 players in the world. Anil too went on to attain hitherto unattained heights for an Indian at the international level.

Having gone our different ways after college—Anil to Harvard and I to Stanford—we met in Mumbai, rather providentially, at the turn of the century. I cherish the meeting as it was one at which I was able to plant the seeds of an idea that has since then borne fruit and, for which, I can truthfully claim some little credit.

I tried to persuade Anil to put pen to paper to record, for posterity, his inspirational squash career in two countries—India and the US—in the historical backdrop of the time when his parents migrated to Mumbai from Pakistan in the bloody aftermath of the Partition. Anil parried my efforts with characteristic modesty, saying, 'It'll be nice to have *you* write it,' knowing fully well that my commitments and frequent travel left me no time to undertake the project.

But I'm happy to say that although it took persuasive attempts on my part over a decade and a half, in India and the US—where the Nayars now live—to coax, cajole and convince, they finally culminated in helping complete the eminently readable biography *Lucky* written by his immensely talented wife Jean, who worked with a publishing firm for many years in New York. Approaches to many publishers in Mumbai and New Delhi having failed because of the time that had elapsed between Anil's glorious playing days and the present, it took the fanatical sports lover/promoter/book publisher, Sachin Bajaj's initiative to publish the handsomely produced book.

I was delighted to accept when 'Lucky' requested me to write the Foreword to Jean's book and to speak at the well-attended book launch at Mumbai's Royal Bombay Yacht Club.

In my Foreword, I wrote:

> As an unabashed admirer of Anil 'Lucky' Nayar, I consider it a privilege to be asked by him and his wife, Jean, to introduce this unputdownable book, which is at once erudite and down to earth. A labour of love, it is a cerebral yet sensitive tour de force of the sports career of an exemplary human being and principled squash champion who played at two ends of the world—in India and the US.
>
> Notable for its flair and professional finesse, *Lucky*, the book, sheds light not only on Anil's razor sharp squash acumen but also his intellect.
>
> And this account of his illustrious squash career should be required reading for young and old involved with the game of squash in both India and the US. as well as other parts of the globe.

NINETEEN

PURSUITS...

'Run For Fun'—a Mass Movement for Fitness

In hindsight, it was the availability of sports facilities—the sports field at St Mary's in particular—from an early age that initiated my friends and me into that magnificent world. Compulsory physical education was an integral part of our curriculum, with time set aside daily for regular PT classes followed by regular periodic tests. The school sports field, although not quite the size of a standard soccer, hockey, cricket or athletics field, was adequate in instilling love for and, at the least, lay the foundations of an invaluable character-building activity. That is the reason why I find the decision of the St Mary's high school authorities to permit the sports ground to be converted into a housing society reprehensible.

Many years later, when I started *Sportsweek* magazine in 1967 and ran it for 20 years, my prime endeavour was to start a mass movement to promote health and fitness through sports.

The magazine took the initiative to try and make sports a compulsory subject in schools and colleges and to introduce members of families to take to running by organizing 'Run for Fun' events on Sunday mornings in different congested areas of Mumbai, by rotation, with the objective of attracting members of the public. We wanted people to run (even walk) for the sake of their own health.

In a city that was fast becoming a teeming metropolis and was notable for the average citizens' inherent insouciance as regards participation in sports, this was akin to taking 'the Mountain to Muhammad.'

◆

In the absence of even a modicum of essential playground facilities in schools and colleges, indeed in the city at large, which was being transformed into an unhealthy eyesore of a concrete jungle, we had the satisfaction of reaching a stage where we had an average of 30,000 runners on any given Sunday morning.

But one can say—with hand on one's heart—that *Sportsweek* magazine played a significant, but unpretentious, role in lighting the spark for spreading the gospel of health through exercise in our burgeoning metropolis.

It has been such a joy over the years ever since the 1970s, when the movement began to see people of all ages embrace the culture of walking and running not only for fun—but for their mental and physical well-being.

CHAMPS Foundation

An invitation from Sunil Gavaskar to serve as a trustee of his Champions Foundation along with himself, his wife Marshneil, brother-in-law and legendary cricketer Gundappa Vishwanath and Mumbai sheriff Nana Chudasama was a privilege.

The CHAMPS Foundation (CHAMPS is an acronym for Caring, Helping, Assisting, Motivating, Promoting Sportspersons) continues its outstanding work of financially helping former Indian sportsmen who have fallen on bad times. In the words of 'Little Master' Gavaskar: 'Starting 1999, we have helped 19 Indian hockey, badminton, boxing, billiards, football and cricket sportspersons with financial support.'

An inaugural fundraising event of the foundation was a double-wicket cricket competition in which members of the Indian team that won the 1983 World Cup paired with industrialists, film stars and other dignitaries.

I shall never forget the thrill I got when I shared the CCI dressing room with luminaries such as Gavaskar himself, Viv Richards, Kapil Dev, Gundappa Vishwanath, Dilip Vengsarkar, Sandeep Patil, Mohinder Amarnath, Ravi Shastri, Kirti Azad, Roger Binny, Syed Kirmani, Krishnamachari Srikkanth and the like.

I was teamed with Sandeep Patil and was particularly thrilled to face the bowling of the affable Viv Richards, my dear friend and cigar ('logie' as he termed it) smoking companion after his retirement.

Terry Fox Run

When in Dubai, I had participated in a fundraising event called the Terry Fox Run which was organized by the *Khaleej Times'* rival paper, *Gulf News*, and was greatly inspired seeing a film about Canadian athlete Terry Fox.

Fox was diagnosed with osteogenic sarcoma (bone cancer) and forced to amputate his right leg at the tender age of 18. The prognosis of the Canadian doctors was 'poor' and stemmed from a lack of research into treatments for cancer. Faced with such a life-altering diagnosis, Terry decided to turn his story around to raise money and awareness for cancer research.

He decided to run across Canada and thus began a journey called 'Marathon of Hope.' Terry died before he could complete his run as the cancer spread to his lungs after which his health deteriorated rapidly. But by the time he passed away at 22, Terry Fox had raised over CAD$23 million for cancer research. Today Terry Fox's legacy has raised funds in support of cancer research all over the world.

◆

When I relocated to Mumbai from Dubai, I happened to meet Gul Kripalani who is now Honorary Consul General for Iceland in Mumbai. We got talking about charity and fundraising and I mentioned the Terry Fox Run to him. The next thing I knew, I was being asked by Gul to join him on the organizing committee of Mumbai's own chapter of the Terry Fox Run. Unfortunately, I had to gratefully decline because of some prior commitments. Instead, I suggested the name of former Olympian sprinter Adille Sumariwalla, who was then working for *Mid-Day*. I understand Adille has been of tremendous help to Gul through the newspaper and personally in the commendable activities of the Run.

But I did take part in the Run, down Mumbai's Marine Drive, for two years in succession and was honoured by an invitation to distribute prizes at one of them. On one occasion, Mumbai Police Commissioner Julio Ribeiro joined me, and we ran a fair distance for the cause.

Whenever we meet, Gul is effusive in his thanks for helping him during the nascent stages of the Run. In all honesty, the credit goes entirely to him and his team. I was only an instrument in igniting a miniscule spark.

◆

This reminds me of the tale about the husband who loves his wife dearly. Sadly, his wife passes away prematurely so he has the undertaker inscribe the epitaph 'the flame of my life has been extinguished.'

A few years later he re-marries. One evening, he happens to be in the vicinity of the graveyard and decides to stop by to pay his respects to the dear departed.

As it turns out, he has, unforgivably, forgotten all about his epitaph. A man for all seasons, he promptly rings the undertaker and instructs him to add the postscript—'P.S: I've struck a new match.'

Cricket Club of India

'Mr Cricket' Raj Singh Dungarpur, president of the BCCI and the CCI, suffering from poor health in his twilight years, suggested he would like to see me succeed him as president, a suggestion I had to turn down.

'Enough is enough,' I told Raj, given my other commitments.

However, I did agree to his offer of an Honorary Membership of the CCI, a world-renowned institution, which I considered an honour.

In the course of my impromptu acceptance speech at the function conferring the membership, I couldn't resist saying: 'I've been a life member of our Club since 1963, now you've made an 'or'nary' (meaning ordinary) Ansari, an *anari* (a duffer).'

I'm not sure if the distinguished audience caught the drift but, if the lack of reaction to what I considered my 'clever' play upon words was any indication, it certainly did not.

Bombay Gymkhana

Although I had joined the Bombay Gymkhana (founded 1875) as far back as 1970, I hardly ever used its facilities. It is among the city's leading sports institutions with a lofty tradition that includes staging the first Test match on Indian soil in 1933–34 and the first Test in history that included cricket on a Sunday.

In due course, proximity to work at JWT induced me to shift my squash routine to the Gymkhana and play the occasional cricket friendly on Saturday afternoons in the company of Tiger Pataudi, Behram and Mehli Irani, and others.

In those days, the club was essentially a sporting institution with hardly any social activity, which meant that the prime real estate in the heart of south Mumbai was barely used for the greater part of the day. Its lingering old-world British stuffiness was evident from the fact that mail to members was, for example, addressed as: 'Khalid A-H Ansari Esq' until almost the 1980s.

In time, the club's activities deteriorated, as did efficiency of management and, in turn quality of membership. This is when some irregulars like me decided to get involved and try and get the venerable institution back on track.

Some well-meaning members, including 'Balu' Sule, MD of Mahindra and Mahindra, met at the Worli home of the late Virenchee Sagar, MD of Nirlon and son of Gandhian and freedom fighter (Is that an oxymoron? Can a Gandhian be a fighter?). Vithalbhai Jhaveri of Nanubhai Jhaveri, the reputable jewellery firm. We drew up a plan of action and handpicked members to contest the next elections of both the managing and balloting committees.

The fact that every single candidate we put up to contest on the two committees was elected testifies to the widespread dissatisfaction among club members with the then existing state of affairs.

◆

In time I was elected president of the club. My three-year term was personally fulfilling since we as a team were able to turn things around and set the institution on course for future generations.

On the occasion of the Gymkhana's Founders Day celebrations on its 142nd anniversary in 2017, some past presidents and I were asked by the magazine committee's editor to pen our reminiscences of our terms as president.

My report to members may be of interest:

Previously the Bombay Gymkhana was largely a British colonial expatriates' and boisterous bachelors' watering hole which became distressingly funereal at sunset. We changed it to a respectable family institution with respectable sporting camaraderie as its raison d'être. This may be said to be the Managing and Balloting Committees' most important contribution during my tenure as President.

With the passage of time this metamorphosis has happily led to the opening of Club membership to ladies.

'Bhalu' Sule, then MD of Mahindra and Mahindra, was unanimously chosen the team's first president (with yours truly his 'vice').

Those elected to the two Committees included the legendary 'Tiger' Pataudi, world billiards champion Michael Ferreira, national golf champion Raj Kumar Pitamber and founder-publisher of *Gentleman* magazine Minhaz Merchant.

Also, Asian junior badminton champion Gautam Thakkar, national swimming champion Lalu Bajaj, squash patron Ranjan Sanghi along with luminaries from the world of business and finance, leading bankers, doctors, lawyers and the like.

Looking back, I'm delighted that during my tenure as President, our Committee:

- Carried out urgently needed structural repairs and renovations in our heritage but (architecturally) tired club house.
- Brought about major changes in the culture, governance and membership profile of the institution, making it among Bombay's, if not India's, most prestigious sporting institutions.
- Renovated Gym's Inn, the pub, and the dining room, making the Club a magnet for members, families and guests on weekday and weekend afternoons and evenings.
- Converted what was previously a dump for old furniture on the first floor—prime real estate in the commercial heart of Bombay—into an elegant but sensibly-priced upscale restaurant, The Far Pavilion and the Rear Pavilion, a party venue.
- For the first time in the history of the Gym, we set up an airconditioned, well-stocked library and gymnasium and improved overall sporting facilities. Aerobic classes for both men and women were started.
- The illustrious Khushwant Singh, Ram Jethmalani, Anil Dharker (to name just a few) and other celebrities became regular users of the club's sporting facilities;
- The introduction of the International Sportsmen's Category, under which the likes of Sunil Gavaskar, Dilip Vengsarkar, Mahesh Bhupathi and Adille Sumariwalla became eligible for membership, lent credence to the claim that we are, indeed, a coveted sporting club.
- Training and coaching schemes in different sport disciplines were set up and a number of club tournaments started with young members and members' children in mind.
- The prestigious but deceased all-India Aga Khan Hockey Tournament, once incontrovertibly India's leading hockey tournament, was revived with the nation's best teams participating.
- Given the rapidly evolving demographics, lifestyle and consequent value systems in our dynamic city heading into the '90s, our Balloting Committee assiduously endeavoured

- to retain the quintessential sporting character of the Gym by having all applicants for membership undergo a strict sporting performance test.
- The Committee started the practice of inviting membership applicants for a formal interview and, if considered suitable on the sporting ability criteria, offered them temporary membership. During this period the candidate was required to regularly bring along his family to the Gym to enable assessment of their general behaviour and deportment.
- We adhered strictly to the norm of sporting ability, especially in the case of applications for Corporate Membership which we introduced for the first time in the history of the Club, to alleviate our chronic financial malaise.
- At the same time, as custodians of the Gym's future, we were extremely circumspect as regards candidates' educational and professional background and overall 'clubability' in electing members.

Posterity will judge our committee's performance. But I can say, with hand on my heart, that serving the Gym was for us a magnificent obsession—and that, at all times, we tried our very best to function in the best interest of our beloved institution.

◆

> I shall never forget the time the Bombay Gymkhana Premises Committee decided to carry out repairs to the ladies' toilets that fall under the city's heritage laws.
>
> The secretary, deciding to get the work done on a particular day, dictated a memo to his steno intimating female members that the toilet would be closed for use during certain hours on a particular day, because of work on 'fittings,' regretting the inconvenience caused.
>
> While typing the memo, the steno misspelt the word 'fittings' and instead typed 'sittings.' The secretary failed to spot the typo, signed it and had it displayed on the notice board to his great embarrassment and the good-natured hilarity of the ladies.

Eyeball to Eyeball with Datta Samant

During the tenure of our Bombay Gymkhana's Managing Committee, a (customary, but legitimate) demand for substantial increase in wages was made by our staff union led by the firebrand Dr Datta Samant.

The managing committee deputed me to deal with the Union. At the first meeting, before Samant arrived (he was typically late as part of his psychological gambit), I called his Union leaders into the committee room, asked them to take a seat—something they had never done next to the *burra sahibs* (big bosses), nor hoped to do in their wildest dreams—and served them refreshments, leaving them gobsmacked.

When he arrived, Dr Samant tried the usual bullying tactics by resorting to threaten my business. The experience will remain forever etched in my memory for my one-to-one, no-holds-barred encounter with the formidable leader who had no compunction to threaten corporates that his demands be accepted...or else.

Although Samant's ability to willfully destroy business houses—and there were many—was well-known, I retaliated that his union members are as much my 'sons' and their interests as dear to me as they were to him. I challenged him to go on strike if he considered it in their best interest, saying they would be the ones to suffer.

I also used backchannel tactics (to use an expression from the lexicon of diplomacy) to informally convince the staff union leaders that I was sympathetic to their demands. At the next committee meeting, I convinced members that the union's demands were legitimate given the abysmal salary structure and galloping cost of living.

The outcome, in all fairness, was a 'draw' with neither side winning or losing. Both our staff, who were always unquestioningly at our beck and call, as well as the general body of our Gym members were happy at the outcome.

The staff raised a chorus of 'Datta Samant zindabad,' 'Khalid Ansari zindabad' (Long live, Khalid Ansari) as we emerged from the committee room, which I discouraged, saying that the club members may misinterpret it as suggesting that I had sold their interests down the river to the union!

Supremacy Surrendered

Among nineteenth-century English writer and politician Edward Bulwer-Lytton writings is this one passage about the sport of hockey: 'And on the common [public ground] were some young men playing at hockey. That oldfashioned game, now very uncommon in England, except at schools...'[46]

Hockey legend Dhyan Chand, father of the mercurial Ashok Kumar, wrote in his autobiography: 'The game had been taken to India by British servicemen, and the first clubs were formed in Calcutta in 1885,' adding, 'the Beighton Cup (Calcutta) and the Aga Khan tournament (Bombay) had both commenced within 10 years.'[47]

Bombay Gymkhana's Aga Khan hockey tournament, then run by British expatriates, in time became a prestigious event with the country's best teams clamouring to participate on the club's beautiful grass surface. This was particularly conducive to the traditional Indian style based on skill, rather than speed and brawn.

Starting with the Olympic Games in 1928, India won all 10 of its games without conceding a goal, and went on to win gold medals in 1932 until 1956, and then in 1964 and 1980. Pakistan won gold in 1960, 1968 and 1984.

The International Hockey Federation (Federation Internationale

---

[46]Edward Bulwer-Lytton, *Delphi Complete Works of Edward Bulwer-Lytton* (Illustrated), Delphi Classics, 2014.
[47]Dhyan Chand, *Dhyan Chand, Goal: An Autobiography with Hockey Hints*, Sportstar, 2018.

de Hockey—IHF) has continued to grow and now consists of 112 member associations, spread around five continents.

It is no secret that the international powers-that-be, who then controlled the destiny of the sport (even as our own insouciant representatives at the international body licked their boots), conspired to introduce the synthetic turf called 'astroturf' which favoured the bigger and stronger European hockey players and their rugged style of hockey. Combined with changes in the rules of the game, this skulduggery has brought about massive changes not only in its aesthetic appeal but also shifted the balance of power intrinsically in favour of European countries, as well as Argentina, a country that previously had languished in the basement of world hockey.

◆

When I was Bombay Gymkhana president, the Mumbai Aga Khan Council, which governs affairs of the Indian Ismail community in Mumbai, informed us of its intention to disassociate itself from the now world-renowned tournament, the second oldest hockey tournament in the world, after Kolkata's Beighton Cup.

While I was determined to see the famed tournament continue, all our efforts to make the Aga Khan Council change its mind failed, and therefore we started to scout around for a solution. There were many offers of sponsorship but with the proviso that the tournament be renamed after the new sponsor. As far as I was concerned, that was an absolute no-brainer. It was a Bombay Gymkhana tournament and I wanted it to remain that way. As a last resort I called upon Ismailbhai Padamsee (of the then renowned Eagle Vacuum Flask group), an influential office-bearer of the Aga Khan Council.

He pleaded his inability to help but was appreciative of our efforts to retain the council's umbilical cord relationship with the event. Saying he had just hit upon a solution, he requested time to come back to us.

Ismailbhai was as good as his word: imagine our joy when he informed us subsequently that the council had said 'no' but that he had been successful in persuading the members to put their hands in their pockets and raise the sponsorship amount privately.

Overjoyed, we put our shoulder to the wheel and organized a

successful tournament with some of the country's leading teams taking part in it.

◆

Although we had been able to bring it back from the jaws of extinction in 1975, the tournament was not held again until 2001 when the committee, under the presidentship of the late Ashok Kapoor, non-executive chairman of Yes Bank, staged it in 2001.

Reportedly because of the indifference of the club's office bearers, the tournament again lapsed into catalepsy for 10 years when inveterate sports lover president Ashok Rao revived it under the joint sponsorship of the Development Credit Bank, ONGC, Indian Oil Corporation and Rabo India.

I'm told the tournament has not been held subsequently.

Change being the ineluctable rule of life, it is futile for sentimentalists such as me to mourn the death of a beloved, prestigious hockey tournament such as the Aga Khan tournament.

Mumbai Club Life

The passing of an earlier sports-crazy generation is taking its inevitable toll on our club culture. The increasing emphasis on scholastic excellence in the age of the Internet at the expense of sport as a means to development of what we considered a well-rounded personality, is eroding the nature of clubs that used to be truly sporting institutions.

Although serious problems continue to plague our economic well-being as a society, the matrix of Indian club culture has undergone a sea-change brought about by impressive improvement in our peoples' discretionary incomes consequent to impressive economic growth. The disparity in incomes is no longer as vast as it used to be in both rural and urban areas. The profile of our citizenry now travelling by air, going on holidays, eating out, indulging in pastimes hitherto considered expensive, extortionate, or unaffordable, has metamorphosed beyond recognition. In sum, our society has become refreshingly more egalitarian. A younger demographic population, greater longevity, widespread and better education, affordable domestic and international travel, exposure to television, among other factors, have led to a broadening of mental horizons and made us confident and aspirational people. Which is all to the good.

On the flip side, at a micro level, this has also led to a drastic transformation in the definition and understanding of club culture.

At the risk of seeming snooty: our clubs—old and new—are increasingly becoming boorish social and gambling haunts for the moneyed pretentious with skewed values and execrable behavioral norms. Sadly, sport has been relegated to a sorry state.

My wife Zeyna and I do not frequent the sports clubs, of which we are privileged to be members, but are disappointed at the overall erosion of values and sharp decline in ethical and behavioural standards.

The Bombay Gymkhana, lamentably, is no longer the envious sporting institution it used to be. It has become predominantly a social club with emphasis on eating, drinking and the shuffling of playing cards. The internecine squabbling, back-stabbing and jockeying for position and power among some of its members puts even our netas to shame. With many of the members' children either studying abroad, busy socializing, obsessively or in an umbilical relationship with social media, it is becoming increasingly difficult for the club to even muster 11 players to constitute soccer, hockey or cricket teams for a game.

Sadly, the situation is no different at the other 'prestigious' sporting institutions in Mumbai, namely Willingdon Sports Club (WSC) and the CCI, which we use sporadically. I do not know much about the other institutions to which I have access: Garware Club House and Malabar Hill Club, so prudence demands that I refrain from passing judgement.

For the most part, the CCI still retains its sporting persona and traditions, but one wishes one could say the same about the Willingdon (Sports!) Club—once considered the most prestigious club in the country with the crème de la crème of society as members.

In a classic example of '*kaise kaise aise waise ho gaye, aise waise kaise kaise ho gaye*' members of substance advisedly stay away from affairs of the club.

A distinguished member of the club, a cultural cognoscenti, once made a tongue-in-cheek remark about the managing committee of his time: 'The Willingdon is today the only mental institution, run by its own inmates.'

Sadly, the WSC has become less and less a 'sports' club and increasingly a social, card-playing club. More than reflecting the preponderance of seniors in its membership profile, the large number of wheelchairs at the entrance that greet visitors are an indication of the general decrepitude afflicting the institution. From what I have observed, there is a steep decline in quality (narcissistically termed 'clubability' by committee members) as regards educational, social and ethical eligibility, which was once considered 'a gentleman's second home' of captains of business, commerce and industry, and movers and shakers of society.

The Willingdon Club was started by the governor of Bombay of the same name in 1918 because he was refused permission to invite a maharaja as a guest to the old Bombay Byculla Club. This club, as also the Bombay Gymkhana and Royal Bombay Yacht Club, then allowed only Europeans, and Governor Willingdon, therefore, decided to start a club that both Indians and Europeans could go to.

Jockeys, horse trainers and people in the film industry, who were previously frowned upon, are ineligible, WSC membership has been closed since 1985 with only members' children now being admitted. Corporate membership is opened sporadically but at an amount that is obscene. Founding members must be rolling in their graves at the general state of affairs at the once exclusive and enviously run club.

It would need a tome to recount instances of gross incompetence and inefficiency in the management of the club.

To cite only one example: it took almost eight—yes eight—years to build a vaunted sports complex with a classic Greek design that is totally incongruous with the classic Doric architecture of the main club house. Meanwhile a whole generation of players, leave aside potential squash, badminton and table-tennis champions have been denied essential facilities vital to their health.

On a personal level, the enforced break has brought on for me muscle amnesia rendering impossible a return to the game I have greatly enjoyed for 60 years and to the great detriment of my physical fitness.

This may sound like self-aggrandizement but my health is no less precious than anybody else's. That this happens to be my personal experience ought not to come in the way of my right to freedom of speech.

I know of at one least one more such case. There must be many others in other disciplines at the Willingdon.

As these memoirs go to press, one learns of increasing and shocking instances of communal groupism and yes, even corruption at the WSC, as, indeed, at some others! Sad! But then why should clubs be any different from other institutions in a country which is increasingly losing its *imaan* (faith).

Clubs, after all, reflect society at large.

In Memory of a Dear Friend and Champion

I was in Beijing in 2008, covering the Olympic Games, when I received the shattering news of the passing away of dear friend Gautam Thakkar, the only Indian junior Asian badminton champion.

On my return home, I spoke to friends and well-wishers—and he had many—of our Dubai-based mutual friend Shyam Bhatia's suggestion to start a badminton tournament to commemorate our friend's memory.

I invited Sunil Gavaskar (Gautam's regular badminton partner at the Bombay Gymkhana courts), legends Nandu Natekar, Prakash Padukone, Shyam Bhatia (who made a munificent donation to kick-start the event) and Ranjan Sanghi to join me as trustees. We raised a corpus of ₹50 lakhs with the help of Gautam's many friends and well-wishers.

Since Gautam was my successor as Bombay Gymkhana president, it was only fitting that the event was staged at that historic venue, a suggestion to which the club's managing committee very kindly agreed.

We inducted the club's former president Ashok Rao, another partner of Gautam's at the club's courts; businessman and badminton regular Ratu Ramchandani, formerly of *The Statesman*, Kolkata, and Mahendra Agarwal as trustees.

◆

In an article headlined 'In Gautam's Memory' in *Mid-Day*, dated 21 November 2012, Sundari Iyer wrote: 'Carrying forward the legacy of one of the city's most stylish shuttlers, Gautam Thakkar, who was also India's first and only Asian junior champion, the second edition of the tournament for juniors was announced at the Bombay Gymkhana yesterday. The Gautam Thakkar Memorial Badminton Association (GTMBA) will organise the ₹10 lakh prize money for All India Junior Masters badminton tournament (November 22 to 25) at the Bombay Gymkhana.'[48]

◆

We conducted three editions of the tournament from the corpus, which was fast getting depleted in the absence of advertising revenue despite the best efforts of the advertising concessionaires. Unfortunately, committee members, being honorary and active working people, were finding it difficult to find time to attend to the running of the tournament. This left me as the sole working trustee, which was an enormous burden for one person. The problem was exacerbated by my frequent absences from Mumbai (I was spending more time in Australia after handing over the reins of *Mid-Day* to son Tarique).

Unable to do justice to my responsibilities, I approached the Bombay Gymkhana badminton committee, along with Ashok Rao and Ratu Ramchandani, to take over the tournament. The Gymkhana expressed their inability. I had no option other than to resign as trustee and chairman, following which the association was closed down and its audited balance funds handed over to Sunil Gavaskar's CHAMPS Foundation.

Sports aficionado and philanthropist Shyam Bhatia, who has also set up an impressive cricket museum in Dubai, has now come forward to perpetuate Gautam Thakkar's memory on his own along with the Gymkhana. He conducted a very successful tournament in 2019 at the club's courts.

Sadly, the event could not be held in 2020 because of the COVID-19

---

[48]Sundari Iyer, 'In Gautam's Memory', *Mid-Day*, 21 November 2012, https://www.mid-day.com/amp/sports/other-sports/article/In-Gautam-s-memory-189791. Accessed on 15 November 2021.

pandemic. It is hoped the tournament will continue in the years ahead. Here's wishing Shyam Bhatia the very best in his commendable initiative in memory of his—and our—dear friend Gautam.

TWENTY

UNITED COLOURS OF NATIONS

United Nations

The naughty Gadha was at work again!

Although I had met Natwar Singh only once before (at the *Inquilab* Golden Jubilee celebrations) he turned out to be a man of his word. In his capacity as minister of state for external affairs, Natwar was instrumental in getting my name included in the list of delegates to the United Nations so that I could 'get a taste of diplomacy' as he told me later.

An official intimation, followed by a press release, stated that I had been included as member of the Indian delegation to the forty-third session of the UN General Assembly which consisted of nine non-official members, including Atal Bihari Vajpayee, MP. The other non-official members named were Anand Sharma, Khurshid Alam Khan, Purushottam Kakodkar, Vishwa Bandhu Gupta, Tarun Kanti Khosh, Vayalar Ravi, Mrs Amarjit Kaur and myself. All non-official members were MPs, except for Vayalar Ravi, who was an MLA, and Mrs Kaur and yours truly, who were neither. Atal Bihari Vajpayee was to be the leader of the delegation which also included K.K. Tewari and the aforementioned Natwar Singh.

It was no secret that Atal Bihari Vajpayee had been a last-minute inclusion at the insistence of Prime Minister Rajiv Gandhi; they were often adversaries on the floor of Parliament but respected each other immensely. It was also common knowledge that the BJP leader's inclusion was as much for the importance of the session—the fortieth anniversary of the Universal Declaration of Human Rights—as for the opportunity to get his suspected cancer checked at the world-renowned Memorial Sloan Kettering Cancer Center in New York.

I must mention that, despite his indifferent health, which necessitated spending hours at the hospital, Vajpayee was by far the most able, affable and assiduous of all the non-official members of the delegation, not to mention his oratory skills and grasp of subtleties of the art and craft of diplomacy.

Barring days on which he had to go for treatment, Vajpayee was regular, unfailingly punctual and well prepared for the various sessions at the General Assembly. And, once the sun had set, he was the most gracious, cerebral and genial guest imaginable; his poetic renditions, homespun anecdotes and contagious humour made him the life of the party.

The UN General Assembly

The meetings of the UN General Assembly are a fascinating phenomenon, to say the least. The forum can become the Tower of Babel, where people like Krishna Menon of India speak on Kashmir to stonewall proceedings for eight hours and bore the delegates to tears. Or where leaders like Nikita Khrushchev, first secretary of the Communist Party of the Soviet Union, who dramatically bang their shoes in protest at a speech by a delegate from the inconsequential Philippines.

A lot of hot air is blown in the six official languages of the UN which, despite translations, are of little interest to (or go over the heads of) most delegates. I had the privilege, and dubious excitement, of speaking twice in the Assembly Hall—on both occasions, as it turned out, on the issue of human rights since both times were on two separate anniversaries of the establishment of the United Nations Commission on Human Rights. The impressive Assembly Hall, that one sees in photographs, was understandably nowhere near as full as when Ronald Reagan or Mikhail Sergeyevich Gorbachev spoke, not that I expected a full house for my magnum opus! But, for me, what *was* extremely discomfiting was that seemingly everybody in the delegates' seats, which the podium faces almost full on, was either reading sheafs of briefing papers, dozing, chatting or meandering on their way to or returning from toilets. It was quite a deflating experience, believe me. That said, a great deal is achieved in the elegant confines of the Delegates' Lounge through what in diplomatic jargon is termed 'backchannel diplomacy' (a euphemism for horse-trading!) via informal discussions.

Despite the criticism that is often levelled against it for being impotent (just as its predecessor, the League of Nations, allegedly was), its balance sheet in the 76 years of its existence has many positive achievements to its credit. Though the results are largely intangible and understated, the General Assembly has been undeniably successful in, generally, promoting and maintaining an element of sanity in our crazed universe.

The three pillars of the United Nations are: (i) Human Rights, (ii) Peace and Security and (iii) Development. By dedicatedly working with people, the United Nations seeks to help everyone make the world a better and safer place through initiatives such as health interventions, providing food aid and peacekeeping.

◆

Speaking of Nikita Khrushchev: there is this story about the time he visited India in 1955, along with his Premier Nikolai Bulganin, and received a rousing welcome to beat all welcomes.

Almost two million people gathered in Kolkata's famous maidan at Chowringhee; the crowd was bigger than the one that Nehru got when he previously visited the USSR in the same year.

It is said that in the city that lies the bank of the Hooghly, the open car carrying the dignitaries broke down, and so did the KGB chief who was escorting the Soviet dignitaries. Panicking at the sight of the crowds surging towards his leaders, General Serov demanded that the troops be called out to fire upon the sea of people who had enthusiastically shown up to witness the event. He had to be restrained while Bulganin and Khrushchev were packed into a police van and taken to Raj Bhavan.

Wherever they went in the country, whether it was Punjab, Mumbai, Bengaluru, Chennai or Kolkata, even if they were smaller towns or just hamlets, the Russian leaders were greeted by milling throngs. In a British Pathé film of that time that details highlights from the momentous visit, the announcer talks about the sheer scale of the decorations, remarking that 'half the gardens in Delhi must have been emptied to provide all these flowers.'[49]

---

[49]British Pathé, 'Bulganin In India (1955)', YouTube, https://www.youtube.com/watch?v=ApWkI9kG-J0. Accessed on 19 November 2021.

IN LIGHTER VEIN

Before departure for New Delhi, at the airport press conference in Moscow, a journalist asks Khrushchev: 'Sir, do you believe in God?'

'What kind of a silly question is that?' barks Khrushchev irritably. 'Don't you know we Communists are atheists?'

The party lands at Palam airport in New Delhi and is faced with the same journalist, the same question and the same reply at the press conference.

The VIPs go around the country and at every stop are faced with the same reporter, same question and give the very same annoyed reply.

After an impressive ceremonial farewell at Palam, the party returns to Sheremetyevo airport in Moscow. Again, it is the same reporter and the same question. But then comes the reply from Khrushchev: 'Before going to India, like a good Communist, I did not believe in God. Having returned from there, *I do*. Only God can help that country.'

Nikita Khrushchev

Mikhail Gorbachev was the first Soviet leader to visit New York since the two trips undertaken by Nikita S. Khrushchev in 1959 and 1960.

My first dispatch to *Mid-Day* from the UN (there were many, but shall reproduce only two of them here) read:

> The colourful Khrushchev's first exposure to this megapolis was during a state visit at the invitation of President Eisenhower and the second during which he banged his shoe on the desk during a debate in the UN General Assembly.
>
> It came at a time when relations between the two superpowers were less than cool following the shooting down of an American U-2 spy plane.
>
> Khrushchev met Fidel Castro during that visit when he is reported to have come out with his now famous quotable quote: 'Thank God I'm an atheist.'

◆

In his memoirs *Khrushchev Remembers: The Last Testament*, the irrepressible Soviet leader wrote:

> My only impression was of a huge noisy city with an enormous number of neon signs and cars, hence vast quantities of exhaust fumes that were choking people. Nothing new, intellectual or profound there—from a person we were brought up to consider a 'great' leader!

New York is like any other capitalist city: It had great wealth and luxury, and it had terrible poverty and slums.'

Meanwhile, efforts continue to move the debate on the Palestine question during the current session of the UN General Assembly to Geneva. At press time last night, the resolution seeking a revision of the US decision to not grant a visa to the PLO leader Yasser Arafat to enter the US to address the UN during the debate on Palestine today and tomorrow was about to be moved. Only the United States and Israel were expected to withhold assent.

A more confrontational approach is advocated by some diplomats who oppose the move to Geneva. They have suggested that Mr Arafat's speech should be broadcast into the General Assembly Hall by satellite.

Dismantling of Glasnost, Perestroika

One of my dispatches from the UN detailed the Soviet withdrawal from Afghanistan and went as followed:

[The departure of Soviet troops] heralded the historic dismantling of *glasnost* and *perestroika* by Gorbachev, the man who played a key role in ending the Soviet Union's post World War II domination of eastern Europe.

He also helped take down the long-standing Iron Curtain separating eastern Communist states from the western ones. Along with Ronald Reagan he helped lessen the military and political tension between the two countries and helped end the Cold War.

The final phase of the withdrawal of the Soviet troops from Afghanistan was expected to be the focus of the address of the Soviet leader Mikhail Gorbachev, to the 43rd General Assembly of the United Nations on 7 December 1991.

Gorbachev faces disturbing economic problems and mounting pressure from conservative elements over ideological issues at home, ethnic unrest in Armenia and Azerbaijan and demands for autonomy from the Baltic republics of Estonia, Latvia and Lithuania. He is expected to summon his charisma, affability and acknowledged powers of persuasion to invest the withdrawal of troops with an element of face-saving dignity and respectability.

As it turned out, the hawks won the day on the controversy regarding the visa to Arafat and we all adjourned to meet again—in Geneva—just to listen to Yasser Arafat. The rest is history.

◆

This reminds me of the apocryphal yarn about Russian president Boris Yeltsin who was a guest of Prime Minister John Major over a weekend at his bucolic country estate, Chequers, during an official visit to the United Kingdom in 1992.

Yeltsin was well known for his fondness for the hard stuff, which he could reputedly knock back in enormous quantities at any point of time. It is said that he was so inebriated during a stopover on his way back home after a trip abroad, that he was in no condition to deplane for his hosts' morning reception at the airport.

The story goes that on another occasion, after breakfast, Major asked Yeltsin if he was ready to begin talks as per the agenda. '*Nyet*,' (No) came the reply.

A little later, the very same question was repeated. And pat came the same reply.

An hour went by, and yet, Yeltsin remained consistent with his replies.

Major changed tacks and asked Boris if he would instead fancy a game of golf. '*Nyet*' again.

Out of exasperation, Major then suggested that they go to a delightful pub down the hill for drinks.

Yeltsin, with eyes lit up, replied, 'Of course!'

So they walked down to the pub, only to find the front door shut with a sign on it that said 'Closed on Sundays.'

Frantic, Yeltsin knocked at the door repeatedly, but there was no answer.

The security staff joined Boris in his desperate knocking and yelled, 'Open up! It's the President of Russia!'

'Oh yeah?' came the reply, 'I'm the Emperor of Prussia!'

◆

The number of real and invented bloopers by dignitaries (especially about Donald Trump), many unsubstantiated, keep proliferating in this age of social media.

There's the one about former vice president of the US, Dan Quayle, who wasn't exactly reputed for his mastery over the English language. He reportedly told school students during a visit to South America that the perennial and popular root vegetable native to the Americas was spelt 'potatoe.'

There's also the one about Quayle expressing regret for not having learnt Latin at high school since 'it would have helped during my visit to South America.'

Then, there's the story concerning George Brown, British foreign secretary under Prime Minister Harold Wilson. It is said that during his official visits, there wasn't a single country where Brown didn't behave abominably.

Brown was in Venezuela, where he arrived after having consumed a few glasses of his favourite scotch at Heathrow VIP departure lounge. More of the same continued on the flight across the Atlantic and at the Arrivals VIP lounge in Caracas, Venezuela.

At the official reception for him by the Foreign Minister of Venezuela that evening, Brown did a repeat while he was seated at the head table: he had some more scotches, followed by champagne for the toast and, then some more scotches, followed by wine.

Following speeches (and more scotches, more wine), later in the evening, Brown espied a pretty young thing, all dressed in red.

He got up from his seat, weaved his unsteady way between tables to the person on the dance floor and gushed: 'Good evening you lovely, gorgeous, delectable, delightful lady in red. May I have the pleasure of this dance with you?'

> She replied: 'You certainly may *not* dance with me. To begin with, you are disgustingly drunk. Next, this is not music to dance to, it's the national anthem of Venezuela. And finally, I'm not a "lovely, gorgeous, delectable, delightful lady in red." I'm the Archbishop of Caracas!"'

Dismantling of Glasnost, Perestroika

United Nations Preparatory Committee (PrepCom), New York

In 1992, I received a call from Pranay Gupte, author and former staff reporter and foreign columnist for *The New York Times* and *Newsweek International*.

He said he had been tasked by environmentalist and New York industrial relations lawyer of repute Ted Kheel to publish a newspaper for the Preparatory Committee (PrepCom) to be held at the UN Headquarters at New York ahead of the UN Earth Summit scheduled for 1996 in Rio de Janeiro, Brazil.

He asked: 'Would you be interested in being its editor-in-chief?'

He went on to explain the importance of the PrepCom as a prelude to the historic Rio Summit at which issues of crucial importance to Mother Earth—and therefore humankind—would be addressed.

Was I interested?

'Do bears love berries?'

So New York, New York, it was.

◈

The Afternoon Despatch and Courier reported:

> If we were a little melodramatic, we would say that Mumbai's loss is planet earth's gain.

Mr Khalid A-H Ansari who, after building his own strong house (the *Mid-Day* group of publications) moved on to set the Arab world's *Khaleej Times* on the road to success, then set up an international communications centre in Dubai, has moved to New York as editor-in-chief of *Earth Summit Times*, an independent newspaper brought out in connection with the forthcoming Earth Summit in Rio de Janeiro.

Mr Ansari has been heading an international team of journalists, and the paper, considering the universality of its subjects, has been sent to specialists and concerned bodies all over the world.

In characteristic style, Mr Ansari declares in one of his front-page editorials: 'Given the chasm of major issues between immovable objects and irresistible forces—the North and the South—and the understandable desire of the non-governmental organizations to assert themselves, we are cast in a manner of speaking, between Scylla and Charybdis, a rock and a hard place, as the expression goes in the US of A. Be that as it may, we have balanced to the extent possible, the concerns, aspirations and perceptions of the North with those of the South.'

◆

The newspaper for PrepCom at the UN headquarters in New York was called the *Earth Summit Times*.

To work with me, I was given an outstanding team of journalists, some retired and senior staff from *The New York Times, Daily News, Washington Post, Wall Street Journal,* NBC television, as also some trainees who made me wonder what they were doing in that distinguished team.

It was a tremendous learning experience for me on a personal level and I was pleased that the paper was well-received among the discerning readers of UN delegates from member-countries, resulting in my being asked to go to Rio de Janeiro for the Earth Summit.

◆

My front-page editorial at the end of the PrepCom read:

United Nations Preparatory Committee (PrepCom), New York

To say 'goodbye", as the aphorism goes, 'is to die a little'. So it is with us as we bid farewell, adieu, arrivederci, sayonara, shalom, au yong, haydo, dosvidanya, namaste, khuda hafiz and their multifarious equivalents to our readers from all over the world with this our final issue. It has been a memorable experience for all of us who have been privileged to be involved with the magnificent obsession of helping save the Planet Earth.

◆

In a 'Publishers Message', Ted Kheel replied:

In the 27 years I have been directly involved in newspaper affairs, I have never encountered a more dedicated and devoted group of journalists than those we have assembled for our newspaper.

Under the most trying of circumstances they have laboured for 12 to 20 hours a day—and sometimes more—to produce a newspaper of quality and relevance.

Our editor-in-chief, Khalid A-H Ansari, has taxed himself in excess of the demands he has made on the staff. In his regular work, Mr Ansari is owner and publisher of a group of newspapers in India, including *Mid-Day*, the largest afternoon newspaper in India.

Hailing from a distinguished publishing family that participated in India's freedom movement, Mr Ansari now leads a multi-professional life. In addition to his publishing responsibilities he heads a communication company based in Dubai. His vast experience has helped him cope with severe and onerous challenges.

In view of Mr Ansari's experience in publishing, Mr Yazaki and I have asked him to assist us as Advisory Publisher and Mr Ansari has graciously accepted this formidable assignment.

Earth Summit, Rio de Janeiro, 1997

There had been a great deal of conjecture as to whether or not the US president would attend the unprecedented 160-nation summit. Although keen to attend the high-profile session, Bush Jr was opposed to an agreement that would have bound the United States to specific reductions in emission of greenhouse gases.

However, he did attend, prompting *The Los Angeles Times* to editorialize: 'Bush's visit gave the Rio session a prominence previously accorded only to summits addressing security or economic issues.'[50]

Coverage of proceedings at the Earth Summit in the *Earth Summit Times* was too detailed and abstruse to warrant inclusion in these recollections. However, one report was of special relevance to India and is being reproduced here:

> Of all the factors impeding progress in developing countries, corruption is perhaps the most pernicious.
>
> The pervasiveness of the malaise is assuming alarming proportions during the critical take-off stage in many emerging societies.

---

[50]Douglas Jehl, 'Bush Decides to Attend Earth Summit in Rio', *The Los Angeles Times*, 13 May 1992, https://www.latimes.com/archives/la-xpm-1992-05-13-mn-1677-story.html. Accessed on 20 October 2021.

It is bleeding economies, draining precious natural resources, negating the benefits of welfare programmes, diverting energy and focus away from the important task of nation-building.

Sadly in many cases parasites, in the form of politicians, who fatten on the national wealth, are plundering the very people who have appointed them their leaders, the custodians of their country's assets, the arbiters of their destinies.

At a time of growing concern about corruption throughout the world, the findings of the 1996 International Corruption Perception Index issued by Transparency International assume special significance.

Based on 10 international surveys of business people, the index, although not professing to be definitive or exhaustive, reflects the perception of corruption in 54 countries.

Prepared as a 'poll of polls', it provides insights into perceptions which have an impact on how private companies, particularly in Japan, North America and Western Europe, operate in the rest of the world.

In the survey led by Dr Johann Lambsdorff and a research team of Goettingen University, a '10' indicates a perfectly clean country, whereas a '0' refers to a country where business transactions are entirely perpetrated by corruption involving immense sums of kickbacks, extortion, fraud, etc.

Following are the rankings of the index in descending order of corruption among the top and bottom five (including India):

1.	New Zealand	9	42.	India	2
2.	Denmark	9	50.	China	2
3.	Sweden	9	51.	Bangladesh	2
4.	Finland	9	52.	Kenya	2
5.	Canada	8	53.	Pakistan	1

Given the gravity of the situation, this is a wake-up call for the international community and governments to address themselves to the cancer of corruption in all seriousness and with the utmost urgency.

TWENTY-ONE

THE GAME CALLED LIFE

Return to Mumbai

So I was back home, and it was back to business as usual. In the words of the Urdu proverb: *'Jaan bachi to lakhon paye, laut ke budhu ghar ko aaye'* (In a difficult situation when our life is saved, that is the equivalent to having gained millions.).

By now son Tarique had learnt the ropes of the publishing business. At the same time, he branched out impressively into outdoor advertising, commercial printing, Internet and the FM radio broadcasting business (in joint ventures, first with Capital London radio station and BBC Radio, projects that later functioned under the nomenclatures of Radio Mid-Day and Radio One).

Tarique and I are both uncompromisingly independent in our styles of running businesses (as in fact, long back, my father and I were as well!). It would have been calamitous to try and conduct the multi-dimensional businesses with two captains in command.

It was prudent to let Tarique continue the good work he had settled into even as, with the advent of digital media, we both started hearing unmistakable low-decibel—but distinct—rumblings at the base of the well-established edifice of the newspaper publishing business.

In hindsight, we were perhaps the first to see the writing on the wall and decide on a plan to evacuate while the going was good.

Even as Tarique took charge of the nuts and bolts of the business, I was semi-retired from the business, which left me ample time to concentrate on my late father's charity for the girl-child—the Abdul Hamid Ansari Charitable Trust.

The trust is now 60 years old, but in a new avatar that is the Khalid and Zeyna Foundation, (more on that later).

We were fortunate to have the unstinted support of our trustees Dr Altaf Patel; Saleem Fazelbhoy; Rukya's lawyer-niece Yasmin Shaikh, lawyer and active social worker on former police commissioner Julio Ribeiro's mohalla committee and Aziz Khatri, who has been associated with the family businesses for almost 50 years.

We endeavoured to help, in particular, orphans (since father started life as one) and the girl child in an effort to empower and make them financially independent through vocational training.

'Doin' What Comes, Natur'lly'

I had my own interpretation of what life was all about at that stage of my life and where I wished to go.

It soon became a personal challenge for me to unearth and file a daily newsworthy, publishable column called *Khalidoscope* from wherever I was travelling in the world, a thousand-words-a-day column on any topic under the sun for the various English, Urdu and Gujarati publications in the group.

Space restrictions come in the way of reproducing the columns (written between 2000 and 2010) in these recollections. Apart from the ones quoted earlier, I am reproducing just one (on sport, *mais oui!*), from the many sent daily from Beijing during the 2008 Olympics.

BEIJING OLYMPICS 2008:

Should we celebrate?

Quoting from coverage of the Beijing Olympics: 'I am flabbergasted at the euphoria that has seemingly gripped India over our winning three meagre medals at the Beijing Olympic Games.

The *wah-wahs* (well-dones) over what was essentially a dismal performance from our contingent of 57 competitors are symptomatic of our *chalta-hai mentality*. (Journalists from all over the world covering the Beijing Olympics, too, are amazed at reports of jubilation and dancing in Indian cities over the winning of what an American journalist described as 'one measly' gold.

Some journalists here in Beijing do not hide their amusement at learning that it has taken India 108 years to win its first Olympic individual gold medal and that a mere bronze medal winner has been gifted an airline ticket for life!

The adulation showered upon the three medal winners has been so disproportionately over the top that the China Daily, the nation's leading English newspaper, has been regularly publishing stories of *shabaash (*congratulation*)* celebrations in India, which are positively embarrassing.

If you look at the medals table, you will find India, with a solitary gold and two bronze medals, languishing at number 50 (out of 204 competing nations) behind countries that are much smaller and underdeveloped.

On the other hand, China, with which it has become fashionable for us to compare ourselves as regards achievements, tops the table with 51 repeat 51 gold medals, 21 silver and 28 bronzes, a total of 100!

And we are patting ourselves on the back over the fact that, with a population of 1.2 billion (and growing by the minute!) we have won just one gold and two bronze medals! Big deal!

To put matters in correct perspective, tiny Jamaica, with a population of just 2,714,000, has won 11 medals, of which six are gold.

Forget the top five powerhouses: China (pop 13.25 million), USA (total 110 medals, pop. 305 m.) Russia (72 medals, pop. 142 m.), Britain (47 medals, pop. 58 m), Australia (46 medals, pop. 21 m) and Germany (41 medals, pop. 82 m).

Bahrain, a nation with a population of only 760,000 and hardly any sporting culture worth the name, also boasts a gold medal, but has not been trumpeting its achievements, as India has been doing.

Indian sports administration is rotten to its core. Its time all concerned in our sports administration stopped patting themselves on their backs and got down to the serious business of running our sport efficiently, not only for national glory, but also the physical and mental well-being of the youth of our country.

Mens sana in corpore sano (a healthy mind in a healthy body).

'Doin' What Comes, Natur'lly'

A Crisis of Grave Magnitude

Running a daily newspaper in a crime-ridden metropolis like Mumbai has afforded me the opportunity to befriend some exemplary members of the police force, such as the legendary Julio Ribeiro, of whom we should be proud.

Of others that I have known well, I had the utmost respect for upright commissioners such as D.S. Soman, Satish Sahni, Hasan Gafoor, Surender Pathania, Ronald Mendonca, M.N. Singh and Ahmed Javed (who was named ambassador to Saudi Arabia after retirement), to name a few.

Unfortunately, the Mumbai police force, which once had an enviable international reputation for its exemplary discipline, efficiency and probity, has sullied its name in the recent past because of some alarming happenings that give rise to serious concern. Without mincing words, it can be said that the police force is facing a crisis of conscience and a plethora of other critical problems, including, notably, corruption.

The need of the hour is to combat the cancer manifest in cases of rampant lawlessness across the country such as the latest occurrent concerning the SUV carrying explosives and a threatening letter that was parked near Antilla, the residence of business tycoon Mukesh Ambani.

As editorialized by *The Times of India*:

The structural problem here is successive governments' failure to implement police reforms, wherein the Supreme Court way back in 2006 had outlined various mechanisms for insulating police from extraneous pressures, making it autonomous in personnel matters, and ensuring high levels of accountability. In the years since, governments have expanded police's roles but without commensurate investment to modernise their functioning, or upgrade their autonomy and accountability.[51]

Having known some of the luminaries listed above, I choose to keep my faith in the force in the belief, more than mere hope, that the police reforms will be implemented and worthy men and women will emerge from the ranks to restore the image of the police force to its pristine prestige.

◆

An incident concerning Commissioner M.N. Singh, best known for having thrown the rule book at Bal Thackeray, comes to mind:

In his own words:

> Yes, I'm never tired of narrating that story when Khalid helped me prevent a serious crisis building up in Mumbai in 2001 during my tenure in Mumbai.
>
> The news came that a copy of the Quran was burnt in Delhi which resulted in some disturbances over there and caused some commotion among Muslims in certain Mumbai areas. Next day, after Friday prayers in Hari Masjid at Kurla, the Delhi incident came to be mentioned. This infuriated the large gathering of Muslims and they decided to take out a protest rally in the city the next day.
>
> My counterpart in Delhi informed me that the news was false and that it was just a rumour spread by some mischief mongers.

---

[51] 'The Waze Trap: Political Crisis of MVA Government Has Its Roots in Failures to Undertake Police Reforms', *The Times of India*, 21 March 2021, https://timesofindia.indiatimes.com/blogs/toi-editorials/the-waze-trap-political-crisis-of-mva-government-has-its-roots-in-failures-to-undertake-police-reforms/. Accessed on 20 November 2021.

He also told me that the situation had returned to normal after a brief period of turmoil and Delhi was quiet.

I directed my officers to fan out in their respective jurisdictions and inform the Muslim masses that as the news of Quran burning was false there was no need to take out a protest rally.

As I was driving back home that evening, I recalled that I had a dinner date with Nana Chudasama, the late Sheriff of Mumbai who lived on Nepean Sea Road.

Nana and his wife Munira were great hosts besides being among the prominent citizens of the city. As their house was located on my way to Worli Sea Face, I decided to take a detour, visit them briefly and make a quick exit.

As I reached Nana's house, curious queries started flying across about my late arrival. I started telling them about the tension building up in the city over the news of the Quran burning in Delhi and that my problem was how to convey it to the Muslim masses in the city since it was too late to call the press.

My main strategy was to somehow diffuse the tension or else the protest rally was sure to result in serious riots as had happened in the past over such issues.

The intelligence report had hinted at the possibility of disturbances over this issue as the tempers were running high.

No sooner had I finished narrating my predicament, Ayaz Memon, well known sports journalist and a good old friend, who was standing nearby, suggested that I should speak to Khalid Ansari, another prominent journalist, a Padma Shri awardee and a good friend of mine who had helped me build a Squash Court in the Police Gymkhana.

I asked Ayaz what he could do in the matter. I did not know until then that Khalid was also the owner of prominent Urdu newspaper *Inquilab*. Ayaz, who had worked with him, suggested that Khalid could help me.

To my great relief, Khalid was present at the party. Good Samaritan that he is, Khalid took no time to phone his editor and tell him firmly to do as the Police Commissioner desired and handed over the phone to me.

The next morning, *Inquilab* came out with a prominent headline quoting me that the Delhi police had denied the occurrence of the Quran and made an appeal to Muslims to maintain peace. I felt like I had already won the war.

Achilles Heel

In Greek mythology, Achilles was the son of Peleus, a Greek king, and Thetis, a sea nymph or goddess. When Achilles was an infant, his mother dipped him into the river Styx to make him immortal. But since she held him by one heel, that particular spot did not touch the water and remained mortal and vulnerable; it was here that Achilles was mortally wounded.

And so it has been with me: to begin with, there's no business acumen in my genes that I know of, going back at least to my grandfather, who was a teacher. As I've always maintained with reference to myself that a barber only knows how to cut hair. I have known only how to start publications *not* to sustain them in the long run. For me, the latter are alien functions to be discharged by superior humans: whiz-kids, accountants and differently wired financial geniuses.

Nor did I learn even the rudiments of business or commerce in my educational career. Whatever little success came my way in my quixotic business undertakings was the result, very largely, of either accidental, albeit apt, timing, being at the right place at the right time, and sincere, devoted hard work by my colleagues, all of which bring me back to the fable about the One Above and the mischievous Donkey.

But this Donkey is also two-faced and capable of delivering a lethal kick at the most unexpected time and for reasons known only to himself.

◆

Basically, I have been lucky to never hanker after *money*—that ugly five-letter word which, through history, has been the root of all evil.

Indeed, I do enjoy the good things in life and am grateful to the One Above for making the good life in the Aristotelean sense possible for me. But overall, reaching my destination *my way*, with minimal, perhaps foolish, disregard for money in an essentially business endeavour, has been exhilarating. Starting with *Sportsweek*, down to KANZ Communications and then *Mid-Day* (and its allied publications), the thrill of the chase was infinitely greater than winning the prize.

As long as *gaadi chal rahi thi* (as long as the vehicle was running), I had neither the time nor the patience to check the engine. The ride was all-important. As long as my ventures were keeping their heads above water, I didn't worry about the lurking dangers beneath the surface. Profit, the be-all-and-end-all of most commercial activity, was my least concern.

Espousing causes, fighting for principles I cherished (right or wrong!), taking on the big boys, rocking the boat, cocking a snook at the established market leaders made for an indescribable high, not the balance sheet. It was the ride that mattered, as was the case with the frenzied Formula One driver, the legendary Brazilian Ayrton Senna, who died in a crash in the San Marino Grand Prix in 1994. Or Austrian Niki Lauda, three-time world champion, who was almost burned to death (and even administered last rites in the hospital) in a horrific accident at the 1976 German Grand Prix at Nürburgring, only to make a remarkable comeback in 1984 as the world champion.

◆

For the most part, I just refused to see the wood for the trees, didn't know, or wished to know, top line from bottom line, profitability from liquidity. Despite dire warnings from accountants and auditors, I wilfully refused to see the looming dark clouds of disaster: I was living in a haze even as the businesses hurtled towards financial apocalypse.

I have been blessed to have son Tarique, whose grasp of business and finance is truly brilliant, and who has been the guardian—the lifebuoy and saviour—of our family's financial stability. It was he who brought sanity into the proceedings, persuaded me to shut down *Sportsweek* and injected fiscal discipline into an adventure that was fast careening to misadventure.

◆

Lord Thomson of Fleet, who owned the *Times* newspaper of London, once famously said in jest (but only with tongue half in cheek) editorial matter is 'just the stuff between the Ads.'

The more I tried to grow the business in different directions—*Mid-Day* in New Delhi, *Sunday Mid-Day* in Bengaluru, Urdu *Inquilab* in Delhi, *Sportsweek* in Hindi, Gujarati *Mid-Day* in Mumbai, *Sunday Mid-Day* in Bengaluru—the more northwards did our financial problems escalate.

To make matters worse, my old-fashioned values—inherited from my father—which considered ownership of media almost a hallowed trust for the public good, rendered any thought of going public or even joining hands with a financially sound organization, a mercantile heresy. I regret making the same mistakes as my father and not spending enough time with my children when they were growing up. But for Rukya's loving parenting, they could have gone astray.

Tarique's achievements are impressive and he will certainly go down in the history of Indian publishing for blazing new trails of which the Ansari family is proud.

Writing on the Wall

Seeing the writing on the wall over the plight of newspapers in many developed countries in the face of relentless assault from the electronic media, Tarique and I decided to opt out from the publishing business.

It was Tarique who masterminded our exit strategy and, ultimately sale, to the Jagran Prakashan group in 2014, after prolonged and dexterous negotiations. The sale of our group of publications included *Inquilab* Urdu daily (established in 1937), *Mid-Day* (Mumbai, Delhi, Bengaluru and Pune—established in 1979) and *Gujarati Mid-Day* (Mumbai, established in 1983).

Jagran Prakashan, the new owners, closed down the Delhi and Bengaluru editions of *Mid-Day* in 2011 and the Pune edition of *Mid-Day* in 2012.

◆

We're delighted the result of endeavours of three generations of the Ansari family, starting with orphan boy Abdul Hamid, down to me and, finally, Tarique and Sharique, are now in the hands of the descendants of the late Shri Puran Chandra Gupta, a freedom fighter like my late father.

Jagran's vision statement says: 'Just like the morning sun that dispels darkness and brings warmth to the world, the vision of Jagran is to transform lives through enlightening and enriching experiences.'

We wish the Gupta family, the new custodians, every success in the fond hope that they will look after the *Inquilab* and *Mid-Day* groups of publications—the fruits of our blood, tears, toil and sweat—with the same integrity, devotion and loving care that we tried to put into them for 73 years.

In the words of the poignant patriotic song penned by Pradeep and sung tearfully by Mohammed Rafi:

*'Hum laaye hain toofan se kishti nikaal ke
Is desh ko rakhna mere bacche sambhaal ke'*

(We have brought the boat (of life) out of the storm,
Take great care of this country, my children.)

Life Down Under, Mate

Even as negotiations for sale of our newspapers were in progress, Zeyna and I decided to ride into the sunset and spend the rest of our lives in Sydney, which had enchanting memories for us (having first met there on Millennium Eve, 1999), as mentioned in an earlier chapter.

Zeyna had built a successful retail business of pet animal memorabilia and would have loved to settle down in the laidback city with its comfortable lifestyle in the 'back of beyond' (as I teased her!), in the antipodes or Down Under.

Although quintessentially a shy and retiring person, she had made a few close friends in Sydney, whose company she enjoyed. But the prospect of living the rest of her life thousands of miles away from New Zealand, where she had family and friends going back to her childhood and fond memories of, was an exciting adventure, something to look forward to.

Having had, in a manner of speaking, a trial run, living in two apartments (at different times) with front seat views of the gorgeous Sydney Harbour Bridge and the Opera House panorama over five intermittent years, I was mesmerized by the city's riveting beauty. I was in thrall of its relaxed ambience, sporting culture, eclectic cuisine, polyglot mix of people and hail-fellow-well-met, backslapping mannerisms. Drawn inexorably to the Emerald City, we decided to set up home in Sydney.

Now fully retired, I divided my time between Sydney and Mumbai, continuing my daily column without a break even as we indulged our passionate love for travel to the far corners of the world, in the course of which we have taken over 30 ocean and river cruises.

I shall never forget the time we were on an island of the archipelago of Fiji and, having finished my column on the insurrection in that country, went down to the hotel reception to fax my *Mid-Day* article home. The man on duty gave me a quizzical look: 'You crazy or what? You been writing a newspaper article on this beautiful island? Nobody works here mister. Nobody like you comes here…everybody else comes to have a good time!'

It so happened that the hotel had never had facsimile facilities and I had to reconcile myself to the (disgraceful) fact that my column did not appear the next morning and had to take an enforced break for the next three days as long as we were on that island. This was a professional irreverence for the first (and, thankfully last) time in my close to 50-year writing career. Never before in my entire life had I missed a deadline, leave aside a publishing date in my whole life. Shame on me!

◆

We had settled down well in Sydney and made a cross-section of varied and interesting friends: cricket patrons John and Evelyn Geber, owners of the renowned Chateau Tanunda Wineyards in Borassa Valley; Gina and her management consultant husband Colin Knowles; academician Piyush Bhatt and his wife, Poornima; doctors Deepak Malhotra (now deceased) and Rajan Parhawk and wife Ujita; marketing honcho Gautam and his spouse, Samta Sharma; businessman Noshir Irani and wife Maggie; restauranteurs Surjit Singh and Paresh and wife Latha Pandya and marketing manager Hartley Anderson and his wife, Pam.

Much as we were enjoying our carefree Sydney lifestyle, I was often troubled by its crassness and overall lack of intellectual stimulus. I soon came face to face with the irresistible magnetism of *aamchi* (our) Mumbai—warts and all—and which shall always remain my spiritual home.

Mumbai, I realized, has for me an appeal that far transcends the ephemeral superfluity of most Western cities. It embodies a particular sort of zeitgeist that is unique. It must be the basic elements: the *panchamahabhutas*, the basic elements of earth (*prithvi*), water (*jala*), fire (*tejas*), wind (*vayu*) and space (*akasha*) in my mental, physical and spiritual makeup that somehow respond to the filth, dust, garbage, pollution of the beloved city of my birth and keep pulling me back.

I started longing for Mumbai.

What finally settled the conundrum was a seemingly throwaway but, in essence, sincere and touching remark, by Nana Chudasama in the stag company of Dr Altaf Patel (Medical Director, Jaslok Hospital), businessmen Ranjan Sanghi, Saleem Fazelbhoy, Ratu Ramchandani, Rajan Patel, Abbas Jasdanwala and (the late) Srikant Ruparel, at a sundowner at our home during one of our trips to Mumbai.

'*Arre yaar wahan dozakh mein kya kar rahe ho—tumhari yahaan zaroot hai*, asked Nana (Hey buddy, what the hell are you doing out there in the Styx, we need you here). The others joined in and harangued me all evening to convince Zeyna and me to return to Mumbai.

The remark left an indelible impression and was compounded by bouts of miserable homesickness that I had periodically experienced abroad over the years for now-obvious reasons of insecurity. More importantly, despite all of Sydney's shallow blandishments, I was victim to a feeling of huge emotional and intellectual vacuity, an outlier recoil from the meaningless superficialities, hedonistic in-your-face larrikinism that so characterizes everyday life Down Under. In short, I was desperately hungry for intellectual stimulus. After much soul-searching during future trips to Sydney and Mumbai, Zeyna and I decided to make Mumbai our *jeena yahan marna yahan* (live here, die here) abode.

Zeyna had travelled to India a few times, met my family and friends and felt quite comfortable at the prospect of spending the rest of her life with me in *aamchi* Mumbai. She loved our spiritual and cultural values, our innate religiosity, our history, culture and heritage, the kaleidoscope of colours in our everyday lives, the razzle-dazzle of our big fat ugly weddings. But the omnipresent poverty and misery of our pavement dwellers, caste system, appalling treatment of animals, the erosion of our cultural values and galloping religious intolerance vitiated against her essential gentle and compassionate nature.

Life Down Under, Mate

Giving Back to Society

Following our decision to move back to Mumbai, Zeyna sold her business in Sydney, and we relocated to Mumbai to pick up the lost threads of the Abdul Hamid Ansari Charitable Trust.

My late father had started the charity to help the cause of education of the girl child, especially orphans (since he himself had started life as one) with the objective of empowering them to be financially self-sufficient.

We initially continued the practice of accepting donations from friends and well-wishers but soon learnt from unpleasant experience that doing so meant leaving ourselves open to ridiculous accountability. It made us answerable to multifarious authorities whose sole purpose in life was to view all charities with utmost suspicion and treat them as criminals, often with selfish intent of extracting money. This prompted us to convert our trust (this was another Himalayan task!) to a 'foundation' for legal purposes, discontinue the practice of accepting donations from outsiders and set up our own private foundation.

Hence the Khalid & Zeyna Ansari Foundation, which continues our welfare activities strictly from our own private funds.

In any event, the income tax benefits that donors now receive under our Indian laws are insignificant, if not downright laughable. It's no wonder large business houses and wealthy Indians in larger numbers are not incentivized to make more munificent donations (if at all) to charity.

It's no wonder so many foreign philanthropists have made well-meaning mention of our 'fat cat' multi-billionaires who seem to have no conscience and live off the fat of the land with minimal social responsibility.

WWW.ANSARIFOUNDATION.ORG

'We ourselves feel that what we are doing is just a drop in the ocean. But the ocean would be less because of that missing drop.'

– Mother Teresa

The Khalid & Zeyna Foundation is endeavouring to provide that 'missing drop'.

For the needy and readers who may be interested, our activities comprise:

- Cancer detection and treatment at the Tata Hospital in conjunction with the Tata Trust.
- Animal welfare activities in conjunction with the Tata Trust and Bombay Society for the Prevention of Cruelty to Animals (BSPCA)
- Vocational training in courses such as computer, pre-school teachers' training, beauty culture, fashion design at AIPTECH, Pune.
- Higher education in courses such as editing and graphic design, pharmacology, computer engineering, medicine, dentistry, medical lab technician, dentistry, biotechnology, para medical training, chemical engineering, accountancy, banking, insurance, electronics and IT in conjunction with the Nargis Dutt Foundation and the Women's India Trust (WIT).
- Nursing training at the Parsi General Hospital (Mumbai) and WIT.
- Education of street children in courses such as hotel management, film making, architecture, chartered accountancy and fashion design in association with Salaam Balak Trust.
- Eye camps in slums and depressed suburbs of Mumbai (in conjunction with Adityajyot Foundation and Vision Foundation of India) in Mumbai and Pune (pan-India as of 1 October 2021): providing free check-ups, subsidized eye-

glasses, medication and conducting cataract surgeries.
- Providing cochlear implant equipment and surgical procedures to eight children in north-eastern India through the Ali Yavar Jung National Institute for Children with Hearing and Speech Disability for acutely deaf children to enable them to have a normal life and, equally importantly, receive school education, which we fund.
- Breast cancer treatment at the Sancheti Cancer Care Mission in Pune.
- Animal welfare—giving finance to pet angels who support animals. We believe animals are just as important as humans.
- Involvement with the World Wildlife Fund (WWF), women's welfare in tribal villages in northeastern India, Super Sniffers Programme to end wildlife trafficking across 20 states with forest departments and the Railway Protection Force (RPF).
- Ad-hoc care where needed, e.g. providing education for needy children, and others within our orbit.
- During emergencies such as COVID-19, making urgent supplies of essential goods e.g. laptops and mobile phones to students for online learning, providing cooked food and ration to migrant workers and giving interest-free loans to needy self-employed tradesmen.

Detailed information can be had from our website: www.ansarifoundation.org.

Afterthoughts

Personally, if there was a silver lining in the pall of doom and gloom that the scourge of the COVID-19 pandemic inflicted, it was that it finally wrenched me out of my insouciance to resolve, finally, to write these memoirs (*aap beeti*, or *sawaan-e-hayaat* in Urdu).

With nothing better to do during the enforced home confinement, even as utensils were clanged all over the country, prayers recited, diyas lit on windows and balconies at the impetuous urging of our Prime Minister Narendra Modi, I finally resolved to buckle up and go down memory lane. It took five months in Goa, Udaipur, Pune and a staycation in Mumbai to complete these reminiscences.

At the time, the appellation 'COVID' was as outlandish as the 45-letter word 'pneumonoultramicroscopicsilicovolcanoconiosis.'

Not even the most cynical of scientists and doctors could have envisaged the havoc the virus would wreak on Mother Earth, a scourge that has bewitched, bothered, bewildered the most erudite scientists and medical geniuses from all schools of medicines.

Although my family and I have been personally fortunate—thus far at least—to be spared the wrath of the scourge, some of the staff at Rupa Publications, my New Delhi-based publishers, have not been as fortunate, with the result that production has been delayed but the consequences could have been immensely worse! One is grateful!

What this has meant is that with at least one event with devastating global repercussions—COVID-19—and a host of other less significant ones but of immense importance taking place during my lifetime, I could not possibly have, in all conscience as a journalist, avoided their inclusion. They merit at least a perfunctory mention without which these memoirs would have been incomplete.

Therefore, this chapter titled 'Afterthoughts,' includes commentary on some of the significant events that took place in the period between the submission of my manuscript to the publishers and the launch of this, my fourth book publication.

DOOM AND GLOOM

Although Prime Minister Narendra Modi demonstrated an admirable grasp of the war-like criticality of the coronavirus situation, a capacity for bold decision-making backed by urgent action, his seemingly frenetic knee-jerk decision to impose a nationwide lockdown overnight turned out to be a case of the remedy being almost worse than the disease.

The lockdown precipitated a nationwide tailspin of the sputtering economy, which was still reeling from the body blows dealt by the ill-advised demonetization followed by imposition of the deleterious general sales tax (GST).

The consequent walloping blows to the mind, body and psyche of the nation, against the backdrop of disturbing obscurantist incidents over alleged cow slaughter, love jihad, *ghar wapsi* (a term used by Hindu right-wing fronts to convert, or reconvert, non-Hindus to Hinduism) and the like shook the fundamentals of religious tolerance and peaceful co-existence that have been the bedrock of traditional Indian society.

But the manifest increase in the disturbing numbers of corona cases brought the economy to its knees, causing in its wake widespread unemployment and mass emigration out of the urban areas—the engines of our economy—as well as deaths as the result of hunger and starvation reminiscent of the 1943 Bengal famine.

The nation reeled under the devastation of the COVID-19 pandemic, the passing of the Citizenship (Amendment) Act (CAA) in 2019 and its attendant National Register of Citizens (NRC), followed by the

Presidential Order of 2019 rendering all but one clause of Article 370 inoperative. The result was mass protests all over the country.

INFRACTIONS OF CONSTITUTIONAL SAFEGUARDS

Then there were blatant violations of constitutional safeguards of the independence of the judiciary and freedom of the press. These were then followed by flagrant disregard for the fundamental rights of citizens, which resulted in the non-violent 24/7 sit-ins at Delhi's Shaheen Bagh and the Mumbai Bagh agitations following police interventions against the students of Jamia Millia Islamia.

With Donald Trump in New Delhi in the course of his ballyhooed visit to India in February 2020, riots broke out in the capital city during the annual conference of the Tablighi Jamaat. There are different accounts of when the Tablighi conference ended in March, but what is clear is that many people, including around 250 foreigners, chose to stay on. It is (allegedly) thought that many of them were carrying the COVID-19 infection that ravaged the country. Even as the national (especially television) media went berserk and shouted itself hoarse while conducting a kangaroo trial of its own and pronouncing the jamaat's followers guilty, a Delhi court absolved 36 foreigners of guilt.

The Chief Justice of India (CJI), Sharad A. Bobde, reprimanded the Union government. *The Hindu* reported the following about the proceedings: '[The CJI] on Thursday pulled up the Union government for mistreating the Supreme Court for having a "junior officer" file an "evasive" affidavit containing "unnecessary, nonsensical" averments on petitions challenging the discriminatory and communal coverage of the Tablighi Jamaat incident by some sections of the media. "You cannot treat the court the way you are doing in this case… A junior officer has filed your affidavit. We find it extremely evasive and brazenly short of details. It even says the petitioners here do not point to any instance of bad reporting…" Chief Justice Bobde addressed Solicitor General Tushar Mehta.'[52]

---

[52]Krishnadas Rajagopal, 'Supreme Court Slams Centre on Tablighi Affidavit', *The Hindu*, 8 October 2020, https://www.thehindu.com/news/national/sc-slams-centre-on-tablighi-affidavit/article32801548.ece. Accessed on 18 November 2021.

Then followed the police intervention and shambolic handling of the Delhi riots after the landmark Supreme Court judgement on the Ram Janmabhoomi-Babri Masjid case and the farcical acquittals of the accused, the Jawaharlal Nehru University (JNU) imbroglio and the profligate Central Vista project (named the 'vanity project'), all of which elicited widespread criticism of the government across the country.

Daily Mail wrote of the vainglorious Central Vista project:[53]

> As millions suffer in pandemic, India's narcissistic Prime Minister is building a vast folly at a cost that could fund 40 major hospitals. Now his nation is in uproar.
>
> Yesterday, pathetically-paid minions skittered about the vast construction site and giant cranes lurched overhead. Within a mile or two, people were still dying for lack of care in the dusty streets.
>
> Despite the death and despair all around him, however, this shameless demagogue—who on Tuesday agreed a £1 billion trade deal with Britain during a virtual summit with Boris Johnson—insists that the drive to complete the new building, derisorily dubbed 'Modi's Dream', must continue apace.

With misguided storm-troopers running amok during and after the Delhi riots, there was a pronounced feeling of fear and insecurity among some sections of the Indian Muslim community who resented the distrust and having to prove their 'Indian-ness' day after day.

As the pandemic galloped out of control amid accusations of centre-state differences; ham-handedness in handling of the prevention, control and cure of the pandemic; accusations of under-reporting of casualties on social media and, more seriously, exports of desperately needed vaccines to foreign countries, the Modi government came under fire from various quarters across the length and breadth of the country. Supra-loyal supporters, the government and the ruling party didn't help matters by asininely bleating in the media, and at international

---

[53]David Jones, 'The monstrous monument to Narendra Modi's ego', *Daily Mail*, 5 May 2021, https://www.dailymail.co.uk/news/article-9547379/DAVID-JONES-millions-suffer-pandemic-Indias-narcissistic-leader-building-folly.html. Accessed on 18 November 2021.

fora, that India had overcome the dreaded pandemic and retained its status as the 'pharmacy of the world.'

RIGHT TO INFORMATION ACT

The passing of the vexatious Right to Information (Amendment) Bill, 2019 in supersession of the commendable, original Bill passed in 2005 led to apprehension among the opposition parties, RTI activists and diverse sections of society that the amendment bill would weaken the RTI, which arguably was the most potent weapon available to Indian citizens for fighting corruption.

Any amendment to the Bill, which has unearthed so many corruption scandals, was bound to be seen with suspicion in the context of the alarming number of whistle-blowers, policemen and RTI activists who have been harassed, threatened with social ostracism, assaulted and killed across the country in their efforts to promote transparency and accountability in the workings of public authorities in the country.

The latest reports say that in the last 16 years or so, 'at least 95–100 RTI applicants have been killed while 190 others attacked, while dozen committed suicide and hundreds of them reported being harassed from powerful lobby.'[54]

Shockingly, many threats and attacks have gone unreported by a timorous media, reminiscent of the contemptible Indira Gandhi-imposed Emergency, of which L.K. Advani said to journalists: 'You were asked only to bend, but you crawled.'[55]

(I'm grateful I am no longer part of the media. The present milieu, in which a shockingly large number of owners and practitioners have

---

[54]Press Trust of India, 'Harassment, Murder Of RTI Applicants Rising, Protection A Challenge: Report', NDTV.com, 11 October 2021, https://www.ndtv.com/india-news/harassment-murder-of-rti-applicants-rising-protection-a-challenge-report-2572038. Accessed on 19 November 2021.

[55]'The Darkest Phase in Indira's Tenure as PM', *The Economic Times*, 31 October 2019, https://economictimes.indiatimes.com/news/politics-and-nation/democracy-interrupted-some-lesser-known-facts-about-emergency-1975-77/emergency/slideshow/69940337.cms. Accessed on 19 November 2021.

execrably sold their souls, would have made life a living hell for me).

Amidst debate over the effectiveness of the RTI, citizens have begun to demand safety because they fear that if no questions can be asked, the authorities will be emboldened to do whatever they please sans accountability.

An article in *The Wire* more than appropriately sums up the situation: 'When conscientious and well-meaning citizens are attacked for "acting rightly", is the government "acting rightly" by not doing enough to safeguard them?'[56]

Bluntly put, the Right to Information Act has not been implemented in letter and spirit, which is why the number of RTI appeals and cases are on the upswing.

AMNESTY INTERNATIONAL

In its 2020 report on India, Amnesty International, the international non-governmental organization, which claims to have seven million members and supporters worldwide, said: 'Freedom of expression was guaranteed selectively, and dissent was repressed through unlawful restrictions on peaceful protests and by silencing critics. Human rights defenders, including students, academics, journalists and artists, were arbitrarily arrested, often without charge or trial.'[57]

The vigilant watchdog that is the organization which at times tends to run ahead of itself, has listed in its report the Citizenship (Amendment) Act (CAA), denial of freedom of expression and assembly, unfair trials, unlawful attacks, and killings, some amounting to extrajudicial executions with impunity, and hate crimes including excessive use of force, violence against Dalits, Adivasi communities and religious minorities.

In February 2020, communal violence broke out in the capital.

---

[56] Venkatesh Nayak, 'As Number of Murdered RTI Activists Rises to 67, It Is the Modi Government That Needs to "Act Rightly"', *The Wire*, 12 March 2018, https://thewire.in/rights/as-number-of-murdered-rti-activists-rises-to-67-it-is-modi-government-that-needs-to-act-rightly. Accessed on 19 November 2021.

[57] 'India 2020', Amensty International, https://www.amnesty.org/en/location/asia-and-the-pacific/south-asia/india/report-india/. Accessed on 19 November 2021.

According to government data, 53 people died in the riots and more than 500 were injured.

In the build-up to the Legislative Assembly elections in Delhi held on 8 February, several political leaders made hate speeches against the anti-CAA protesters.

On 27 January 2021, referring to the protesters at Shaheen Bagh, the epicentre of peaceful sits-ins against the CAA, a Union minister encouraged the crowd to chant 'shoot the traitors of the nation' as the participants responded with '*Goli maro saalon ko.*'

The police used unlawful force and committed various other human rights violations, abusing laws to intimidate people and silence dissent on behalf of the union government. During the February communal violence in Delhi, members of the police pelted stones alongside rioters, tortured people in custody, dismantled sites of peaceful protest and stood by as rioters attacked peaceful protesters and destroyed public and private property. No independent investigation was launched into these acts.

As the COVID-19 pandemic unfolded, the discriminatory enforcement of the lockdown restrictions by the police heightened human rights concerns. The majority of those arrested for violating the lockdown guidelines belonged to marginalized communities such as scheduled castes, scheduled tribes, denotified tribes, Muslims and low-income workers.

In March 2021, migrant workers who were travelling back home were forced by the Uttar Pradesh police to crawl on the road carrying their belongings as punishment for breaching the lockdown guidelines.

On 18 April 2020 in Uttar Pradesh, Rizwan Ahmed, a daily-wage worker, died in a hospital two days after being beaten by police with batons because he had stepped out to buy vegetables during the lockdown.

In the aforesaid report, Amnesty International said: 'The handling of the COVID-19 pandemic exposed weaknesses in the public health care system. It also resulted in unsafe and poor working conditions for those who lack adequate social and economic protection, such as community health care workers and religious minorities.'

The government accused members of the Muslim Tablighi Jamaat minority of spreading the coronavirus disease, and as a result, health care facilities were reportedly denied access to Muslims. Instances of hospitals refusing Muslim pregnant women and cancer patients surfaced in April 2020.

In the months following the nationwide lockdown of March, social media and WhatsApp groups were flooded with calls for social and economic boycotts of Muslims, alongside fake news stories and other misinformation.

In April 2020, the government launched the mobile app Aarogya Setu, purportedly to speed up contact tracing and ensure timely access to essential health services and public health information. No information was provided regarding which government bodies would actually have access to the data collected through the app. Aarogya Setu's code was not open to the public in violation of the government's own policy. The Ministry of Electronics and Information Technology maintained that downloading the app was not mandatory. However, many government departments and private companies, including the Airport Authority of India, made it mandatory for their staff to install it.

FARMERS' AGITATION

The growing farmer agitation spearheaded by members of the Bharatiya Kisan Union has been going on for almost a year.

It led to the Bharat Bandh at the end of September 2021 and indicates their growing agitation. However, there are no signs that they may go back on their demands, despite all efforts by the BJP to allay their fears over three contentious farm laws.

There is growing anger among Haryana, Punjab and Uttar Pradesh farmers, who have been protesting at Delhi's borders against the farm laws since November 2020 demanding the legislations be repealed.

The imbroglio in the Punjab Congress Party involving former Congress chief minister Amarinder Singh, of the former Patiala royal family, and maverick ex-Test cricketer Navjot Singh Sidhu, a stormy petrel if ever there was one, has not helped matters either.

In Punjab and Haryana, resentment also raged over postponement of the paddy procurement with farmer agitations getting violent day after day. Meanwhile, the central government maintains that postponement of procurement is in the overall interest of farmers and consumers as well because untimely rains have delayed maturity of paddy grains.

Recently the Supreme Court pulled up a protesting farmers body for seeking permission to continue its blockade of the highways and holding satyagraha at the Jantar Mantar in the national capital. It remarked that, through their agitation, the farmers have 'strangulated' the entire city, obstructing traffic alongside the highways, blocking trains and had plans of entering Delhi and the National Capital Region (NCR).[58]

In a surprise turn of events, on 19 November 2021, on the occasion of Gurupurab, Prime Minister Modi announced the government's decision to repeal three the farm laws. Bharatiya Kisan Union leader Rakesh Tikait thanked the PM for his decision but maintained that the protests would not cease until the laws are formally repealed in Parliament.

A SHARP DIVIDE

As may be expected, the tumultuous events listed above brought about a sharp divide in the body politic of the nation, resulting in fierce debate in conventional and, even more so, on social media, befouling relations and fostering enmity between communities and across party lines.

Pushed on the back foot because of the unrelenting exposes of the ruling dispensation's so-called 'sins,' the prime minister's fervid polemicists in the print, television and social media closed ranks and unleashed a propaganda blitz the likes of which had not been witnessed since the freedom struggle.

However, as the truism goes: The truth often lies betwixt and between.

---

[58]Sohini Goswami, 'Strangulated city, now want to come inside: SC to Farmers' Body', *Hindustan Times*, 1 October 2021, https://www.hindustantimes.com/india-news/strangulated-city-now-want-to-come-inside-supreme-court-to-farmers-body-101633067779514.html. Accessed on 19 November 2021.

By way of countering the offensive of Amnesty International and the unrelenting critics of the prime minister and the ruling party, the following pedagogic post widely circulated on WhatsApp illustrates the evangelical zeal of the faithful:

> My friend who is Anti Modi, asked me to give one reason to Vote for Modi.
> I gave him 200.
> Here are 200 reasons to vote for Modi:

True to its promise, the post goes on to list 200 extremely impressive but, sadly unsubstantiated, initiatives and achievements of the PM and the ruling party.

Constraints of space preclude their detailed listing. Readers desirous of accessing the post may contact the BJP offices.

BHARATIYA JANATA PARTY

Whereas the veracity of portions of the above-mentioned thesis cannot be denied, the complex figures and supporting data adduced are extremely wide-ranging, sketchy, difficult to verify and, therefore, neither incontrovertible nor acceptable as gospel truth, since truth is seldom absolute in politics.

But, as far as I'm concerned, the prime minister's performance balance-sheet is truly impressive although sullied by the numerous minuses parroted by the naysayers.

In brief (since this is not a treatise on politics): in its run-up heading to the end of its second avatar towards the twenty-fourth Indian general election, the ruling party's pluses overall are impressive. That said, the achievements are undeniably tarnished, judged by many yardsticks, especially when it comes to law and order and human rights.

BATTLING THE PANDEMIC

The reality, however, is that accelerated production of the indigenous COVID-19 vaccine, astute management, aggressive marketing, distribution and administering of the Covishield, Covaxin and Sputnik V vaccines on a war-footing seems to have brought the elusive virus with hydra-headed mutants under a semblance of control.

To have achieved this after a myopic start and despite the enormity of our problems due to our country's size, population, notorious indiscipline in a crisis, partisan politics endemic to the democratic system of government, and a plethora of festivals across the length and breadth of the country, we have done remarkably well in countering the accursed pandemic.

(The central government claims that India has, to date, administered more than 570 million doses of the three approved manufacturers. With more international players jostling to enter the country, the target is to vaccinate all adults by the end of 2021.)

As these memoirs head closer to the press, official figures would have us believe that the country recorded its lowest number of daily cases in over 200 days with the month-end tally falling to below 20,000 for the first time in six months. The portents appear promising, what with the upcoming extension of the vaccination programme to those under 18.

In the words of Anand Mahindra, 'Economists are concerned about the slow rate of vaccinations… India just hit a high of 12 million in 1 day; Sadly, our large population makes the task tough but unless I'm wrong, we are vaccinating the equivalent of 1 Australia every 3 days!'[59] That said, it would be foolhardy to postulate that the country is over the hump, considering the vast number of ignorant or misled nay-sayers, selfish zealots, and plain nincompoops, who obdurately refuse to get themselves vaccinated, with scant regard for their fellow human beings.

On Gandhi Jayanti, over 4,724,876 deaths were reported worldwide. According to the World Health Organization, over 7,370,902,499 vaccines have been given worldwide[60] even as the pandemic continues

---

[59] 'Anand Mahindra's Reply to Economists: India Vaccinates One 'Australia' Every Three Days', *Mint*, 1 September 2021, https://www.livemint.com/news/india/anand-mahindra-s-reply-to-economists-india-vaccinates-one-australia-every-three-days-11630462154012.html. Accessed on 20 November 2021.

[60] 'WHO Coronavirus (COVID-19) Dashboard', World Health Organization,

to shellack the mental, physical and emotional well-being of Homo sapiens the world over.

Having said that, India's achievement in administering one billion COVID-19 vaccination doses is impressive, if not mind-boggling, by any yardstick. Add to it, the ambitious initiatives taken by India in combating climate change, its increasing heft in international geo-politics, Prime Minister Modi's charisma in his interaction with world leaders and the country's impressive economic growth despite the pandemic, have undeniably elevated it to the status of a world power.

OVER THE MOON AFTER THE OLYMPICS

Even as the nation came to grips with the pandemic and the economy crawled back towards normalcy, there were other manifestations which proved that although India, as a nation, had taken a massive body blow, its spirit was far from broken.

The 2021 Tokyo Olympics marked a watershed moment for India in the Games. It brought about a refreshing cheer and kindled a huge surge of national pride and confidence when the nation was reeling in the throes of the pandemic, compounded by execrable political mismanagement.

Being only an infinitesimal, but by no means unimportant, part of human activity the world over, viewership of international sport on television such as the Olympics is numero uno as validated by authoritative TRPs (Television Rating Points Index).

The latest edition—there have been 29 in all—of the quadrennial Olympic Games, were originally scheduled to be held in 2020 in Tokyo but had to be postponed to 2021 because of COVID-19. They were finally held in July–August 2021 after now-on-now-off tempestuous jousts involving sports administrators on the one hand, and politicians, commercial interests and health authorities on the other.

India sent its largest-ever contingent of 121 (53 female and 68 male) amid great optimism but uncertainty about whether the Games

https://covid19.who.int/?adgroupsurvey={adgroupsurvey}&gclid=CjwKCAiAnO2 MBhApEiwA8q0HYVN0S83_4NafxyofV-J3aZ8TCvMdvRW_8D0gjpbsjas7j6cQl hk4BxoCdjcQAvD_BwE. Accessed on 20 November 2021.

would, after all, take place, which they did, and one might add, to the great credit of the host nation. Overall, India's performance was impressive, its best-ever, but rather disappointing compared to the expectations that were heightened by our national sports bodies and our unfailingly optimistic media.

To be fair, deplorable COVID-related crisis management by our national sports bodies (compared to those of other countries) came in the way of better performances because of managerial ineptitude and below-par preparation.

With seven medals—one old, two silver and four bronze—the Tokyo Games were our most fulfilling. The upliftment in national mood, the 'we-are-second-to-none' boost in pride and confidence and, for me, kindling of enthusiastic interest in sport across our vast country thanks to media reach, were priceless accomplishments, which bode extremely well for the future.

Given the measly financial assistance that our successive governments have allotted to Indian sport over the years (despite the untiring efforts of Field Marshal Manekshaw's All India Council of Sport, of which I was a frustrated member), one can now reasonably hope that present and future governments will be more supportive. Importantly, this should also encourage corporates (to whom a great deal of credit should go for enabling us to hold our heads high, post-Tokyo) to substantially increase their involvement in, and assistance to, sport.

I write this in the wider context of not just enabling our young sportsmen of the future to bring glory to the country and themselves. The Games are also the harbinger of wide-ranging change not only in helping the physical and mental development of future generations of Indians but also making them better human beings via the beneficial attributes of sport.

Soon after the end of the moving Closing Ceremony (which are invariably tear-inducing events for me, this sentimental fool), *Mid-Day* sports editor Clayton Murzello, (who I am proud to refer to as my protégé), called to say he had started on his Facebook page a discussion on India's performance at Tokyo and was wondering if I would like to be quoted. I happily agreed. Extracts of my post, which elicited heart-warming response, appear below:

I'm over the moon, Clayton. Here below my response to your query:

In all modesty—and without meaning to appropriate any undeserved personal credit, the assiduous, unceasing efforts of we sports journalists over many years to spread the culture and ethos of sport to promote mental and physical well-being in our country, have borne fruit.

As have our unceasing efforts to attract financial support from our national and state governments and corporates, compel our parasitic and apathetic sports associations to mend their wayward ways, attract foreign coaches etc. Neeraj Chopra's epic feat is only one manifestation of our humble efforts.

(Javelin thrower Chopra became the second Indian in Olympic history to win a gold medal—in javelin throw. The first was air rifle shooter Abhinav Bindra at the 2008 Beijing Olympics).

We can now justifiably hold our heads high in the sporting world, including the Olympics, in which our past performances have been embarrassing given our potential, our so-called 'third world' economic rating, notwithstanding.

Most significantly, almost all our medals at Tokyo '21 have been won by women, and that too from rural areas and impecunious backgrounds, which portends well for the future. It is verily an occasion to celebrate for all those in Indian sports journalism—past and present—whose contribution over the years cannot be overlooked.

THE SPORTS EUPHORIA CONTINUES: TOKYO PARALYMPICS 2021

In the Paralympics that followed in Tokyo, India brought home more Olympic medals of 19 of different hues (with more near-misses) in one edition than in the country's entire history of participation, since the 1968 Tel Aviv Games for the physically disabled.

Close calls are the name of the game in sport. That said, India had as many as six fourth finishes (with one medal taken away because of disqualification), which underlined the need for mental toughness in Paralympics as in the Olympics. It is hoped that, with greater realization of the tremendous importance of sports psychology in our administrative set-up, the number of near misses will diminish with proportionate increase in number of medals won. But, let me hasten to add, the winning of medals should never be the sine qua non, the be-all-and-end-all of sporting endeavour.

Meanwhile, the nation's state of mind was at its lowest ebb: death and disease were the order of the day with no relief in sight. The centre and states continued to indulge in mutual recrimination even as horror stories of corpses lying unattended in crematoria and hospital corridors abounded.

There were reports of gross mismanagement, of desperately inadequate availability of vaccines, partly because of the grossly ill-advised export of vaccines. There was acute shortage of medical staff, ambulances and worse, of food and rations, not to mention the sale and profiteering of fake vaccines, peripheral medicines, oxygen cylinders and the like.

It was a disgraceful, despicable demonstration of the most demeaning, disgusting attributes of Homo sapiens—of a living hell!

Meanwhile, our contemptible netas, never ones to miss a trick, jumped into the fray, claiming credit for the deeds of our brave frontline workers, of dedicated doctors, nurses, paramedics and volunteers, who were all side-lined in their frenetic quest for undeserved glory,

DELIRIOUS WIN AFTER 38 ALL OUT

Even as the nation wallowed in the Slough of Despond, redemption struck for millions of cricket deewane in the country in the form of an unexpected 2–1 series victory over arch rivals Australia, which included a pulsating last-day win at Brisbane to seal the series that was adjudged the 'ultimate Test' series by the ICC.

What made the win sensational was the way in which India fought back despite the COVID-induced nationwide melancholia. Blown away for an ignominious 36 (their lowest score in Test history) in the first Test—a veritable 'horror show' in Adelaide—a rudderless India with charismatic captain Virat Kohli missing because of household duties, stormed back like the champions they are.

Captained by deputy Ajinkya Rahane and with front-line players Ishant Sharma and Mohamed Sami injured, the lesser lights in the Indian team snatched an electrifying three-wicket victory to win the series 2-1 in the last hour of the last day of the last Test.

After the Adelaide drubbing, Kohli had nonchalantly brushed off his team's performance promising that his team will bounce back, thereby attesting to his team's indomitable spirit.

Even for those who do not have time for cricket, this win was the ultimate morale-booster imaginable under the circumstances.

MORE MORALE BOOSTERS

With the pandemic in its dreaded second-wave stage, India scored a morale-boosting 3–1 Test series win against 'old enemy' England in India, followed by an 2–1 ODI series win and a heart-warming 3–2 victory in the T20 series.

With the pandemic continuing its relentless march worldwide, the legion of Indian fans at least had the valiant exploits of Virat Kohli's storm-troopers to keep their spirits high despite the setback in the final of the World Test Championship against New Zealand in England.

Then, during the tour of England in mid-2021 there was the 3–1 home series winning lead over England in which Indian spirits were further buoyed by the come-from-behind heart-stopping Independence Day Test at Lords that India won by a convincing margin of 151 runs.

Wishful expectations among Indian fans were left unfulfilled when the last Test at Old Trafford was cancelled amidst rancour because of a corona outbreak among some members of the Indian support staff on the morning of the Test.

Disappointment among Indian cricket deewane turned into despair when Virat Kohli's World Cup warriors were delivered lethal knock-out punches first by Pakistan and then, New Zealand, such that successive victories over Afghanistan, Namibia and Scotland failed to ameliorate.

Furthermore, changes in the team's war council pursuant to the completion of a jaded Ravi Shastri's term as coach, making way for the appointment of the cerebral Rahul Dravid and Virat Kohli's stepping down from captaincy of the ODI team, enabling Rohit Sharma to assume charge have allowed winds of change to blow through the top echelons of Indian cricket.

As these memoirs go to press, the Indian team has just completed a 2–0 (with one drawn) shellacking of the world Test champions New Zealand in a little over three days by an overwhelming 372 runs in Mumbai.

WOMEN'S CRICKET

By way of exemplifying the spirit of the new India, there was the memorable women's pink ball four-day cricket match in Australia at Carrara, Gold Coast, wherein the touring Indian team did itself proud to stake a claim to be acknowledged as the leading women's Test cricket team in the world.

For male cricketers, tournaments involving the pink-ball format are becoming more common, but for the women's team, this was their first-ever international experience of playing with the mysterious and unpredictable ball.

To begin with, the team had to undergo 14 days of quarantine upon arrival in Australia. To make matters worse, the match, originally scheduled for Perth, had to be relocated to Carrara at short notice because of COVID-related issues. The new location experienced cyclonic weather on the first two days. Not only did this affect the Indian team's training schedule, but it also deprived them of invaluable practice time under the lights. Under those circumstances, only two training sessions were possible.

India had never defeated the home team in a Test in Australia. Cynics had predicted a rout for them—this was their first experience of playing a Test against Australia after 15 years, when India were handed a hiding to nothing.

Expected to be a 'trial by fire,' the match at Carrara, marked a leap for India. The wicket was generally expected to help the rampaging

Australian quicks (bowling with the pink ball), make life hell for Indian captain Mithali Raj's side on a lively green pitch. Cricket pink balls have been known to dominate the bat in men's cricket, but pundits were curious to see how the Indian batters would handle the 'twilight zone' when the pink ball becomes difficult to pick and makes batting a true test.

Although inclement weather forced the match to be drawn (India dominated proceedings from start to finish and almost scored one of Indian women's cricket's major upsets), it turned out to be a memorable one for many reasons. For the Indian side, the match shall remain notable for many reasons: apart from overall skill possessed by the team (their mental, emotional and physical attributes), it was their refusal to be cowed down by alien conditions, sheer determination, raw courage in the face of adversity and, above all, an indomitable will to succeed. But for rain which washed out play for most of two days out of four, India would almost surely have emerged triumphant.

Going away from women's cricket for a bit: junior Dhanush Srikanth won the 10-metres air rifle gold medal at the ISSF Junior World Championships in Lima, Peru, on 1 October 2021.

And, news has just come that student Naamya Kapoor, all of 14, has become the youngest Indian shooter to win an international medal when she clinched the women's 25-metre pistol gold at the same event. Another Indian shooter, Manu Bhaker, finished fourth.

(At the Tokyo Olympics, another young unfancied Indian—golfer Aditi Ashok—had shot into the international limelight when coming out of oblivion to narrowly miss the bronze medal competing against the biggest names in world women's golf).

And in early October, in chess, a less popular sport, fourth-seeded India finished runners-up to favourites Russia, in the final of the prestigious FIDE World Women's Team Chess Championship in Stiges, Spain.

Indian chess grandmaster Vishwanathan Anand has made it a habit of winning title after title in country after country against the likes of legends Garry Kasparov, Magnus Carlsen and Vladimir Kramnik, making one wonder what the Monopolies Commissions is doing about these flagrant violations!

But, as in many other endeavours in life, retiring Indian sportsmen are passing on the baton to a young generation of fiercely driven future champions, spawned ironically during a malevolent pandemic.

Coincidence apart, the above-mentioned and other examples, too many to enumerate, provide ample evidence of the new 'can do' mindset of young India, helped, admittedly, by the government and corporate support.

I, for one, see a resplendent future ahead.

SENSEX AT SIXTY

To continue on a buoyant, upbeat note:
According to a piece in the Mumbai edition of *The Times of India*:

In November 2017, Ridham Desai, one of the top equity strategists at global financial major Morgan Stanley, told a business channel that he expected the sensex to touch the 100,000-point mark in 4-5 years. This was at a time when the index was hovering around the 33,500-level and almost every fund manager worth his roar was finding it difficult to make money on Dalal Street. Desai had said the Indian market was on the cusp of a big rally as the drivers for the same were in place.

Market players then were a divided lot on Desai's comments. For most it was either an audacity of crystal gazing or temerity of stupidity. For a small lot, it was an expression of hope. But none could stick their neck out and support such a bullish call. Since memes were not in vogue then, Desai was spared from being trolled for his predictions.

Almost four years to the date since Desai made that prediction, as the sensex scaled the 60k mark in early trades on Friday, investors on Dalal Street now believe that the 1-lakh mark is within their reach. They also believe India's market capitalisation could soon go above the $5-trillion mark, from about $3.6 trillion now, and front-run the GDP to hit that magic figure. They see a smooth glide path for the Indian market as several tailwinds are visible. [61]

---

[61]Parth Sinha, 'Sensex at Sixty', *The Times of India*, 25 September 2021,

INDIA OVERTAKES FRANCE IN MARKET CAPITALIZATION

Around the time of Navratri in September 2021, the unabated rally in the stock market took India past France in terms of market capitalization.

On 16 September, the index rally moved past the 59,000 mark for the first time ever. It closed at 59,141 points, an increase of 418 points on the day.

The rally took India's market capitalization to nearly $3.5 trillion, ahead of France's $3.4 trillion, almost on par with fifth-placed UK, which has a market cap of $3.7 trillion, as per data on Bloomberg.[62]

CHANGE OF MOOD

Getting into the Dussehra season, Prime Minister Modi oozed confidence by insisting that the mood had changed and there was a marked change in public sentiment, while the Reserve Bank of India stated that people 'are generally less pessimistic about the state of the economy on all fronts and are optimistic about spending, employment and household income. However, they are still wary of prices a year from now.'[63]

◆

I have full knowledge and belief that 'playing the market' is a hazardous endeavour...audacious, perhaps even stupid and tantamount to 'crystal gazing.'[64]

---

https://timesofindia.indiatimes.com/business/markets/sensex/sensex-at-sixty/articleshow/86498284.cms. Accessed on 20 November 2021.
[62]'Sensex Tops 59,000, India 6th Most Valued Market', *The Times of India*, 17 September 2021, https://timesofindia.indiatimes.com/business/markets/sensex/sensex-tops-59k-india-6th-most-valued-market/articleshow/86281158.cms. Accessed on 20 November 2021.
[63]'Mood Has Changed, Consumers Bullish on Economy: RBI', *The Times of India*, 11 October 2021, https://timesofindia.indiatimes.com/business/india-business/mood-has-changed-consumers-bullish-on-economy-rbi/articleshow/86923961.cms. Accessed on 20 November 2021.
[64]Ibid.

I believe I'm neither greedy nor a gambler. As mentioned in an earlier chapter, I'm an absolute ignoramus in all matters financial, which I leave entirely to my fund managers and in whom I have tremendous trust built over many years.

My brief to my consultants is that I desire nothing more than to sleep soundly which, I must say to their credit, they have ensured diligently and unfailingly over the years.

On balance, I believe India is showing unmistakable signs of emerging out of this COVID-induced purgatory and heading towards serendipitous Elysian fields. On this sunny note, this Donkey would like to bray a hopeful *'munh mein ghee, shakkar'* (may there be ghee and sugar in your mouth).

The future looks rosy, indeed. Yes, it *is* indeed a wonderful world!

Epilogue

Chuck Feeney is an Irish-American billionaire who made billions of dollars from a duty-free shopping empire and has achieved his lifelong ambition: giving away his $8-billion fortune while he is still around to see the impact it has made.

The following is an excerpt from *The Guardian* newspaper:[65]

For the past 38 years, Feeney, an Irish American who made billions from a duty-free shopping empire, has been making endowments to charities and universities across the world with the goal of 'striving for zero ... to give it all away'.

This week Feeney, 89, achieved his goal. The Atlantic Philanthropies, the foundation he set up in secret in 1982 and transferred almost all of his wealth to, has finally run out of money.

As he signed papers to formally dissolve the foundation, Feeney, who is in poor health, said he was very satisfied with 'completing this on my watch'. From his small rented apartment in San Francisco, he had a message for other members of the super-rich, who may have pledged to give away part of their fortunes but only after they have died: 'To those wondering about Giving While Living: try it, you'll like it.'

---

[65] Rupert Neate, 'Billionaire Chuck Feeney Achieves Goal of Giving Away His Fortune', *The Guardian*, 19 September 2020, https://www.theguardian.com/business/2020/sep/19/billionaire-chuck-feeney-achieves-goal-of-giving-away-his-fortune. Accessed on 15 November 2021.

Feeney, who gave most of his money away in secret, said he hoped more billionaires would follow his example and use their money to help address the world's biggest problems.

'Wealth brings responsibility,' he often said. 'People must define themselvesor feel a responsibility to use some of their assets to improve the lives of their fellow humans, or else create intractable problems for future generations.'

He said the one-time $8bn man would encourage the likes of Jeff Bezos, the Amazon founder and world's richest person who has an estimated $186bn fortune, to 'pick a global problem that interests you and invest your wealth and get involved'.

Feeney was influenced by Andrew Carnegie's essay The Gospel of Wealth, with its declaration that 'the millionaire will be but a trustee for the poor'.

◆

In the context of philanthropy, it would be impertinence of the most unforgivable kind for Zeyna and me to ever talk of Feeney, Buffett, Gates, even the likes of our own Mukesh Ambani, Azim Premji and ourselves, in the same breath.

Even though I say it myself: being prudent by nature, Zeyna and I have a decent standard of living, made possible initially, and largely overall, thanks to the accident (the Donkey's luck again being responsible!) of being introduced by a friend to the investment advisory firm Merrill Lynch as it was then known. Our standing brief to our consultants has been: 'We're not greedy, nor are we gamblers... We like to sleep in peace.' We are delighted they—our investment 'guru' Pradeep Bihani, in particular—have handled our portfolio with the utmost responsibility and acuity.

In any event, comparisons are always invidious and best avoided. I wince at the mention of the term 'wealth management' from the lips of so-called 'wealth gurus' but I marvel at the impressive wealth that Buffett, Gates, Ambani and Premji (all epitomes of humility and compassion) have amassed in their lifetimes, and importantly, with uttermost regard for the straight and narrow path.

When Zeyna and I first read about Chuck Feeney, we were deeply touched by his noble, almost superhuman compassion, his 'striving for zero ... to give it all away' in one's own lifetime since 'the world is full of people who don't get enough to eat'. We were inspired when we read that Feeney's generosity spurred Bill Gates and Warren Buffett to establish The Giving Pledge, under which the world's richest people commit to giving away at least half their wealth to charity. And finally, we were moved beyond description when Buffett described Feeney as 'my hero. He is Bill Gates's hero. He should be everybody's hero.'[66]

I would like to end these recollections on this humble note: we fully realize that the little that Zeyna and I are giving back to our poor and needy fellow human beings is but a drop in the ocean.

Is it enough? Certainly not. We, as trustees for the poor, can surely do much, much more.

Leaving aside the banal, self-righteous excuse that we all tend to make that we are neither saints, like the recently beatified Mother Teresa, nor the eminently virtuous philanthropists mentioned earlier and innumerable other munificent noble human souls, the fact of the matter is that we are 'chicken,' neurotic, even subconsciously frightened of the unexpected, the what-may-happen, the accident, the crisis, the disaster. But, if we were to be absolutely sincere, people are essentially covetous, grasping, comfortably ensconced in our little Valhalla and not yet prepared to take the definitive step in our evolution as human beings. Zeyna and I are no exceptions.

I worship truth and courage but lack unconditional compassion. I must learn to stop thinking about an afterlife and learn to be righteous at all times for its own sake, and help my fellow beings in the here and now.

Looking back, I've had to work assiduously in life; it's been one hell of a struggle, a very rough ride at times but, hand on my heart, in the words of Louis Armstrong: 'I think to myself, what a wonderful world!'

I've been blessed with wonderful, loving parents; exemplary, caring

---

[66]Bill Murphy Jr., 'Warren Buffett and Bill Gates Call This Man Their Hero and Role Model', *Inc.*, 26 September 2020, https://www.inc.com/bill-murphy-jr/warren-buffett-bill-gates-call-this-man-their-hero-role-model.html. Accessed on 15 November 2021.

wives who have been and continue to remain sincere friends; loving, respectful, educated children and grandchildren who do me proud; sincere, trustworthy friends and caring, responsible workmates and employees. What more can a mere mortal ask for in one life? Yes, indeed, it has been *la dolce vita*!

Hopefully, the Donkey of this narrative—me, the 'I' of these memoirs—who has all along been showered by the blessings of the One Above, will definitively have the moral courage, wisdom and strength to 'give it all away.'

In the words of Robert Frost, from the poem 'Stopping by Woods on a Snowy Evening,' that was purportedly transcribed by Jawaharlal Nehru and kept by him at his bedside: 'We have miles to go before we sleep, we have miles to go before we sleep.'

Index

2021 Tokyo Olympics, 506
2021 Tokyo Paralympics, 508

Abbas, Zaheer ('Zed'), 88, 89, 199, 250
Abdul Hamid Ansari Charitable Trust, xxv, 492
Air Marshal Idris Hasan Latif, 292
Air Marshal Nur Khan, 82, 85, 91, 100
Akbar, M.J., 156
Akhbar-e-Hilal, 7
Akhtar, Javed (Siddiqui), xxviii, 63, 156, 274
All India Council of Sports, xxiv
Ambani, Dhirubhai, 268, 343
Ambani, Mukesh, 105, 480, 517
Amnesty International, 500
Ansari, Abdul Hamid, xxiii, xxv, xl, 4, 5, 6, 7, 10, 11, 12, 13, 15, 425, 492
Ansari, Alya, 47
Ansari, Amina Begum, xxxix, 14
Ansari, Emraan, 49, 50
Ansari, Imaan, 47, 48
Ansari, Rukya, xli, 34, 43, 44, 49, 50, 53, 54, 55, 56, 57, 58, 88, 107, 108, 111, 115, 116, 120, 121, 122, 123, 124, 125, 126, 131, 132, 136, 138, 142, 152, 210, 211, 219, 268, 292, 337, 347, 375, 476, 486
Ansari, Safiya, 49, 50
Ansari, Sharique, xxi, 14, 20, 34, 44, 47, 49, 50, 86, 111, 142, 152, 273, 331, 346, 487
Ansari, Tarique, xxi, 14, 20, 34, 44, 47, 48, 49, 52, 55, 56, 108, 111, 120, 124, 125, 126, 131, 132, 138, 142, 152, 171, 172, 273, 285, 331, 332, 346, 348, 406, 453, 475, 485, 486, 487
Ansari, Zeyna (Tomasevich, Mattie), 399, 400, 423, 426, 449, 476, 489, 491, 492
Asiad Chronicle, xxiv, 180, 181, 256, 259
Asian Games, xxiv, 87, 161, 180, 184, 195, 197, 234, 253, 254, 256, 258, 259, 291

Bedi, Bishan Singh, 89, 164, 166, 199, 209, 222, 224, 225, 250, 362, 363, 364, 365, 366
Behram Contractor, 62, 257, 259,

267, 269, 270, 277
Bhutto, Zulfikar Ali, 86, 91, 93
Bobde, Sharad A., 497
Bombay Cricket Association (BCA), 94
Bombay Gymkhana, xxii, xxv, 93, 414, 439, 440, 442, 443, 445, 446, 449, 450, 452, 453
Brabourne Stadium, 93, 140, 141, 153, 233, 234, 274, 292, 293
Bradman, Don, 88, 163, 222, 251, 252
Brittenden, Dick, 231
Butt, Khalid, 85, 87

Cathedral and John Connon School, 47, 91
Celebrity magazine, 280
Chagla, Mohammadali Currim (M.C. Chagla), 21, 134
Chainani, Raju, 372, 373, 374
CHAMPS Foundation, xxii, xxv, 435, 453
Chandrasekhar, Bhagwat, 224, 225, 229, 362
Chappell, Greg, 199
Chappell, Ian, 199, 368, 423
Chappell, Trevor, 232
Chudasama, Nana, xxii, 414, 435, 482, 491
Citizenship (Amendment) Act (CAA), 496, 500, 501
Commonwealth Games, xxiv, 90, 101, 160, 162, 170, 180, 196, 375
Commonwealth Heads of Government Meeting (CHOGM), 317
Congress, 6, 7, 8, 75, 105, 113, 405, 409, 410, 411, 425, 502
Contractor, Nari, 17, 199

COVID-19, 35, 311, 318, 364, 407, 453, 494
Cozier, Tony, 164, 231
Cricket at Fever Pitch, xxiv, 173, 198
Cricket Club of India (CCI), xxiv, xxxvii, 89, 93, 94, 151, 152, 153, 157, 166, 202, 210, 233, 308, 427, 429, 435, 438, 449
Cricket Hall of Fame, 231
Currimbhoy, Aziz, 152, 153, 154, 164, 268, 274

de Grooth, Geerhard (Gerry), 96, 97, 98, 99
Delhi and District Cricket Association (DDCA), 364, 365, 366
Donkey, xxvii, xxxi, xxxii, xxxvii, 138, 145, 151, 152, 155, 159, 258, 277, 338, 399, 410, 414, 426, 484, 515, 517, 519
Dravid, Rahul, xxix, 199, 202, 240, 250, 252, 354, 511
Dubai, xxv, 31, 63, 72, 96, 105, 117, 166, 171, 244, 296, 337, 338, 339, 342, 344, 347, 348, 349, 378, 406, 408, 436, 452, 453, 469, 470
Dungarpur, Raj Singh, xxiv, 199, 237, 420, 438
Durrani, Shahid Ali Khan, 229

Earth Summit Times, xxv, 469, 471
Earth Times, xxv, 52
Eden Gardens, 212, 234
Engineer, Farokh ('Rookie'), 88, 163, 167, 199, 217, 268, 359, 360, 361, 371
Evening News of India, 165, 267, 268, 277, 280

Feeney, Chuck, 516, 517, 518
Field Marshal S.H.F.J Manekshaw (Sam Manekshaw), xxiv, xxvii, 199, 283, 302, 303, 306, 419
Fielden, Edward J. (EJF), 132, 133, 134, 137, 138
Flower Power, 120
Fox, Terry, 436
Free Press Bulletin, 277, 280, 284

Gadha, xi, xxvii, xxxi, xxxiii, xxxiii, 348, 419, 426, 457
Gaekwad, Fatehsinghrao ('Jackie Baroda'), 242, 243, 256
Galadari, Abdul Rahim, 3, 4, 338, 339, 340, 346, 347
Gandhi, Indira, 83, 134, 289, 290, 304, 305, 319, 499
Gandhi, Rajiv, xxiv, 85, 256, 258, 315, 317, 318, 320, 332, 409, 457
Ganguly, Sourav, 240, 354, 365
Gavaskar, Sunil, xxii, xxv, xxix, 88, 89, 120, 164, 172, 173, 174, 182, 199, 228, 229, 240, 250, 251, 252, 308, 353, 354, 355, 356, 357, 362, 368, 370, 371, 414, 435, 441, 452, 453
General P.P. Kumaramangalam, xxiv
Gentle, R.S., 163, 255
Gibson, 'Pat', 208, 209, 210, 211, 212, 220
Gorbachev, Mikhail Sergeyevich, 459
Government Law College, xxv, 17, 328
Greig, Tony, 208, 209
Grossman, David, 52
Grossman, Leah, 51, 52
Grossman, Noah, 51, 52
Grossman, Tehzeeb, 14, 34, 44, 47, 51, 52, 136, 141

Gulf News, 338, 339, 341, 436

Hawn, Goldie, 311
H.H. Prince Karim Aga Khan IV, 293
Hindustan Times, 113, 222, 230, 258, 362, 503
H.R.H Tunku Imran, (Tunku 'Pete' Imran), 101, 199, 373, 375

Independent, 63
Indian Olympic Association (IOA), 184, 256
Inquilab, xxiii, xxix, xl, 4, 5, 6, 9, 10, 11, 12, 13, 14, 15, 41, 52, 54, 55, 56, 60, 63, 75, 83, 133, 143, 144, 145, 154, 155, 157, 158, 160, 269, 271, 284, 315, 331, 332, 384, 406, 410, 425, 457, 482, 483, 486, 487, 488
International Cricket Council (ICC), 88, 101, 232, 239, 251, 363, 369, 509
International Hockey Federation (FIH), 95, 168, 194, 253
International Sports Writers Association (IHSWA), 95

Jagran Prakashan, 52, 487
Jaisimha, M.L., 140
Jamaluddin, Javed, 3, 5, 7, 8, 9, 10
Jamia Millia Islamia, 497
Jawaharlal Nehru University (JNU), 498
Jones, Dean, 222
J. Walter Thompson, 54, 55, 132

Kalam, A.P.J. Abdul, xxiv, xxxv, 85, 329
Kanz Communications, 342, 348
Karanjia, Russi, 280

Kerry Packer's World Series Cricket competition, 90, 224, 238
Khaleej Times, xxv, 72, 117, 171, 296, 338, 339, 342, 343, 346, 347, 348, 349, 408, 409, 436, 469
Khalid & Zeyna Ansari Foundation, 400, 492
Khan, Imran, 164, 199, 250, 252, 268, 308, 348, 349, 369
Khan, Latasha, 429
Khan, Shabana, 429
Khan, Yusuf, 10, 427, 429
Khrushchev, Nikita, 459, 460, 461, 462
Kohli, Virat 250, 252, 354, 360, 509, 510, 511
Kotnis, Sharad, 63, 156, 212, 213, 216, 274

Lollobrigida, Gina (La Lollo), 309
Lord's, 23, 219, 230, 233, 240, 247, 355, 356, 357, 368, 370

Major, John, 328, 465
Mazhar, Farooq, 95
Melbourne Cricket Ground (MCG), 90, 227
Mid-Day, xxiii, xxviii, xxix, xxx, xxxix, xl, 47, 52, 60, 62, 63, 64, 72, 141, 156, 158, 165, 168, 173, 186, 198, 202, 244, 257, 258, 259, 267, 268, 269, 270, 271, 272, 274, 276, 277, 278, 279, 280, 282, 283, 284, 285, 286, 287, 292, 296, 315, 318, 322, 331, 332, 333, 338, 343, 349, 372, 373, 374, 383, 384, 385, 389, 398, 406, 421, 422, 423, 437, 453, 462, 469, 470, 475, 485, 486, 487, 488, 490, 507

Mid-Day A-H Ansari Squash Academy, 373
Mid-Day Multimedia Ltd, xxiii, 47
Mid-Day's Plan For Citizens (ACT), 285
Modi, Narendra, 405, 495, 496, 498
Monroe, Marilyn, xxx, 123, 124, 309
Mumbai University, 38
Murzello, Clayton, xxix, 168, 173, 198, 507
Muslim League, 7

National Register of Citizens (NRC), 496
Natwar Singh, 83, 118, 409, 425, 457
Nayar, Anil 'Lucky', 429, 430
Nayudu, C.K., 233, 244, 370
Nehru, Jawaharlal, 9, 134, 137, 256, 320, 400, 498, 519
Non-Aligned Movement (NAM), xxv, 291, 320, 322, 400

Olympic Games (Olympics), xxiv, 18, 87, 95, 97, 170, 177, 178, 179, 180, 183, 184, 185, 186, 189, 193, 195, 253, 254, 344, 375, 400, 428, 445, 452, 477, 506, 508, 509, 512

Padma Shri, xxiii, 410, 482
Palkhivala, Nani, 292, 293, 419
Pardiwala, Jal, 17
Partition, 12, 91, 92, 331, 429
Pataudi, Mansoor Ali Khan ('Tiger'), 140, 163, 168, 182, 263, 359, 439, 440
Prabhudesai, Devendra, xxix, xxx
Prabhu, K.N., 183, 199
Premji, Azim, 21, 105, 517

PrepCom, 468, 469
Press Institute of India, 145
Prohibition, 109, 112, 113, 127

Qureshi, Omar, 91, 92

Raj, Mithali, 512
Ram Janmabhoomi-Babri Masjid case, 498
Ribeiro, Julio, xxv, 420, 437, 476, 480
Richards, Viv, 164, 172, 250, 252, 355, 435
Right to Information (Amendment) Bill, 2019, 499
Rotary Club, xxv, 254, 283, 308, 418
Run for Fun, 297, 433
Rutnagar, D.J.S., 163

Sachin: Born to Bat, xxiv, 173, 198, 199, 200, 202, 308
Samant, Datta, 443, 444
Sangghvi, Malavika, 269, 362, 421, 422
Schumacher, Michael, 377, 378
Shaheen Bagh, 497, 501
Singh, Giani Zail, xxii, 419
Smith, Ian, 322
Society magazine, 277, 278
Sport and Pastime, 152, 155, 156, 157, 164, 170, 263, 264, 266
Sportstar, 219, 263, 264, 266, 365, 445
Sportsweek, xxi, xxiii, xxviii, xxx, 60, 63, 64, 149, 151, 152, 155–174, 180, 182, 183, 184, 185, 189, 194, 197, 209, 212, 213, 216, 218, 219, 221, 231, 232, 244, 255, 256, 259, 263, 264, 265, 266, 268, 269, 270, 271, 274, 276, 277, 278, 297, 301, 302, 315, 331, 354, 363, 423, 433, 434, 485, 486
Sportsworld, 263, 264, 266
Squash Rackets Federation of India (SRFI), 427
Squash Racquet Association of Maharashtra (SRAM), xxiv, 427, 428
St Agnes, 16, 34, 44
Stanford University, xxiii, 54, 66, 105, 107, 109, 110, 115, 122, 337
St Mary's, 17, 19, 20, 21, 22, 23, 24, 34, 42, 76, 108, 433
St Xavier's College, xxv, 17, 23, 24, 32, 33, 42, 93
Sunday Mid-Day, xxiii, 60, 141, 158, 270, 279, 280, 331, 332, 333, 343, 486
Swaminathan, Nurjehan (Nuru), 132, 134, 135, 136
Sydney Cricket Ground (SCG), 221, 236

Tablighi Jamaat, 497, 501
Talyarkhan, Ardeshir Furdorji Sohrabji 'Bobby' (AFST), 153, 154, 274
Tata, JRD, 292
Tendulkar, Sachin, xxix, 198, 199, 200, 202, 240, 250, 252, 354, 397
Thakkar, Gautam, xxii, 379, 427, 440, 452, 453
The Afternoon Despatch & Courier, 62
The Examiner, 110
The Free Press Journal, 155, 156, 272, 276
The Hindu, 152, 164, 219, 263, 497
The Illustrated Weekly of India, 165

The Times of India, 63, 84, 138, 139, 160, 164, 183, 197, 229, 254, 269, 276, 277, 284, 364, 480, 481, 513, 514
The Wanderers, 239
Turfite, 60

United Nations, xxv, xxxvi, 52, 457, 459, 460, 464, 468
United Nations General Assembly, xxv, xxxvi

Vajpayee, Atal Bihari, xxiv, xxxvi, 85, 100, 383, 410, 457
Vengsarkar, Dilip, 199, 354, 355, 358, 362, 370, 371, 372, 435, 441
Vishwanath, Gundappa, 354, 370, 435

Wadekar, Ajit, 169, 182, 199, 234
Wankhede, Sheshrao, 94
Wankhede Stadium, 211, 241
Western Australia Cricket Association (WACA), 226
Williamson, Kane, 230, 250
Wills Tribute to Excellence: Champions of One-Day Cricket, xxiv
Wisden, 219, 239, 354, 355, 359

Zaiwalla, Sarosh, 328